PEERLESS AND PERILED

PEERLESS AND PERILED

*The Paradox of American Leadership
in the World Economic Order*

Kati Suominen

Stanford Economics and Finance
An Imprint of Stanford University Press
Stanford, California

Stanford University Press
Stanford, California

Printed in the United States of America on acid-free, archival-quality paper

Library of Congress Cataloging-in-Publication Data

Suominen, Kati, author.
  Peerless and periled : The paradox of American leadership in the world economic order / Kati Suominen.
    pages cm
  Includes bibliographical references and index.
  ISBN 978-0-8047-8154-1 (cloth : alk. paper)
  1. United States—Foreign economic relations.   2. United States—Economic policy—2009–   3. International economic relations.   4. International finance.
5. Finance—Government policy—United States.   I. Title.
  HF1455.S857 2012
  337.73—dc23

                                                                    2011036935

Typeset by Newgen in 10/14 Minion

Special discounts for bulk quantities of Stanford Economics and Finance are available to corporations, professional associations, and other organizations. For details and discount information, contact the special sales department of Stanford University Press. Tel: (650) 736-1782, Fax: (650) 736-1784

To Robert J. Michela

Contents

Acknowledgments

T HIS BOOK BUILDS ON THE WORK OF SOME OF THE WORLD'S
finest scholars and draws on countless discussions with policy
makers, bankers, and analysts in the course of the past two years. Too numerous to thank in person, these individuals have shaped the thrust and recommendations of this volume more than they will ever be able to appreciate.

I am particularly grateful to the two dozen senior US, European, and
Asian government officials who so readily agreed to candid off-the-record
conversations amid their crisis-driven agendas. Their diligence and dedica-
tion give confidence that a thriving world economy is within reach.

A number of individuals have enriched this volume with insights and comments at various stages. My very special thanks to J. Lawrence Broz, Mark E.
Buchman, Douglas Elliott, Todd Fox, Gary Hufbauer, Steffen Kern, Phil Levy,
Ted Moran, Sean Mulvaney, Joseph Nye, Alex Pollock, Joseph Quinlan, Andrew Small, and Bruce Stokes. I am also grateful to the anonymous referees; it
was their comments that led me to discover my argument and rediscover my
voice. All errors remain mine alone.

I am indebted to the superb team at the Economics Program of the German Marshall Fund for their steadfast support of my work and their perennially great spirits that give it perspective.

Often one needs only one other person to believe in an aspiration in order
to realize it. My agent, Don Fehr, is that person for this book. He took a leap
of faith with me, believed in the project, and was tireless in seeing it through.
My very special thanks.

I am deeply grateful to Margo Beth Fleming at Stanford University Press for her outstanding editing and patient guidance. Many thanks also to Jessica Walsh for her excellent work in making a book from a manuscript.

I dedicate this volume to Robert J. Michela, a soldier, loyal friend, and fine sportsman whose courage in adversity will be a lasting source of inspiration.

Preface

WHAT ARE AMERICA'S INTERESTS IN THE TWENTY-FIRST-century world economy? And how can Washington attain them?

The energetic debate on the recent global economic convulsions has been devoid of answers to these enormously consequential questions for the United States and the world. The purpose of this book is to start filling this gap. This is an assessment of the US-led postwar global economic order, an account of the changes and challenges to it, and a road map for Washington to advance global growth and stability in the new century. This is also a call for leadership in the global economy and an assertion that the United States is the only nation able to exercise it.

Such a starting point may sound heady. After all, the past few years have been extraordinarily difficult for America. The United States has become portrayed as a nation divided at home and discredited abroad, its economy sullied by deficits and stifled by disinvestment, its global primacy overtaken by a near-audible power shift from West to East. In all too common depictions, America is passing the baton of global stewardship to emerging nations. A new world order led by China is said to be waiting in the shadows.

However, such arguments have analytical flaws. They assume linearity, seeing a world where emerging markets inexorably rise and America falls, when most of world history has been capricious and nonlinear. They regard the world economy as a zero-sum game in which China's gain is America's loss, when global economics are about mutual gains. They consider power fungible, with economic prowess automatically translating into political power and the size of a nation's GDP determining its capacity to lead, when leadership is about much more than guns and butter. And they are premised on structuralist determinism, whereby big-wheel economic transformations supersede policy, institutions, and ideology, rather than being shaped by them.

This book takes issue with the gloom about America and its world economic order. I argue that there are no substitute leaders for the United States in world affairs, just as there are no rival paradigms of global governance that would match the growth and globalization generated by the American order. But we are also not home free. The institutions of the American order are hard-pressed to deal with the challenges in the twenty-first-century world economy and manage the competing demands of the old and new powers. Meanwhile, the United States, the indispensable core of the system, is ailing at home and failing to lead abroad.

How to best further global growth and stability against this backdrop is one of the greatest questions of our time, and it is the quintessential challenge facing US economic policy makers. This book strives to provide answers. Rather than a new theory of economics, this is a pathfinder for policy makers. Rather than a study of the patterns of global trade or finance, this is an international political economy account, centering on politics of and among nations. And besides an analysis of the challenges to the American order, this is an assessment of clashing policy proposals and a display of their sponsors contesting the global economic future in governments, influencing it from Wall Street, and shaping it in academia.

At its very heart, this book is a call for renewed America's global leadership.

This book is at the crux of global economic policy, financial affairs, and US foreign policy literatures. A large body of literature, including Peter Kenen's *The International Financial Architecture: What's New? What's Missing?* (Institute for International Economics, 2001) and Barry Eichengreen's *Globalizing Capital: A History of the International Monetary System* (Princeton University Press, 2008), examines the global financial architecture. However, these works are aimed at the international policy community, rather than analyzing US interests and policy options.

Kenneth Dam's *The Rules of the Global Game* (University of Chicago Press, 2001) and John Taylor's *Global Financial Warriors* (Norton, 2007) offer insider accounts on Treasury's international operations, but they are more centered on past events than the future, and they predate the global economic crisis. Nouriel Roubini and Stephen Shim's *Crisis Economics: A Crash Course in the Future of Finance* (Penguin, 2010), Raghuram Rajan's *Fault Lines* (Princeton University Press, 2010), and Simon Johnson and James Kwak's *13 Bankers* (Vintage, 2010) touch on issues dealt in this volume, but they are geared to explaining the causes of the financial crisis instead of systematically examining America's interests and projection in the twenty-first-century world. Gideon Rachman's *Zero-Sum Future: American Power in an Age of Anxiety* (Simon & Schuster, 2011) addresses similar concerns as this book does about the future of US power but does not focus on the institutions of the American order.

The extensive series of books about Wall Street in the throes of the crisis, such as Michael Lewis' *Big Short* (Norton, 2010), Sebastian Mallaby's *More Money Than God* (Penguin, 2010), and Andrew Ross Sorkin's *Too Big to Fail* (Penguin, 2009) and its dozen namesakes, have little to say to US foreign economic policy makers. Meanwhile, renowned volumes about US foreign policy, such as Joseph Nye's *Soft Power: The Means to Success in World Politics* (PublicAffairs, 2004) and *The Future of Power* (PublicAffairs, 2011), Charles Kupchan's *The End of the American Era: U.S. Foreign Policy and the Geopolitics of the Twenty-First Century* (Knopf, 2003), Robert Kagan's *The Return of History and the End of Dreams* (Knopf, 2008), and Andrew Bacevich's *The Limits of Power: The End of American Exceptionalism* (Holt, 2008), tend to glaze over financial and economic policy, and instead focus on pivotal world regions and national security issues.

This book will doubtless be paralleled by dozens of new volumes on global economic affairs and US foreign policy—lighter, ephemeral journalistic accounts, historical surveys, and technical studies inaccessible even to many sophisticated readers. I seek to merge these approaches: claim rigor while aspiring for accessibility, give scope while focusing on the near future. The method here is to "summon and translate"—compile discussions with leading policy makers and some of the best academic and policy analyses into a new whole, and decode the complexities for policy makers and interested nonexperts.

My hope is to bridge different streams of literature, and technical and nontechnical audiences. Above all, my aspiration is to inform American economic policy making in the years ahead.

A world that depends on the strength of our economy is now watching and waiting for America to lead once more. And that is what we will do.

—*US President-Elect Barack Obama in Fairfax, Virginia, 8 January 2009*

The absence of alternatives clears the mind marvelously.

—*Former US Secretary of State Henry Kissinger, Time, 2 January 1978*

Introduction

Leadership Renewed

A MERICA'S GREAT CONTRIBUTION IN THE TWENTIETH century was to champion a set of institutions and an economic paradigm that would promote open markets and economic stability around the world. The US-led order paved the way to globalization and produced prosperity unimaginable only a few decades before. As the core of the system, the United States served as the world's economic locomotive, fueled by its innovation economy, first-rate institutions, and global economic vitality. But as the Great Crisis of 2008–2009 unfolded from America across the world, a chorus of critics rose to declare the United States a declining nation and call an end to the American order.[1]

The US-built Group of Eight (G8) leading economies was indicted for ignoring the crisis warning signs and succeeding only at groupthink. The International Monetary Fund (IMF), the US-conceived guardian of global stability, was called too meek to prevent the debacle and too slow to halt it. American financial regulations, the blueprint for countless nations, stood accused of serving the regulated. The dollar's reign was declared over as America's deficits soared and China launched a bid for a new global currency. Confidence in independent central bankers, trusted stewards of price stability, eroded as the housing bubble was linked to years of low interest rates and the Federal Reserve's bank bailouts burgeoned. With forecasts failing to herald the disaster, the very premises of modern macroeconomics became unhinged.

America, meanwhile, ailed as the financial devastation ravaged the real economy. The US economy ground to a halt, unemployment soared, and fiscal deficits ballooned as the government struggled to forestall a depression. Foreign nations were livid, blaming the United States. America's free-market capitalism, only a few years ago viewed as the universal epitome and endpoint in the evolution of societies, seemed to have lost its polish. American polity, already divided by partisanship, was further splintered by a contest cast as Main Street versus Wall Street. US financial markets, while still drawing investors even more fearful abroad, were deemed suspect for long-term bets as America's deficits ballooned. The deleveraging American consumer would not, most everyone agreed, deliver the world from the debacle, not this time around. The architect of the postwar world economy was down—and seemed to be out.

Dozens of articles echoed Helene Cooper of the *New York Times*, who declared, "[G]one are the days, from Pax Britannica to Pax Americana, when the US and the UK made the rules that others followed."[2] The mantle bearer at the helm of the world would be China, the next global order run by a multipolar medley of emerging and advanced nations.

Fast-forward to the present day. The American order persists, and it even thrives. The aftermath of the crisis has only reinforced it. The G20, the new steward of global economic policy, is but a US-launched sequel to the US-built G8. The IMF's resources have been tripled, largely at America's behest. The US dollar has gained in prominence as the euro has lost investor confidence. The Federal Reserve has not been closed, and capitalism has not died.

The United States also did not depart the world stage when the crisis broke. Instead, Washington claimed its traditional role as the agenda setter and prodder of laggard nations in the global economy, securing buy-in from emerging nations to G20 commitments and pushing Europe to arrest its debt crisis and match America's new financial regulations.

The outcome reflects a fact of global governance: there are no rival orders that would match the growth and globalization produced by the American order. But while the American order is peerless, it is also periled. Financial instability has become more frequent, fatal, and global over the past decades, but the institutions of the American order are failing to confront it. At the same time, as the core of the order, the United States is ailing at home and failing to lead abroad. Even as reformed, the American order remains defenseless. This is the Achilles heel of the American order and one that jeopardizes its existence: a defective order will cease to garner support from the adherent nations. A downfall of the American order would pull down growth and globalization in its wake, spelling disaster for all nations. Reforms and leadership are required, but divisive power politics among nations and self-defeating Washington bickering stand in the way. This book is a road map through them. A thriving twenty-first-century world economy is within reach, but America must reach harder than ever for it.

Unfolding

In the wake of World War II, the United States reigned supreme. As an allied victor, America saw its global power and prestige soar. The US economy, even if pressed by debt, towered over that of war-torn Europe. American exports boomed, and the United States became the world's premier creditor and growth engine. US economic reach was limited only by the rise of the communist bloc, which carved Europe and the world into two camps connected only by the Cold War.

Although the most powerful nation and itself a continental economy, the United States needed a prosperous and peaceful world. The raw memories of the wartime devastation prompted Washington to search for a new international economic order, one that would preempt the economic turmoil and discriminatory nationalism of the 1920s, and bind the fortunes of nations together so as to make war unthinkable.

The drive for a new world order led the United States, along with European powers spearheaded by Britain, to stage the Bretton Woods Conference in 1944. Washington and London shared a conviction: a prosperous global economy required global institutions. Bretton Woods became a watershed: it led to the establishment of the International Monetary Fund (IMF) and the World Bank, and it paved the way for the General Agreement on Tariffs and Trade (GATT). The conferees also minted the US dollar as the global currency, a convertible medium of exchange for nations to treasure in their vaults.

A new regime arose, one based on transatlantic aims of free and open markets, economic growth and stability, and worldwide prosperity. Nations around the world intent on sharing its benefits joined *en masse* in the subsequent decades. The new institutions became genuinely global in their reach, claiming the loyalties of members from Asia to Africa and, in the 1990s, postcommunist Eastern Europe.

Other transformations unfolded. After the United States broke the dollar's gold peg in 1971, Washington and three leading European nations, Britain, France, and Germany, set out to coordinate their exchange-rate and macroeconomic policies. Within half a decade, the foursome welcomed Japan, an ascendant Pacific economy. As Italy and Canada joined, the group was enshrined as the G7, a body that would become the world's premier macroeconomic guardian.

National economic paradigms shifted. As the economics profession developed and the failures of socialism became glaring, private enterprise was given the reins, and the state, previously the manager of entire sectors of the economy, was made a regulator. Efforts were made to distance economic policy making from politics. Starting with the US Federal Reserve and the Bundesbank in the years surrounding World War II, governments accorded their central banks greater independence to make monetary policy. The early 1990s Washington consensus—aimed at defeating developing world debt crises and rampant inflation with macroeconomic discipline and economic openness—globalized the mantra of free markets and good governance.

Wall Street changed. The division codified in law between investment banking and savings and loans institutions started eroding as the latter found speculative opportunities too lucrative to miss. By the 1970s, new technologies that connected banks to customers across borders obliterated geographic boundaries for bank operations. A wave of deregulation followed across America and, by the 1990s, around the globe. Banks consolidated, financial markets integrated, and new operators—hedge funds, private equity firms, venture capitalists—sprang up. Fresh talent was hired to devise derivative instruments that multiplied the potential of credit.

The institutions of the evolving economic order delivered results. The successive Gs—G4, G5, G7, and G8—helped coordinate macroeconomic policies among the leading economies and faced down global financial imbalances that burdened US trade politics. The IMF spread the Washington consensus across Latin America and Asia, and shepherded transition economies toward capitalism. Bank deregulation and financial liberalization made credit more available and affordable, propelling consumption and entrepreneurship the world over. The US dollar, the world's venerable reserve currency, economized global transactions, fueled world trade, and allowed central banks to have smooth exchange-rate fluctuations. Seven multilateral trade negotiation rounds brought down tariffs and other barriers to global commerce, and culminated in the establishment of the World Trade Organization (WTO) in 1994. Better insulated from politics, central banks helped produced the Great Moderation, by now a quarter century of low and steady inflation around the world.

The world economy awakened to its potential. Beneficiaries of economic reforms and the integrating world economy, previously backward nations became vibrant emerging markets. The "Asian tigers"—Singapore, South Korea, Taiwan, and Hong Kong—that boomed in the 1980s were in the 1990s joined by the awakening giants, China, India, and Brazil, along with nations of Southeast Asia such as Thailand and Indonesia. In the decade between 1987 and 1996, emerging East Asia grew by 9 percent per year, powered by China's 10-percent annual growth. India took off with a 6-percent annual growth. Latin America harvested the results of its late-1980s and 1990s macroeconomic reforms, seeing regional inflation drop to single digits after years of hyperinflation, and growth rise to a solid 5 percent by 1994. Europe also overcame its 1980s "eurosclerosis" and went on to grow robustly at the turn of the decade. Embattled by the oil shocks of the 1970s, the stagflation of the 1980s, and the recession and Gulf War of the early 1990s, the United States thrived as the unquestionable core of the system, the hub of global trade, finance, and investment.

Slowed by Shocks

But the world was not perfect. Growth and globalization were not matched by stability. Financial and banking crises became more frequent and on occasion truly global, a testimony to excessive leverage and the shortcomings of national institutions in interfacing with the complex, interconnected world economy.

Developed economies went through a series of banking crises—Spain in 1977; the United States in 1988; Finland, Norway, and Sweden in the early 1990s; and Japan during the 1990s. Financial markets were volatile from the American Black Monday in 1987 to Europe's Black Wednesday in 1992, the collapse of hedge fund Long-Term Capital Management in 1998, and the end of the dot-com bubble of 2001. The emerging markets of Latin America and Asia experienced "sudden stops," rapid investor flight that undermined local currencies and canceled the newly found growth. Latin America's 1982 debt crisis delivered a lost decade, a period during which per capita income regressed by a percent each year. In 1994, right after signing the North American Free Trade Agreement with Mexico and Canada, Washington watched its southern neighbor collapse again, now under the 1994 peso crisis. The Southern Cone economies, Brazil and Argentina, suffered from what became known as the Tequila Effect.

The celebrated rise of Asia was interrupted by the 1997–1998 regional financial crisis that engulfed Thailand, Indonesia, Malaysia, and Korea. Sparked in part by hidden problems in the region's financial markets and banking systems, the crisis ground the regional economy to a halt and quickly spread to Russia and Turkey, sending shock waves through the world economy. Emerging markets suffered from chain reactions. After Russia defaulted, investors lost faith in Eastern Europe and Latin America, especially Brazil; as Brazil seized up and its currency collapsed, Argentina, dependent on exports to its neighbor, also ailed. Unnerved, investors deemed the United States the world's safe haven. The trouble resumed in 2002, when Argentina, the reputed star reformer of the 1990s, collapsed and defaulted on its $100-billion debt obligations to global investors.[3]

Instability cost. According to conservative estimates, bank bailouts took a toll of 2 percent of GDP in Norway in the early 1990s, 2.7 percent in the United States in the 1980s, 8 percent in Japan in the 1990s, and a high of 29 percent in Chile in 1981.[4] On the basis of data starting from year 1800, Harvard's Kenneth Rogoff and University of Maryland's Carmen Reinhardt calculate that the total costs of responses to banking crises—bailout of the financial sector, shortfall in revenue, and fiscal stimulus packages—have increased central government debts by an average of 86 percent in the three years after a crisis.[5]

In emerging markets, outside help was needed to end the hemorrhage. Throughout the 1980s and 1990s, America and the IMF acted as the world's shock absorbers, issuing politically consuming, multibillion-dollar rescues. Quelling the 1994 peso crisis alone required a US loan of $50 billion; rescuing the Asian nations took some $120 billion from the Fund and from other sources.

Order Tarnished   The stormy decade discredited the postwar institutions. The G7 was seen as a mere rich nations' country club with no stomach for hard commitments to steady global exchange rates, address economic contractions in the advanced nations, or end financial crises in the emerging world.[6] The IMF became the culprit for Argentina's collapse and was criticized for tough loan conditions in Asia that traumatized the recipients. Around the world, financial regulators seemed dwarfed by the expansion of global banking and financial markets. The conduits of free markets—deregulation, privatization, liberalization—were tarnished in developing nations disgruntled by stubborn poverty and inequality. Protectionism raised its head. Not unlike Europe in the 1960s and 1970s, emerging markets from Russia to Brazil, India, and a number of emerging East Asian nations reintroduced capital controls. An army of academics labored to rewrite the world economic order.[7]

But urgency was absent. Although blame abounded, challenges to the existing order were nebulous. Washington pursued some reforms both to placate critics and monitor emerging markets' policies. At the initiative of President Bill Clinton, in 1999 the G7 finance ministers began to meet with their emerging-market counterparts in a G22. Seeing gaps in the multilateral Basel Accord on global capital requirements, the United States and other leading economies devised a sequel, Basel II, in 2004. The Bush administration engaged emerging nations in talks to expand their influence in the IMF's governance.

With minor modifications, the global order remained intact. Power was not changing hands, either. Even after the blow of the September 11, 2001, terrorist attacks and the implosion of the dot-com boom, the United States reigned as the sole superpower. As the millennia turned, the status quo had prevailed.

Rebound
The bitterness of the 1990s lifted as the world economy rebounded. Globalization—cross-border trade and finance—roared, and economies grew increasingly interdependent. While global GDP expanded four-fold between 1980 and 2008, world trade expanded by a factor of six to $15.8 trillion and foreign direct investment by a factor of 20 to similar levels. Cross-border financial flows soared from less than a trillion dollars in 1980 and $1.5 trillion in 1990 to more than $11 trillion in 2007.[8] That year, total global financial assets, foreign and domestic, topped almost $200 trillion, or three and a half times the size of the global economy.

Financial liberalization propelled profits and entrepreneurship the world over. The free flow of trade and capital produced prosperity unattainable through domestic means and lifted millions out of poverty.[9] Advanced nations regained growth and prosperity.[10] Japan hibernated for more than a decade after its real estate market imploded in 1989, but growth resumed at a decent 2 percent in 2003. The European Union went on to thrive on the new common currency, central bank, and eastward expansion of its integration project. By 2007, five decades after being founded by six nations, the European Union would claim 27 member states and the world's largest single market, with almost 30 percent of global output.

America was back, growing at a handsome 3–4 percent annually. Stock markets boomed. Between October 2002 and October 2007, the Dow Jones Industrial Average soared by 94 percent, from 7,286 to 14,165 points. Consumers gained wealth and confidence, spending lavishly and borrowing to buy houses whose soaring values would back further spending. Private savings fell from some 4–5 percent of income in the late 1990s to 1 percent in 2005.[11] Not yielding even to hurricanes Katrina and Rita or the surge in global energy prices, growth would slow only in 2006 as the housing boom tapered off.

However, it was the emerging markets that stole the show. Goldman Sachs famously coined the term BRICs—Brazil, Russia, India, China—as a synonym for fast-growing juggernaut economies, projecting they would grow to rival the G7 economies by 2035.[12] Growth rates across Asia were staggering. India boomed by 8–9 percent each year in 2003–2007 on the back of growth in manufacturing and services—hotels, banking, telecommunications, and information technology. Its output expanding at double digits, China surpassed Italy, France, and the UK in 2004–2005 to become the world's fourth-largest economy, outpacing Germany in 2007. Global inequality came down as wealth spread across the most populous nations. Between 1981 and 2007, the share of Chinese in abject poverty declined from 64 percent to 15 percent; and of Indians from 55 percent to 35 percent.[13]

East Asia grew to a good extent by trading, often with the United States. In an implicit bargain labeled "Bretton Woods II,"[14] the United States stoked Asian growth by importing goods from the region in exchange for Asian investment to help sustain US consumption. In turn, Asia's insatiable demand for raw materials for manufacturing industries propelled Latin American commodity producers and Middle Eastern oil exporters. Emerging markets around the world grew and built reserves with which to invest abroad, often targeting the world's safest asset, US Treasuries. Emerging-market sovereign wealth funds, government-run private investment vehicles, set out to acquire assets at times deemed strategic across advanced nations, including stakes in America's crown jewel companies. In 2007 the China Investment Corporation invested a total of $8 billion in Morgan Stanley and the renowned US private equity firm Blackstone, and Dubai's Mubadala Development Company bought a 7.5-percent interest in the Carlyle Group. The reversal in global capital to flow "upstream" from poor to rich countries belied economic theories.

Economic transformations reverberated in global politics. China and Korea asserted themselves, challenging the decades-old Japanese hegemony in Asia. As a rising services economy with nuclear weapons, India became America's strategic linchpin between the tense Middle East and the ebullient Asia, serving as a counterweight to China. Encouraged by their nascent prowess, emerging nations formed their own G, a G24, which called for greater decision-making powers on the world stage, from the United Nations Security Council to the Bretton Woods twins, the IMF and the World Bank. Debate brewed on the rise of a multipolar, post-American world.

But the boom times cooled the fervor for an institutional shakeup. Not only did governments focus on sustaining growth; the contested institutions seemed to become increasingly irrelevant as well. The largest emerging nations, such as Brazil and China, while borrowing from the World Bank, transformed from aid recipients into lenders to needier nations. And armed with growing reserves, emerging markets graduated to higher credit ratings, ostensibly obviating the need for IMF's sovereign insurance.[15] Berkeley's Barry Eichengreen characterized the Fund as a "rudderless ship adrift on a sea of liquidity."[16] A hammer in a world devoid of nails, the IMF's future was narrowed to two options—to shrink it or to sink it. Washington was flooded with the résumés of laid-off Fund economists.

Unraveling

The Great Crisis upset the global political equilibrium. For the first time, the structural changes in the world economy—the potent rise of emerging markets—coincided with a stunning shock to the US economy and prestige.

The hypothesized drivers of the crisis are several—US government's housing policies, flawed mortgage underwriting standards, gaps in financial regulations and supervision, off-balance sheet finance, opaque securitization, perverse incentives for ratings agencies, low interest rates, global financial imbalances, interconnectedness of banks, excessive leverage, among many others—and they will be subject to academic research for years to come. Most arguments about the causes are thus far but opinions tainted by their advocates' ideology, politics, and professional positions. Even, or perhaps in particular, serious academics have fallen in the ideological trap, working backward to look for evidence to support their precrisis claims. In a caricature, Washington blames Wall Street, Congress blames the Federal Reserve, Democrats blame Republicans, and all blame the Chinese.

Refuting reality that does not fit in one's theory may be politically more expedient than doing the opposite. When firmer evidence does come in, it will dispel the argument that the crisis was only a Black Swan event, a random and rare confluence of events. Rather, it will be deemed a perfect yet preventable storm of many factors, domestic and global. The most plausible story is just that, one where Washington, Wall Street, and Main Street alike were at fault, each aided by willing foreign enablers. Loose money in America and loosened credit constraint resulting from foreign lending conspired with lax mortgage underwriting standards and federal support for sub-prime mortgages, producing the supreme housing boom and mass leverage across America. The securitization of toxic housing assets built wealth without worth—a fact that many did not understand and most who did ignored—that was traded across the Atlantic and around the world. Once the fallacy of the underlying asset grew evident, the collapse of the castle built in the air was only a matter of time.

But blame has no patience for research. As the turmoil unfolded from America in the epic fall of 2008, it was the United States that bore the bulk of the blame. Safely on the sidelines, critics around the world pointed at Washington. Emerging markets and Europe alike traced the debacle to America's housing frenzy and financial regulations. The punishment would fit the alleged crime. America's economy ailed more severely than at any time since the Great Depression. In 2009 GDP contracted by 2.6 percent, unemployment soared to double digits, and credit markets seized up. With the economy languishing and Washington responding with a $787-billion stimulus, America's fiscal deficit rose to 13.5 percent of GDP, more than double the level of 1983, when the United States was emerging from a deep recession. Europe, the region most keenly connected to American financial markets, followed in close tow.

With advanced nations on the brink, the entire world looked into the abyss. By 2009, global growth hit zero, world trade shrunk by 12 percent, and capital repatriated the world over. While all nations suffered, the pain was uneven. Cushioned by reserves earned from exports and strengthened by the reforms made after the late-1990s regional financial crisis, Asian economies would emerge as the oasis of growth in the insipid world economy. Economic resilience boosting their confidence, the regional economies, particularly China, set out to claim the center stage in global politics.

The economic shifts coincided with a renewed unhappiness with post-war institutions. Claims about their irrelevance turned into criticisms of their ineffectiveness. The press portrayed the G8 leaders as more interested in a sumptuous banquet at their July 2008 Hokkaido Summit than in pre-venting the rising storm.[17] The floodgates of resentment opened, with crit-ics from Mumbai to Moscow blaming the advanced economies for failing to solve practically all global problems, from climate change to food price crises, poverty, and wars.[18] Though having sounded alarms about the US housing bubble, the IMF was criticized as being oblivious of the depth of the problem and too optimistic about the world economy still in the spring of 2007, only months before markets turned turbulent.

With the US dollar trading at a record low of $1.57 against the euro in July 2008, the future of the world's anchor currency seemed dim. As Lehman Brothers fell, in September 2008, the world lost faith in America's free-range capitalism and the Federal Reserve's enigmatic inflation hawks. The 1990s as-surances about the end of history, an inevitable convergence of all nations to capitalism and democracy, seemed outdated; assertions that technocrats had at last unveiled the mysteries of macroeconomics sounded outright preposter-ous. Markets were deemed to be out; the managerial state was back in.

The world arrived in a fork on the road that to many commentators her-alded a dispersion of global growth, diffusion of global economic power, and, possibly, disintegration of the world economic order. With America subdued and the pillars of its order revealing cracks, the table was set for reform.

Peerless Order

The United States would not stand by and watch its construct unravel. The frantic search for ways to forestall a depression inspired changes to the global order largely at America's behest. The first reaction in Washington, shared in Europe, was that the emerging players would have to be made an integral part of the solution; the subsequent consensus was that the existing institutions and instruments of the American order needed to be retailored to defeat the hydra-headed problems of the twenty-first-century world economy.

It was the United States that in the fall of 2008 assembled the leaders of the G20 nations to their first-ever summit in Washington and that a year later at the group's Pittsburgh Summit originated its leitmotif, the "Framework for strong, sustainable and balanced growth" aimed at taming global financial imbalances. It was the United States that proposed a tripling of the IMF's resources to respond to the spreading crisis and that subsequently persuaded a reluctant Europe to expand the powers of emerging nations in the world body. It was also the United States that first drove for an overhaul of financial regulations and envisioned the Financial Stability Board (FSB) as the global regulatory coordinator of the stature of the IMF, World Bank, and World Trade Organization. As the world doubted the dollar, it was the United States that rose in defense of the greenback as critical to the US and world economies, and pledged fiscal discipline to buttress it. And while others hesitated, it was America that first picked up the lessons of the Great Depression and pushed back the impending collapse with its entire fiscal and monetary policy artillery.

The thrust of US actions, many designed by the Treasury's seasoned civil servants, was not unfamiliar or surprising. The intent mirrored that of the United States since the mid-twentieth century: to further America's interest in global economic growth and stability, the economic expressions of the enduring US national interest in peace and security for its citizens, by creating, fostering, and, when necessary, reforming global economic institutions. Washington's pursuit was premised on the same notions that guided US policy when the allied victors crafted the postwar order at Bretton Woods: the United States benefits from a global economy, and a global economy requires global institutions. The liberal postwar paradigm was to be kept intact; only the institutions created to advance it would need to be retailored to meet the economic needs and political demands of the new century.

The measures were not altruistic. They were geared to driving the interests of an inherently global economic power, one keenly integrated with practically every economy and each day more dependent on the fortunes of the world economy for its prosperity. They were also deeply rooted in crisis-torn America's pressing domestic political imperatives to promote growth, propel exports and jobs, and preempt discrimination against US economic interests. And they reflected America's vested interest in the postwar order and Washington's impulse to preserve it.

Even if in the lead, Washington was hard-pressed to drive its agenda. The Bush administration showed strong strategic sense by convening the G20 in Washington, but it was also consumed by crisis management at home and the struggle to pay full attention to the broader questions of global governance. Battling against time, Washington fashioned policies of consequence on the fly. Treasury Secretary Henry Paulson, seconded by Federal Reserve Chairman Ben Bernanke, was at pains to convince the incredulous Congress to release $700 billion for the Troubled Asset Relief Program (TARP).[19] The Fed purchased more than $1.7 trillion in Treasury and mortgage debt, and partnered with the Treasury to rescue companies such as Citigroup and American International Group, awakening Americans' suspicions of central bankers captive to Wall Street.

After power changed hands in January 2009, a good share of the Obama Treasury team remained on the sidelines, awaiting Senate confirmation through the administration's first year in office. Both White House and Congress were less focused on global economic policy than on the epic health care reform. Captive to union lobbies, the president shunned his predecessor's trade liberalization agenda; eager to respond to voters infuriated by Wall Street, he put forth financial regulatory reform aimed at cracking down on banks. Facing an indignant world harboring pent-up hopes for dovish US foreign policy, the administration chose to self-censor abroad, projecting an image of an apologetic America. It was only at the third G20 Summit in Pittsburgh in the fall of 2009 that Washington seemed to awaken to the responsibility to lead.

Order Imperiled

The past few years have been extraordinarily difficult and divisive in America. But they have hardly undone the American order. Rather, they have reaffirmed it. The new institutions, the G20 and FSB, are but US-conceived sequels to US-created entities. Investors have deemed America the safe haven in the recoiling world economy, and the dollar has persevered as the world's reserve currency. The mission and capacities of the Bretton Woods twins, the IMF and the World Bank, have only been expanded. No country has resigned from these institutions; rather, outsiders are clamoring for a seat on the coveted IMF Executive Board or an invite to the charmed club of the G20. Nations have opted into, not out of, the American order.

Core ideas have survived. Capitalism and free markets have taken but nonfatal blows, open trade regimes have largely prevailed, and central bank independence is defended more vocally than it is criticized. Albeit contentious and critical, the global policy debate has not been about overhauling the world economic order; it has been about reforming what already exists. Proposals may have changed, but the paradigm persists.

The durability of the American order reflects its merits and the absence of alternatives. The American order is designed to advance growth and globalization and safeguard global stability. It is a coherent institutional and intellectual framework—one of rules-based institutions premised on free markets and good governance. It is a liberal order rooted not on notions of international anarchy or the failed experiment of history—coercion—but on open markets, private property, and, when those are met, democracy.[20] It is not an order imposed, but an order adopted. It has prospered because of its built-in promise of mutual economic gains to its adherents—gains unattainable by other means. That practically all countries have joined it in the past six decades is a testimony to its exceptionalism.

The American order is an inherently American order, for its values are the founding values of the United States. There are no competing paradigms for global governance, for there are no substitutes to the institutions and ideals of the American order. There is a reason why there is no second IMF or a WTO, no shadow G20 in waiting, no grand scheme to dissolve global financial markets, no real rivals to the dollar, no match to independent central banks, no ideology better than capitalism for harnessing individual incentives in the interest of common prosperity. The leading nations have chosen their institutions and held on to them. There may be regional currencies or regional financial arrangements, but they are at best imperfect substitutes for the institutions of the global order.

But Washington has no room for complacency. The American order is peerless, but it is also periled. It is increasingly hard-pressed to weather twenty-first-century global economic challenges and manage conflicts among the leading nations. And US leadership is falling short.

The Threat

The paramount threat in the twenty-first-century world economy is systemic, global financial instability. The threat has been present for centuries—between 1300 and 1800, Austria, France, Germany, Portugal, and Spain defaulted on their external debts on a total of 19 occasions, a telling sign of repeat turmoil.[21] But except for the Great Depression, the effects of instability have not been as global, malicious, or systematically devastating, particularly in the advanced nations, as in the Great Crisis. The crisis is a case study of the prowess of instability—credit crunch, unemployment, public debt, toxic politics. No country remained immune, and not one could be secured quickly enough. The crisis literally drove the threat home. The adversary crystallized.

Financial instability occurs when a large number of parties—consumers, households, companies, and/or governments—experience financial crises that collectively amount to negative macroeconomic effects.[22] It is not a microeconomic event—a shock affecting a few households or a set of firms—but a macroeconomic one. As such, it affects the economic and financial behaviors of even those consumers and businesses that are mere innocent bystanders. Global financial instability is a grade greater: regardless of its epicenter, it gushes over bystander nations.

The causes of financial instability vary from one crisis to the next, defying scholars and policy makers each time. In a broad generalization, crises in the nineteenth century were largely bank failures; between the 1940s and the 1960s, crises combined bank failures and sharp devaluations; while in the 1980s, 1990s, and now the 2000s, the origin was real estate booms and busts, accompanied by excessive leverage.[23] But despite the differences in place and time, the buildup periods to crises share familiar features—an asset bubble followed by financial euphoria, risk taking, and accumulation of debt.[24]

Abetting the treacherous sequence of events are thorny interactions among discrete problems and snowballing, self-fulfilling prophesies. The Great Depression is the premier example of both forces at work. A leading scholar of the era, current Federal Reserve Chairman Ben Bernanke, argues that the debacle was caused by a "financial accelerator," or amplification of a series of smaller financial shocks in the course of 1930–1933 that made credit more expensive, which lowered investment and aggregate demand, which, in turn, turned a recession into the Great Depression.[25] Another way in which smaller shocks are augmented is a psychological one: euphoric or fearful, financial actors tend to engage in self-destructive herd behaviors. The effects are familiar: changes in consumers' wealth and buying patterns, and havoc in firms' balance sheets and investment decisions.

Into Turbulence

Scholarship on the causes of the Great Crisis will become at least as voluminous as that on the drivers of the Great Depression. Causal relationships now regarded as facts will be refuted, new determinants uncovered, and previously hidden fractures exposed. "Robo-signers" who cleared as many as 10,000 home foreclosures represent just one example of surprises that once eluded analysts. But though much remains to be learned, three facts already stand clear.

First, while long the norm in the world economy, instability has become more frequent in the past 40 years. After the Asian crisis, a team of leading economists systematically explored the odds of a banking and/or currency crisis in 21 advanced countries in four periods—the pre-1914 era of globalization (1880–1913), the interwar period (1919–1939), the Bretton Woods era (1945–1971), and the end of the twentieth century (1973–1997). The likelihood of a crisis in at least one economy in any given year in the latest (1973–1997) period was nearly 10 percent, or only somewhat less than during the traumatic interwar era and well above the time of the gold standard of the immediate postwar years.[26] When 35 emerging markets are added in the data, the odds of crises at the end of the twentieth century rise to 12.2 percent—meaning that any one country has a one-in-eight chance of being struck in any given year. Coming to 2010 and looking back a quarter century reveals a crisis every three years.[27]

Predicting the odds of crises in the twenty-first century is next to impossible. But countless economists now foresee a continuation, perhaps even a rise, of the recurring instability. As interdependence among nations grows, emerging markets ascend, financial markets expand, and politics and economics intertwine, complexity is high and tail risks tall. The Great Crisis of 2008–2009 may have been a consummate crisis, but it was also a crisis *inter pares*, and it is feared to be a harbinger of travails to come.

Second, even small flames can turn into bonfires torching entire economies because of the magnitudes of markets. Even in 2008, a dreadful year in the global economy, global financial assets stood at $178 trillion, or more than three times the global GDP. The assets of global banks rival the economies of entire nations: assets of the infamous three Icelandic banks that collapsed in the historic fall of 2008 amounted to six times the island nation's output. Banks are large even for large economies: HSBC's assets equal UK's GDP, and BNP Paribas's assets equal French GDP, while Deutsche Bank's assets are more than four-fifths of the German economy.[28] The US mortgage market, a source of great troubles in the latest crisis, is the size of three-quarters of the entire US economy.

The third known fact is that while the causes of instability can be domestic (such as excessive leverage) or international (such as exchange-rate volatility), the effects always risk being global.[29] One reason is global financial flows that connect markets to one another. Before the crisis, cross-border financial flows amounted to $11 trillion, more than the GDPs of Japan and China combined. Portfolio inflows can quickly go in reverse when a country is hit with an adverse shock. Global capital tends to be pro-cyclical, flowing to markets when times are good and getting out when things go sour, and providing no cushion for rainy days.

As the conduits of financial flows, financial institutions are themselves global. For one, banks play a role in many economies. Upon its fall, Lehman Brothers sported 2,598 outlets with a staff of 26,000 in more than 50 countries. The Icelandic banks, when collapsing, froze accounts in numerous European countries to the effect that host nations had to bail out depositors who were their nationals. When a bank's mother ship ails, many nations can get hurt. Moreover, financial institutions are keenly interdependent, inherently able to take one another down. Lehman's fall resulted in up to $100 billion in losses to its unsecured creditors holding its bonds and commercial paper around the world. There were psychological aftershocks: the crude realization that financial giants could be allowed to fail raised the cost of credit to such Wall Street stalwarts as Goldman Sachs and Morgan Stanley.[30]

Economies are linked not only by flows but also by perceptions: as long as investors group together economies with similar characteristics and risk profiles—such as "emerging markets," "frontier economies," or the infamous "PIGS" (Portugal, Italy, Greece, and Spain)—the demise of one nation undoes confidence in the others. In the 1990s the Tequila Effect of the Mexican crisis in Brazil and Argentina—economies with only tenuous trade and financial ties with Mexico—and the reverberations from the Asian crisis across the emerging world were indicators of contagion at work. More recently, as the depth of southern Europe's fiscal deficit came to light, the future of the highly indebted California fell into doubt. As America lost its triple-A status, the credit ratings of the debt-laden European economies were thought to be at risk. The Russian saying "Fear has big eyes" is apt for global financial markets.

Even nations whose banking systems withstand the external shock, as those of China, Canada, and Australia did in the Great Crisis, will suffer once financial tremors start straining real economies. The negative secondary effects on trade in goods and services and on foreign direct investment travel through countries engaged in economic exchange. As trade and financial flows are interregional and global, so are crises. For example, by closing down advanced nations' foreign direct investment and import demand, the Great Crisis reduced growth in Africa, hardly the eye of the financial storm, by an estimated 2–4 percent in 2009 alone.[31]

Besides contagion, crises can be created by so-called synchronous shocks. In the 1980s, Latin American economies collapsed after the US interest rate hike that made their dollar-denominated debts too expensive to service. In the fall of 2011, Washington's budget standoff and its lackluster resolution engendered a roller coaster in global markets. In a globalized world economy, there are few isolated incidents, and there is nowhere to take cover.

Imminent Danger   The renowned economist Anna Schwartz, who in the 1950s established the fundamentals of monetarism with Milton Friedman, has made a distinction between "real" financial crises, marked by a scramble for liquidity requiring action by a lender of last resort, and "pseudo-crises," collapses in asset values that lead to losses in wealth but do not require the lender of last resort.[32] Both are devastating. Troublingly, elements of both are looming.

The headliners *du jour* include the Southern European debt crisis, America's budgetary morass, inflationary pressures in emerging economies, and soaring global oil and commodity prices. Responses to each have been garbled. Europeans have for two years failed to converge on a plan bold enough to once and for all assure markets. Washington has been agonizingly divided, delayed, and devoid of presidential leadership in confronting the fiscal problem. China and other emerging economies, torn between the need for growth and the necessity of stability, have reverted to the old bad habit of employing capital controls to control inflation—instead of swallowing the right medicine: macroeconomic and monetary tightening. The cocktail of economic volatility and policy uncertainty creates noise in financial markets, conspiring to keep investors on the fence and businesses from investing.

There are further troubles in sight. America's price stability is at risk. In the 1970s, inflation became hyperinflation even though the 10-year Treasury bond yields never anticipated it. The situation now is not dissimilar. In September 2010 the yield on the 10-year Treasury note was 2.8 percent, the lowest points since 1955, and inflation a mere 1.3 percent. By July 2011, yields had not picked up, but inflation had, to 3.6 percent, as food and gas prices kept inching up. Rising costs eat into companies' bottom lines and discourage savings, reducing funds that could be used for productive invest-ments. If inflation soars, it will have to be brought down, as in the 1980s, with an interest rate hike that will inevitably kill any growth in America and around the world.

Now consider exchange rates. Volatility in currency values can turn com-panies' overseas investments into losing propositions practically overnight. In a Deutsche Bank survey, exchange-rate risk ranked as the top strategic issue facing executives, above market risk, commercial risk, and others.[33] The risk is all the more relevant now that emerging nations are resorting to capital controls and engaging in currency wars to export their way out of the eco-nomic trough. Add to that the talk about the dollar's demise in the face of America's debt problems, low interest rates, and current-account deficits.

Much of the pessimism is overblown—the dollar has survived many eco-nomic and political challenges during its postwar reign. But the greenback faces a thorny dilemma. The demand for fresh reserves, resulting from future expansion of the world economy and trade, risks overwhelming the US ca-pacity to supply them without mass deficits—which, in turn, could undercut the dollar. At the same time, there are no good complements that would al-leviate the dollar dilemma. The most feasible co-currency, the euro, is amid a crisis of confidence thanks to the European debt crisis and governments' procrastination in responding to it. A third of Germans, the very creators of the vaunted single currency, now believe that the euro will be replaced by old national currencies within a decade. Consulting firm McKinsey is raising the specter of an "unmanaged" global currency regime of "greater exchange rate uncertainty and destabilizing shifts in cross-border capital flows."[34]

Global imbalances pose yet another threat. The imbalances reached a historic 5 percent of world GDP in 2006, with US trade deficit soaring to an unprecedented 6.5 percent of US GDP. The pattern is rebounding, as global oil prices are expanding the current-account surpluses of Middle Eastern oil exporters, as China and Germany perpetuate their export-led growth para-digms, and as the United States is bound to borrow from overseas to cover its gaping budget deficit. Without adjustments, the imbalances will climb to their historic precrisis heights, where they can only worsen hidden fissures in financial systems. Worse, a re-rise of the imbalances could herald a hugely perilous "Bretton Woods III" system, where global growth is supported not by US private demand but by America's fiscal spending.[35] No longer distant, such a scenario would wreak lasting havoc on American finances and trade policy.

Protectionism sentiments would be shared by other current-account-deficit nations pressed by import penetration.

What about another bubble? Many bubbles are less hideous than the housing one yet still inflict pain. The dot.com bubble, in which high-flying tech stocks sold in excess of 100 times earnings, did not devastate the US economy upon crashing, but it hurt, in America and abroad. The several recent tech IPOs have arguably had inflated valuations. A further bubble of potentially much greater consequence is building up in the bond market, where investors have flocked in escape of uncertainties in stocks. True, bond bubble fears have been percolating for a number of years, but they are also warranted. Jeremy Seigel and Jeremy Schwartz point out that if the interest on the 10-year Treasuries were to rise from 2.8 percent to 3.15 percent, bondholders would suffer a capital loss equal to the current yield.[36] If the rate were to rise to 4 percent, the capital loss would be more than three times the current yield. Perhaps a global crisis would be averted, but even so, the outcome would be harrowing.

Why Instability Matters

Instability matters not only because it can destroy livelihoods; it also matters because it undermines growth and places globalization at risk. Sustained growth hinges on stability.[37] So does globalization. Granted, economic openness helps transmit shocks, but it is not their cause. Openness and globalization are often blamed for instability, but the causal relationship is the reverse and inverse: instability causes protectionism. When stability and growth go, voters vouch for keeping foreigners out and jobs in. Capital controls, tariffs, laws, and loans emerge that are favorable to local firms. And yet such measures cancel out the gains from globalization and only arrest the odds of growth further, besides introducing new, destabilizing frictions in the global economy. Beggar-thy-neighbor tariff protectionism amid the Great Depression was the nail on the world economy's coffin. The grand paradox is that right when open markets are needed for reviving growth and employment, those fearing for their jobs start opposing openness.

Free and open markets remain the optimal policy. They are a source of strength and a pathway to prosperity. Financial openness has resoundingly been shown to increase the availability of credit and deepen financial systems—which, in turn, are found to reduce the volatility of economic growth.[38] The ultimate effects of turmoil often depend not on the extent of openness but on the institutions of the affected nation. Countries that are open and have gone through serious crises yet have good institutions capable of halting and weathering instability are likelier to grow faster than closed nations without crises. Compare Thailand, a liberalized economy that has been on an economic roller coaster, with India, the much less open economy that has practically been on a steady train ride. India's GDP per capita grew by 99 percent between 1980 and 2001, but Thailand's grew by 148 percent—despite the Asian financial crisis of 1997–1998, which devastated the Thai economy.[39]

The solution to instability is not to close down markets or revert from globalization: that would cancel the growth gains of the past decades and impoverish the world. The benefits of free markets, economic openness, and globalization far outweigh any trade-offs. But as long as there are free markets, there will be business cycles; as long as there are credit markets, there will be speculation and asset bubbles. As long as economies are interlinked, the contagion of crises cannot be undone. Rather, it must be managed. How to best do that is the quintessential question of our time. And it is the existential question facing the American order.

Order Imperiled

In contrast to the early-twentieth-century "orderless" era that delivered the Great Depression, beggar-thy-neighbor policies of the 1930s, and two world wars, the American order has been a stunning success. A midwife of growth and globalization, it has also been a shock absorber and automatic stabilizer. It has time and again cushioned against crises and combated their reemergence. But it has also been more successful in generating growth than in ensuring sustained stability. And it is now wearing thin. Even as refurbished, the American order appears dwarfed by today's global economic challenges.

Consider the IMF. Even with the new $750 billion in lending power, the Fund's armory is but a fifth of the $4 trillion that the United States had committed domestically by spring of 2009 to stem the crisis. While America's is a large economy, it is only one-quarter of the world total. A future shock facing a group of countries of roughly the same economic size as America, but without the resources that Washington has at its disposal, would overwhelm the Fund. The Fund's modus operandi chips away at its effectiveness. It is a reactionary body that lacks levers to preempt crises before they flare. Yet fixes are elusive. Expanding the Fund much further would be unwise, inspiring moral hazard among spendthrift nations. There are also organizational limits to a wholesale mission: the Fund's lean staff is already struggling to juggle its duties in an institution seen more as a single-minded hedgehog than a multitasking fox.

The largest economies have sizable domestic resources to respond to crises, but they too are exposed. In America, the Treasury and the Federal Reserve's epic bank bailouts, credit expansion, and zero interest rates softened the fall, but did not save the nation from the worst economic calamity since the Great Depression. The trade-offs were steep, from a massive expansion of the public debt to politicization of central banking. The main limit to the government's response was not political or self-imposed, but economic: two years after Lehman's fall, Bernanke confessed that the Fed had simply lacked the means to salvage the Wall Street giant.[40]

Across the Atlantic, the boundaries to action are political. Failing to marshal an indigenous response to the Eurozone crisis, Europeans resorted to the IMF for additional resources and experience in disciplining spendthrift economies. And even at $1 trillion, the continental rescue program failed to quell investor anxiety about the Greek budget and the Spanish housing market.

Even East Asia, a region with more than $4 trillion in reserves and an incipient $120-billion regional rescue fund, fell hard. Regional economies hit by the crisis, such as Korea, had to resort to emergency swap lines from such nations as China, Japan, and the US Federal Reserve as its banks and companies ran out of foreign currencies to repay their external debts. Singapore also needed the Fed's help. Ad hoc improvisation took over, and the world economy sank.

What of preventing crises altogether? As the Great Crisis became traced to shortcomings in financial regulations and their enforcement, regulatory reform was made the centerpiece of the response. But despite the claims of Washington Democrats, the new regulations will neither prevent crises nor extricate taxpayers from the burden to bail out banks. The 2,319-page Dodd–Frank Act has serious holes—for instance, it does nothing to address the defamed mortgage giants Fannie Mae and Freddie Mac, which helped perpetrate the very crisis. Worse, the law is counterproductive. Saddling banks with multiple requirements and such straitjacketing regulations as the Volcker rule cuts into bank profits and only accentuates the kind of reckless risk taking that the regulatory spree was said to curb.

Blind faith in regulations is also foolish, for two reasons. First, as long as financial markets are global and regulations national, the bite of America's regulations is blunted by rules and events elsewhere. Suspect policies in one part of the world will have repercussions in others just as quickly as instruments issued in a bank in Hong Kong find their way to counterparts in New York and Frankfurt. Yet the regulatory overdrive in the United States and Europe is matched by under-delivery in international coordination on issues that matter, such as cross-border bank resolution. Second, regulations are an inherently imperfect defense against instability because of the method of making them—a myopic focus on regulations. Systemic risks tend to result from a confluence of factors, rendering regulations a sliver of the solution. Regulators cut some trees, but not the entire forest.

Granted, policy makers have sought to transcend myopia and address global imbalances, alongside regulations the leading contender for the main culprit for the crisis. However, the G20's balanced growth agenda is thus far words more than action. Countries necessary for rebalancing—China, the United States, Japan, Germany, Saudi Arabia—will not alter their policies just because they may have committed to doing so at the summit table, let alone if the other members thought a change in course was desirable. The G20 process can at best expose the countries most at fault and build pressure on them. Rebalancing ultimately requires unilateral measures: cuts in the US budget deficit; a commitment by China and East Asia, Europe, and the Middle East to stimulate domestic demand; and an end to China's currency mercantilism. Remedies are known. Results have yet to show.

Could central banks prevent crises? The lack of Fed action in culling the housing bubble has been widely criticized. But there are countless political and technical questions for central banks trying to identify bubbles—essentially, they would be in the business of determining "correct" asset values. If a veritable bubble were identified, bursting it with an interest rate hike could be ineffective and extremely counterproductive: rates are too dull a tool for bursting specific bubbles, yet they are hugely consequential for the overall US and global economies. A bubble might get killed, but so might economic growth. Moreover, the empirical evidence on the contributions of monetary policy to the rise in housing prices is mixed. The lesson from studies is that while loose monetary policy can contribute to asset bubbles, it may not drive economies into crises—while tightening may only make things worse.

Prisoner's Dilemma

Across the board, economic instability now overpowers the tools designed to gird it. All countries share an interest in growth and stability, and many of the weaknesses in the world economy, from global imbalances to exchange-rate volatility, debt buildups, and lack of concerted responses to multinational bank failures, could be mended by better international coordination among the leading economies. As the Great Crisis unfolded, the leading powers did issue commitments to cooperate to jump-start global growth. However, rapport became tenuous as the urgency of the crisis lifted. Instead of coordinating policies and rallying behind the common institutions, the major powers—United States, China, Germany, India, Britain, Japan, France, and Russia—are trapped in a destructive prisoner's dilemma, clashing over policies to prevent the next crisis, elbowing for an edge in world financial markets, and jockeying for power in global economic institutions. Some of them, like China, are at odds with the very American order.

The drive to tame global imbalances epitomizes the problem. Needing exports for growth and employment, China and Germany disagree with the United States, the UK, and other deficit nations on the G20's rebalancing effort. China cites domestic structural constraints to boosting domestic consumption, and faults the US budget deficit as the source of the global pattern. Running the world's largest budget deficit and continuing to battle deflation, Japan has few tools to spur domestic consumption. Germany deflects the problem, claiming it to be a US–China one, and has resolved to export its way back to growth. Europeans and the United States clash with Beijing on China's undervalued exchange rate, an Asia-wide phenomenon and one of the drivers of the imbalances. Tokyo is reluctant to criticize Chinese economic and exchange-rate policies so as to avoid antagonizing its next-door trade partner and rising military power. At home, Washington is deeply divided over the road to fiscal solvency, giving China and Germany reasons to claim that America is at fault.

The divisions have diluted policy. Take the G20's commitment in the June 2010 Toronto Summit to halve government deficits by 2013 and "stabilize" debt loads by 2016. The pledge is not international cooperation, but merely a statement that describes national policies that were already in place. Entailing that all countries can adopt the policies they want to adopt, the group struck a balance between thrifty and spendthrift nations, respectively spearheaded by Germany and the United States. This reflects the familiar fact of international

relations: fiscal policy is a sovereign prerogative. But Europe's fiscal retrenchment and US spending, coupled with the weak euro and Asia's continued export drive, reaffirm the US role as the world's consumer of last resort.

Also, the IMF's future is contentious. The United States and Europe favor
the Fund's leadership in global crisis management, while emerging nations in
Asia, still resentful of the Fund's loan conditions during the 1997–1998 Asian
crisis, prioritize self-insurance and regional financial arrangements. With a
vested interest in the IMF and hopes to continue spearheading Asian integration, Japan falls in between, counseling gradualness in the Asian schemes.
Europeans and Chinese clash over the Fund's mission, with the former keen
on preserving the work in small developing nations, the latter seeking to focus the Fund on the largest economies. The United States, while placing the
Fund at the heart of its global financial policy making and eager to increase its
scrutiny of emerging-nation policies, is uneasy about multilateral judgments
on US economic policies.

The latest fault line at the IMF is the use of capital controls. Emerging
markets have claimed that the US Federal Reserve's quantitative easing, along
with Europe's monetary loosening, has created a destabilizing gush of global
liquidity that stoked inflation in the emerging markets and justifies their capital controls. They have rejected the IMF's proposed guidelines on certain permitted controls—which implicitly bar capital controls not on the list.

Disagreements over substance are exacerbated by discord over structure.
Emerging markets, especially India and China, call for an ever-larger role in
IMF governance. The United States has sought to accommodate the rising
powers, supporting a 6-percent expansion in their voting quota and calling
on European nations to relinquish some of their eight seats on the fund's
24-member board. Europeans, whose interest in the postwar order translates
into reluctance to reform, resist changes as the likeliest losers in any power re-
shuffling in the institution over which a European has traditionally presided.
At the same time, emerging markets are failing to converge on IMF policies or
back a common candidate to spearhead the institution, as evinced by the lack
of support in 2011 for Mexico's Agustin Carstens, the first serious emerging-
market contender for the IMF's managing director, by Africans and China.

Politics hampers coordination on financial regulations. To be sure, global
regulatory harmonization would be as foolish as it is unfeasible. However,
common principles to guarantee open, free, and nondiscriminatory global
financial markets are in America's interest, especially as new financial centers

aiming to displace London and New York as global financial hubs are sprouting across Asia. Yet regulatory nationalism is raising its head. Transatlantic discord has flared over European rule blueprints that favor continental institutions over foreign ones, and the United States and Europe are on different pages on rules on derivatives, hedge funds, and accounting standards. Less-scathed nations such as Canada and Australia resist US and European politicized regulatory zeal. The BRICs are decidedly unenthusiastic about blanket rule prescriptions emanating from Washington and Brussels, and instead argue for restraints on American market capitalism, IMF surveillance of large countries, and new global currencies. And as capitals prioritize politically expedient reforms such as caps on bankers' pay or piling regulations on the "too-big-to-fail banks," issues of real importance risk falling through the cracks.

 The dollar has fallen prey to politics. During the crisis, China and Russia sparked a crisis of confidence in the dollar by setting out to lobby for a system based on special drawing rights (SDRs) housed at the IMF in place of a dollar-centric order. Beijing is also working to expand the reach of the renminbi in its bilateral trade relations and across Southeast Asia, worrying Japan, the once-envisaged core of an Asian yen bloc, and India, a regional currency contender. Meanwhile, the United States and Europe vehemently defend the importance of the dollar's primacy to the world economy. Yet in America, policy makers clash on policies to curb the fiscal deficit, undermining the world's faith in the greenback.

 Today's politics renders economic stability precarious. Politics also hampers global growth. Deep and encompassing global trade liberalization would give the world economy a much-needed jolt and do so without new stimulus dollars, but the odds of progress are slim. The Doha Round talks collapsed in July 2008, as India, backed by China, torpedoed the deal, citing US and European agricultural subsidies and tariffs as an excuse for not opening its market to foreign competition. China resists deepening its trade commitments made in 2001, when it joined the WTO. And, catering to union supporters, the Obama White House has been uncommitted to free trade and has seemingly scant regard for the global trading system that America has assiduously built over the past six decades.

 The stakes in the Doha Round span the billions of dollars that would immediately result from new liberalization. The deal would also curb the ability of emerging economies to jerk up their multilateral tariffs at whim, and it

would deliver so-called dynamic gains of trade opening, such as new investments that thrive on trade, and healthy competition—creative destruction—
in the shielded emerging economies such as Brazil and India. It would also
give new impetus to the WTO, whose credibility has suffered tremendously
by Doha's travails and whose respected dispute settlement system risks irrelevance as long as trade negotiations keep failing. Nations around the world
are searching for an edge in global commerce by pursuing bilateral free trade
deals that, while liberalizing some channels of commerce as talks in Geneva
languish, can balkanize the world trading system into mini-blocs that complicate the operations of big and small global companies.

Politics stands in the way of fixes to the American order and only exacerbates its weaknesses. Most difficult, the very underpinnings of the American
order are questioned. The United States, Europe, and Japan appreciate the
existing order and its rules-based institutions. Many emerging nations, such
as India, Brazil, Mexico, and Korea, are predisposed to it, even if sensitive
to power structures unfavorable to them. But China, albeit with little choice
but to opt into the prevailing order lest it be a pariah, is philosophically at
odds with the very notion of global governance. Also Russia is lukewarm to
the world order that it considers crafted and choreographed by Washington.
Moscow takes on multilateral responsibilities reluctantly and rarely issues
constructive proposals.

Leadership Void
The twenty-first-century international political economy pits global institutions against regional schemes, global rules of the game against calls for
sovereign prerogatives, and aspirations for a global marketplace against as-
sertions of state power. Common threats pull nations together; national interests draw them apart. The conundrum is a familiar one in international
relations, yet the past is not instructive in the present. The main powers of the
twenty-first century are economically weightier and politically bolder than at
any time in the postwar era, able to constrain, even derail, US policy. US–UK
pacts behind the Bretton Woods consensuses would no longer have wings.

Yet the central tenet of global economic governance is that someone has
to coordinate the play, that somebody has to keep it all together. During the
critical 1945–1948 construction of the global economic order, the world came
and was kept together due to American strength, vision, and leadership, not
because multilateralism was in vogue and everyone had a say. The leading

nations were able to launch institutions that would shape the course of the twentieth century because there was a towering actor aware of its national interest in an integrated world economy. It was American power and leadership that created and subsequently sustained the world economic order. Helpfully, the leading nations' interests were aligned with those of the United States: the transatlantic consensus was to build institutions that would tie countries' fates together and make war unthinkable.

A global power with global interests, the United States kept it all together. America paid a disproportionate share of the workings of global institutions, brokered differences among nations, and provided critical global public goods—a global reserve currency, deep and predictable financial markets, an open trade regime, and vigorous economic growth. Aiding the American paradigm was a dichotomous world, a contest of capitalism versus communism where nations able and willing to join the American camp opted for free and open markets. But leadership was never easy: there was resistance by allies to America's aspirations, recurring protectionist pressures at home, and volatility and wars that diverted Washington's attention. The United States has always faced constraints on the world stage and even in its own backyard: America's keen engagement notwithstanding, Nicaragua fell under Sandinista rule, and Haiti frequented the lists of failed states. Still, the United States got global economic integration done.

Leadership is again required. And again it must be American. There are no substitutes for US leadership: although the cast of characters on the global stage is larger than it was in the mid-twentieth century, leadership runs thin.

China, a rising power that plays a savvy game of *realpolitik* and expands its reach with the power of its purse, does not claim other nations' loyalties and remains reluctant to shoulder global responsibilities, instead casting itself as a "developing country."[41] It is a mercantilist, transactional nation uninterested in universal values, multilateralism, or providing global public goods. While views of the usefulness of the postwar order vary within China, the current leadership sees them as Western constructs antithetical to Chinese interests, devices to entangle China in pursuits not of its choosing and restrain its rise.[42]

Beijing engages selectively, primarily in the interest of national security, but also as window dressing to mollify Western powers that demand it be a responsible stakeholder.[43] Cantankerousness has prevailed over cooperation in China's foreign policy. Backing India, Beijing helped perpetrate the deadlock in the Doha Round. It maneuvered with Brazil, India, and South

Africa to undermine the global climate change agreements in Copenhagen. It has truncated the G20's global rebalancing agenda and resisted curbs on capital controls. Although a member of the IMF and the World Bank, China has long lent to developing nations without the conditions of good economic governance demanded by the multilateral bodies—yet with conditions to access the recipients' raw materials and secure some degree of political acquiescence. At home, Beijing has only complicated the operations of Western companies located in China with red tape and discrimination, continued to arbitrarily block foreign investment, and failed to curb the rampant intellectual property violations of foreign products. Even US companies with thriving operations in China have grown weary of protecting China's honor in Washington.

When China sparks interest, it sparks economic interest; when it inspires, it inspires worry. And even if uncomfortable with the order in which it became a global economic power, China has at best a vague vision of the kind of international relations that would be most amenable to it. China, in short, is a global player and it is a major power, but it is not a world leader.

India does better in terms of soft power but, though transcending its geographic location with trade in services, has a long way to go economically. Japan, albeit a linchpin in Asia-Pacific politics, remains trapped in a decade of deflation and is neither economically nor politically powerful enough to lead—nor is it fixed on seeking global supremacy, instead exercising restraint on the world stage.

Europe, preferring the welfare state to economic dynamism, is constrained by a lack of growth and perennial politicking among its nations. The repercussions of the debt crisis cloud Europe's economic future, and the continent faces an epic demographic challenge of rapidly aging populations. To be sure, Europe is increasingly integrated, with common trade policy, financial regulatory principles and supervision, as well as foreign policy. In September 2010 the EU's foreign policy chief, Catherine Ashton, unveiled the list of the first 28 EU ambassadors of the new European External Action Service. But it is national governments that ultimately shape their own financial and foreign policies. Each nation has a foreign policy toward European foreign policy, and all fiercely contest European-wide policy initiatives.

When needing to exercise hard power that a global leader has to exercise—such as prevent genocide in the Balkans or stop an invasion of Kuwait—Europeans have waited for Washington to take charge and pay up and make it right. President Obama's apologetic 2009 statement, "'[I]n

America there is a failure to appreciate Europe's leading role in the world," should have been reserved for a time when Americans do have a reason to be impressed and no reason to be derisive.[44] Europe is simply too divided, unprincipled, stagnant, and nostalgic to lift the world and point the way forward as America has time and again done. Europeans know it: witness the sigh of relief from Berlin to London upon the election of Obama, whom Europeans idolized as portending a restoration of sturdy multilateralism in global affairs.

When aspiring to ignite its economy or exercise a coherent foreign policy, Europe continues to compare itself to America, its traditional yardstick—when America compares itself to no one, except on occasion to its past self.

Groups of countries fall short of global stewardship, as well. The Northeast Asian threesome, Japan, China, and Korea, each vie for influence in Asia and are unlikely partners to lead the world. The BRICs is an acronym developed on Wall Street and based on economic characteristics, not a like-minded group able to converge on detailed policy agendas. The G8 is not only increasingly obsolete, but only as cohesive as Western Europe is itself.

This leaves the United States. But America is not only a leader by default. It is also the only nation capable enough by its power, invested enough by its interests, and persuasive enough by its order and its temper to lead.

Mirage of Decoupling   The United States is the overwhelmingly wealthiest and most powerful nation. It is the world's predominant economy by any measure. The US economy makes up nearly a quarter of global output and is almost three times larger than the Chinese economy. US exports and imports make up some 14 percent of world trade; China's total is still one-half of that. US financial assets make up almost a third of global financial assets, and New York, with London, continues as the world's financial hub of unrivaled depth and scope. Yes, these figures have changed and are changing as others gain wealth. That is fine: America thrives on the prosperity of others, not their poverty. The point is that America will be a leading economy for decades.

Some would argue that the fortunes of the United States matter less to the emerging economies as the latter grow and trade more with one another. However, a global "super-cycle" driven by emerging economies is a distant prospect: emerging-market consumption remains too limited to offset dips in US consumption, and there remain steep barriers to seamless integration among the emerging economies. Indeed, rather than diverging, the fortunes of emerging and advanced economies are converging: the correlation of their outputs has tripled over the past decade.[45] The world's two-speed postcrisis recovery notwithstanding, emerging markets continue to need advanced economies to thrive.

Those arguing that America is becoming an actor *inter pares* tend to presuppose that political power flows from economic prowess alone. America's primacy spans economic power. It is not a stretch to say that the Bretton Woods system came together and the Berlin Wall fell because of the ideals and enlightened policies of the United States, and because America's power and moral authority gave it the license to lead. America's repertoire of power—economic, military, diplomatic, cultural—dwarfs those of other nations. While others may be gaining wealth, the United States is still supreme in world politics, a nation whose policy choices and relationships are more consequential than those of any other. America's global relations are mature and entrenched; China's are younger and based on economic interests rather than on shared values or security.

No other nation has as compelling an interest—economic, strategic, or vested—to secure the world economic order as the United States does. US interests are inherently aligned with those of the many nations that seek prosperity by way of integration in the global economy. While no longer (if it ever was) a hegemon, the United States is still the only nation able to continually bring nations together to define solutions to common problems.

The American order undergirding the international system also renders America the leader. While some, such as Robert Kagan, argue that America is now in a *realpolitik* balance of power game with China and Europe, the characterization does not capture the essence of the global polity.[46] True, in the classic realist world, states operate in a state of anarchy, and the most powerful states—states with the largest economies, militaries, populations, and so forth—are conceptualized as poles, with the global polity altering between various types of polarities. Europe of the mid-nineteenth century was a multipolar system, the Cold War was a bipolar one, and the system afterward was unipolar. But global affairs are not conducted in anarchy or on the basis of pure market interactions, as presumed by the traditional conceptualization of international relations. Instead, states are better viewed as interacting in hierarchies where they exercise varying degrees of authority over one another not necessarily because of their capacities, but because some states recognize that other states have authority—a legitimate right—to issue certain orders, or to "rightfully rule."[47] Based on a social contract among the dominant state(s) and subordinate ones, hierarchy is a political order that holds as long as subordinate states see the prevailing order as worth the loss of autonomy.[48]

The American order has been based on the mutual economic gains that it delivers to nations around the world. It is an implicit global social contract, and it reaffirms the hierarchical global polity with the United States at the top. Providing stability and predictability, the American order has helped dispel anarchy and multiple equilibria in global economics and politics. The price for the United States has been to lead—to serve as the coordinating core, the stabilizing broker, and the supplier of global public goods. The price will have to be paid again.

Slippage of Our Choosing

Arguing that America is disqualified from leading because the current crisis began in the United States is futile. Not only are global economic challenges insolvable without America; there are no substitute leaders. Just as the global economic order of the twentieth century cannot be understood without grasping the role of the United States, so the twenty-first-century order cannot be crafted without America. The United States may be down, but it remains the indispensable nation.

Yet America's economic troubles are very real. US leadership is withering as America struggles with epic deficits, uncertain growth prospects, and morale-busting unemployment, all precursors to protectionism and isolationism. In a recent poll, 49 percent of Americans believe that the United States should "mind its own business" and let other nations get along on their own, up from 30 percent in 2002 and the highest figure in 40 years of polling.[49] And 43 percent of Americans believe China is now the leading economic power, as opposed to 38 percent vouching for the United States.[50]

America's economic problems are raising questions about the US ability to lead, but it is US willingness to lead that should be the subject. The Obama administration's policies have led to a dramatic expansion in the US fiscal deficit and have done precious little to revive the economy and create jobs. The gaping budget deficit hurts the dollar, exacerbates global imbalances, and stifles America's economic dynamism—and undermines America's preeminence. At the same time, the administration has failed to do away with the excessive taxes and regulations that stifle the engines of recovery and jobs, America's small and large businesses. Its $30-billion package for small-business loans launched in 2010 remained untapped due to lackluster domestic demand. And Obama's National Export Initiative unveiled in 2010 to double US exports in five years lacks the resources to get the job done.

US fiscal policy is a disgrace. The budget impasse in July 2011 unsettled world financial markets and delivered the first-ever downgrade of America's gold-plated triple-A status. The deal was timid, and the failure to lock in a long-term plan for America's fiscal health would have made the United States a global laughingstock were the specter of a new American crisis not so terrifying. A perverse triumph was that America was still viewed by most investors as the safe haven in a world economy bedeviled by the endless Eurozone crisis and foggy growth forecasts for emerging economies. The fiscal problem is acute; the need for Washington to undo it is urgent.

The United States is not matching its calls for free and fluid financial markets with deeds. Treasury Secretary Geithner has rightly demanded that Europe not enact a number of discriminatory financial regulatory proposals circulating in Brussels and Paris. But at home, Washington is enacting rules that will undermine competition in America's financial markets, the twentieth-century global envy. The Obama-sponsored Volcker rule curtails banks' proprietary trading when such trades had practically nothing to do with the crisis. It echoes the Glass–Steagall limits on bank operations that unnecessarily elevated Americans' cost of credit and limited banking services for more than five decades. There is fault at both ends of Pennsylvania Avenue. The Dodd–Frank Act supercharges the new Financial Stability Oversight Council and Bureau of Consumer Financial Protection Agency to a point where financial institutions, large and small, may decide to focus on appeasing Washington more than engaging in the kind of hard-knuckled competition that is the essence of American market capitalism.

Politicking gone awry has also jeopardized central bank independence, the crowning achievement of twentieth-century economic policy making that spread from the United States to other nations to produce a quarter-century of global freedom from inflation. As the Fed pulled down interest rates and opened credit lines, some congressional representatives sought to take advantage of the Fed's credit window for political ends, while others rose to accuse monetary mavens of interfering with fiscal policy and stoking moral hazard, and sought to curb their independence. Congressman Ron Paul's books on abolishing the Fed rose to the best-seller lists.[51] Central bankers from London to Seoul, Berlin, and Tokyo faced similar politicized attacks. The scrutiny is only bound to intensify now that central banks have been vested with vast regulatory powers.

America's trade policy is adrift, hurting US broader foreign policy objectives. As the crisis breezed through, Washington sent the wrong signal abroad by enacting such discriminatory measures as the "Buy American" provision attached to the stimulus bill. Congress resumed its calls for trade barriers against China to retaliate against Beijing's currency manipulation. Catering to its union supporters, the Obama administration took almost three years to seek the ratification of three pending bilateral free trade agreements (FTAs) negotiated by the Bush administration with South Korea, Colombia, and Panama. The action came only after unemployment persisted in near double digits and the administration wanted to expand the Trade Adjustment Assistance (TAA) benefits for workers laid off due to foreign competition. Republicans accepted the TAA as a quid pro quo for the FTAs. The problem with the packaging is that it perpetuates the flawed perception that trade deals undermine American jobs.

The bright spot in US trade policy is the Trans-Pacific Partnership (TPP), which Washington pursues with eight small Asia-Pacific markets. But while promising to be a gold standard deal, the TPP will have little economic impact, as the United States already has free trade deals with four of the eight partners. For the TPP to deliver real economic gains and be of strategic value, Japan and Korea would need to join the deal. Persuasion by the Oval Office would make a difference.

Multilateral trade liberalization is the first-best trade policy, but the global Doha Round lies dead in the water. The fault is to a large extent in emerging economies such as India and Brazil that hold on to their barriers against foreign manufactures and services and fear that further opening would flood their markets with cheap Chinese goods. But it is also the case that the United States does not appear committed to the talks and to getting more from cantankerous India and China. America's slippage on trade gives license to other nations to cut corners. Global tariff protectionism has been rather muted in the aftermath of the crisis, but the G20 nations alone introduced more than 500 discriminatory trade policy measures between the first summit in November 2008 and the start of 2011, despite repeated commitments to forego protectionism and finish Doha.

America's languishing trade agenda hurts US relations with key allies in Asia and the Americas. It undermines the world trading system that America has built and that has opened markets for US industries around the world. And it weakens Washington's hand in dealing with US trade deficits and global imbalances: America's calls for open trade regimes abroad sound hollow when Washington is not living up to its end of the bargain.

The sense of drift spans trade. President Obama has failed to articulate a clear grand strategy for US foreign policy. It is not clear that he has one. In the words of the renowned Democratic foreign policy scholar Zbigniew Brzezinski, rather than strategizing, President Obama sermonizes.[52] The lack of clarity of purpose notwithstanding, some threads running through Obama's first three years can be detected: modesty instead of assertion of America's prerogatives on the world stage; an accommodating stance regarding difficult states and rivals such as China; taking a backseat in such multilateral decisions as the selection of the IMF managing director; "leading from behind" amid the political convulsions of North Africa and the Middle East; and an attempt to shift some of the burdens of running the world to other nations.

Such approaches have premises. One appears to be that America is weakened and has to make way for the rising nations; another is that other states would reciprocate an accommodating stance as well as step up to the plate if America withdraws. Granted, the setting has been extraordinarily difficult for the administration: America in an epic economic crisis and emerging nations elbowing for power. But in international relations you do not necessarily get the behavior you think you reward. Others have not exactly reciprocated—witness for starters Chinese cantankerousness on the currency, India's intransigence on trade, and Russian reluctance for a "reset" in its relations with America—and they have not stepped up to the plate. Neither has America. President Obama has opted for convenience, backpedaling from US pledges made at the Pittsburgh Summit to conclude the Doha Round by the end of 2010 and reduce the deficit to tame global imbalances. This has let other nations do the same. The result has not been multilateral governance, but reciprocal unilateralism.

When America's eye should be on the ball, focused on restoring US and global growth and economic stability, it is deviating to political convenience. Self-defeating Washington deadlocks and divisive "Wall Street vs. Main Street" rhetoric hamper solutions to the nation's troubles, and "foreign policy leadership" is becoming an oxymoron. The onset of the 2012 presidential race promises to postpone fixes.

Triple Risk

The world is facing a triple risk. It is a risk of frailties of the institutions of the American order, deepening divisions among major powers, and a global leadership vacuum. The setting is hugely consequential for the twenty-first-century world. A perfect storm of the three risks would deal a severe blow to US interests. It would undo the American order and unleash a world economic disorder of mercurial financial markets, widening global imbalances, spread of state capitalism, and beggar-thy-neighbor protectionism. It would also change the global polity, eroding mutual economic gains and resulting in a world without order, a scenario with a sorry past that is abhorred by all nations. The downfall of the American order would imply the onset of a non-polar world or multipolar balance of power politics. Neither is desirable. The former is a near impossibility, for it is hugely unstable; the latter is a frequent phenomenon, especially at regional levels, but prone to conflict. Can such a world be avoided?

Remake

It is impossible to prevent all crises, but it is possible to manage their wrath. The American order is designed to safeguard stability, just as it is aimed to advance growth and globalization. Its properties—rules-based institutions and the ideals of free markets and good governance—must now be preserved; its success story, economic growth, restored; and its menace, economic instability, tackled. An order that proves defenseless will lose its credibility and, with it, its resilience.

The stakes are high. The world economy will be drastically different if the American order thrives than if it crumbles.

The starting point offers opportunities. The grounds for growth—economic liberalization, globalization, the creation of wealth, and the expansion of middle classes across the emerging world—are unprecedented. The institutions and policies that have advanced growth and stability are also now systematically present.

The goals are clear. The aim must be a world where crises are prevented, not reacted to only after they reach a raging gale. A world where risks are assessed today, not weighed only after they converge into a catastrophe. A world where instability is promptly managed away, not perpetuated by confusion or political contention. Yet also a world where the quest for stability does not trump the pursuit of growth. In such a world, economic openness is embraced as a conduit of strength and stability, not shunned as a source of vulnerability, where incentives for financial innovation and entrepreneurship are stoked, not killed off by zealous wholesale policies, where the private sector is prized as an engine of prosperity, not demonized as the avaricious adversary.

Global growth and stability are foremost US interests, and they are not antithetical. Sustained growth requires stability. But economic stability is of no use without growth—and lackluster growth can in and of itself be destabilizing.[53] Drives for the twin goals must be kept in a healthy tension, with the pursuit of one checking and abetting the quest for the other.

This is easier said than done. Stable growth is elusive. There can be unforeseen shocks beyond any government's grasp, from commodity price swings to exchange-rate volatility and political uprisings. There will be new unknown unknowns. And as throughout history, economic trends will not be neat and linear, but impose new, sudden demands on policy making.

What is more, fostering the world economic order is difficult, for it is a political endeavor. Economic policy turns on political economy. The future of the global economic order depends on the politics of and among nations— and right when national politics must align, they clash. Not all policy makers and nations see the postwar economic order as more legitimate, relevant, and effective at furthering their aims than conceivable domestic and regional alternatives. And few are resolved to aspire for long-term benefits if it means foregoing gains today.

Strategic Multilateralism

Reforms and regimes are not automatic. They require leaders to prosper. Only the United States can help the world transcend this dangerous moment. America is the indispensable leader of the peerless order. America must uphold its order, and only it can. But indispensability does not equal influence. The United States is perhaps more constrained than at any time in the postwar era, both home and abroad. Although the other players do not match US leadership, they condition it; even if America has raw economic and political power, it faces financial trade-offs. The setting begs better strategies.

The first pillar of US leadership needs to be strategic multilateralism. Multilateralism is often used as a convenient fall-back strategy among US foreign-policy makers struggling to articulate a vision for the rapidly changing, postcrisis world. At the same time, it remains critical. It is critical not because it is a high-minded principle or an internationally expedient cliché, but simply because US economic objectives in the twentieth-first-century global economy are hard to attain without it. A global power in a globalized world economy needs global approaches.

Multilateralism implies working with all main nations at once. It is most effective when embedded in economic institutions predicated on America's values. The United States has assiduously built such institutions in the past six decades. For a global power such as the United States, multilateralism economizes negotiations, actions, and transactions: it allows Washington to work with all important nations simultaneously across issues. Unwinding global imbalances, critical for containing asset buildups and defusing the anti-trade mood in Congress, calls for adjustments by all the main surplus economies (China, Germany, Japan, and the Middle East); ensuring fair treatment to US banks takes a commitment by European and rising Asian financial centers alike to good regulatory principles; safeguarding global price and financial stability requires all main economies to pursue sound economic policies.

Multilateralism is of further instrumental worth: it reinforces America's benign intent. It helps claim the loyalties of others by providing assurances of restraint in US foreign policy. It is consistent with a conservative foreign policy, for it preserves the American order and upholds America's primacy. Coupled with the application of American values, multilateralism is a self-imposed check that lends America power. David Lake elegantly writes that "to grant authority to another state is one of the most profound acts any country or people can make. Countries do so only when they believe the dominant state will exercise its authority fairly and in the general interest."[54]

Some have advocated opportunistic "minilateralism" or "manylateralism."[55] For the United States, such prescriptions require nuance, for they have trade-offs. America is a global power whose bilateral and regional relations affect the multilateral agenda, and it is both a Pacific and Atlantic nation whose actions in one theater reverberate in the other. The United States is a preeminently multilateral actor. Yet selectivity is of the essence. Multilateralism must be strategic: in a world of multiple demands and manifold players, the United States must choose those that truly matter. And constrained for means, it must play its hand right.

Two priorities run through this volume. The first is revising instruments and policies to effectively tackle economic instability—global imbalances, contagious financial crises, exchange-rate instability, the specter of protec-tionism. One part of the answer is to upgrade multilateral, system manager institutions. For example, the IMF should be made into a bridge between pri-vate and public insurance markets in order to harness the resources of the pri-vate markets to combat financial crises. Another part is recrafting US bilateral and regional policies, such as taking a more muscular approach to confront China on its currency manipulation. Still another part is domestic policy—restoring US fiscal health and growth and cementing central bank indepen-dence are key to buttressing the dollar-centric currency order and reducing global imbalances.

The second priority is to get back to the task of integrating the world econ-omy. This means two things. One is to expand global trade and investment at the multilateral and regional levels. The multilateral trade regime needs to be restored by concluding the Doha Round and launching a new round with a fresh modality to negotiate plurilateral deals among coalitions of the willing. At the same time, America must reinvigorate the pursuit of deeper access to American goods, services, and investments in the fast-growing markets. The passage of the FTAs with Colombia, Panama, and Korea must be followed by a comprehensive transpacific free trade area and plurilateral economic inte-gration schemes in the Americas and the Middle East. Replacing the drift on trade and investment policy with such vigorous agendas is one of the most cost-effective ways to expand America's exports, ensure fair treatment to US investors, and reengage America's friends and allies at a time when they are courted by China and other powers.

Integration also means averting a balkanization of the world economy. In contrast to the 1940s, the international institutional ecology is now hugely diverse, one where global institutions are paralleled by a mosaic of regional and bilateral arrangements. Regional arrangements have many benefits. For example, regional financial schemes in Asia and Europe and, perhaps in the future, Latin America can buttress the IMF's surveillance and crisis-manage-ment functions. Their members have front-row seats to regional dynamics and the keenest interest in extinguishing local financial fires. Regional "first responder" funds would also help the IMF weather crises beyond its means and turn down some of the political heat for rescues incurred by one admin-istration after the next in the United States, the Fund's largest shareholder.

But relying on regionalism alone would be risky, complicating efforts to spot and contain globalizing crises. Regional schemes fail to harness the potential of the global economy and fall short of managing global crises: they can only complement, not substitute for, a global order. But in a world of multiple overlapping institutions joined by the quest for growth and stability, purist multilateralism is elusive, and it is foolish. Rather, the policies and actions of regional arrangements must be better synchronized with those of multilateral instances.

Getting Pivotal Powers to Play   America's success at managing instability and advancing integration in the world economy depends on engaging and influencing the emerging economies. Part of the answer both in the Bush and the Obama administrations has been to align emerging nations' political power in multilateral venues with their growing economic weight. The G8 has been expanded, with the G20 now seating many of the nations resentful of its predecessor. The FSB also doubled the membership of the Financial Stability Forum to 24 nations. The IMF's quotas were rebalanced, even if rather modestly, in favor of underrepresented nations, particularly China.

Whether giving emerging economies a seat at the table translates into buy-in is far from clear. But absent a stake in the system, emerging markets are guaranteed not to play by it. Preserving the postwar multilateral economic order requires tying emerging markets into it. The world economy has no enforcement authority: common commitments will need to be self-enforced, and thus inherently in the key nations' interest. Policies cannot fly if the weightiest are not on board.

The point is not to aspire for some kind of international legitimacy, a term that has been overused in recent years. With all nations having an equal say, legitimacy might be maximized, but so would inefficiency and ineffectiveness. The point is also not to make accommodations as gestures of goodwill or to futilely attempt to turn rivals into allies. And the point certainly is not to call for dogmatic multilateralism, let alone internationalism in American foreign policy, for opportunism and pragmatism are immensely valuable amid the convulsions of the global economy. The point is simply that integrating the emerging players in the system America has built is more useful for influencing them than leaving them out would be. We may not like what they have to say and vice versa, but at least we are talking.

Yet Washington must not issue blank checks. This is no time for altruism. For every new right, emerging nations must assume new responsibilities. If they do not and instead keep breaching the common rules of the game, giving them a seat at the table will enfeeble the US-built institutions. This is a huge dilemma facing America's policy makers. The Obama administration is becoming trapped into it with China, conducting quiet diplomacy and helping China gain greater powers at the IMF, when Beijing has only grown more pugnacious on the world stage.

Professed good intentions by Beijing, New Delhi, or Moscow are not enough and must not be taken at face value; only manifest actions matter. What are those? For starters, articulating constructive policies rather than opposing Washington for the sake of opposing in multilateral forums; living up to commitments to forego trade protectionism, arbitrary barriers to investment, and discrimination against foreign companies; enforcing intellectual property rights; and putting an end to currency manipulation and capital controls. Such measures do not force any nation to mimic "American-style" capitalism, but merely to safeguard globalization. And they are not impossible. There are examples of rising nations that have quickly grown into responsible stakeholders. South Korea, the host of the 2010 G20 Summit, is a case in point, as is Mexico.

It is far easier to call for the emerging economies to deliver such desirables than to get to them to do so. In fact, rewarding certain behaviors with greater say at the multilateral level is meaningless unless the supposed beneficiary values the reward. It is not clear that China, for instance, does. How Washington can influence the rising powers to act in US interests is the quintessential question facing US policy makers in the twenty-first century. The diplomatic chess game poses an enormous challenge, and its outcomes will be immensely consequential for America's economy and its role in the world.

Tenets of Diplomacy   How should the United States manage its relations with the leading powers? Start with the region critical for US foreign economic policy in the twenty-first century, Asia-Pacific. America cannot neglect the importance of its relationship with China. Even if often opposing Washington's agenda, Beijing is a necessary counterpart for arresting global imbalances, reorienting the IMF, coordinating financial regulatory principles, undoing the deadlock in global trade talks, and preempting world inflation.

Beijing's actions will critically affect America's attainment of its interests in the world, but moving China is difficult. It prioritizes its own agendas and schedule, where a decade appears to equate the American half a year. It disagrees with a range of US policy objectives, from RMB appreciation to firmer investor protections and enforcement of intellectual property rights, to name a few. And China has only grown more confrontational abroad and toward foreign business interests at home. Disconcertingly, as leading China scholar David Shambaugh writes, "2009–2010 will be remembered as the years in which China became difficult for the world to deal with, as Beijing exhibited increasingly tough and truculent behavior toward many of its neighbors in Asia, as well as the United States and the European Union."[56]

The US relationship with China has often been one of false hopes and repeated frustrations. It is also one of asymmetric information: while the United States calls for transparency, China prefers discreteness and secrecy, arguably as a means to perpetuate Washington's uncertainties about its true intentions and capabilities.[57] But disagreements and obstacles do not warrant disengagement. While opening American ties to China in the 1970s, Secretary of State Henry Kissinger remarked that "we can do more to advance the day when China will be able to recognize it is in her interest to join in rational and constructive relationships with the outside world."[58] In the 1990s, as China crushed the Tiananmen Square protests, many in Washington argued for an embargo against China until it addressed human rights concerns. But engagement won the day, and economics tied the United States and China together. The policy carried over from the Clinton administration right to Henry Paulson's desk.

The Obama administration prioritized the US–China relationship, sparking speculation about a "G2" duopoly at the helm of the world economy. Some, including Kissinger, have since argued that a privileged relationship with China would have negative strategic repercussions for US alliances in Asia and Europe.[59] But that depends on how the other relationships are managed. And a close relationship with China should help more than hurt outsiders' interests: after all, it is Washington, not Brussels or Tokyo, that needs to work to secure Chinese collaboration on issues also of interest to US allies, such as on imbalances, trade, climate change, nuclear proliferation, and North Korea. But thus far it is the case that America's pivotal Asian allies, India and Japan, do feel slighted by Washington's intense focus on China.

America's accommodating stance regarding Beijing is also misguided. In lieu of quiet diplomacy and deference, the United States has to take a more muscular stance with China—be more vocal and critical of China's currency, trade, and foreign policies, and much more forcefully summon allies to the cause. One immediate measure at the bilateral level is to better harness the potential of the bilateral Strategic and Economic Dialogue (S&ED). The dialogue remains an assortment of episodic bilateral talks on numerous topics and has very limited impact. It should be upgraded to a system of year-round working groups that would tie China to permanent interactions with the United States in good times and bad.

Clear from the outset is that success with China depends in part on playing America's hand right with the rest of the world. Beijing tends to respond better to events and pressures outside the bilateral US–China relationship than within it.[60] The idea is not to craft an anti-China block or incite tensions, as that would only make China belligerent. Rather, Washington must keep engaging China but use its alliances and friendships as a lever with Beijing. With most emerging economies uneasy about the ascent of China and Beijing's currency, trade, and foreign policies, intellectual property rights violations, and flailing product standards, the United States has a chance to play the China card—convince others that managing the rise of China requires them to invest in the rules-based international order. Korea, Mexico, India, Brazil, South Africa, and the ASEAN states all share this basic understanding. Washington must also avert fissures in the Western alliance and persuade Europeans to work much more vigorously in prodding China and other emerging nations.

US policies in East Asia will be critical. Washington must hone America's special relationships with allies and pivotal partners—Japan, Korea, India, the largest ASEAN nations, and the quasi-arbiter among Asians, Australia. Each of these partners is important on its own for US trade, investment, and strategic interests, and strong bilateral economic and political ties with these economies can be leveraged in dealings with China. America also has to deepen its reengagement with ASEAN, a growing region courted by each of the Northeast Asian powers; fuel the alliance with South Korea; and keep working closely and firmly with Japan, the pillar of US forward presence in the Asia-Pacific for more than 60 years and a nation with an overwhelmingly positive view of America and Americans that prefers multilateral and trans-pacific approaches to intra-Asian ones. After a keen focus on China and an accommodating stance toward Beijing in the first two years in power, the Obama administration showed much improved strategic acumen and interagency coordination in the fall of 2011, as the president toured Asia, announcing various security and trade measures with America's traditional allies.

However, bilateral approaches are not enough. While regional jealousies and disparate national agendas make most Asians prefer bilateralism with Washington, bilateralism has four pitfalls if pursued alone.

First, many of the global issues discussed in this volume, from global imbalances to exchange rates, the future of the IMF, financial regulations, and the global currency regime, depend on not a few but several Asian nations and, most importantly, on bargains among them.

Second, a regional approach helps defuse claims that America is ganging up against China. An explicit intent to encircle China would unnecessarily create tensions and would be unlikely to appeal to smaller East Asian economies that are now intricately interlinked with China's economy and worried about its future military capabilities.

Third, bilateral approaches are inadequate for addressing America's economic interests in Asia because those interests are inherently region-wide. To a large extent, the Asian nations are in US economic interests *by virtue of* being hugely interconnected with one another in trade and finance. Asia's main attraction is its economic integration. American companies transact throughout the region and trade and invest regionally, rather than only bilaterally. As long as it is based on open regionalism, Asian economic integration is in the US interest, and Washington needs to encourage it.

Fourth, a regional approach enables the United States to engage the many economic integration schemes in Asia, which, while beneficial, risk both dominating Asians' attention and becoming exclusive blocs unless their members are also connected interregionally. The United States has participated in the meetings of some of the key arrangements, most notably the ASEAN summits. Continued US involvement is critical, especially in light of China's inroads into the region.

Such subregional efforts need to be couched in broader regional engagement with formal US involvement. America's joining the 18-nation East Asia Summit process in 2010 at the initiative of Hillary Clinton's State Department is a very positive step to fuller engagement in the Asia-Pacific. The Asia-Pacific Economic Cooperation (APEC) forum, which was founded by the United States with various Asia nations in 1989 and which propitiously also includes Russia, Australia, New Zealand, Canada, and Mexico, among others, is another useful transpacific lever for America. APEC offers a counterweight to the ASEAN+3 and ASEAN+6 arrangements, among other pan-Asian organizations, and is critical for the US foothold in the region.

However, APEC is not doing what it set out to do in the early 1990s: free Asia-Pacific trade and investment by 2020. Unleashing the region's full economic promise requires a more concentrated focus and deeper commitments to integrate the Pacific Basin in terms of trade, investment, and finance. With skillful diplomacy, the TPP can become a docking station that all APEC nations can join when ready for a binding commitment to liberalize trade and investment in the vast region. Japan and Korea's joining the TPP talks would overnight reshape the economic and strategic landscape in Asia Pacific to America's advantage—yet another reason why the TPP is of strategic importance.

Washington must continue deepening transpacific regionalism as a hedge against fortress Asia and a means to prosperity in the region crucial to US economic interests. The United States has clout in Asia: 13 percent of Asia's total trade and a much higher share of its trade in high-tech goods are with the United States. Many regional nations are deeply concerned about potential US security and economic disengagement. US allies in Latin America that border the Pacific are enthusiastically pursuing integration with Asia and can be tapped as partners in America's Pacific policy. Three US trade agreement partners of the region, Peru, Chile, and Mexico, are already APEC members. Brazil, a Western Hemisphere power that is growing more assertive yet is amenable to cooperation with the United States, has found an insatiable market in Asia for its commodities and airplanes.

Strong bilateral relationship with India, a US ally in a volatile region, is crucial. The Clinton and Bush administrations rightly upgraded US–India relations with agreements on peaceful nuclear cooperation and intensified security and economic cooperation. But the strategic purpose has withered in recent years as President Obama has prioritized ties with China and decided to withdraw from Afghanistan, raising New Delhi's concerns over Pakistan's next moves in the region. Despite torpedoing the Doha Round in 2008 with China, India has a troubled relationship with China. They two have simmering border tensions, and New Delhi worries about Beijing's flexing its military muscles in the neighborhood and overall regards Beijing warily as a rival in South and Southeast Asia. The Obama administration may have made a mistake in 2009 when it promoted US–China cooperation in South Asia. It needs to reengage with Nepal, Sri Lanka, and Bangladesh to counteract China's heavy presence in India's neighborhood.

Granted, Indians have not played nice in the past few years. They have become more antagonistic on global trade and climate initiatives, dragged their feet on meaningful domestic economic policy reforms, and disappointed on bilateral economic opportunities, such as rejecting US combat aircraft in India's biggest defense deal yet and failing to enact legislation necessary for US companies to develop India's nuclear industry.[61]

However, worried about China and prizing its strategic ties with the United States, India's leadership wants to reinforce rather than undercut US leadership in Asia and around the world. New Delhi also sees America as key for India's economic development and rise on the world stage. The United States has to reassure India about our commitment to the strategic partnership and to counterbalancing Chinese influence around India. And the US–India investment treaty needs to be retrieved from the Washington bureaucracy and implemented as a precursor to a deeper and more encompassing economic integration agreement.

Now come to the Americas. Washington's engagement in the Western Hemisphere has receded dramatically in recent years as the administration has stressed Asia in US foreign economic policy. Yet Latin America is growing more prosperous and remains critical for US economic and strategic interests. The US relationship with Mexico is complex and intricate, but the strategic sense that NAFTA and the decade of its implementation gave is withering. President Obama hardly has the commitment that George W. Bush did for close cooperation with Mexico. The US relationship with Brazil is also underwhelming and underused, marked by clashes over the Nuclear Non-Proliferation Treaty, Brazil's protectionist trade policies, and US cotton subsidies. The Summit of the Americas process, launched in 1994, has deviated from the aspiration for a Free Trade Area of the Americas and become a white elephant—largely because of the discord between Washington and Brasilia.

The United States must reengage, both to retain its status as the number-one outside economy in Latin America at a time when China has made extensive inroads across the region, and to integrate the Americas economically. The several bilateral free trade deals the United States has in the region offer a ready platform, and knitting them together would create an eleven-nation free trade and investment bloc, a process that some Latin American countries are already pursuing. Such a deal would reaffirm the US relationship with key allies Chile, Colombia, and Mexico; advance economic integration in the Pacific Rim; and pressure Brazil and Argentina, Latin America's reluctant liberalizers. The Brazilian penchant for smooth diplomacy in lieu of confrontation and President Vilma Rousself's positive view of the United

States do offer an opportunity for connecting the hemisphere's two largest markets and building rapport between Washington and Brasilia at the international level. Yes, the United States should phase out barriers to trade in agricultural products that vex Brazil, but do so because that would be good for America. Concessions to the South American giant must entail reciprocity: access to US goods and services in the protected Brazilian market.

As the co-author of the Bretton Woods world, Europe is central to advancing America's economic interests. It is the most like-minded partner with a vested interest in the American-led postwar order, and a critical partner in buttressing democracy and free markets around the world. Despite its woes, Europe is also a necessary partner in the remake of the global economic order. Transatlanticism is a tool for setting and driving the global economic policy agenda. By working with Europeans, and Germany and the UK in particular, the United States can set the global agenda on issues large and small, from the future of multilateral institutions to new financial regulations and common product standards in global commerce.

America's tie with Europe is so strong that the Old Continent fears and complains about being taken for granted in Washington. Many observers in both Washington and Brussels agonize over the perceived lack of high-level strategic vision in the US–European relationship. But while perhaps comforting, such grand schemes are not essential with Europe. The continent shares America's intellectual backdrop, mature domestic laws and regulations, and vested interest in global institutions and free markets. With joint interests self-evident, the focus is freed from diplomatic niceties to the arcane authoring of practical rules that make transatlantic and global finance and trade flow. The current focus is rightly on the Eurozone crisis; on the longer haul, a comprehensive transatlantic FTA would give the bilateral relationship fresh impetus and a new focal point for the various ongoing sectoral and regulatory discussions, replacing the current piecemeal and disaggregated agenda.

Having a strong relationship with Asia gives America bargaining power with Brussels. Closer trade integration with Asia helped Washington compel Europe to finalize the multilateral Uruguay Round in 1994. Transpacific initiatives have also been multilateralized: the Information Technology Agreement (ITA) incubated in APEC was by the mid-1990s adopted by the WTO as a way to free global trade in the sector. The demands are several on the world stage, but retaining the focus on institutions conducive to a growing and stable twenty-first-century world economy will channel bureaucratic energies in the right direction.

Economic Leadership

None of America's multilateral or regional goals can be attained without restoring US economic leadership.

America has been a policy entrepreneur and a wayfarer in the postwar world economy. It is an example to nations large and small on ways to meld good governance, economic openness, and free markets to produce the world's most dynamic economy—one that rewards risk taking and entrepreneurship. Today, the US economy is not exactly the global beacon. Unemployment persists at its highest levels in a quarter-century, growth forecasts remain uncertain, and the fiscal deficit is at its deepest since World War II, diverting necessary investments in US productivity. Economic frailties exacerbate threats to US interests and undermine efforts to defeat them.

Restoring America's economic prowess is key for meeting global economic problems, for they cannot be met without the United States. It is imperative for US international engagement, for engagement requires economic resilience. And it is critical for the credibility of US leadership. A nation that squanders its own economy will not be granted the authority to lead.

Washington did well in steering the immediate global response when the Great Crisis broke. But bad policies have been seeping in during the past few years. They do a disservice to Washington's credibility with friends and foes, and undermine the pursuit of global growth and stability. And they highlight the current lack of Washington's grasp that it is American leadership that holds the world economic order together.

The United States must reform at home to lead abroad. As long as America does not fix itself, live up to its pending commitments, and take on new responsibilities, it cannot drive others to do so. And if the United States does not lead, no one else will. Leadership has a steep price, but it must be paid: at this pivotal moment in history, it is the price of prosperity. It requires Washington to reengage globally, recommit to the aspirations for free flow of finance and trade, and reinvigorate the institutions of the American order. It does not mean America cannot be the benevolent power it is; it does mean that the United States must reassert its interests, revitalize its alliances, and reward reciprocity only. It takes statesmanship at the very top. And, critically, it requires mending America's own economy.

That problems exist in the United States does not mean that they cannot and will not be fixed. The future is not preordained. Good policy, along with technological advances, has time and again disproved the waves of claims about America's decline. The Obama administration has made domestic economic vitality a key aspiration in its foreign policy rhetoric and sought to justify new spending initiatives in innovation, infrastructure, and education as keys to US competitiveness. In his 2011 State of the Union speech, the president argued America was in for a "Sputnik moment." The linkage between domestic and foreign economic policies is a correct one; the problem is that the administration's domestic economic policies are not reviving the American economy.

The premium on good policy is at its peak. Making the United States a European style welfare state would be an epic tragedy for America and the world. It would sap US economic dynamism and entrepreneurship, and end America's economic leadership. Instead, needed are uncompromising fiscal discipline; ironclad central bank independence; cuts in taxes and red tape on American business; reforms to entitlements; restoration of free, competitive, and vigorous financial markets; and a lock on long-term policies that harness the productivity of America's next generations and newcomers.

Conclusion

Instability in the world economy and institutional stress in global governance are not new, and often the former has triggered the latter. Countless commentators have blamed the American order for global downturns, relegating it to the graveyard of international experiments. Each emerging-market crisis has resulted in stern questioning of the IMF's mission, governance, and purpose. Banking crises have compelled changes in financial regulations and been followed by often intractable international disagreements over the reach and rigidity of proposed global rules. America's periodic economic travails have unfailingly made the dollar fair game among global commentators and resulted in debates on a new global currency regime. Episodes of inflation and economic turmoil have been trailed by political interference with central bank independence, and raised broader questions about the division between governments and markets. Yet the premises and properties of the postwar world economic order have not only persevered; the order has actually grown more resilient. Will it now?

The question is imminent. Never in the postwar era has the risk of economic instability been as global and consequential. Perhaps never before have the institutions of the postwar world economic order been questioned as sharply or simultaneously. And seldom have the global economy and polity been amid such a mixture of transformations, of coinciding challenges and opportunities. For the United States, this is not a time to revert from the world, for global economic problems cannot be solved without America, nor can America's economy be restored without engagement with the world. This is also no time to abandon leadership, for a gaze at the global stage registers an absence of contending leaders. This is a defining time, and a time to restore American leadership. Let's get it right. The next chapters show how.

1   Rebalancing the World Economy

I call on the surplus countries . . . to find the political gumption to stimulate
their economies without reigniting the fires of inflation. It must be
recognized that the health of the world economy does not hinge solely on
US budget policy. As US budget and trade deficits decline, other countries
must pick up the slack, particularly on imports from developing countries.
Our focus—and this means all of us—must be on achieving balanced
growth and more open economies.

—*President Ronald Reagan, IMF–World Bank Annual Meetings, Washington,*
29 September 1987

A S THE WORLD BEGAN EMERGING FROM THE FINANCIAL CRISIS,
global imbalances rebounded. In a lopsided pattern whereby
the United States and many other nations such as France, India, and UK imported and borrowed, while China, Japan, Germany, and Middle Eastern oil
producers exported and lent, imbalances soared in the early 2000s, reaching
some 5 percent of world GDP by 2006. That year, US current-account deficit
peaked at an unprecedented 6.5 percent of US GDP, a level widely viewed as
unsustainable. Confidence in the US economy was expected to erode, and the
dollar was deemed to fall. Exasperated by the mass influx of imports, Congress threatened steep tariffs against China. Perpetuating low US real interest
rates that, in turn, stoked the housing bubble, the imbalances became one of
the main culprits for the Great Crisis. It would also take the crisis to unwind
them.

The risks of a world out of balance are several, from bouts of currency
wars to trade protectionism and a new global economic crisis sparked by a
hard landing in America. The International Monetary Fund (IMF) argues
that imbalances are "a major concern for the sustainability of the recovery
over the medium term" and that advanced-economy current accounts will
"make increasingly negative contributions to growth."[1] The European Central

Bank echoes the warning, stating that imbalances "pose a key risk for global macroeconomic and financial stability."[2]

At Washington's prodding, the G20 has made the imbalances the centerpiece of its agenda and created a peer review process of the members' economic policies. Success at rebalancing will be the key barometer of the G20's relevance. Unlike the other items on its agenda—financial regulations, reform of the IMF, global trade liberalization, and so on—that will ultimately be dealt with in other forums, global imbalances are the G20's core competence. Indeed, the story of the various prior Gs, starting with G4 in the 1970s, is a story of imbalances—and it is a story of US economic fortunes and clashing national interests. The group has addressed the imbalances grudgingly, only when the US economy ailed and Congress reverted to a staunchly anti-trade mood. The collaboration, while difficult, had its successes, most notably the historic Plaza Accord of 1985.

The stars may seem to be aligned for rebalancing. Three of the critical factors that propelled the adjustments in the 1980s are again in place: floundering American demand, sour US trade politics, and a forum that encompasses all actors required for a solution. However, none of the main surplus nations—China, Germany, or Japan—is poised to adopt consumer-led growth strategies, while the United States is running steep budget deficits that continue to require heavy foreign borrowing. The G20 has no enforcement mechanisms to compel rebalancing, and no major economy will comply with its international commitments if those clash with domestic political imperatives—let alone overhaul its policies because other G20 nations decide it should. At the same time, Washington's bilateral carrots and sticks that compelled Japan and Germany to adjust their policies in the past—security guarantees and a credible threat of steep tariffs—are not available against China, America's main counterpart in the global cycle of money. Why the failures to tackle imbalances in the past? And what measures should the United States take to tame them—before they undo the global economy?

Uneven Balancing

The global hegemons of the past two centuries, the UK and the United States, have repeatedly run current-account deficits. Britain went through a century of chronic trade deficits from Waterloo in 1815 to World War I, despite holding captive export markets and serving as the creditor to its vast empire. The

US current account was in the red for most years in 1790–1875, the heyday of America's expansion, as the New World brimmed with investment opportunities and lacked savings.[3] Foreigners—particularly the British but also the Germans, Dutch, and the French—stepped in, funding America's railroads and canals and helping to create a continental economy.

The pattern rebounded in the late twentieth century. After World War I, the United States replaced the UK as the world's largest creditor nation; after World War II, America emerged as the premier global exporter. But as Europe and Japan recovered and industrialized, the United States, an open and fast-growing market, was on its way to becoming a net importer.[4] Declining in the 1960s, US trade balance turned negative in the early 1970s. The Kennedy and Johnson administrations sought remedies, such as persuading European nations to purchase military hardware from the United States in order to offset the negative impact of US military expenditures in Europe on US balance of payments.[5] But the Vietnam war–related deficits, tight labor market, and loose monetary policy decreased the US current account. Paul Samuelson, the future winner of the Nobel Prize in economics, argued that US balance of payments policy had turned "from benign neglect to malignant preoccupation."[6]

The Nixon administration's solution, in 1971, was to break the straitjacketing gold peg. But floating exchange rates gave rise to a new worry: that countries with devalued currencies would pose unfair competition in global commerce. This was a disquieting prospect at the time, when soaring oil prices and inflation were already causing economic havoc. Worried, Treasury Secretary George Shultz convened his counterparts from West Germany, France, and the United Kingdom in Washington in April 1973.

Grudging Cooperation

Schultz's "Library Group," named after its venue, the ground-floor library of the White House, quickly became an institution. It worked on common macroeconomic problems—the terrifying specter of economic contraction as countries tightened spending and interest rates, and America's worry, global imbalances. The foursome soon proved too few for resolving the main problem vexing America, current-account deficits. In the fall of 1973, the G4 welcomed Japan, the rising counterpart of America's trade gap. The G5 was born; by 1975, the G meetings were elevated to leaders' level. In the next two years the group invited Italy, a nation with political heft in Europe, and Canada, a US ally, growing into the famous G7.

What was the tally? The Gs came together only reluctantly to address the imbalances and had trouble living up to their commitments. However, co-ordination was successful when it truly mattered—when the United States was about to turn protectionist and when imbalances held global trade talks hostage.

The quad's main weapon was exchange rates. In September 1973 it agreed on policies that made the dollar depreciate against the German mark. The measure, along with congressional action the following year to relax the criteria for American companies to seek trade remedies, paved the way for the launch of the multilateral Tokyo Round trade negotiations.[7]

The G7 Bonn Summit in 1978 was another of the better efforts. Each nation shouldered some of the burden to revive global growth and cut the imbalances. Japan and Germany pledged fiscal expansion, and the United States promised to deregulate oil prices to bring down the world price of petroleum.[8] Trade again followed, as the group committed to concluding the Tokyo Round. But even Bonn failed to work exactly as intended, in part because the interventions came past their time and in part because of unpredictables—the Iranian Revolution and the 1979 oil shock.[9]

The best effort yet came in the mid-1980s, when Japan became the overwhelmingly largest creditor nation and the United States the main debtor. With a large share of Japanese overseas investments flowing in US bonds, the two nations created a symbiotic relationship: America sustained Japan's export-led growth model and provided a safe haven for Japanese investments, and in return Japan funded America's growing fiscal deficit.[10] But the pressure of Japanese imports and the lack of reciprocity with Tokyo aggravated Congress. Journalist James Fallows quipped that the legendary Japanese Ministry of International Trade and Industry (MITI) seemed to Americans like "Trade Surplus Central."[11]

Although the Reagan–Thatcher revolution spelled an end to interventionist policies, the second Reagan administration relented under congressional pressures and set out to pursue what became known as "strategic trade policy." The aim was to sharpen US companies' edge in global markets and ensure reciprocity with American trade partners, particularly Japan. The administration also decided on multilateralism.[12] Summoning the G5, Treasury sought to both harness the three European G5 members to pressure Tokyo and to shift some of the cost of US fiscal adjustment to other nations, thereby strengthening its hand with Congress in the deadlocked fiscal policy discussions.[13]

Seeing the US fiscal deficit as the main driver of the imbalances, Germany and Japan were loath to act, despite their genuine fears about US protectionism. For its part, the United States argued that the surplus nations were failing to do their fair share to stimulate demand. However, everyone saw the need for action. Critically, with Japanese export interests and MITI worrying about market access in the United States, domestic politics in Japan aligned behind the required adjustments.[14] The Reagan administration pledged to curb the fiscal deficit.

The commitments were enshrined in the 22 September 1985 Plaza Agreement among the G5 finance ministers. The United States was to rein in the budget, Japan to boost private demand through tax reform, and Germany to cut taxes to stimulate its economy.[15] All five were also to intervene in foreign exchange markets to bring down the value of the dollar. To be sure, Germany—Bundesbank in particular—resisted, and Plaza entailed practically no changes to German fiscal or monetary policies.[16]

Plaza had an immediate effect. The following day, the dollar fell 4.3 percent against other major currencies; in the next several months, it dropped by more than 30 percent, both thanks to Plaza and because of lower oil prices and flickers of growth in Japan and Europe.[17] The dollar's descent was so remarkable that by early 1987, the G6 finance ministers met in Paris to halt it. The Louvre Accord pledged realignments and coordination on fiscal and monetary policy matters, including major cuts in US and French budget deficits.[18] Overall, the episode was one of successful rebalancing. The Uruguay Round that would culminate in the creation of the WTO was set in motion in 1986, and after peaking at 3.6 percent of GDP in 1987, US current-account deficit closed at 0.16 percent of GDP in 1991.[19] The price of US goods in Japan was literally halved.

Waning Salience
Underpinning the G5 and G7's success at rebalancing were US global power and leadership. Other major economies and US allies, in particular, agreed to policies to balance America's current account as a price for the security and economic benefits of US presence in world affairs. In the 1960s Europeans accepted US proposals to control current-account shortfalls in exchange for

America's security umbrella. Even if reluctantly, the Japanese acquiesced to Plaza and Washington's bilateral trade agenda as a quid pro quo for open US markets. The Middle Eastern nations that paid for part of the first Gulf War helped terminate two decades of US current-account deficits.

In the 1990s the salience of the imbalances dissipated. Granted, governments still intervened to realign exchange rates—strong yen in 1995, weak yen in 1998, and weak euro in 2000, respectively—when they failed to match the underlying economic fundamentals.[20] But the imbalances dissipated as the Japanese economy imploded in a real estate crash. US current-account deficits settled below 2 percent of GDP in most of the 1990s and even in 1998 were still moderate, at 2.6 percent. US exports and economy thrived, and with growth averaging almost 4 percent in 1995–1999, the fiscal deficit narrowed and ultimately vanished. Americans were more positive about trade than they had been in years.[21] The North American Trade Agreement (NAFTA) passed in 1993, and the Uruguay Round was completed in 1994. The European G7 members were focused on their own affairs. Germans were steeped in the reunification process, and Western Europeans in general labored to integrate the Eastern half and launch the euro and the European Central Bank.

Macroeconomic policy coordination was also less useful. Developed nations established inflation-targeting regimes, effectively tying their hands in monetary policy making. The effectiveness of interventionism was questioned as the foreign exchange market grew too large for governments to move.[22] The G7 shifted its focus from mutual adjustments to global economic challenges—the Asian financial crisis of 1997–1998, IMF reform, global macroeconomic surveillance—and expanded into such noneconomic topics as counterterrorism, nuclear security, and environmental protection.

Collectively Consistent?

By the mid-2000s, the imbalances came back with a vengeance. As in the 1980s, the pattern was again primarily transpacific—one where the United States consumed, imported, and borrowed, and Asia, especially China, saved, exported, and lent. In 2006 the US current-account deficit stretched to a historic 6.5 percent of US GDP, with Chinese imports making up a third of the total. The quadrupling of oil prices between 2002 and the summer of 2007, in part a result of Asia's insatiable demand for raw materials, added insult to injury. Imbalances stretched to some 5 percent of world GDP in 2008, the year the world would enter the worst financial crisis since the Great Depression.

Reacting to the global financial firestorm and recognizing the importance of emerging markets for mending the world economy, in November 2008 the George W. Bush administration convened the first-ever summit of the leaders of the twenty leading economies. Rather than the usual group of seven or eight, now the heads of industrialized powers would write a plan for ending the crisis and reviving the global economy with such ascending economies as China, India, Brazil, and Indonesia. The *Economist* announced this was "not a new Bretton Woods—but a decisive shift in the old order."[23]

While historic, the event did not represent an abrupt shift in global affairs. The G20 had been launched already in 1999 at the level of finance ministers and central bank governors as an outgrowth of a discussion between President Bill Clinton and Singaporean Prime Minister Goh Chok Tong on ways to further economic dialogue between the G7 and emerging nations.[24]

The Clinton administration had a number of reasons to expand the G system. Reverberating across the emerging world, including the pivotal Russia and Turkey, the Asian crisis showcased the effects of financial contagion on US economic and strategic interests, while the costly rescues soured relations with Congress.[25] Closer vigilance would be required to keep the rising economies in line. The US economy was also growing more dependent on the emerging markets. By the end of the 1990s, almost a third of US trade was with emerging and developing nations, and some 40 percent of US FDI went to markets other than the European Union or Japan, particularly Asia and Latin America.[26] There were further market opportunities to cultivate, as well: the G20 represented 4.2 billion consumers out of the planet's 6.8 billion, more than five-fold the 750 million in the G7 nations. Leadership on Wall Street and in Washington galvanized opinions, as Goldman Sachs singled out the BRICs as the coming world growth engines and the Brookings Institution called for adjusting global governance to reflect the economic transformations.[27]

America's Growth Imperative
In just a year, the G20 produced a long list of commitments for reigniting global growth, regulating financial markets, and expanding the IMF's role in insuring against crises. By the third summit, in September 2009 in Pittsburgh, the group took up a familiar theme: imbalances. The chosen tool was the

US-sponsored "[f]ramework for strong, sustainable and balanced growth," whereby each member would subject its economic policies to a Mutual Assessment Process (MAP), a peer review process managed by the IMF. The G20 subsequently defined "indicative guidelines," national economic variables by which the IMF would assess the G20 members' movement toward rebalancing and determine whether the members' policies were "collectively consistent" with the balanced-growth goals. A nation deemed to fail to move toward that goal would be scrutinized and called to change its policies—or to make a case for why its policies did not pose a threat.

The main impetus for the framework was America's economic collapse. Its phrasing reflected bureaucratic priorities: the Treasury was keen on securing the "balanced" term, while the White House, worried about American jobless recovery, insisted on the "strong" part. The framework fit President Obama's campaign platform of job creation and enforcement of trade laws against unfair foreign practices. Since its maiden G20 summit in April 2009 in London, the Obama administration had argued that other nations would have to bear their share in jump-starting global growth and stimulating American jobs and exports. US trade policy was aligned with the pro-export aim. Without committing to concluding the multilateral Doha Trade Round or pushing through Congress free trade agreements that the Bush administration had negotiated with Korea, Panama, and Colombia yet which union lobbies opposed, Obama launched an initiative to double US exports in five years, and privately pressured China to revalue the RMB.

The G20 was a natural forum for tackling the imbalances, and multilateralizing the issue was seen as a way to recruit other deficit nations to bring pressure on Beijing and also to highlight the role of other surplus economies. Many other deficit nations, such as the UK and Australia, embraced the agenda, but the surplus nations wanted something in return—Germany, a commitment to address executive pay and financial regulations; China, a reform of the IMF and the World Bank.

Why Out of Balance?

Why did the anomalous pattern, where capital flowed "uphill" from poorer, emerging markets to richer, capital-abundant nations, develop and soar to such magnitudes in the early 2000s? Those coming to the answer from the current-account perspective attribute it to exchange rates and comparative advantage in global commerce. Asia enjoyed abundant supplies of cheap labor, and the region's undervalued currencies perpetuated the market-driven depreciations following the 1997–1998 Asian financial crisis, entrenching the export-led growth model. Exports were a crucial lever for politicians to propel economies with limited domestic demand and investment but also with growing populations eager for jobs. Export revenue conveniently also helped build—and was in many countries pursued in order to build—a reserve buffer against future crises.[28] China drove the regional currency politics: as Beijing kept the RMB undervalued and pegged to the dollar, other Asian nations, concerned about their competitiveness with China, followed suit. US expansionary policies, including the monetary loosening after the September 11, 2001, terrorist attacks, traveled around the world.[29]

Those explaining the imbalances from the capital-account perspective advance a number of different stories. One of the most cited ones, advocated by many on Wall Street, is the "money glut" theory: low taxes and interest rates aimed at overcoming the post-9/11 uncertainties gave Americans too much money with which to buy houses and purchase a record number of imports.[30] Another argument, advanced among others by Federal Reserve Chairman Ben Bernanke and *Financial Times* columnist Martin Wolf, places the starting point in the Asian "savings glut": because Asian companies and consumers saved, the region had to find export and investment targets abroad.[31] It was the United States that became the main deficit nation because the US served as the global safe haven and reserve currency issuer, and because of the rapid growth in US household wealth and housing appreciation, something that did not occur to the same extent in other large economies such as Germany or Japan.[32] The flow of money into housing rather than equipment or, say, software was linked to gaps in supervision and regulations in the mortgage underwriting business and the overall financial sector.[33] Washington was slow to react, as Wall Street kept slicing risky housing loans into tranches and repackaging them into supposedly low-risk securities, perpetuating credit, America's housing boom, and, by extension, lending from Asia.

The imbalances were reborn from a perfect storm. Asia's cheap exports and vast reserves conspired with the US housing boom, low interest rates, and seeming infallibility as an investment haven to keep money and trade flowing to America.

Exacerbated by the Crisis

Washington did make numerous attempts to reduce the imbalances, but its instruments to tackle imbalances were blunt. Relentless congressional trade threats—which culminated in the proposal by veteran senators Charles Schumer of New York and Leslie Graham of North Carolina to impose a 27.5-percent blanket tariff against China unless Beijing revalued the RMB—made China agree to a modest 2.1-percent revaluation in July 2005. The RMB ended up rising by 21 percent against the dollar until July 2008, when it was again fixed.

The token measure reflected Beijing's concerns about the congressional pressure and the effect on US–China relations, and its interest in showing deference to Washington in world affairs. However, the currency adjustment did little to alter trade balances or quiet Congress. The 109th Congress, in office in 2005–2007, introduced 27 pieces of anti-China trade legislation.[34] Its successor put forth some dozen China bills, many aimed at China's exchange-rate regime.[35] Political pressures were magnified by the fact that while at 5–6 percent of total US economy, the current-account deficit accounted for more than 20 percent of US *traded* goods production.[36]

At the other end of Pennsylvania Avenue, the Bush administration struggled to find the right frequency with Beijing. The G7 could not be used to deal with the issue, for China was not a member. There was also no appropriate bilateral US–China forum. The relatively low-level US–China dialogue did not sway Beijing, and Washington's singular focus on the currency distanced the Chinese further. The administration's change of tactics from public persuasion to quiet diplomacy also failed to work, and multilateral pressure backfired. As Washington enlisted the IMF to serve as an honest broker among China, the United States, Europeans, Japan, and Saudi Arabia, the surplus nations agreed that the low US savings rate was the main problem.[37]

Unlike in the Plaza years, it would take a global financial crisis to undo the imbalances. Dampened demand in the deficit nations and, initially, reduction in global commodity prices that cut into oil and other commodity exporters' trade balances practically halved the imbalances between 2008 and 2009. Although the stubborn slowdown in the advanced economies and the appreciation of the Japanese yen helped hold imbalances back through 2011, the IMF projects that they will rise closer to precrisis levels and remain elevated in the following years (see Figure 1). The main counterparts in global imbalances, the United States and China, will see their current-account gaps widen. The US current-account deficit is bound to surge to 3.4 percent in 2016, while China's current-account surplus is estimated to be 7.8 percent in 2016, a tall figure, albeit below the 10.6 percent reached in 2007.

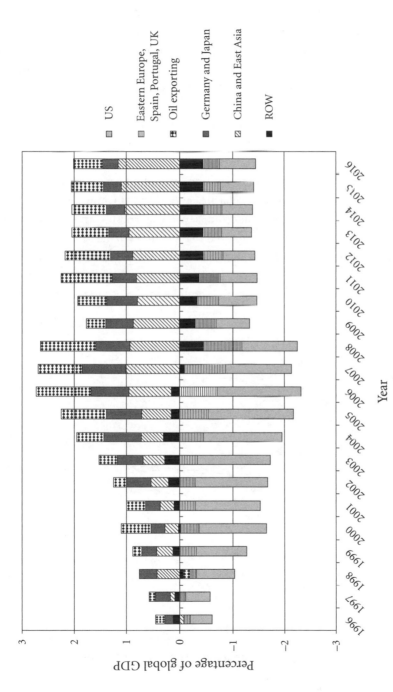

FIGURE 1 Global imbalances as a percentage of global GDP, 1996–2016 by country/region

SOURCE: IMF *World Economic Outlook* (2011).

Apart from America, the UK, Canada, Australia, India, Turkey, France, and the southern European nations will run trade deficits. The mirroring surplus nations will be familiar—primarily China and East Asia, but also Germany, Japan, and the oil-producing nations, including Russia. The global pattern is replicated within Europe, where the northern economies, especially Germany, run current-account surpluses, and the southern ones and the UK and Ireland are seeing deficits.

The global financial crisis exacerbated many of the structural and policy distortions that drive the imbalances.

First, the crisis only entrenched the precrisis policies in the surplus economies. East Asian economies saw the episode as validating reserve accumulation as a means to buffer against volatility and are reaffirming the strategy, even though it diverts investments from, say, infrastructure and education. The reserve buildup is now also employed to preempt exchange-rate appreciation, which helps preserve export competitiveness. At the same time, emerging East Asia continues to under-consume: regional savings are projected to exceed precrisis levels in 2013 and grow overall by some 1.25 percentage points of the regional GDP through 2016 (see Figure 2).

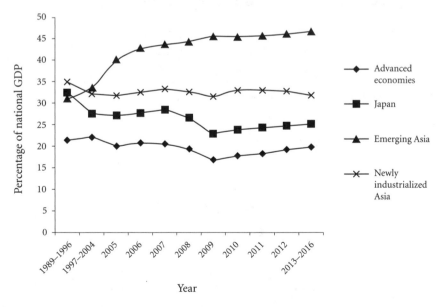

FIGURE 2 National savings as a percentage of GDP in Asia and advanced economies, 1989–2016
SOURCE: IMF *World Economic Outlook* (2011).

Much of the increased savings trend is driven by China. The shutdown of its key export markets amid the crisis revealed to China the perils of the export-led growth strategy. Beijing compensated by issuing a $587-billion stimulus package and some $1 trillion of loans to state-owned enterprises, tax rebates, and infrastructure investments. China is back at hoarding reserves and promoting exports at all costs, and is unlikely to abruptly break with the key tenet of its growth formula or be able to propel domestic consumption sufficiently to dent global imbalances. Most of the stimulus money and new investments are channeled through state-owned enterprises (SOEs), which, instead of passing profits to households and private companies to stoke consumption, recycle profits internally. SOEs have gained influence in the Chinese economy and politics after the crisis, perpetuating the county's savings glut. Worried that the stimulus spending would create an asset bubble, Beijing accumulated further reserves to hedge against investor exit.[38]

Exchange-rate challenges were also worsened by the crisis, reaching a fever pitch in the second half of 2010, as more than a dozen countries— Brazil, China, India, Indonesia, Israel, Japan, Korea, Malaysia, the Philippines, Singapore, South Africa, Switzerland, Taiwan, and Thailand—intervened in foreign exchange markets and/or effected capital controls to curb currency appreciation, much to the dismay of the United States and other deficit nations. For their part, emerging markets claimed that the US Federal Reserve's quantitative easing, along with Europe's monetary loosening, had built a destabilizing gush of global liquidity that stoked inflation in the emerging markets and justified their capital controls.[39] Asian and Latin American governments also reacted to retain their relative competitiveness with the other emerging economies, particularly China. In the eve of the Seoul G20 Summit in November 2010, advanced-country exchange rates were somewhat overvalued (by 2.8–5.6 percent) while Asian rates were significantly undervalued (by 6.6–14.8 percent).[40]

Granted, China terminated the RMB's peg to the dollar in June 2010 to combat inflation and has since allowed the RMB to appreciate slightly, by 5.4 percent at the time of writing, against the dollar, but the move is far too modest to dent global imbalances and may be ended as Beijing worries about dampened growth in Europe, its main export market. Besides, the RMB's value also reflects the depreciation of the dollar: measured against a basket of trading partners' currencies, the Chinese currency's effective exchange rate has only fallen.[41]

Japan is also in dire straits. The crisis mired Japan only deeper in debt and deflation—it is the advanced economy most prone to a double-dip recession—and Tokyo is unlikely to raise interest rates from near zero. The crisis also rendered Europe an even less likely source of global consumer demand than it was in the past. The continent's postcrisis fiscal retrenchment—including Germany's '95-billion austerity measures through 2014 and belt-tightening in the UK and southern Europe—and lackluster demand reemphasize America's role as the consumer of last resort. Germany is growing robustly, but it is a surplus economy and is resolved to restore its status as a manufacturing export power rather than propel domestic demand. Dire uncertainties created by the southern European financial crises depress the continent's growth and perpetuate global and regional imbalances: the stronger economies, especially Germany, are rebuilding their capital stock, while the slower ones, primarily the southern deficit nations, struggle to attract investment.

Debt Overhang

The drivers of the imbalances were exacerbated also in the deficit nations, particularly the United States. US private savings surged from the near-zero range before the crisis to about 5 percent in 2011, and Americans' debt loads have fallen. However, public debt, ballooning on the back of the fiscal deficits Washington ran during the crisis, is projected to rival the wartime record highs, likely requiring even more expansive foreign borrowing that will perpetuate America's twin deficits.[42]

The debt deal reached in August 2011 raises the US debt ceiling by $2.4 trillion in two stages and cuts spending by $917 billion over 10 years. The subsequent failure of the debt committee paved the way for automatic cuts of $1.2 trillion by 2013. The measures hardly herald a balanced budget. Projections by the Congressional Budget Office (CBO) show that under a benign scenario, the deficit would be 2.3 percent in 2014.[43] With the deficit persisting through 2020, debt held by the public would rise from 62 percent of GDP in 2010 to 66 percent in 2020, the highest since the early 1950s and double the levels attained in 2001. Under an alternative scenario of significantly lower revenues and higher outlays, debt would reach 87 percent of GDP by 2020 and a stunning Japanese-style 185 percent by 2035, while the fiscal deficit would be 16 percent of GDP. The projections of the administration's Office of Management and Budget fall in between these two scenarios. The fiscal deficit would be 3.9 percent in 2011, and the debt held by the public would rise to 72.9 per cent of GDP by 2015, the highest since 1946.[44] The increase in debt and interest rate hikes once the economy recovers is expected to triple interest payments between 2010 and 2020.

There is no necessary link between budget deficit and current-account deficits: the United States had a moderately deepening current-account deficit while its fiscal deficit was coming down in 1996–2000, and some other countries deep in arrears, like Japan and Germany, run current-account surpluses. However, most of recent American and international economic history has shown that by causing total national savings to decline, budget deficits tend to increase borrowing from abroad. One recent study calculates that a 2-percentage-point reduction in the fiscal deficit lowers the current-account deficit by 0.6 percentage points of GDP.[45] The IMF calculates that a 1-percent decrease in the share of fiscal deficit of GDP leads to an over half a percent reduction in the current-account deficit, as imports decline and exports rise.[46] The magic works largely through the exchange rate.

The debt burden can have dramatic implications for the US current account. Economist William Cline estimates that in a benign scenario where growth is a decent 2.75 percent annually and fiscal deficit only 2 percent of GDP through 2030, the US current-account deficit would still be a notable 4–5 percent of GDP. However, in a scenario where the fiscal deficit escalates to 10 percent in 2030, America's debt would be 140 percent of GDP and more than 700 percent of exports, and the US current-account deficit would soar to 5.2 percent in 2015, 7.5 percent in 2020, and 16 percent in 2030, two-and-a-half times the historic 2006 level.[47] The value of the dollar would surge more than 20 percent, undermining America's export competitiveness and fueling the imbalances.

Known Unknowns

If economic fundamentals and policies in the main deficit and surplus economies augur poorly for global rebalancing in the years ahead, a number of factors obscure the short term.[48] Higher interest rates and tightened fiscal policies in the emerging markets to cool off economic overheating could markedly undermine global growth and widen imbalances, especially between East Asian economies and the advanced economies. An end of the Chinese real estate rally would have similar effects. To be sure, an Asian demand shock would likely also reduce commodity exporters' surpluses, as would OPEC's agreeing to increase oil production. Of course, persistently high petroleum prices and rapid wage increases in China could make US companies repatriate some export-oriented manufacturing. Continued lackluster growth in the United States and much of Europe would also stem the imbalances, but such an outcome would not be in any nation's interest.

Why Imbalances Matter

National accounts do not need to be balanced, and imbalances do not have to result from distorting or unsustainable policies. Instead, they can reflect cross-national differences in rates of return on capital, propensity to save, and degree of risk.[49] But if imbalances result from distorting regulatory, currency, and/or trade policies, as they now do, they can impair macroeconomic performance. And large imbalances can only exacerbate fragilities and distortions in financial markets and perpetuate discord between surplus and deficit nations. In addition, the imbalances pose three immediate threats to the global economy.

The Rise of Protectionism

One of the main threats of global imbalances is to open markets around the world. The current-account deficit has historically been the surest predictor of protectionist impulses in the United States, and it is proving so again. Just as it was no accident that the agreements by the G5 to undo imbalances laid the groundwork for global trade rounds, it is no surprise that growing shares of Americans started seeing trade as a threat in the 2000s as the trade deficit soared. At the end of 2010, 53 percent of Americans saw free trade agreements as hurting the United States, while a paltry 17 percent saw them as helping, a record low.[50] In an echo of precrisis attempts to curb imports from China, in September 2010 the House of Representatives approved by an overwhelming margin a bill that is interpreted to open the door for an imposition of trade remedies against alleged currency manipulation.[51]

Protectionist sentiments go beyond US–China relations. To be sure, protectionism in the global economic crisis was orders of magnitude less than perpetrated by the beggar-thy-neighbor policies during the Great Depression. International commitments made over the past six decades to liberalize world trade and finance—defended by thousands of proponents of free markets ensconced in industry, academia, the media, and governments—preserved the open global economy. But there has been worrisome slippage: the G20 governments have implemented well over 500 discriminatory measures since the end of 2008, most of them against China, despite repeated commitments to forego protectionism and conclude the Doha Round.[52] The reemergence of trade deficits, particularly if accompanied by a Doha failure, could herald further corner cutting: absent Doha, many economies, especially the emerging nations, have a great deal of "water" between their applied and multilaterally agreed bound tariffs, which gives them a blank check to raise tariffs at a whim.

Currency Wars

The second threat posed by imbalances is a long currency war. Before the crisis, Washington and Beijing clashed over the value of the RMB, with the US Congress repeatedly threatening tariffs to retaliate against Chinese currency mercantilism. This policy of containment was not perfect, but it did secure at least token cooperation from the Chinese while keeping Washington's trade threats from translating into actual barriers. In the postcrisis world, the terrain is harsher. The pie of global demand is not growing fast enough, and contests over the slices are increasingly vicious—as attested by the exchange-rate manipulation by more than a dozen nations. As the deficit nations look to export their way to growth and surplus nations seek to hold on to their export-led growth strategies, currency is a convenient weapon of choice.

At the heart of such craftiness is global economic interdependence. The fates of nations are increasingly tied to one another, and the talk of global decoupling notwithstanding, the fortunes of emerging markets continue fluctuating with demand in the United States, the world's largest economy and importer. But whether accomplished by capital controls or other means, currency manipulation by China and other surplus nations only fuels protectionist sentiments in the deficit economies. Besides, capital controls are in their own right hugely problematic, not least because of their chilling effect on global trade, finance, and FDI alike.

The sheer uncertainties created by currency wars, capital controls, and exchange-rate instability undermine global trade and investment flows, and sow antagonism in international affairs, which, in turn, complicates multilateral rebalancing efforts.

The Next Crash?

The third major threat posed by global imbalances is a new global economic crisis. To be sure, the extent to which the imbalances can damage the world economy is disputed and has polarized academia since the mid-2000s. At the time, alarmist opinion leaders such as Nouriel Roubini, Brad Setser, Maurice Obstfeld, Kenneth Rogoff, Robert Rubin, and Martin Wolf argued that America was in for a sudden stop and a hard landing—loss of confidence in US economy resulting in capital flight, followed by the collapse of the dollar, a rise in interest rates, and a major decline in output.[53] The predicted trigger of a sudden stop was generally set at current-account deficit in excess of 5 percent of GDP. Obstfeld and Rogoff, remarking that "the US current account deficit [is] a sword of Damocles hanging over the global economy,"[54] suggested that an excessive trade deficit would make the dollar drop by 30–40 percent.[55] In a speech in London, then-president of the New York Federal Reserve Timothy Geithner also noted that "these imbalances are unsustainable and . . . need to unwind at some point.[56] Cited factors that would worsen the trade deficit were many—declining US private savings, growing budget deficits, rising energy prices, Asia's focus on tradables, and relative exchange rates. In a systematic study of 26 current-account adjustments in industrialized countries, Caroline Freund and Frank Warnock argued that unwinding from large current-account deficits takes a long time and is associated with slow growth, and indeed precipitates currency depreciation.[57]

The more optimistic analysts saw the imbalances as a symbiotic pattern that channeled surplus-nation savings to safe and liquid destinations, which, in turn, enjoyed greater availability of credit. In this so-called "Bretton Woods II" world of capital flows from the "peripheral" economies of Asia to the "center" economy, the United States, the US current-account deficit would be near-permanent, and as long as fiscal deficits were kept in check, they would also be sustainable.[58] Then-chairman of the Federal Reserve Alan Greenspan claimed that since capital markets were becoming more flexible, not only would America be more able to borrow, but the world economy would absorb any US adjustment better than before.[59] A 2005 Federal Reserve technical study, exploring historical data, argued that a disorderly adjustment was less likely than the alarmists were presuming.[60]

Others argued that the ado was about very little. In a self-ascribed "contrarian view," Harvard's Richard Cooper pointed out that America's savings rates were larger than commonly thought, since the measure for them, formulated in the 1930s industrial age, failed to account for savings in America's knowledge-based economy.[61] His Harvard colleagues Ricardo Hausmann and Federico Sturzenegger maintained that the large difference between US net assets and debts was "dark matter" that reflected accounting problems, not reality.[62]

Still others argued that America's three unique attributes kept the country safe from sudden stops and hard landings that had time and again bedeviled emerging markets. First, the United States was arguably too big to fail: US capital markets are so large relative to the world market that by departing, investors would undermine the world economy and thus their own fortunes.[63] And why, and where, would they go? The United States had high productivity, a world-class investment climate, and a government highly unlikely to default. Second, because the US dollar is the global reserve currency and America's debts are denominated in dollars, depreciation would not cause US liabilities to rise in relative terms. The United States thus hardly shared the precariousness of the many emerging markets whose dollar-denominated debts multiplied as their currencies collapsed. Third, because the difference between the returns that America receives on its foreign assets and those that it pays on its liabilities is persistently positive, the United States can arguably enjoy positive net capital inflows despite large net debts.[64]

This Time **Will Be** *Different?*   The Great Crisis seemed to vindicate the optimists: as the crisis globalized, money flowed not out of but into the United States to escape turbulence elsewhere. Treasuries gained 14 percent in 2008, and as the global economic recovery fell in doubt, net purchases of US government notes and bonds soared to $100.5 billion in June 2009, a historical monthly high. Purchases by the Chinese and the Japanese were the largest on record. The crisis expected by the alarmists did not occur, even if many of them subsequently defended their views.[65] However, by 2010, most prominent observers, such as Ben Bernanke, had turned to seeing regulatory failures as the leading cause of the crisis.[66]

But arguing that the Great Crisis was not caused by a US hard landing is not to posit that the next global crisis could not be. True, America's unique qualities stressed by the optimists are still in place: the United States is still too big to fail, the issuer of the global reserve currency, a world-class economy, and—the credit rating downgrade notwithstanding—the world's safe haven. The problem is that the positives are now threatened by the US budget deficit.

An insightful imbalance analyst, Jörg Bibow, suggests that the emerging global regime might be a "Bretton Woods III," where US public deficits sustain global growth. Such a system would be hugely perilous.[67] Catherine

Mann, who in 1999 accurately projected US trade balance to soar to 5 percent in 2005, argues that should the current-account deficit rise to 16 percent of US GDP by 2030, other nations would need to devote over 65 percent of all their offshore investments to dollar assets, more than double the share that foreign holders currently allocate to investments in the United States.[68] The scenario would also imply that the United States would each year have to transfer 7 percent of GDP—about the annual output of the state of New York—to its foreign creditors in debt payments, a daunting figure that would test America's ability to pay.

Bluntly, the deficit could reach a point where foreigners would cease to be both willing and able to serve as America's loan officers. Seizing on this prospect, countless economists have now joined the alarmist camp. In fact, the United States would have to undergo a serious economic adjustment—a sizable drop in the value of the dollar and reduced domestic consumption and investment—well before such an astronomical current-account deficit was reached. But even more damaging would be a scenario where an adjustment did not occur, as prolonged foreign financing could allow the fiscal gap to widen further, entrenching America in a vicious cycle.[69] While an American sudden stop is distant, it is in US domestic and global economic interests to avert even speculations about such an outcome. Warning signs are big and bright, and they must be heeded.

Can Imbalances Be Tamed?

What are the odds of global rebalancing? On the one hand, the mix of factors that paved the way for the Plaza Accord are again present: uncertain American demand, sour US trade politics, and a forum, the G20, that encompasses all actors required for a solution. Unlike in the Bush years, there is also a systematic peer review process, and Washington now also has the Strategic and Economic Dialogue (S&ED), first launched by Bush's Treasury Secretary Henry Paulson to engage with China. The State Department's taking leadership of the process with the Treasury during the Obama administration expands the opportunities for bargains and broadens the dialogue to address the overall US–China relationship, something Beijing has tended to care about.

On the other hand, absent a major short-term change in energy sources, Washington lacks leverage over a key driver of the imbalances, global petroleum prices. Countries' rebalancing commitments at the S&DE and G20 are

consistently trumped by their domestic political imperatives. While US engagement with China is positive, Beijing has not taken adequate steps to undo
the imbalances, such as substantial goods and services trade liberalization,
currency appreciation, and pro-consumption initiatives. Meanwhile, the G20
process enables the members only to shed light on, scrutinize, and monitor
one another's economic policies, and bring pressure to bear on misbehaving
members. The group lacks enforcement mechanisms, and none of the main
economies will change its policies just because the G20 decided that might be
desirable.

Instead, governments let one another off the hook when that serves their
own interests. Emblematic was the G20's commitment in the June 2010 Toronto Summit to halve government deficits by 2013 and "stabilize" debt loads
by 2016. Striking a balance between thrifty and spendthrift nations, respectively spearheaded by Germany and the United States, the pledge merely
described national policies previously in place and essentially entailed a reemergence of the imbalances. The outcome was not international coordination but reciprocal unilateralism—and a failure of leadership. Beijing pledged
token RMB revaluation days prior to the summit to turn the spotlight away
from currencies and onto US criticism of German and UK fiscal tightening, a
strategy that succeeded.

The G20 has also failed to set a clear goal. In the Seoul Summit, surplus
nations rejected the Obama administration's idea to set a global threshold
for identifying large imbalances at 4 percent of global current-account surpluses. The initiative was criticized as global central planning, but its thrust
is a correct one: the amorphous terms *balanced* and *sustainable* must be defined in order for the G20 to meet these objectives. However, the politics of a
numerical target is intractable. Instead, the G20 agreed to develop "indicative
guidelines" for identifying imbalances that would be composed of a range of
macroeconomic and trade indicators. China truncated the effort by removing
a reference to current-account imbalances in favor of the more narrow trade
balance and practically blocked the use of critical variables: exchange rates
and currency reserves.

Feeble Levers

Such outcomes are not surprising. Domestic macroeconomic policies
and binding international agreements have never mixed. Governments
jealously guard their main levers in domestic politics—monetary policies,

exchange-rate policies, and fiscal policies. Cooperation is particularly difficult in the case of the imbalances, as trade surpluses make for good politics in
the surplus economies.

Washington's carrots and sticks to prod the surplus nations bilaterally
are also in short supply. Plaza happened because of a credible and meaningful threat by the US Congress to block trade with Japan, especially in high-
technology and strategic sectors.[70] Heavily invested in America, the Japanese
were also concerned about the sustainability of the US current-account deficit.

Trade policy threats are far fewer today. Granted, direct pressure has had
some impact with Beijing in the past, even if China argues that it is counterproductive. The modest RMB appreciation in 2005 was due to such pressure;
dwindling attention by the lame-duck Bush administration enabled China to
revert to the dollar peg in the summer of 2008. But the effects of even a high
US tariff would unlikely affect Chinese currency policies for very long. About
a fifth of China's exports go to the US market. A 25-percent blanket tariff in
2010 on China would cause a 1-percent drop in Chinese GDP. However, China
would eventually be able to find substitute export markets in Asia and other
parts of the world.[71]

The United States is unlikely, and would be foolish, to erect tariff barriers
that would seriously threaten China's exports, and China knows it. Indeed,
while China's economic growth model based on US-bound exports is similar
to the one adopted by West Germany and Japan after World War II, Beijing has
engaged in unprecedented currency mercantilism and resisted the currency
appreciation to which West Germany and Japan consented.[72] Washington has
one fewer lever after Beijing secured US backing for its 2001 WTO membership.

The two other surplus economies, Germany and Japan, are unaffected by
congressional trade threats and see the United States as the world's most open
major economy and as unlikely to renege on its multilateral trade commitments. They also trade much more as a share of their total trade with their
regional partners in Europe and Asia, respectively, than in the 1980s, when
they relied more on the US market. Berlin and Tokyo also provide scant additional pressure on China. Although Germany would benefit from changes in
China's commercial and currency policies and greater Chinese consumption,
it has joined the rebalancing drive only reluctantly, providing little additional
leverage to Washington in dealing with the East Asian nations.

Carrots are also fewer. Pledges to lower the fiscal deficit do not work as a
bargaining chip the way they did in the 1980s, as other nations full well know

that any deficit cuts are made out of domestic political reasons, not because of some international grand bargain. National security is also a less potent quid pro quo than in the past: while Japan and Germany used to depend on the US security umbrella, China is a rival that is vying to convert itself into a military might—an aim at full display in Beijing's shows of force around East Asia and its hacking of the computer systems of the Pentagon and other US government agencies.

The Obama administration has not helped this state of affairs. Engagement with China is imperative, but it is the content of US policy regarding China that has lacked muscle. The administration has largely opted for quiet diplomacy, preferring to work behind the scenes rather than confront the Chinese openly with currency or trade policy qualms. It has also given China plenty of concessions, such as railing against Europe by sponsoring a larger Chinese quota at the IMF and, much like its predecessors since 1994, finding that while Chinese currency is undervalued, China does not manipulate its value.

China has done precious little in return. In fact, Beijing has only grown more assertive and less cooperative in the Obama years. It has not changed its cantankerous multilateral trade policy stance since torpedoing, with India, the Doha Round in 2008; it truncated the G20's rebalancing process; it has only complicated the lives of US companies in China further with red tape and discrimination—bureaucratic licensing procedures, information restrictions, uneven enforcement standards, product and trademark piracy, preferential treatment of local companies, and requirements for using local technologies.[73] It has continued to arbitrarily block foreign investment and failed to curb the rampant intellectual property rights violations of American products, instead issuing "indigenous innovation" policies aimed at bringing to market Chinese technologies in favor of those offered by foreigners. Beijing's celebrated gradual opening is going in the wrong direction, toward less liberalization.[74]

One of the very best ways to influence China is by working with allies also concerned about China's rise. But the administration's upgrading the relationship with China has caused consternation with critical allies, Japan and India—which robs America of a lever and only emboldens China. America's domestic policies do not help either; the fiscal deficit is making the United States deferential to China. To be sure, after two years of not getting the behavior it thought it was rewarding, the administration did toughen its stance, and Beijing has taken some useful steps, such as pledging to improve fairness in government procurement and allow US and other foreign firms to sell auto insurance and mutual funds and other investments in China. Overall, however, America is facing a cantankerous and uncooperative China.

Global rebalancing will not result from annual G20 summits or US–China dialogues, but ultimately from unilateral measures, motivated by domestic political imperatives, by the leading economies. Absent enforcement, rebalancing policies will have to be self-enforcing and thus in the leading economies' domestic political interest. Such a prospect is distant.

China's Self-Made Trouble

In the 1990s a tectonic shift occurred in the Asia-Pacific: China eclipsed Japan as the premier US counterpart in the global cycle of trade and credit. For Beijing, the pattern has been a blessing and a curse. On the one hand, it has served as a political lifeline for a country where leadership sees 8-percent annual growth as critical for political stability and where foreign trade has been a major source of growth since the 1970s. Exports make up an estimated 40 percent of China's GDP, and the government has long demonstrated a keen interest in bolstering them.[75] A by-product of the strategy is the massive, $2.7-trillion reserve pool that garners prestige at home and can be invested abroad.

On the other hand, China has tied its economic fortunes to those of the United States. Holding at least $1.2 trillion of US government debt at the end of 2011, or 8 percent of all US government debt (and about a third of all US debt held by foreigners and more than a third of all Chinese reserves), it cannot divest its holdings without undermining the value of the dollar and hurting the global economy—which, in turn, would undercut Beijing's own remaining dollar assets and exports, leaving factory workers in Guangdong Province and port personnel in Shanghai unemployed. At the same time, import demand in the advanced-economy markets promises to be too insipid to propel Chinese economic growth. The RMB is chronically undervalued, continuing to aggravate US–China ties.

If China's economic model has such downsides, why not wean off it? Beijing has, after all, recognized the problem. The 2004 Central Economic Work Conference endorsed a transition to a more domestic-consumption-driven growth, and Beijing issued payment programs for 75 million low-income people, increased pension payments, and tripled total health care expenditures to expand health insurance coverage to an additional 400 million Chinese by 2011.[76] However, these commitments had no impact on the soaring global imbalances. The twelfth Five-Year Plan, issued in early 2011, yet again promises a "strategic readjustment" of the Chinese growth model and major pro-consumption initiatives, such as support to rural incomes, expansion of the social safety net, and development of large-scale consumer-services industries. But whether Beijing will and can implement the pledges is hardly clear.

The leading reason for the stickiness of the Chinese growth model lies in China's industry. The more than 150 state-owned enterprises are politically important even if they hog China's savings. Chinese corporate profits and savings have soared since the Asian financial crisis, and China's enterprise after-tax saving makes up three-quarters of its aggregate savings and over 20 percent of GDP, more than household saving. The pattern is driven by policy: energy and land subsidies, cheap credit, low wage costs, and lax environmental standards.[77] Labor market distortions, such as limits to the mobility of labor within China, keep wages low, subsidizing producers further, and SOEs are also shielded from foreign competition. Negative real interest rates on corporate bank deposits have compelled SOEs to reinvest all of their retained earnings—even when expected returns are low or even negative.[78] Corporate dividend policies have also favored the practice.

Policies toward SOEs are rooted in politics. Albeit reformed in the 1990s, SOEs tend to be led by local officials and executives appointed by the Communist Party, who use them as a source of fiscal revenue and political patronage, including millions of jobs.[79] The importance of SOEs as a political lever only increased as the Great Crisis undercut foreign demand. SOE politics has precluded Chinese consumers from consuming; rather, it is Chinese households that subsidize SOEs. But SOEs not only absorb the resources that could be used to propel a consumer-led economy; heavily subsidized and practically handed the bulk of Chinese demand across multiple sectors, they also immediately limit the market potential of American companies looking to serve the Chinese market.[80] The damage to US investors and exporters from China's coddling of SOEs is much more significant than that of the undervalued currency.

Will the Chinese Consume?   Beijing has placed its bets on massive public investment as a means to propel further urbanization and the consumption that comes with it. But promoting urbanization is easier said than done—Chinese surveys reveal reluctance among the public to move to the cities and eagerness by young urbanites to move back to the countryside. Worse, the by-product of the strategy is a further emboldening of the SOEs, the recipients of public investments—even though they are inefficient and now also pressed by high commodity prices. Besides indebting the central and local governments even further, the investment spree risks the proliferation of bad loans in the banking system and overcapacity in the Chinese economy. At the same time, inflation, especially in the urban areas, is canceling out gains in Chinese consumption power. Small wonder that Beijing dreads the prospect of a middle-income trap, a stagnation of middle-class incomes, a political powder keg after years of heady growth.

There is a gulf between China's macroeconomic data and Beijing's stated pro-consumption policies, between Chinese politics and policy actions. Even if Beijing did implement many of the reforms contemplated in the latest five-year plan, it might not move the needle much. According to McKinsey, enactment of practically all conceivable pro-consumption policies in housing, credit, education financing, health care, pensions, and investment to labor-intensive sectors would raise consumption only glacially, to some 45–50 percent of GDP in 2025, still far below the levels of United States, Europe, or such emerging economies as Mexico and Brazil.[81] Such measures also do not go to the heart of the SOE problem or pave the way to changes in trade policies. China's economic policy direction boils down to politics: whether expanding consumption and reducing inflation is politically more important than keeping with the status quo, which benefits export lobbies and SOEs—neither of which builds a vibrant services economy or stokes consumer-led growth, and both of which compel China to keep the RMB undervalued. For now, Beijing is locked in an intractable political equation of its own making.

The Renminbi Trap   With domestic consumption constrained, China needs to keep investing and exporting any which way. Before joining the WTO in 2001, China promoted its exports with trade and industrial policies. But because WTO rules bar such policies, Beijing turned to the exchange rate. Between the summer of 2008 and the end of 2009, the RMB depreciated by some 5–10 percentage points in trade-weighted terms, making it overall 25–40 percent undervalued.[82]

The weak currency fueled China's export-led growth and reserve buildup. It allowed Beijing to cater to demanding export lobbies that encircle local and national leaders.[83] Although the Chinese central bank has favored appreciation, the commerce ministry is eager to boost exports and appears to have prevailed in Beijing's bureaucratic politics. China's top leadership has consistently maintained that the imbalances are not driven by the exchange rate, but by US budget deficits and structural challenges in the Chinese economy.[84]

True, RMB revaluation would not undo global imbalances. Exchange rate is only one of the many parameters affecting trade balances, and China competes on a number of other factors, most prominently low labor costs (that are rising but still just half of Mexican labor costs). To start closing the US–China trade gap, Chinese revaluation would likely have to be large, perhaps at least 25 percent.[85] According to C. Fred Bergsten, a critic of the currency regime, an overall 25–40-percent revaluation would reduce the US trade deficit by $100–150 billion annually and add 750,000–1,000,000 US jobs.[86]

However, a large-scale overnight appreciation would be a political nonstarter in China. If not done *because* domestic demand was on the rise, currency appreciation would dent growth. Dani Rodrik estimates that a 25-percent RMB appreciation in real terms would reduce China's growth by more than 2 percentage points as the economy would shift toward nontradables from tradables, which would bring growth below the annual 8-percent threshold deemed critical by Chinese leadership.[87] Action on the RMB is also blocked because of fears of speculation. As it revalued the RMB in 2005, China saw investors bet on further appreciations, which propelled capital inflows and raised the RMB's value.

In contrast, a gradual, staged revaluation starting at 10–15 percent (perhaps converging to a floating regime) would be in China's interest. It would help alleviate Beijing's high exposure to the US economy, help preempt speculation, and be unlikely to hurt growth. According to IMF research, countries that in the past 50 years have enacted policies to end their current-account surpluses have not lost any growth or exports, but only gained in employment, capital, and imports.[88] A revaluation would also improve US–China relations by mollifying the US Congress and signaling China's willingness to at last become a responsible stakeholder in the world economy, an American aim practically since Nixon went to China.

The economic effects would of course be more gradual—changes in exchange rates seldom have immediate effects—and US domestic goods are unlikely to benefit much.[89] The United States might incur some negative effects. There is little overlap between American and Chinese production, so US-made goods would not simply replace Chinese imports; rather, imports

formerly originating from China would only come from higher-cost locations, or simply continue to flow from China, only more expensive. Even if
China were to increase its imports, US exports per se would unlikely to see a
benefit.

Over time, however, revaluation should have positive effects: relieve
pressure on the US current account and dollar, and reduce China's massive
reserves and dollar exposure, which makes Beijing criticize US fiscal management. However, the road to lasting currency reform and rebalancing will need
to run through a reform to the Chinese growth model. Nominal exchange-
rate appreciation will translate into real appreciation only if it is accompanied
by increased spending on nontraded goods.[90] As long as corporate and government savings are not released to consumption, such a translation will not
occur. Politically, industry and export interests will continue to be powerful
as long as other economic forces with an interest in domestic demand and
strong RMB, such as producers of services, fail to rise as a counter-lobby.

Back to the Eighties

Germany and Japan, in part fearful of inflation and fiscal deficits, in part
counting on exports and the revival of the American consumer, are unlikely
to emerge as global demand poles. Japan has suffered from low (below 1 percent) average annual growth since 1992 despite the near-zero interest rates.
The trouble started when the government hesitated to provide liquidity in
response to the collapse of the real estate market. Monetary loosening, when
it came, only produced deflation as consumers remained cautious. The tested
and tried export-led growth strategy served as a safety valve.

Two decades later, Japan still has near-zero interest rates and a sluggish
economy. At 225 percent of GDP, its public debt is the largest among the major economies and rules out major spending initiatives. Exports are a lifeline,
making up a third of the country's output. With saving outpacing investment,
Japanese current-account surplus has persisted through periods of strong and
weak yen for nearly three decades. Much like in China, the corporate sector is
the hub of national savings, and the productivity of the services sector is poor
and declining, only one-half of that of foreign entrants.[91]

The Japanese consumer is steadfastly frugal. In 1989 Bill Emmott of *The
Economist* published *The Sun Also Sets*, which analyzes a number of long-
term trends, such as aging, that might work against Japan's rise.[92] At the time,
Japanese savings rates were expected to start dwindling and turn negative

once baby boomers exited the workforce. But Japan's retirees defied analysts: while personal saving rates have declined, they remain remarkably high for Japan's demographic structure, partly because of uncertainties about the future of the country's public pensions.[93] Although the household saving rate did fall from more than 10 percent of GDP in the 1990s to 2.2 percent in 2007, Japan's consumption is still but a third of US consumption.[94]

For their part, Germans have reacted to economic downturns just like they reacted to the latest crisis: with a national resolve to revive exports. Interests of labor and business have been aligned through collective bargaining arrangements, where labor agrees to wage cuts and business to investments and providing jobs.[95] The stealth wage discipline has limited consumption, and a 19-percent VAT increase in 2007, sold to voters as a means to boost exports, further curbed incentives to spend.[96] That year, the German savings rate was 10.8 percent of disposable income, at a par with France, Belgium, and Switzerland, but well above the 1.7 percent registered in the United States, 2.2 percent in the UK, and 3.3 percent in Japan.[97] Germans also have more rigid labor markets, higher tax burdens, and less household wealth than Americans have, all of which encourage savings.

Granted, even if Germany were to bring its overall trade surplus to zero, the US trade deficit would be reduced by a mere 0.2 percentage points.[98] After all, 60 percent of Germany's trade surplus arises from within the Eurozone. But German adjustment would alleviate intra-EU imbalances that abet the Eurozone crises and be useful for persuading China and other surplus nations to adjust. However, Germans see global imbalances as a US–China problem caused mainly by the US fiscal deficit, and the Merkel government has since the first G20 meetings claimed political constraints on spending. Voters still recall the hyperinflation of the 1920s as an era that hurried in Hitler and are also resolved to reattain, by 2013, the 3-percent fiscal deficit target set by the European Growth and Stability Pact. Expanding the share of services—let alone financial services, as the United States has done—in the German economy is seen by most Germans as imprudent. Berlin sees few reasons to change its policies.

Plan of Action

With surplus nations' policies in a collision course with US rebalancing objectives, the odds of a breakthrough at the G20 are slim. But the limitations of a policy do not mean it should not be pursued. The status quo makes everyone lose in the end. If pushing exports at all costs, the surplus nations, especially China, could send off rounds of trade protection around the world and only perpetuate the imbalances. Continued government spending in the United States would be similarly shortsighted, requiring increased foreign borrowing and torpedoing the US economic future. Currency warriors headed for a battle are on a suicide mission.

There is also no time to wait for structural transformations to undo imbalances. Genuine consumer-led growth in emerging markets is still distant—China and India are bound to produce some 500 million new middle-class consumers, but not until 2030—while it is unattainable in aging Europe and Japan.

Washington should not expect the G20's peer review process to rebalance the world economy. At best, the process will help bring forth good data on other nations' policies, publicize China's unfair policies without negative fallout to Washington, and bring to the table other nations with an interest in rebalancing. But the United States can give the process sharper teeth. Continuity is critical: imbalances must be dealt with regularly, not only when they grow too large and political to be undone only by a good crisis. The G20 leaders and finance ministers must reserve a regular meeting on their agendas for the imbalances, issue bold language to single out laggard nations, and ensure that the IMF has adequate powers and resources for its assigned tasks. In addition, they must make the MAP process fully transparent. All data and IMF analyses must be published in full in order for outside analysts to make informed assessments and craft policy recommendations. Although it would be harder to accomplish, a lack of progress toward rebalancing should trigger tangible measures, such as a special meeting among G20 finance ministers or an IMF consultation, as well as an extensive follow-up process involving analyses and public reports.[99] The United States should pursue four additional policies to manage imbalances.

Can We Make Them Buy?

First, Washington needs to encourage structural changes in the emerging surplus economies. Large imbalances will cease no sooner than their leading cause is terminated. Asia's industry mix needs to change and its policy bias against services end. While the United States has little sway over the politics of Chinese industry, it can encourage investment in Asian services industries. Greater social security and public pension benefits would help reduce the Chinese penchant to save, and an efficient services sector would lead them to spend—and it would be much more effective than an improved social safety net for raising consumption.[100] The impact of such policies could be especially powerful if combined with financial development: if Chinese savers had access to safe instruments guaranteeing high rates of return, they would be likelier to spend a larger share of their incomes. Washington needs to keep tapping the World Bank and the IMF to advance financial development.

The United States should enlist Europe behind these efforts. Europe shares an interest in averting the negative repercussions of global imbalances, and much like the United States, both Germany and other European nations should have an expressed interest in a rise in consumption across Asia as well as in China's trade and currency policies. European nations with steep trade deficits such as the UK, France, and Spain are natural allies for the United States. In contrast, the German resolve to export its way to growth has caused much anguish in Washington (and, more recently, admiration of Germany's manufacturing prowess). Granted, Germany could do itself and the deficit nations a favor and liberalize and stimulate its tightly regulated services sector, which, after all, is also the backbone of an efficient manufacturing sector and would promote consumption. It could also cut the time and costs involved in starting a business, which, like in Japan, are among the highest in the world and impede structural changes.[101] But Germany is not nearly as important for rebalancing from the US point of view as China is. Rather than blaming each other for global imbalances, Washington and Berlin need to work together to address economic policies in East Asia—and the United States has to keep driving the message home in Europe.

Getting Serious About Currencies

Second, exchange rates are only part of the rebalancing exercise and are contingent on structural reforms. But the fact is that the RMB is significantly undervalued because of Beijing's currency manipulation. Granted, RMB revaluation would have to be substantial, 40–50 percent, to help undo the US trade deficit, but a change of such magnitude would undercut Chinese and global growth. However, a more gradual appreciation would be beneficial, and even better would be a coordinated exchange-rate adjustment across Asia, as it would double the impact of Chinese revaluation.[102]

The currency issue risks serious international tensions spanning US–China relations, but it will have to be dealt with sooner or later. Both multilateral and bilateral approaches can be employed.

The multilateral approach, most feasibly at the IMF, should be comprehensive—addressing both capital controls and exchange-rate manipulation simultaneously. The IMF and, more cautiously, the US Treasury have broken with their uniform rejection of capital controls, with a few IMF staff papers proposing a set of criteria when controls could be permitted. But allowing some capital controls is perilous: the trade-offs of capital controls outweigh their presumed benefits. Although there will likely be little concrete action to limit capital controls or exchange-rate manipulation regardless of what the IMF does, multilateralizing the issue would keep the issue on the table and in the public eye, help bring together all leading nations interested in changes in China's currency policies, shed light on the other East Asian nations' undervalued currencies, and address the widespread ad hoc currency manipulation by emerging economies to counter quantitative easing policies in advanced economies or to mimic each other.

Bilaterally, US tone should be tougher. There are a number of policy options. The first is the countervailing currency intervention proposed by C. Fred Bergsten in the fall of 2010.[103] When China (or Japan) buys dollars to keep its currency substantially undervalued, the United States could sell an equivalent amount of dollars to neutralize the impact. The signal to the Asian economies would be clear, even if the impact of counter-intervention, especially in the case of China, would be muted, as the RMB remains inconvertible. The policy tool would help address the RMB's value and lessen congressional pressures to erect tariffs, even if would not undo global imbalances.

The second option is to tax the earnings of Chinese official holdings of dollar assets, which should dampen the Chinese drive to fatten their reserve trove.[104] The policy, proposed by Gary Hufbauer, is particularly useful as effecting it would be gradual, with each step bringing greater pressure on China. The first step would be to terminate the US–China tax treaty, followed by a congressional exemption for the Treasury to impose a withholding tax on interest and dividends paid on dollar holdings by any nation that sports a current-account surplus and an undervalued currency.

Third, the United States could call for a World Trade Organization dispute settlement panel to judge whether Chinese currency manipulation violates WTO Article XV ("frustration of the intent of the agreement by exchange action").[105] WTO rules on currency matters are long overdue, notwithstanding the methodological difficulties in assessing currency manipulation, and a US–China case would set a powerful precedent. However, there are two risks to this approach that would need to be carefully weighed: the risk of losing and the risk that the WTO would interpret Article XV, which is rather open-ended, in ways that will end up hurting US interests in the future.

A further option to preempt currency wars would be to address the symptom instead of the cause and revise the global currency regime, an expressed wish of many an idealistic analyst. But any fundamental change is distant, as will be discussed in Chapter 4, as no other currency enjoys the economic prowess and liquid financial markets that underpin the US dollar.

No to Tariffs

Third, the United States must ward off the siren call of protectionism to counter the imbalances. In early 2010 Paul Krugman echoed the sentiments of congressional Democrats, advocating a 25-percent US across-the-board tariff on China should China fail to appreciate its currency.[106] Such policy would be foolish for numerous reasons.

First, as discussed above, it would not hurt China for too long, but it would hurt US workers, consumers, and companies importing from China. Nearly 60 percent of Chinese exports come from (and imports are bought by) foreign multinationals in China.[107] The tariff would thus penalize the many US and other companies that export from China to the United States. A tariff on goods imported from China that are produced in a global supply chain could also hurt American jobs in such areas as engineering, design, finance, marketing, and retail while not hurting China to the same extent: on average, 50–61 percent of the value of goods exported from China is added in countries other than China, including in the United States.[108]

Also hurt would be US consumers and retailers sourcing from China, such as Walmart. Because China and the United States hardly (or no longer) produce the same goods, a tariff would not entice Americans to purchase US goods. If the tariff on China were prohibitive, it would shift the Chinese share of US imports to another, higher-cost producer and only exacerbate the US trade deficit. A lighter tariff might trap Americans into buying the still competitive yet now more expensive Chinese goods.

Second, a unilateral tariff could make China counterretaliate with trade barriers. Protectionist ricochet would not be out of character for Beijing. In

2009, for example, China retaliated against US anti-dumping measures with steep tariffs.[109] A Chinese tariff on the United States would have an impact. China is America's third-largest export market after Canada and Mexico, absorbing some 7 percent of the total in 2009. If resulting in 1 percent of lost American exports, Chinese retaliation could cost 6,500 US jobs.[110] Beijing could also complicate the operations of US companies in China, one of its increasingly frequent habits.[111] Sufficiently incensed, China might also only further devalue the RMB, promote exports by other means even at a risk of a WTO case, and/or project its wrath onto other policy arenas—such as torpedo the Doha Trade Round, as it did in July 2008. There are better get-tough policies than tariffs.

Third, US tariff retaliation against China could have thorny global implications. It would place America's Asian allies, Japan, India, and Korea, in an uncomfortable position of having to choose between Beijing and Washington. If pressed, Tokyo and Seoul might have to take sides in ways that have lasting geo-economic implications for the United States in the Asia-Pacific. A tariff would also violate US obligations at the WTO and undermine the rules-based multilateral trade regime that the United States has championed in the post-war era.[112] Equally bad, it could make unilateral currency retaliation more acceptable around the world. America should not underestimate the extent to which its policies are emulated or retaliated against abroad to the detriment of the global trading system. If currency mercantilism leads to a proliferation of currency protectionism, the global trading system would suffer. By implying that the United States is not going to play by the framework process that it itself has promoted to contain the imbalances, tariff retaliation would decidedly undermine, if not end, the process. There are other ways to force China's hand.

Yes to Trade   Instead of tariffs, US trade policy needs to be for free trade, most-favored-nation treatment, and full reciprocity in the global trading system—policies that would actually further American exports rather than harming American consumers. Part of the answer lies in the Doha Round. Forceful multilateral liberalization would not only inject much-needed confidence and vitality in the global economy, but it must also come with substantial cuts in emerging economies' manufacturing and services industries.

Whatever the fortunes of the multilateral round, the US bilateral and regional trade agendas also need rebooting. The passage of the FTAs with Korea, Colombia, and Panama is not enough; the real prize is the Asia-Pacific region. China matters, for US trade and rebalancing alike. The United States needs to publicly voice its unhappiness with Beijing's trade and investment discrimination and currency mercantilism, and push for greater market access for US exporters and investors in China. A particularly useful tool both for opening new markets and bringing pressure on China is the US-led Trans-Pacific Partnership (TPP), which thus far includes eight smaller Asia-Pacific economies. The United States should secure Korea and Japan's participation in the TPP, negotiate a deal that paves the way to much deeper liberalization than is offered by any Asian FTAs, and use the accord as a springboard to a genuine Free Trade Area of the Asia-Pacific, a long-standing American aspiration. Once encircled by a liberalizing TPP that encompasses ASEAN economies and Japan and Korea, China ought to be inclined to join lest it be left out—an outcome that provides the United States with important leverage.

More generally, deeper economic and political ties in the Asia-Pacific region will help Washington deal with China, as Beijing tends to respond better to events and pressures outside the bilateral US–China forum than within it.[113] This is yet another reason why the TPP is of major strategic importance. Washington must continue deepening transpacific regionalism as a hedge against the multiple intra-Asian economic schemes and as a means to American prosperity in the twenty-first century.

A particularly useful further policy for reducing the US trade deficit would be a comprehensive services agreement with major economies with which the United States does not have an FTA, such as Brazil and India. Services make up some 40 percent of US exports and face barriers in both advanced and emerging nations. The TPP will have comprehensive chapters on services trade, representing an important step in the right direction.

The transatlantic front should not be abandoned. Opening talks for a transatlantic free trade agreement, something the US business community has supported postcrisis, could be employed to bring pressure on emerging economies to get serious about global trade talks. Such a process would also open an opportunity for the United States and Europe to kick-start a global drive to multilateralize trade regionalism as a complement to multilateral talks and a back door to global trade liberalization. And it would create a hook to which the ongoing transatlantic regulatory and sectoral policy coordination processes could be hung, giving the relationship greater strategic feel. With robust services liberalization, the deal would aid US services trade with Europe and improve the US trade deficit.

What We Can Control

Fourth and most critically, the United States must do its own share of rebalancing. Fiscal discipline is a prerequisite for US growth, investor confidence in America, and global rebalancing. It would signal US preparedness to do its share, not exclusively pursue the Obama administration's export agenda or shift the adjustment burden abroad. China in particular is opposed to Plaza-like horse trading, something it sees as an effort to boost the Obama administration's populist export-led growth agenda and avoid less-popular belt-tightening.

Domestic policies are the only way to pursue rebalancing that is squarely in Washington's control. Instilling confidence in US businesses to start investing and hiring takes an ironclad plan for fiscal solvency, tax incentives, cuts in red tape and regulation, and new trade deals.

Rebalancing will not work without US fiscal discipline. Fiscal discipline is also a must for reinvigorating America's economic growth, which in turn will help close the budget shortfall. When not outweighed by a rise in government deficits, the ongoing household saving increases will help boost US exports.[114] There is nothing antithetical about Americans saving. In the 1960s Americans saved 7.5–10 percent of their incomes, almost the level of Germany in the past 15 years; in the 1970s the savings rate was in the 8–12 percent range, slightly less than where France's has been the past 15 years. Still in the boom years of 1994–2000, Americans saved 4–6 percent.[115]

Would stringency hurt US growth prospects? Democrats like to argue that government spending is necessary for jump-starting growth—and some even claim that the Bretton Woods III system is already in place, so US deficit spending is needed to keep the world economy afloat. However, the massive stimulus programs of the past few years have all but failed to restore US economic prowess, and even analysts usually sanguine about public spending now agree that America's long-term economic health requires cutting the deficit. Any negative effects from reduced public and private spending are consistently offset by the positive effect of other factors, particularly by the greater availability of capital investment.[116] Historically, robust investment and economic growth have been sustainable only on the back of domestic saving.

The congressional supercommittee charged with devising policies to lower the nation's debt collapsed after locking horns over taxes. As such, it made the George W. Bush tax cuts into a major political issue on the road of the 2012 presidential race. Democrats ardently support taxes on the wealthy, but heavier taxation is a bad fiscal policy at a time when growth hangs on balance, not least because growth increases tax revenues.[117] In a groundbreaking study of 107 adjustments in OECD nations' fiscal policies in 1970–2007, Alberto Alesina and Silvia Ardagna found that cutting spending and taxes is an effective way to propel growth and reduce deficits, while increasing spending is ineffective—the promised multiplier effect of stimulus dollars is scant—and increasing taxes is recessionary.[118] Spending cuts are expansionary because they signal that tax increases will not occur in the future or that, if they do, they will be smaller. This, in turn, leads to adjustments in expectations: consumers and investors are more willing to spend if they believe that spending and taxes will remain low for an extended period of time. Several rigorous empirical studies echo these findings. Yet they are lost on countless commentators and congressional Democrats who see tax cuts as antithetical to deficit reduction.

America needs a firm commitment to pay-as-you-go rules and, in the longer run, lower taxes. Containing entitlement spending is critical for America's fiscal health. Government needs to exit from markets in order for them to run on their own. Taxes do little to help businesses to invest and plan ahead, and consumers to build confidence and spend.

America and the G20

The G20 is up against the same challenge that has confronted each G, from the G4 to the G8: rebalancing the world economy when doing so clashes with the members' domestic political imperatives. If the group's potential for rebalancing the world economy is meager, should it exit the game? What, if anything, is the G20 worth?

Since the G4, convened by George Schultz, the Gs have served a function distinct from the boards and governors of the various world bodies: they are high-level venues of flexible coordination without heavy obligations. These properties are unique in global governance and should be preserved and prized. They are particularly well-suited for crisis management and for setting sweeping agendas, and, in general, for the world of international finance, where circumstances change rapidly, uncertainties abound, and the treasured prerogatives of national policy making are at stake. The G20 is also well positioned to function like an international board of nonexecutive directors or steering committee of other international institutions and policy agendas. It is a coordinator and leader rather than rule crafter or manager, and a chair-person rather than a CEO. Even if high level and strategic, the G20 members are not aloof; they have waged several specific battles over the future of the IMF, for instance. The G20 has shown glimpses of its longer-term potential—revising such institutions as the IMF and the Financial Stability Board, and setting the global economic agenda.

Lacking enforcement tools, the G20 cannot induce action, but if it had enforcement tools, its coordination function would be stifled, as the leaders would become much more hesitant to discuss policy options and make any commitments. Concerns about the G20 degenerating into a grand photo op are valid, but the proposed cure—making the G20's commitments hard law or demoting leaders to managers of the minutiae of economic policies—could be worse than the anticipated disease.

The G20 leaders and commentators alike must recognize the group's limi-tations and set the agenda and expectations accordingly. They also need to differentiate between the forum and its individual members, such as China. And they should not underestimate the intangible value of the leaders of the main economies regularly coming together to discuss global economic chal-lenges, let alone the intense exchanges among national working groups that precede the summits.

If it avoids overpromising and overreach and bridges advanced and emerging members' interests, the G20 can help steer the world economy and help the United States economize global relationships, logroll with the leading nations, and build coalitions behind American aims. However, that is a major *if*. Repeated failures by the G20 to meet its commitments on rebalancing, the Doha Round, financial regulations, and other policy areas will quickly chip away at the group's credibility and relegate it to irrelevance. The leaders them-selves, starting with President Obama, should not underestimate that fact.

The key factor between success and failure is leadership. Just like the G5 or G7, the G20 requires leadership for generating useful policy ideas and build-ing actionable support around them. And just like in the past, there are only a handful of members that truly matter. Of those, the United States is the most important one and the only plausible leader. Emerging economies have a long way to go in learning to play ball and defining what they want in the G20 beyond the increased political power they covet on the international stage. And, as in the past, the United States leads best by example. That most im-mediately means balancing the budget, pursuing global trade and investment liberalization and integration, and ensuring the viability of the dollar. On those metrics, the Obama administration has a long way to go.

Conclusion

A failure to address global imbalances would jeopardize the gains from open markets scored in the past six decades, exacerbate the fragilities in the world economy, and sow international acrimony. In the 1980s Washington succeeded at rebalancing not because the G5 was a particularly clever coordination mechanism but because the United States was able to pressure Tokyo with credible trade threats and to recruit European allies to the cause. America's main counterpart in the rebalancing process today, China, is harder to move, but the United States still has several policy options. However, much of Washington's act of persuasion can and must be done at home, and it needs to consist of deeds, not words: fiscal policies that clearly signal US commitment to America's economic health—and that would compel others to adjust. There are no better motivators for the surplus nations to reexamine their growth models than fiscal discipline and positive private savings in America. Short of that, Washington should prepare to live in an imbalanced world economy and deal with the threats that it poses.

2　Rescuing the Rescuer

What Should a Twenty-First-Century IMF Do?

An international monetary fund . . . will put an end to monetary chaos.
The fund is a financial institution to preserve stability and order in the
exchange rates between different moneys . . . the fund agreement spells
the difference between a world caught again in the maelstrom of panic and
economic warfare culminating in war—as in the Nineteen Thirties—or a
world in which the members strive for a better life through mutual trust,
cooperation and assistance. The choice is ours.
　　　—*President Franklin Delano Roosevelt's message to Congress, 12 February 1945*

A S THE GREAT CRISIS BATTERED ECONOMIES AROUND THE
world, the International Monetary Fund (IMF), only a few years
ago fading into obscurity in the thriving world economy, sprung back to business. Some of the first rescues went to Ukraine, Iceland, Pakistan, Belarus,
Georgia, and Latvia, followed by Serbia, Romania, Poland, and a number of
Latin American nations, among others. By the fall of 2009, the IMF had committed over $160 billion in new loans and credit lines. Policy thinking on the
Fund's future shifted rapidly, as well. At US initiative, the G20 pledged to triple the Fund's lending capacity to $750 billion, and minted it as the manager
of the G20's rebalancing initiative. Paradoxically perhaps, the crisis rescued
the venerable global rescuer.

The IMF has played a critical role in postwar global economic governance and in advancing US interests. It has issued authoritative commentary on the challenges in the world economy, assiduously surveyed the state
of its 186 member economies, and time and again steadied nations engulfed
in economic turbulence. The Fund's counsel, even if at times criticized as
draconian, has tempered economic policy making around the world. Many

an emerging market would be a declining market were it not for the Fund's emergency lending and policy advice.

Notwithstanding its new windfall and duties, the IMF's effectiveness is under fire. Its arsenal has limits. Economic volatility will recur, but expanding the Fund's kitty could only inspire moral hazard around the world and face stiff headwinds on Capitol Hill, where many a congressperson see Fund rescues as free bailouts of distant nations—especially now that it is Americans who need to be bailed out. IMF governance poses another challenge. Recent concessions by the overrepresented Western European members, made at US prodding, to transfer voting power to emerging markets are unlikely to suffice for China, India, and other underrepresented nations that hunger for greater sway in the world body, including to end the US veto over the Fund's major decisions. Conflicts fester over the Fund's future mission, with emerging nations eager for Fund surveillance of the advanced economies and Washington aiming to keep the spotlight on global imbalances and exchange rates.

Another, growing issue troubling the IMF is the specter of disintegration of the global insurance architecture into regional and bilateral financial schemes—right when the globalization of financial markets and crises alike calls for strong system-wide management. Asian economies, scarred by the Fund's tough policy conditions in exchange for loans during the 1997–1998 regional financial crisis, are busily building national reserves and regional financial arrangements to wean themselves off the Fund's influence. Also, Latin Americans are discussing a regional arrangement. Such indigenous initiatives would not afford America the sway over other nations' economic policies that its leadership in the Fund does. Europe poses the opposite problem. Struggling to end the continent's financial crises even with strong Fund support, Europeans risk dragging the world body ever deeper into a mess that the Fund has little power to fix. Can the IMF contain coming financial storms?

The Global Guarantor

A crowning achievement of the Bretton Woods conference, the IMF was the brainchild of Harry Dexter White, chief international economist at the US Treasury, and the legendary British economist John Maynard Keynes. In the run-up to the 1944 conference, the two economists crafted plans on ways to further global trade and economic stability in the postwar era and prevent the kind of economic devastation that followed the First World War.[1] It was White who prevailed in the vigorous transatlantic debate. His plan prioritized price and exchange-rate stability and envisioned a global insurance agency over Keynes's calls for growth, a world reserve currency, and a global central bank capable of printing money.[2]

The IMF embodied White's ideals. Formally organized in 1945 among the initial 29 signatories, the Washington body would promote exchange-rate stability and serve as a payment system for members struggling with balance-of-payment shortfalls—and thereby forestall currency misalignments conducive to beggar-thy-neighbor protectionism. Each Fund member agreed to peg its currency to the dollar; the pegged rates could be altered only with the Fund's approval in case of a "fundamental disequilibrium" in the troubled nation's balance of payments.

The IMF's initial pool of $8.8 billion was based on the members' subscriptions—25 percent in gold or currency convertible into gold (i.e., the dollar) and 75 percent in the members' own currencies—and quotas that reflected the member states' relative economic weight. Each member was entitled to withdraw 25 percent of its quota immediately in the face of balance-of-payment problems. France became the first nation to draw on the Fund. However, the Fund's armory proved insufficient for meeting the severe postwar balance-of-payment problems across Europe. The United States offered the Marshall Plan as a means to rebuild the war-torn continent.

The United States and the IMF

Terminating the par value regime, the end of the gold peg in 1971 marked the beginning of the IMF's modern history. Keen on revalidating its reason for being, the Fund quickly found a new mission: lending to oil importers struggling with inflation and trade deficits resulting from the soaring petroleum prices. It also expanded its research on the state of the world economy and surveillance of its members' economic policies. But it was in the 1980s when the Fund got in the business it is best known for today—rescuing emerging economies mired in financial crises.[3] The first clients were Latin American nations, whose extensive borrowing in dollar-denominated debt backfired after US interest rates soared in the late 1970s. The plunging international commodity prices exacerbated the region's bind. The Fund's lending was to give countries breathing space to adjust consumption and generate resources to repay their external debts without incurring as dramatic impact on their economies as would be the case in the absence of an external lifeline. Loans would be tied to economic policy reforms by the borrower nation aimed at preventing further calamities, helping to get the creditors on board.

The United States, the IMF's founder and main shareholder, played a central role in its firefighting, both as the first responder and, later, as the Fund's second line of defense. In 1982 the Reagan administration countered the Mexican financial crisis with a series of emergency loans, in 1989 the Bush administration devised the Brady Plan to help Latin American nations service their debts, and in 1994 the Clinton administration lent $50 billion to Mexico, by then America's NAFTA partner, to suppress the peso crisis. In the late 1990s, Washington engineered a series of IMF emergency loans to countries recoiling in the Asian financial crisis, and helped shore up the faltering Russian economy. As Argentina's economy collapsed in the early 2000s, the George W. Bush administration, after much agonizing, agreed to billions of dollars of Fund loans to Buenos Aires.[4]

Washington has justified the repeated rescues as critical to US economic and foreign policy objectives. In Asia the motivation was economic: the rapidly spreading crisis undermined markets increasingly critical for US trade and financial interests, and offered an opportunity to influence longer-term economic policies across the region.[5] In the Americas and Russia, foreign policy rationales led the way. Mexican crises needed to be tamed to avert mass migration across the Rio Grande; the Russian meltdown had to be arrested lest it aggravated the nuclear power issues and undermined Russia's nascent democracy.[6] Turkey needed buttressing as a NATO ally in the Muslim world.[7] Even the package to Argentina, while partly aimed at shoring up exasperated US creditors, could be defended on the grounds that the fall of the star pupil of the Washington Consensus would make other reforming nations lose heart.[8]

Benefits of Pooling   Does the IMF advance US interests? It has certainly been used as an instrument of US foreign and financial policy. For instance, countries that vote in the United Nations with Washington on issues key to US interests are found to be likelier to receive an IMF program than countries that vote against America.[9] Analyzing African countries, Randall Stone has found that the more US foreign aid a country receives, the shorter the duration of punishment incurred by the country for lack of compliance with a Fund program.[10] Lawrence Broz and Michael Hawes show that the amount of US bank exposure in a developing country affects the size of Fund loans that the country receives: US money-center banks likely convince Congress to support loans to nations where their funds are at stake.[11]

If it is a tool of statecraft, the IMF has delivered on US interests. Its involvement has steadied countries critical for US exports: American trade flows with emerging nations that have borrowed from the Fund amount to more than $400 billion *annually*, or almost half of US trade with emerging markets.[12] The Fund has helped rescue nations pivotal to US foreign policy and national security interests, such as Mexico, Pakistan, Turkey, Korea, and Ukraine, and it has spread the tenets of capitalism to Eastern Europe and Russia as they emerged from communism. Granted, the Fund has made mistakes—and it certainly is no magic wand for misgoverned economies, let alone the many nations that fail to complete its programs.[13] But it has also made a veritable difference. When implemented, IMF programs improve countries' current-account and international reserves; contrary to the Fund's critics, its impact on preventing currency crises and reducing macroeconomic imbalances is also positive.[14] The Fund's indirect benefits, even if hard to measure, may be particularly important. For instance, its involvement sets the stage for unpopular policy reforms by allowing the affected country's government to deflect some of the political fallout.

The IMF imparts a further benefit: it economizes bailouts. By distributing the burdens of emergency insurance across the 186-member group, the Fund prevents smaller nations from free riding on the main lenders. Randall Henning has found that US contributions to the Fund are matched more than four-fold by other states.[15] Pooling insurance globally is, in short, efficient. Besides, US contributions are not grants that vanish once allocated: they are exchanges of financial assets in which the United States receives a readily usable claim on the Fund. Indeed, the United States has not incurred any losses on its contributions to the Fund.[16] The bilateral rescues have also been repaid; recovering from the peso crisis, Mexico repaid the IMF well before the due date. The Fund's mere presence reduces the odds that America would need to act as the world's last resort—or, worse yet, act and fall short. And even if only partially, the Fund also shields US policy makers from discontent: the Fund, not Washington, takes the primary hit from anguished populations wrestling with a crisis and the austerity measures to subdue it.

The Stormy Nineties

Its benefits notwithstanding, the IMF was falling from grace in the years leading to the Great Crisis.[17] The first blow came with the 1997–1998 Asian financial crisis, when the Fund imposed tough conditions—tight money and deep budget cuts to tame inflation and external deficits—before dispensing emergency funds.[18] Asians saw the structural reforms as excessive and causing politically taxing austerity.[19] Acidly criticizing the Fund's actions and advice, such opinion leaders as Jeffrey Sachs and Joseph Stiglitz emerged as the IMF-bashers' cheerleaders in the West.[20] Most often unfairly, the Fund was faulted for lack of foresight, blanket prescriptions inapplicable to idiosyncratic circumstances, and even for outright heartlessness. Its counsel was claimed to have turned the regional illiquidity problem into an insolvency problem. The episode created a lasting disdain for the Fund in emerging Asia, contributing to the region's drive to build national reserves and to devise a common swap system.

Critics resurfaced in the early 2000s as the IMF adamantly supported the Argentine currency board, a mechanism that tied the value of the peso to the US dollar. As Argentina's poor fiscal management and economic travails following the 1999 Brazilian crisis undermined investor confidence, a run on the peso depleted Argentine reserves. The currency board was terminated, the peso value of Argentina's dollar-denominated debts more than tripled, and the government defaulted. Finger-pointers accused the Fund of straitjacketing Buenos Aires into the currency board when a floating exchange rate might have averted the crisis.

In addition to the political challenges, the IMF's relevance was questioned. Armed only with the political heft its members could afford it, the Fund proved unable to affect the bigger players. It could do little more than issue warnings about the US housing boom, and it steered clear of berating China for its undervalued exchange rate.[21] And if the Fund was a hammer, there were few nails: macroeconomic conditions during the first few years of the new millennium were stellar in the Fund's erstwhile clientele. Asian nations were growing at near double-digit rates and were increasingly buffered by national reserves resulting from export-led development strategies; Latin American commodity producers thrived on the insatiable Asian demand for soy, wheat, iron ore, copper, oil, and other raw materials. Russia also basked in the global commodity boom. Emerging markets received progressively higher credit ratings, becoming eligible for low-interest private loans. The Fund's future was narrowed to essentially two options—to shrink it or to sink it. Washington was flooded with the résumés of dozens of laid-off IMF economists.

Saved by the Crisis

The Great Crisis resurrected the IMF. As countries around the world crumbled, the Fund issued loans in a rapid sequence. By the fall of 2009, it had committed over $160 billion in new loans and credit lines. The Obama administration supported the funds as critical for saving the world from another Great Depression. National security arguments were revived, as well: Director of National Intelligence Dennis Blair held that the financial turmoil posed the foremost near-term security threat to the United States.[22] While the Treasury worked with the IMF, the Federal Reserve moved bilaterally, channeling $755 billion to other major central banks in 14 bilateral swap lines—temporary sales of US dollars for a specified quantity of foreign currency to aid foreign central banks with their dollar shortfalls.[23] The ECB extended swaps in Europe, as did the Bank of Japan and People's Bank of China.

Policy consensus on the IMF's future shifted practically overnight. At US initiative, in April 2009 the G20 pledged to restock the Fund with $500 billion in fresh lending capacity. Japan, the European Union, and the United States each committed some $100 billion, China promised $40 billion, and Korea $18 billion. Norway, Canada, and Switzerland provided a total of $25 billion. Europe increased its contribution to $178 million. Commitments ended up exceeding the pledged totals, raising the Fund's total borrowed and quota resources to more than $900 billion by October 2010.

The G20 also allocated $250 billion in Special Drawing Rights (SDRs), its quasi-currency unit worth at the time about $1.56, to boost liquidity among the IMF's members. The allocation of SDRs boosts member countries' reserves because SDRs can be turned into usable currencies: countries in need of a hard currency can sell SDRs to countries with strong external finances. At $283 billion by September 2009, the outstanding SDR stock had ballooned by nearly ten-fold. In yet another historic fund-raiser, the Fund sold some of its gold and set out to issue bonds nominated in SDRs. The BRICs were keenest on the measure because the SDR makes for an ultra-safe investment vehicle and because buying it allowed central banks to lower their high dollar exposure. China, proposing the SDR be employed more widely in global economy, was the first customer, with a $50-billion purchase.

The IMF revamped its tool kit. It introduced a new instrument, the Flexible Credit Line (FCL), to respond to contagious crises more rapidly. The FCL allows countries with sound policies that do not need to effect further policy reforms to access Fund resources quickly and free of conditions; Mexico and Poland were the first beneficiaries.

The IMF's mission was also refurbished. Before the crisis, the Fund lacked a clear, compelling long-term task; now, its army of PhDs would be charged with assessing countries' progress toward the high-profile G20 balanced growth agenda. The G20 also looked to the Fund for more extensive surveillance on imbalances and such other systemic issues as asset buildups and exchange rates. In addition, the Fund was tasked to partner with the Financial Stability Board (FSB) in early-warning exercises aimed at forecasting new storms in financial markets, and to complement the FSB's work on coordinating national financial regulations.

The IMF–G20 consortium was a perfect match: an IMF in search of money and mission and a G20 in search of staff. Now an agent of the G20, the Fund was less susceptible to criticism that it lacked political courage. It would do what it does best: perform technocratic, objective, and standardized analyses for the G20 peer review, and leave the G20 to deal with the politics and outcomes of the process. By involving the Fund and thus its 186 members, the G20 hoped the arrangement would engage its nonmembers that nonetheless are IMF members.[24]

The $2-Trillion Challenge

The IMF hardly missed a beat in regaining its footing on the world map after the crisis broke. Its revival owed in part to its managing director, the charismatic former French Socialist finance minister Dominique Strauss-Kahn (DSK)—who in mid-2011 would become a global headliner for rape charges that caused his resignation.

DSK had come to the IMF in 2007 promising institutional reforms.[25] The crisis provided an opportunity, and DSK emerged as an outsized figure in the institution's turnaround. During the crisis, he pushed through reforms for the Fund to dispense large sums rapidly and with fewer strings attached, strong-armed members to permit the sale of a portion of the Fund's gold stock, and charmed emerging markets into contributing more to the Fund's pool.[26] Promising internal budgetary cuts, DSK bought goodwill that helped engineer the partnership with the G20. He persuaded governments of the

Fund's ready brainpower and justified his reform drive by referring to discussions well before the crisis about the needs to revise the Fund's mandate.

These triumphs notwithstanding, the IMF faces daunting challenges. The most immediate one is managing the new diverse demands at an organization seen more as a single-minded hedgehog than a multitasking fox. The larger and longer-term challenge is money. The Fund's capital pool is not deep enough in a world of frequent economic turmoil and trillions in financial assets at stake—no fewer than $178 trillion even in 2008, a dreadful year in the global economy. Even with its new lending powers, the Fund's armory would be less than a quarter of the $4 trillion that the United States had committed domestically by the spring of 2009 to stem the crisis.[27] While America's is a large economy, it is only one-quarter of the world total. A future shock facing a group of countries of roughly the same economic size but without the resources Washington had at its disposal could overwhelm the Fund.[28]

DSK recognized the mismatch between the IMF and the world economy. Having tripled the Fund's arsenal, he set his sights to another $1.25 trillion to bring the total lending capacity to $2 trillion—a sum that he argued was necessary for the Fund to serve as an effective global insurer.[29] The proposal surpassed the $1-trillion package proposed by former IMF Chief Economist Simon Johnson in 2008, but it was politically more feasible than the call by former Inter-American Development Bank Chief Economist Guillermo Calvo to make the Fund the lender of last resort—at least in theory a body of unlimited funds.[30] As the Europeans failed to stem their financial crisis, DSK's successor, Christine Lagarde, also argued that the Fund's war chest would have to be boosted to preempt a deepening of the crisis.

But key IMF members are balking at increasing the institution's resources. In October 2011, the G20 finance ministers rejected a proposal to make permanent a special $590-billion pool of Fund resources, which would have raised total lending power to a record $1.3 trillion.

The politics are thorny. The main emerging nations, Brazil, Russia, India, China, and South Africa, are the main proponents of a funding increase, in part for economic reasons. Despite forecasts by many bullish analysts, emerging markets have not created a new global "supercycle" of widespread growth and prosperity. Instead of becoming decoupled from the advanced economies, emerging economies find themselves held hostage to the transatlantic economic morass. Short of inflationary domestic stimulus, they see in the IMF the best lever to get Europe back on track, reviving global growth and their own economic fortunes. Moreover, the cash-rich emerging nations would provide the lion's share of such a new increase, enhancing their claims to greater powers in the world body.

However, the United States, the United Kingdom, Canada, Japan, and Australia are queasy about such political implications and unenthused to pony up more money. Indeed, although the crisis concentrated minds on the importance of emergency lending, there are good academic arguments against, and serious political constraints to, expanding the IMF any further. The first lies just a few blocks east from its headquarters, on Capitol Hill.

Constraints on the Good Neighbor

Before the 1980s, the IMF was a rather obscure institution with little connection to the average American's existence. But the subsequent bailouts brought the Fund to the center of US domestic politics. The successive rescues entailed increased congressional scrutiny on the Fund's work and effectiveness, and led to progressive greater reluctance to lend.

As Mexico faltered in 1994, congressional leadership rose to the occasion as requested by the administration, but opposition mounted among the rank and file on both sides of the aisle. [31] The Clinton administration decided to circumvent Congress altogether by using executive authority to tap the obscure Exchange Stabilization Fund (ESF) to extend $20 billion in loans and guarantees to the southern neighbor.[32] Congress retaliated by limiting the use of the ESF; however, the strings conveniently expired during the Asian crisis of 1997–1998, freeing the administration to back the IMF up with loans to Indonesia and Korea. Incensed, Congress argued that the rescues consumed America's precious fiscal resources and only created moral hazard problems—excessive risk taking by governments and investors who expect the Fund to spring to the rescue in case of a crisis.[33] Some members of Congress also opposed extending emergency lines to Russia in 1999.[34]

The repeated bailout battles induced Congress to sponsor a commission that would recommend reforms to the various multilateral financial institutions. Led by economist Allan Meltzer, in 2000 the commission came down hard on the IMF and World Bank, arguing that they lacked transparency and suffered from mission creep. [35] It recommended that the Fund be a "quasilender of last resort" and provide short-term funds only to such crisis-torn countries that have met certain preconditions, such as sound macroeconomic governance. Citing moral hazard, the Meltzer Commission argued that Fund loans should carry a penalty in order for potential borrowers to explore other options before resorting to the Fund. Meltzer and his coauthor, Adam Lerrick, also argued investors needed a lesson, writing that "only default and the losses that follow will create the incentives to deter speculative flows in the capital markets." [36]

The ideas of limiting bailouts and rewarding countries for good behavior were not novel: amid the Asian crisis, the Clinton administration had opened a facility favoring well-managed economies, and also a Council on Foreign Relations Task Force had argued the IMF should reward emerging markets for "good housekeeping" and recommended that Fund rescues be limited to 300 percent of the member's quota.[37]

Moral Hazard Meets Foreign Policy

The Bush administration, particularly Treasury Secretary Paul O'Neill, bought into the moral hazard arguments. The position was sound. Research shows that for countries in arrears, the availability of insurance appears to encourage expansive policies that only increase the likelihood that an IMF loan will be needed.[38] Since the 1970s, several countries have used the Fund's lending for a prolonged period of time, some for 7–10 years, and have been repeat borrowers, accessing the Fund's facilities time and again.[39] The odds are that many of them would have got their houses in order had the option to re-resort to the Fund not been available.

There is also considerable evidence that IMF insurance leads to moral hazard among investors. For instance, countries that can access the Fund window have lower bond spreads than might otherwise be expected. A natural experiment proves the point. The fact that Russia was not bailed out in 1997 when its economy flew into turbulence could be expected to have frightened risk-taking investors and profligate nations into believing that the Fund would no longer dash to their rescue. A team composed, among others, of Fund researchers, found that to be the case: the nonbailout had momentous implications, raising the level of spreads around the world and the sensitivity with which spreads reflect country fundamentals.[40]

After its long and principled quest not to bail out the imploding Argentina, the Bush White House had to yield, both because the US creditors—who held 9 percent of the total Argentine debt—demanded resolution, and because the administration ran into similar broader foreign policy concerns that had convinced the Clinton administration to rescue Mexico and Asian nations.[41] This set the administration against the weary congressional Republicans, who had proposed cutting off funds to Argentina. The White House ended up backing IMF rescues also to Argentina's panicked neighbors Uruguay and Brazil, as well as to Turkey. The *New York Times* declared these measures represented "a 30-degree tack, rather than the 180-degree turnaround that the Bush administration had once indicated it preferred when it came to repeat borrowers at the financial bailout window."[42]

The Politics of the Great Crisis

The Great Crisis re-ruptured the fault line between the broad foreign policy incentives of the administration and the parochial interests of congressional representatives. The Obama administration's call for a fresh $108 billion in US commitments to the IMF divided Washington into two camps. The skeptics, including many congressional representatives and long-standing Fund critics, argued against the package on the grounds of US fiscal woes, preexisting commitments to fund two wars, and needs to prioritize constituents hit by the crisis right in America. To add insult to injury, the hostile Iran had circulated into a seat on the IMF Board.

The proponents of the request included a number of Washington think tanks, perhaps most prominently the Brookings Institution, and the IMF's former second in command, renowned economist Anne Krueger. No liberal, she argued that the magnitude of the crisis warranted funding and that any leftover funds could be converted into a useful insurance pool.[43] Krueger also pointed out that without further funding, the IMF staff was "if anything, too lean and too small" to effectively survey the increasingly complex and consequential global economic issues.

The funds, tied to a war-spending bill for Iraq and Afghanistan, were approved in June 2009 after weeks of wrangling.[44] All but 5 of the 175 House Republicans who voted opposed the legislation, largely because of the IMF provision. Some Senate Republicans opposed the idea, as well, but they were overpowered by John Kerry, multilateralist Massachusetts Democrat, and Judd Gregg of New Hampshire, a ranking Republican on the Budget Committee and Obama's initial candidate for Commerce Secretary.[45] However, strings were attached. At the initiative of Kay Granger, Republican from Texas, Congress conditioned the funds on the executive's commitment to vote in favor of health and education issues affecting poor countries; the House approved an amendment with a vote of 429–2. Further clashes emerged in the spring of 2010, as the Senate reacted to the Fund's involvement in rescuing Greece, an advanced economy and part of a potent currency area, with a 94-0 vote to oppose IMF bailout packages to countries that are not likely to repay them.

Rational Parochialism   The Treasury Department has been the IMF's cheerleader ever since organizing a coalition of interest groups in support of the Bretton Woods Agreements Act in 1945.[46] The tactics are many—tasking the White House to advance legislation on Capitol Hill; mobilizing support from other executive agencies, including the Commerce, State, and Defense departments; and persuading key congressional representatives privately, followed by a public relations campaign on Capitol Hill and among interest groups and the media.

Yet Congress has become progressively harder to persuade. Opposition is now reaching a fever pitch as US public debt peaks and many think it is Main Street America, not European welfare states, that should be bailed out.

Resistance to rescues spans partisanship: Republican representatives have opposed bailouts by Republican presidents, Democratic ones have sought to face down Democratic administrations. If the IMF does indeed advance US interests, why the persistent disconnect between the executive and the Congress?

One reason is moral hazard. But there are also four institutional reasons. The first is a collective action problem that also mires US trade policy: while the IMF stabilizes the global economy and thereby buoys the US economy, the benefits are broadly dispersed. Unlike most federal agencies, the Fund does not directly serve any particular constituency. The incentives for any one interest group to rise in defense of the Fund are scarce, by default giving greater voice to groups opposed to the Fund.[47] In addition, lawmakers with blue-collar constituencies may be particularly wary about committing taxpayer dollars to buttress nations that might be America's economic competitors. Lawrence Broz finds that the greater the proportion of low-skilled workers in a district, the likelier a House member is to oppose the executive's pro-bailout agenda.[48]

Second, the collective action problem is compounded by institutional setup. The responsibility for legislation and oversight in Congress is fragmented, with the banking, international relations, and appropriations committees of both houses involved. As such, the IMF ends up being neglected rather than claimed or championed by any one committee or congressman.[49]

Third, IMF funding is but a part of a broader power struggle between Congress and the president over international issues. Congress is quick to showcase its levers. Upon signing the June 2009 funding approval, President Obama argued that the limitations imposed by Congress on Fund loans would interfere with his constitutional authority to conduct foreign policy and negotiate with other governments. Senior Democrats responded with stern warnings for Obama not to overstep the boundaries set in the bill lest he jeopardize further funding.[50]

As cantankerous as the Congress has been, it has not derailed the executive's rescues of nations or the US role in the IMF. But the postcrisis drive to cut the fiscal deficit could herald a change in US foreign operations for years to come. The context calls for renewed attention to moral hazard and for other nations to bear their share. Will they?

A Battle for Power

Besides its limited funds, the IMF is constrained by internal divisions. It has for two decades been caught in a power battle between its founders, the United States and Western Europeans, on the one hand, and emerging markets, on the other. Because a nation's political power at the Fund is supposed to be largely premised on its prowess in the world economy, the rise of emerging economies in the postcrisis world economy has brought the power struggle to a boiling point. The main combatants are the economically weakened yet overrepresented Western Europeans and the rising yet underrepresented East Asians.

The key sticking points are "chairs and shares," namely national representation at the IMF executive board and voting power determined by national quotas.[51] When the crisis broke, the United States held 17 percent of the voting power, enough to give Washington a veto over the rare but important decisions that require an 85-percent majority, such as on the Fund's quota reforms and gold sales. Europeans—EU members plus Norway and Switzerland—claimed a total of 33 percent of the voting power. The BRICs demanded a quota increase of 7 percentage points for emerging markets, sufficient to bring them almost to a par with the advanced countries. China also sought to increase the representation of developing countries, whose cause it claims to champion, in the Fund.[52] In addition, the BRICs also reissued demands for changes in the Fund's board and for a "merit-based" selection of the Fund's managing director, traditionally held by a European.

These demands were not new. After weathering the Asian financial crisis, emerging markets argued for a larger quota, and in 2006 the IMF approved a modest quota increase to China, Mexico, South Korea, and Turkey. Others, such as India, Brazil, Egypt, South Africa, and Argentina, opposed the measure as improvised and inadequate. After intensive US-initiated transatlantic diplomacy in the wake of the Great Crisis, Europeans agreed to expand emerging markets' quota by 6 percentage points by October 2012. The reforms would increase the voting share of China to 6 percent, raising it to the third-most powerful member after the United States and Japan, and just above Germany. India would have 2.6 percent. Washington subsequently forced a showdown with Europe over the IMF board by forcing a resizing of the board from 24 to 20 members, with Europeans taking the hit. The policy was a copy of that pursued by the Bush administration, and it was infused with US frustrations with Europe's resistance to change and unhappiness with European austerity measures and positions on new international banking standards. Washington's pressure bore fruit. Europeans agreed to relinquish two seats by 2014, with the smaller Western European economies likely to lose their seat. The Fund also opened the possibility of moving toward an all-elected board.

US Motives

The United States has long pressed Europe to concede both shares and chairs to the underrepresented nations. Washington's postcrisis drive for the reforms was strongly criticized in Europe as a ploy to sacrifice the transatlantic relationship in order to curry favor with emerging economies. The reaction is unsurprising: reluctance by the leading stakeholders to reform institutional power structures is a familiar theme in domestic and international politics and has been a permanent facet of the IMF's governance. The Allied powers of World War II have been consistently overrepresented at the Fund compared to Axis powers, even though more than six decades have passed since the end of World War II.[53]

The United States has long worried that emerging markets, if further disenchanted with the IMF's governance, would become increasingly difficult to work with—and instead of growing into responsible stakeholders in global governance, drift away from the Fund and set up parallel regional financial facilities where neither the United States nor Europe would have influence.

The epicenter of the problem is East Asia. Sufficiently disgruntled, Asian nations have exit options: many of them have large national reserves with which to insure themselves, and the region has been building an indigenous monetary fund that many members want to see independent from the IMF-centric monetary order. But such a stand-alone regional entity would strip Washington of the influence to affect economic policies in the region—and is feared to fail to set as staunch and objective conditions for good economic governance in exchange for loans as imposed by the Fund. Such concerns are hardly unfounded: in what might be called "mercenary finance," China, a major actor in Asian financial regionalism, has provided bilateral loans and emergency swap lines to Latin American, Asian, and African nations without requiring any policy changes in return. Indeed, China has expressed disdain for the reforms-for-loans quid pro quo that is the essence of the Fund.[54] In the view of many Washington observers and officials, failure to expand the Fund could give only greater powers to China because it would entice countries that do not have adequate reserves to fight off crises to go to nations with ready cash on hand.[55]

Tables Turning?
Europe's caving to US demands is significant and of historic symbolic value, but it does not entail a sea change in the IMF's governance or operations. For one, the quota reform is incremental, as only 2 percentage points of the total 6-percent shift will be cut from the share of the advanced nations. The rest will be from overrepresented Middle Eastern oil exporters and some developing nations of Africa. The shifted total will be distributed across numerous economies.[56] Overall, advanced nations' share will decrease to a still comfortable majority of 55.3 percent, and the share of the 27 EU members would drop only by 1.5 percentage points, from 30.9 to 29.4 percent—a result that presages future power battles.

Europe's board concessions are also limited. The composition of the eight members that have a nonrotating seat—France, Germany, the United Kingdom, the United States, Japan, and three emerging markets, Russia, Saudi Arabia, and China—remains unchanged. Major emerging markets that have lobbied for governance reforms such as India, Brazil, and Thailand are already leading their rotating groups composed of smaller developing countries, and are also thus unaffected by the European concession. Conversely, the smaller European members are not as dominant as often portrayed because they belong to groups of directors, one of whose members is elected to circulate to the board every two years. Depending on how Europe plays its hand, the reform could leave the continent's powers largely unaffected. For example, one European proposal is that Spain move into a fully European constituency (from its current group, which includes such Latin American countries as Venezuela, Mexico, and Colombia) and that Belgium share the directorship of its constituency with (non-European) Turkey to meet the two-seat shift. In such a scenario, Europe would give up very little.

Europeans are resolved to go down only with their boots on. They have long argued that they are entitled to their quota and seats as merely proportional to their contributions; Europe's doubling its pledge to expand the IMF's lending capacity amid the crisis was to cement that argument. It is true that many European countries that trail some of the larger emerging economies in size, such as Spain, put more in the Fund than they gain in votes. Meanwhile, China, India, and Saudi Arabia contribute less than their voting shares suggest.

European governments have used the money argument in efforts to extract concessions from emerging markets in exchange for any reallocation in power. For instance, they have called on China and other emerging economies to be first movers and increase their contributions to the IMF before securing greater voting share.[57] In 2009 the French circulated among European capitals a more daring quid pro quo: that Europe give up the Fund directorship if China agrees to increase its contributions to the Fund.[58] Europeans also rightly demand that emerging nations embrace IMF-managed assessments on global imbalances and exchange-rate policies in exchange for power. The rationale echoes that of the United States: Europe runs a current-account deficit with China and became doubly pressed by Asian imports in the immediate aftermath of the Great Crisis as the RMB's dollar peg fell.

A Short-Lived Truce   The power struggles are bound to continue even if the transfer of chairs and shares proceeds flawlessly because the new reforms are incremental and because Europe still controls the IMF's crown jewel coveted by the emerging markets, the managing directorship. In 2011 Europeans aligned seamlessly behind the candidacy of French Finance Minister Christine Lagarde to head the Fund. The United States is unlikely to press Europeans anytime soon on the issue as that would entail the US being willing to give up the World Bank presidency. Emerging economies are also not posing a unified front. For example, Agustín Carstens of Mexico, the former IMF deputy managing director who ran against Lagarde, did garner support across Latin America but did not secure the backing of China or several Asian and African governments.

Even farther-reaching governance reforms would not create a more co-operative or effective IMF. The main members have distinct visions of the Fund's mission: China wants the Fund to focus on systemic stability and surveillance of the largest economies, while Western Europeans are interested in retaining a strong focus on surveillance of, and technical assistance to, developing nations. The United States is wary of IMF judgments on American domestic economic policy but keen on fostering surveillance of pressing global issues, such as imbalances and exchange rates—something China is uneasy with. There are also tensions over relaxing the Fund's lending criteria to make it more responsive to rapidly escalating crises. While such nations as Japan and UK have voiced support, Germany is a skeptic, citing moral hazard concerns. Such disagreements limit the Fund's scope and potential. For instance, a 2011 IMF proposal for the members to agree on certain parameters for imposing capital controls was torpedoed by emerging markets.

Granted, IMF governance would transform dramatically were the Europeans to combine their votes and seats. A single European seat would give the continent a veto over Fund decisions now only enjoyed by the United States. What are the prospects?

A Coming Duopoly?

Amid the raging European financial crisis, the European Commission made a call for the Eurozone nations to pool their representation at the IMF board into a single seat. The commission's drive was motivated by a sense of a global assault on European powers in the world body. Not only was Washington pressuring Europeans to yield power in the Fund, but in 2011 some of the reserve-rich emerging markets such as China and India expressed willingness to rescue the ailing Eurozone in return for expanded voting shares at the Fund. Although designed to boost the currency bloc's clout at a time when emerging markets are seeking greater powers in the world body, the proposal met with resistance—not in Beijing or Brasilia, but right next door to Brussels, in Berlin and Paris.

The idea of consolidating European seats is nothing new. A decade ago, as finance minister of France, DSK floated the idea of a Franco–German chair.[59]

Reflecting its interest in concentrating power in Brussels, the European Commission launched the single-seat bid for the entire EU membership around the time, and the former head of the European Central Bank, Jean Claude Trichet, has also supported the idea, as has European Council President Herman Van Rompoy.

The single-seat idea is not far-fetched. Europe is a single market with a common currency that is integrating some of the last vestiges of national sovereignty, foreign policy, and financial oversight and supervision. Furthermore, unlike in other world bodies, EU members often agree with one another at the IMF, and the Eurozone members are unified on exchange-rate matters. Also favoring a common stance is the infrastructure in Brussels and Washington. The EU has a subcommittee on Fund-related issues in the Economic and Financial Committee, while an informal committee of EU members meets a few times a week at the Fund.[60]

But the single-seat idea has not gone very far, as no European country wants to yield its national seat. The larger countries cite their size and contributions. For example, France and Britain fear an outcome where Germany remains the only European sovereign in the Fund's weighty top five. And none of these nations would want to negotiate each vote with one another. All bigger European players also worry that quota or seat adjustments would reduce their influence regarding China. There is intra-European politics at play, as well: no European leader wants to pressure his or her counterparts into relinquishing a seat so as to avoid antagonism in regional affairs. Europeans are also loath to abandon their respective pet causes. Germany is most concerned about potential moral hazard and the inflationary effects of rescue packages, the UK is focused on financial regulations and liberalization, France has been focused on the global currency regime, and the Netherlands and the Nordics stress concessionary finance to the poorest countries.[61]

The irony is that the status quo hurts Western Europeans themselves. A single seat, or even a pair of EU seats—one for the Eurozone and another for the non-Eurozone, or one for the EU and another for the non-EU member Switzerland—would make the continent a swing vote, enhancing Europe's leverage at the IMF.[62] But Europe's self-denied claim for the power is not necessarily bad: an IMF with two explicit vetoes would unlikely be any more effective or serve US interests. European parochialism keeps the Fund's governance evolving as previously, through agonized, incremental reforms. Will transformations in the global financial architecture meantime render the Fund moot?

Regionalism to the Rescue

The size and spread of the Asian financial crisis awakened the region to the need for financial cooperation. The Chiang-mai initiative, after its namesake venue in Thailand where it was conceived in 2000, created a new network of bilateral swap arrangements in Asia among the ten Association of South East Asian Nations members and China, Japan, and Korea (or ASEAN+3).[63] The arrangement was paralleled by the Asian Bond Markets Initiative, and it paved the way to discussions on a regional IMF, an Asian Monetary Fund (AMF).

Chiang-mai has a link to the IMF: borrowers can draw up to 20 percent of their bilateral or multilateral swaps, but then need to agree on a Fund program, including the Fund's policy prescriptions, to access the remaining 80 percent. The link is a source of resentment in the region, where the Fund is severely stigmatized after its tough conditions for loans in response to the 1997–1998 Asian crisis. Asians' urgency to foster Chiang-mai accentuated as the Great Crisis breezed through. The need for liquidity in the US and Europe reverted capital flows from Asia, raising risk premiums in the region. And as the region's capital inflows dwindled, equity prices dropped. Worried, Asians expanded Chiang-mai to a total of $120 billion and multilateralized it—made it a regional pool for realizing the very same scale economies that the Fund promotes at the global level. The main powers, Japan and China, agreed to equal voting shares.[64] In June 2011, Chiang-mai was doubled to $240 billion.

As a regional scheme, Chiang-mai is no pioneer. There are a number of other, even if not as widely discussed, regional funds in Europe, the Americas, and the Middle East.[65] Washington has used the Treasury's Exchange Stabilization Fund mostly within the Western Hemisphere. With Mexico and Canada, its partners in the North American Free Trade Agreement (NAFTA), Washington has a limited system of bilateral swaps that can be activated by the North American Financial Group (NAFA), composed of the three countries' central bank and treasury officials. Latin Americans have often relied on regional development banks such as the Inter-American Development Bank for countercyclical lending; following the Great Crisis, the regional finance ministers launched discussions on deeper regional financial cooperation.

The European Union has in the past used the Medium-Term Financial Assistance as a balance-of-payment facility for members that have yet to adopt the euro. The Southern European debt crisis built momentum for a watershed

European regional fund. In the spring of 2010 the German finance minister floated the idea of a European Monetary Fund (EMF), but Europe eventually opted for cooperation with the IMF: rescuing Greece in the spring of 2010, the 17 Eurozone nations and the IMF provided €110 billion. Seeking to restore market confidence in the beleaguered Southern European economies and, by extension, the euro, the Eurozone also created a €440-billion European Financial Stability Fund (EFSF) that can be activated through a memorandum of understanding between the affected country and the European Commission, with expert consultations with the European Central Bank and the IMF. The European Commission gave an additional €60 billion in loans and the IMF another €250 billion, raising the total to a market-moving headliner $1 trillion. The new stability fund was tapped in rescuing the debt-laden Ireland six months later; the €85-billion package also involved European bilateral lenders, financing from Ireland's own cash reserves, and €22.5 billion from the IMF. Portugal was next with a €78 billion, followed by a second loan to the ailing Greece at €109 billion.

The rise of regional financial arrangements will critically shape the future of global financial architecture and the IMF's role in it. One scenario is close cooperation between regional initiatives and the Fund, as in Europe; another is a divorce between the two, which could entail the Fund's withering; still another is cooperation with the Fund by some regions and disengagement by others.

The future relationship between the Chiang-mai arrangement and the IMF will provide one answer. For now, Chiang-mai is more tightly and formally referenced to the Fund than the EU and US schemes ever were. However, given their powers in the Fund, the US and EU schemes have a built-in consistency with the IMF. But Asians, with less weight at the IMF and still resentful of the world body's policy prescriptions, do not necessarily agree on the Fund's policy prescriptions for their region and are more eager to go it alone.

A Runaway Region?

Is Asia looking to disengage from the IMF? Few Asian leaders would dare to claim so in public, although regional officials have become more vocal about the intent to unlink the region from the Fund. Rather, Asians defend the regional plans by arguing that by tackling region-specific issues regional bodies complement and deepen, not replace, global mechanisms.[66] True, Asia does struggle with very different issues from those pressing in Latin America or Africa. For instance, Asia's capital markets have tended to lag behind those of Latin America, and the likeliest potential trouble centers in Asia are banks, not nonbanking bodies as in Latin America. However, it is also the case that Asians harbor desires for autonomy from the Fund. Mercantilist motivations may also be in play: regional mechanisms allow Asians to favor their own banks in crisis insurance and management.[67]

But Asia is not ready to disengage from the IMF for three reasons. First, it is much more integrated with the US and European financial markets than intra-regionally.[68] The global exposure renders the region vulnerable to volatility elsewhere, calling for multilateral engagement. Second, Chiang-mai is still small and untested. It was not the region's liquidity window in the Great Crisis. Hit rather hard, Korea and Singapore turned directly to Japan and China, and Korea performed its largest, $30-million swap arrangement not with Asia, but with the US Federal Reserve. The reluctance to use the Chiang-mai is to a good extent because of the link to the IMF: Asian nations worry that they would ultimately have to be subject to the Fund's conditions if drawing on the Chiang-mai. Third, intra-regional politics complicates financial regionalism.

Thorny Asian Politics   The Clinton and the George W. Bush administrations approved of Chiang-mai, but the initial plans for the AMF, advanced by Tokyo, ran into opposition from the Treasury—as well as into China's refusal to support the proposal at the time.[69] Washington and Europeans have sought to bind the rising Asian arrangements into the IMF's orbit. This is critical: the Fund has no clout over countries it does *not* lend to, even if their policies hurt the global economy. But the United States and Europe now weigh less in the regional calculus than a decade ago: after all, in stark contrast to their bankrupt past, East Asian nations now have a massive $4 trillion in reserves. The future of the regional arrangements in Asia will be arbitrated by regional politics—both between the Asian power brokers, Japan and China, and between the region's creditors and debtors.

China has been seen as unenthused by any international financial schemes, whether the IMF or Chiang-mai. One of its motivations for pursuing greater powers at the IMF is not a new faith in multilateral governance, but a desire to ensure that the United States does not act counter to Chinese interests on the world stage. However, China does tend to see Asia as a more sympathetic arena, and wants to expand its sphere of influence in Southeast Asia. But it is keener to dispense loans bilaterally than via Chiang-mai, where China's sway is limited by the other main members, Japan and Korea. China has deliberately set out to oppose Japan in the various regional forums to carve out its sphere of influence in Asia.

Beijing's interest in disentangling Asia from the Western-dominated IMF is trumping its wariness about Chiang-mai. In 2011 it threw its support behind expanding the Chiang-mai and increasing the share that Asian borrowers can draw from the Chiang-Mai before having to agree to an IMF program of 30–40 percent instead of the current 20 percent. While hesitant to embrace China, most Southeast Asian nations are keen supporters of loosening the Fund link. Beijing is also playing a leading role in creating the Chiang-mai's surveillance unit, the ASEAN+3 Macroeconomic Research Office (AMRO), in Singapore.

Chinese maneuvers are hardly welcome news to Japan, which wants to continue playing its traditional role as the leading power in Asia. It was the Japanese locomotive that in the latter part of the twentieth century pulled the developing Asian nations to the industrial age. Tokyo has led the founding of such entities as the Asia-Pacific Economic Cooperation forum (APEC) and the Asian Development Bank, which it by tradition presides. It is also keen on putting in place institutions of its liking in the Asian financial cooperation process and restraining China's influence in the region.

A likely creditor in the Chiang-mai and the Asian nation with a large stake in the IMF, Japan has conditioned any softening of the Fund link on improvements in regional capacities for surveying the member countries' economic conditions. Seoul, while enthused about Chiang-mai, is similarly level-headed. But sturdy surveillance might not be feasible. There are ample technical capacities in the region for surveillance, but no stomach for peer reviews for political and cultural reasons. Above all, Asians want to avoid losing face and public embarrassment. The main regional watchdog, the Economic Review and Policy Dialogue, has self-censored, refraining from revealing sensitive financial data and berating misbehaving nations.[70]

Japan has revived with China the idea of the East Asian community, an envisioned trade area consisting either of ASEAN+3 or ASEAN+6—ASEAN+3 and Australia, New Zealand, and India. But such a recalibration in Japan's foreign policy should be interpreted as an insurance policy rather than a geopolitical about-face. After all, China is Japan's second-biggest export destination after the United States, and a rising next-door military power. Sino–Japanese political and territorial tensions persist, affecting public opinions. In a late-2010 survey, 78 percent of Japanese said that they do not "feel close" to China, an increase of more than 19 percentage points from 2009 and the worst figure since 1978.[71]

Tokyo's push for regional cooperation, especially in ASEAN+6, is in its own interest: regional cooperation will help Japan tie China into regional institutions and dilute Sino-centricism in Asia. Similarly, Japan has been keen on deeper regional trade integration within APEC, a 21-nation forum that, among others, includes such powers as the United States, Russia, Canada, and Australia. Tokyo has also taken steps toward joining also the Trans-Pacific Partnership (TPP) negotiations among the United States, Chile, Peru, Singapore, Malaysia, New Zealand, Australia, Brunei, and Vietnam that are emerging as a substitute for APEC's lackluster free trade talks, yet exclude China.

Even if Tokyo and Beijing were able to collaborate in Chiang-mai, political divisions not unlike those at the IMF could erupt between them, on the one hand, and the smaller regional nations, on the other. China has intricate economic ties with the ASEAN nations, and there is a large Chinese diaspora in the region.[72] Chinese leadership is also resolved to expand the reach of the RMB in the region, something it has already done through various bilateral swap arrangements. While the ASEAN nations find the advances appealing in light of their trade ties with China and Beijing's promises of infrastructure loans, they are uneasy about China's hegemonic intentions. Like Japan, ASEAN prefers the broader ASEAN+6 to counter China's efforts to build an exclusive East Asian bloc it would dominate.

The regional financial architecture might also have to be sorted out. Asian financial cooperation has evolved organically, not from a grand master plan, and has resulted in a plethora of regional and subregional institutions among differing groups of countries that both overlap and are not linked to one another. While Chiang-mai is the leading initiative, other instances with financial cooperation include ASEAN, ASEAN+6, APEC, the Executive Meeting of East Asia-Pacific Central Banks (EMEAP), the South East Asian Central Banks (SEACEN) Research and Training Centre, and the SEANZA (Southeast Asia, New Zealand and Australia).[73]

For now, Asian nations are likeliest to rely on their tested and tried self-insurance. While for China reserves are a by-product of export-led strategy, many emerging Asian nations pursue reserves as an end in themselves. Asians saw the Great Crisis as validating the reserve buildup and set out to aspire for even sturdier armories, something that many in the region now see as proper vaccination against contagious crises, even as a source of national pride. The strategy is for now the first-best for the region's major nations, even if it de-economized the provision of insurance that the IMF is designed to economize and unnecessarily diverted funds away from investments in public goods. However, the regional economies have widely different levels of liquidity and reserves to defend themselves, especially against another severe crisis. China, with the most cash on hand, could emerge as the default lender, just as Beijing seems to be intending.

The IMF's European Problem

If in Asia the IMF's problem is "can we get in?" in Europe it is "can we get out?"

As the main IMF shareholders, Europeans have an inherent stake in ensuring a seamless relationship between regional arrangements and the Fund. The French have expressed concerns that the Fund's involvement gives the United States a say in European affairs, but German Chancellor Angela Merkel prevailed in insisting on a partnership with the Fund, paving the way for the joint rescues. Besides its role as a cosponsor of European rescues, the Fund is integrated into the EFSF/ESM system decision making. Economic and fiscal adjustment programs and debt sustainability analyses that will form part and parcel of any lending will be carried out jointly by the European Commission and the IMF, in liaison with the ECB. Private-sector creditors will also be treated as they are under Fund rules, and in case of insolvency, they would negotiate a restructuring plan in line with Fund practices.

The arrangement is in many ways useful for the IMF's non-European members such as the United States. It ensures that Europeans keep singing from the Fund's hymnbook that the United States has had a role in authoring. It also keeps the Fund involved in designing and enforcing loan conditions for the recipient nations to get their economic houses in order. In addition, with Europeans providing the bulk of the rescue funding, the Fund's involvement is easier to justify on Capitol Hill.

Europe's cash cow Germany has carried the day. The crisis has been sheer agony for Berlin, which is torn between moral hazard concerns and the need to curb contagion before it is too late, and between the politically hugely unpopular bailouts to spendthrift nations on Europe's fringe and Germany's resolve to do what it takes to rescue its own constructs, the euro and the European integration project. In December 2010, Merkel drove through a proposal to change the European constitution on two scores: vest the EU with powers to suspend the voting rights of Eurozone members that persistently breach Europe's 3-percent limits on national budget deficits and to create, by mid-2013, a permanent financial safety net for the Eurozone, the European Stability Mechanism (ESM), as a replacement of the EFSF for restructuring the debt of countries that cannot repay their loans.[74] Entailing tough conditions on countries that resort to the Fund and losses for bondholders, the ESM is designed to discourage heavy borrowing and lending conducive to crises.

In July 2011 Germany drove through a requirement for private creditors to contribute an additional €50 billion by 2014 via a combination of debt buybacks and swaps to manage the Greek crisis. European leaders also permitted the EFSF to extend credit lines to members attacked by bond speculators, recapitalize troubled Eurozone banks, and buy ailing Eurozone countries' bonds. The bond issuances enjoy a triple-A rating thanks to guarantees from mostly highly rated Eurozone members.

These advances suggested to such boosters as French President Nicolas Sarkozy that a European Monetary Fund was indeed in the making. But the problems in the EFSF preclude a stand-alone fund able to fight off the Eurozone troubles, and steps toward anything suggestive of fiscal federalism also stand no chance with German taxpayers weary of rescuing the spendthrift nations at Europe's fringe. In fact, almost a third of Germans now believe the Euro will be finished in a decade.[75] Besides, Germany has a keen interest in keeping the IMF involved as a means to design and enforce policy conditions. Berlin is right: Europeans have shown that they are no better than Asians at telling truth to power. The undoubtedly strong technical expertise of the EMF would be held hostage by Europeans' reluctance to criticize and impose tough conditions on one another. The IMF has few such problems: it excels at bluntness, to the terror (and benefit) of the loan applicants.

However, the arrangement with Europe is hardly a panacea for the IMF. European responses, worked through repeated summits among 17 heads of state, have been agonizingly slow, revealing the perils for the Fund of partnering with a procrastinating and politically circumscribed regional grouping in fighting fast-moving crises. Moreover, the EFSF/ESM system has several flaws that the Fund will now have to live with.[76]

For starters, the EFSF's €440-billion lending capacity is too limited. Contrast it to the €502-billion debt coming to maturity in 2011 for Greece, Ireland, Italy, Portugal, and Spain and the €470 billion of financial requirements of Spanish central and local governments in 2013. The debts of the most troubled Southern nation, Greece, amounted to €300 billion in mid-2011. Estimates among banks and investors of resources adequate to assure markets range from €700 billion to €2 trillion.

Whatever the sum, Europe's reflexes in activating funding promise to be glacial. The decisions for the terms of loans, loan approvals, bond purchases, and conditions require unanimity among Eurozone finance ministers (unlike the simple majority needed for IMF lending), opening the specter for immense delays and politicization, as any creditor nation can threaten the supposed recipient government with a veto unless the latter curries favor with the former.

Worse, the EFSF design may only magnify the Eurozone's troubles for three reasons. First, just like US mortgage giants Fannie Mae and Freddie Mac, the facility repackages low-grade assets into a product that is then being sold as a triple-A rated security, risking a pileup of suspect assets in the banking systems.[77] Second, the fact that plausible debtors—the southern European nations—are also creditors in the EFSF means that the rescue burden will be ever more concentrated in Germany, France, the Benelux, and Finland. Third, the incentive systems are flawed. If the European Commission, which is required to assess the sustainability of the beneficiary nation's public debt prior to loan disbursement, were to declare the recipient insolvent, the ESM would be allowed to lend only on the condition that the private sector will also be involved. Yet the very fact that a country resorts to the ESM means that investors have deemed it insolvent and will be unlikely to get involved. As such, the sustainability assessment is moot: the Commission would unlikely risk declaring any recipient insolvent. Emblematically, the joint EU, ECB, and IMF mission to Greece in 2011 promptly declared that there were no problems with Greece's sustainability.

The IMF's New Dilemma   The IMF is in a bind. US congressional representatives have expressed repeated concerns about wasting US taxpayer money on bailouts to Greece when the odds of success are uncertain. Many emerging-market members at the Fund share these concerns and also worry that private European bondholders are getting away too easily without having to take serious write-downs. Yet the Fund—and Washington—cannot just march out of Europe, for at least three reasons.

First, the IMF and the Treasury have repeatedly warned that the Eurozone crisis risks global spillovers, which it does. Second, the Europeans have time and again demonstrated their inability to marshal an adequate regional response and imposing tough conditions on one another. And third, Europeans have a major say in Fund involvement to begin with. This is not the emerging-market crisis of the 1980s, where the loan recipients had little say over Fund activities: now the recipient region happens to be the Fund's main shareholder. The stakes are high, and IMF and US involvement is compelling. Yet their leverage is limited.

Swaps: Not Your Saving Grace

The liquidity provided by bilateral swaps amid the Great Crisis was critical in keeping the Great Recession from becoming a Great Depression. Swaps have many advantages over IMF loans: they have no stigma or conditions attached to them; they tend to be capped at $30 billion, as opposed to Fund loans based on balance of payments needs; and they are quick to disburse and of very short duration, up to 3 months as opposed to the Fund's 3.25 to 5 years.

But central banks may not be as willing to dispense swaps in the future or be able to perform swaps systematically to extinguish dangerous financial fires. After all, nations dispensing swaps tend to favor nations with which they have important financial and trade ties.[78] Choices were already made: while the Federal Reserve chose to support Korea, it declined to extend a swap to Indonesia due to high US bank exposures in Korea. Having to choose between potential recipients also places the monetary mavens in an uncomfortable position diplomatically. The US Federal Reserve would likely also face political pressures is staging another major swap scheme. During the crisis, Fed officials were among those summoned to Capitol Hill to explain their swaps to legislators concerned about the crisis right at home.

The IMF board has also considered the so-called global stabilization mechanism (GSM) as a multi-country merger of national swap lines that would be activated only in response to systemic crises. The GSM would make large amounts of money available on short notice to a number of countries at once in the case of a pending global economic collapse and, as such, represent the first tool for the Fund to use to respond to systemic crises across multiple nations. The activation of the GSM would require the IMF board's approval.[79]

Such a centralized system, while requiring changes in the IMF's charter, would replace bilateral lending operations of national central banks and, at least in theory, enhance the consistency of lending and lower risks to all nations, potentially even reducing the odds of mercenary finance. France and the United Kingdom have signaled support for a global stabilization mechanism. But Germany worries that the scheme would make it too easy for countries to obtain loans, encouraging budgetary profligacy and poor economic management. Central banks, including the US Fed, are also unlikely to want to relinquish their authority over swap lines to the finance-minister-run IMF.

Global Versus Regional

Whether the trend toward financial regionalism is driven by politics—the backlash against the IMF—or by the expansion of intra-regional trade linkages, it will likely play a growing role around the world in the twenty-first century. The growth of national reserves, the rise of different pools of sovereign capital, and bilateral financial agreements—witness Asian bilateral swaps and the odd Russian credit line to the sinking Iceland—all suggest that even a well-stocked Fund will not be the only game in town.

The IMF does not need to be a monopoly. Regional funds can be immensely useful. They can serve as the first line of defense in regional crises, and their surveillance can supplement the Fund's analyses and alleviate its propensity for group-think. Regional first-responder funds would also help the Fund weather crises beyond its means, reduce competing claims on its resources, and turn down some of the political heat for rescues incurred by one administration after the next in Washington. For its part, the Fund brings to the table financial resources, sound policy advice, and tough-love policy conditions. This division of labor is desirable as long as it leads to prompt crisis management and policy prescriptions aimed at financial stability—and where the Fund has sufficient leverage to affect outcomes and a clear exit option, a situation quite the opposite from the Fund's gradual entrenchment in Europe.

However, even where they are most vibrant, Asia and Europe, regional funds can be only part of the solution. They are untested, inherently politicized, and hostage to regional diplomatic niceties even at the height of crises. Regional or bilateral rescues not predicated on similarly rigorous conditions for good macroeconomic governance as demanded by the IMF could perpetuate bad policies in the borrower nations while only increasing moral hazard. And a failed or inadequate regional response would only erode market confidence, making the task for the second line of defenders harder, not unlike what has happened in Europe.

Disengagement by any major region from the IMF would spark a vicious cycle: because the value of the global insurance agency would decline as its funding pool shrinks, the departure of any major nation would dampen the enthusiasm of the other members to contribute to the Fund. And a completely regionalized crisis management system would be a bad idea for all nations. It would risk conflicts and gaps among regional responses to global crises and complicate efforts to spot them to begin with. The Great Crisis demonstrated that havoc in New York or London can devastate distant economies, just as turmoil starting in Thailand ravaged emerging markets on the opposite side of the world. With crises disrespecting borders, regional responses are but imperfect substitutes for the Fund. The globalization of economics and crises alike requires sturdy system-wide management. The Fund has technical expertise, institutional memory, and global experience that are unrivaled, and its globalized insurance pool is much more cost effective for the members and better for the world economy than reserve hoarding would ever be.

Better System Management

The IMF is at a crossroads: although the crisis revalidated its role, it also faces challenges of legitimacy and responsiveness. While working to fulfill its new missions, it has to deal with political infighting, the rise of regional and bilateral financial arrangements, and uncertainties about its abilities to meet future global calamities. A continued reserve buildup in East Asia would perpetuate a global savings glut conducive to imbalances and could send the Fund back to the path of an obscure oversight body in which the United States would have little sway over its members' economic policies. The Fund's further entrenchment in the Eurozone could also induce emerging economies to prioritize their regional schemes. Washington needs to pursue four measures to keep the Fund relevant and effective in fighting twenty-first-century financial storms.

What Can the WTO Teach the IMF?
The first reform is to better integrate regional and global crisis management mechanisms. Here, a look into the international trading system is instructive, perhaps in particular for what not to do.

The policy concerns surrounding the rise of financial regionalism are eerily reminiscent of the debate over the past decade that the countless regional trade agreements (RTAs) might balkanize the global trading system. RTAs have proliferated in an ad hoc fashion alongside, yet uncoordinated by, the GATT/WTO system. Two parallel systems, global and regional, are now in place.

This was not meant to happen. GATT Article XXIV stipulates that members notify the WTO about their new RTAs and that the RTAs liberalize "substantially all trade" among the members "in reasonable length of time" and do not introduce new "restrictive rules on commerce." The article also demands open regionalism—that RTA members do not raise barriers to third parties. However, the GATT has numerous problems that offer lessons to the IMF. For one, RTAs among some developing countries are exempted from Article XXIV, which leaves numerous RTAs outside its reach. In addition, the WTO members' interpretations of the sparsely worded article vary widely.[80] For example, "substantially all trade" has at least four interpretations— a quantitative approach geared to a statistical benchmark, such as a percentage of trade between the parties (most commonly suggested are 90, 85, and 80 percent), and a qualitative approach stipulating that no sector (or at least no major sector) should be kept from liberalization, with definitions of "sector" varying widely.

The WTO's efforts, starting some five years ago, to analyze the compliance of the various RTAs with the GATT rules have been limited and constrained by political concerns, and simply overwhelmed by the complexity of the RTA universe. Mappings and economic analyses of RTAs have been crafted mostly by outside experts. Perhaps most importantly, the fact that all WTO members belong to at least one RTA renders any one member reluctant to challenge the RTAs of other members as discriminatory at the WTO's robust dispute-settlement mechanism.

In trade, the regionalism horse is out of the barn, and the WTO is lagging far behind. The nascent efforts to somehow multilateralize the countless RTAs, such as to transpose their so-called "WTO+" features to the GATT and WTO agreements, or even to "converge" them into broader regional and continental integration zones, are proving extraordinarily thorny, both technically and politically.

Financial regionalism is more nascent: the horse is at the gates. Taking the reins now, Washington, working through the IMF, will have an opportunity to institutionalize the relationship between the Fund and regional and bilateral financial arrangements. True, the properties of trade and finance are distinct—for instance, there will never be hundreds of discrete financial arrangements. But bridging regional and global arrangements is arguably even more urgent in finance than it is in trade given that the negative externalities—the global contagion of financial crises—of failed responses are enormous. The idea is already on the world stage: the November 2010 G20 Summit host Korea has called for a "global safety net" as a means to introduce greater coherence and coordination among global responses, regional financial arrangements, and bilateral responses.

Global and regional assets and policies need to be aligned, and spreading thin must be avoided. While reforms to IMF quotas and board can help enhance emerging markets' buy-in for a complementary relationship between the IMF and regional funds, crises afford little time to define what that relationship exactly is. Formal, *ex ante* specification is needed. Financial policy makers can take at least four measures.[81]

First, working particularly with Japan, Korea, and the Europeans, Washington should give the global safety net concept legs by building formal ties between the IMF and further capital sources—regional funds, central banks, and the private sector. The first step in that direction would be to fashion a clear set of principles to define the relationship among the Fund, regional financial facilities, and bilateral arrangements, akin to the principles laid out in GATT Article XXIV, but perhaps more precise. The principles—a "Global Code on Financial Regionalism"—should address both money and policy, or the sequencing of the allocation of the funds from the different facilities as well as potential cost sharing among them; the structure of cooperation between the Fund and regional authorities in designing country programs and enforcing policy conditions; and the powers of the Fund in regional decision making.

Such principles should not be excessively detailed; they need to account for the diversity among current and new regional funds. At the same time, they also ought to leave much less room for interpretation than the GATT's sparse phrasing gives the WTO members. Forging such a code is of course difficult, as especially emerging markets would be loath to have the stigmatized IMF meddle with their affairs. However, it is also the case that nations in any region should have an interest in stability and developments in other regions. Precisely such concerns sparked a mass demand among governments for empirical analyses on RTAs.

Second, Washington should call on the IMF or, politically more feasible, an outside, independent entity to start performing regular, informal multilateral reviews of the various regional financial schemes that map out the dimensions of the regional funds, examine their compliance with the global code, and assess their economic significance in their regions, such as capacities to push back a regional crisis.

Third, the IMF should also bring authorities of the regional funds together to share best practices and lessons learned in such areas as economic surveillance, technical assistance, financial operations, and the relationship of the funds with the private sector. Besides cross-fertilizing each other, regional schemes can serve as useful laboratories and incubators of new practices, the best of which could be multilateralized in the IMF. Washington also needs to consider ways in which any future bilateral financial arrangements could be co-opted to the Fund, perhaps in more flexible ways than through the Fund-proposed GSM.[82]

Fourth, working with Japan and Korea, its postwar linchpins in the Asian economic and security theaters, the United States should work to retain the 20-percent link between the Chiang-mai and the IMF. But it should call for the Fund to study and make recommendations on a range of further, less formal mechanisms to foster synergies between the Fund and regional financial mechanisms, and enhance a sense of ownership among regional economies of Fund policies. For example, members of a regional fund could be given committee status to set the agenda or preapprove IMF packages for their region, and they could gain voting shares in proportion to their contributions to the regional fund in IMF decisions concerning their region.[83] Regional authorities could accompany the Fund in Article IV missions, and also partner with the Fund in early-warning exercises and bank stress tests.

The IMF and regional financial authorities should also develop formal channels of communication on surveillance and economic analysis. Duplication of efforts should not be completely averted, as some overlap helps ensure a diversity of opinions. However, there could be some topical division of labor, with the Fund handling the fiscal issues and analysis and the regions centering on issues most pertinent to them. For example, in Asia regional efforts could focus on asset bubbles, exchange rates, and liquidity issues.[84]

The cooperation between the IMF and the EU has set a useful precedent for a complementary relationship between regional funds and the IMF—

one that Washington and Europeans can reference and leverage with Asia. However, it has also been instructive of the perils of the Fund getting entrapped in a crisis whose resolution lies primarily with the regional authorities. The episode has driven home the importance of a clear delineation of the Fund's role, powers, and exit strategy in any partnership with a regional arrangement—and the need for the Fund to be vested with sufficient resources to have a strong and preferably predominant say in fighting the regional fires it does have to fight.

There is also work to be done bilaterally with Asia. The United States needs to retain a strong presence in the region's financial and economic panorama. APEC should form part of the effort, particularly in discussing financial stability and perhaps even spearheading transpacific financial surveillance. The US joining the East Asian Summit process is also positive, and Washington's commitment to the ASEAN, lapsing since the early 2000s, is critical for a foothold in a region keenly courted by China.

Governance Reforms

The second reform area is governance. Giving emerging Asia, and especially China, more power in the IMF would unlikely—and ought not—undo plans for a regional fund. But it is necessary even if not necessarily sufficient for providing Asians greater incentives to hone the multilateral financial system, be more responsive to the Fund's suggestions, and build complementarities between the Fund and their regional arrangements. Money confers influence, but as President Roosevelt understood in the 1940s, influence can be exercised in ways that ensure the long-term viability of the world economy. Emerging nations will now need to be tied into this paradigm.

Expanding emerging markets' sway at the IMF is no guarantee of improved collaboration or a stronger Fund. Washington's lobbying for a greater stake for the emerging economies also does not automatically enhance US ability to drive its goals with emerging markets: even if the United States did help secure a greater voice for China, Beijing has only become more difficult to deal with on the world stage. Washington cannot issue blank checks. Rather, it has to condition its support to reciprocity—emerging markets' commitment to discuss currency manipulation and capital controls, work on formal ties between the Fund and regional financial arrangements, and, as Europeans have insisted, contribute a share commensurate with their desired voting rights to the Fund's lending capacity. The Fund also has to be a pay-to-play body, not a forum of free riders or a one-country-one-vote United Nations. That the reform ball remains on Europe's court offers Washington an opportunity to work with Europe to offer governance reforms only in exchange for concessions by the emerging economies.

The United States must also shield its own legitimate claim to power. The US veto is largely symbolic and seen by many in Washington as a bargaining chip that needs to be on the table, or something that could be given up without concessions.[85] However, the veto has power even when it is not exercised because it conditions other nations' behaviors: anticipating it, others are unlikely to offer proposals that the United States would oppose. Besides, given America's 20-percent share of the world economy, its voting share is completely legitimate. Of course, the veto could be eliminated without hurting the US quota if the threshold for important votes was reduced to, say, 80 percent instead of 85 percent. However, some emerging markets, such as Brazil, resist such a move on the grounds that they are better able to assemble a vetoing coalition under the current rules.

Going forward, efforts to accommodate emerging and developing nations' calls for legitimacy cannot come at the expense of US influence. An IMF where the United States did not play a role equal to its economic prowess would do disservice to American foreign economic policy and undermine congressional support for the body. Balance has to be found—the quota and seat shift to underrepresented members represents one such balancing act— and most of the recalibration must be done by the Europeans. Washington has to work closely with Europe to handle the selection of the Fund's managing director: after all, Europe's relinquishing its hold over the post would increase pressures on the United States to let go of the World Bank presidency, which is traditionally reserved for an American.

Gazing further afield, the odds of debilitating future leadership battles could be avoided by using an even more objective quota formula based on economic size and presence in financial markets that is automatically adjusted—and so more frequently than during each five-year quota review.[86] The Bush Treasury's quota formula, approved in April 2008, gives pride of place to GDP in determining a member's voting powers, as opposed to such factors as economic openness, which is advocated particularly by small (and very open) European nations. The 2013 review offers an opportunity to simplify the quota further.

Conditioning Conditionality

The third reform area is to make the IMF more responsive to globalizing crises. The Fund became relevant in the crisis, argues the *Economist,* by lending "freely, quickly and with few strings attached."[87] Granted, such lending policies are attractive to potential clients and, because ensuring compliance with loan conditions requires gradual disbursements, accelerate the lending process.[88] But they also raise the enduring tension between responsiveness to crises and moral hazard.

The IMF has long battled its rigidities. After being criticized for its wide-ranging structural adjustment requirements during the Asian crisis, the Fund limited its conditions. It has also sought to engineer special facilities for members that have sound policies yet have become embroiled in a contagious crisis not of their own making. One permutation of this idea was applied during the Asian crisis; another appeared amid the Great Crisis in the form of the Flexible Credit Line. In August 2010 the IMF board approved still another facility, the Precautionary Credit Line (PCL), which is aimed at countries that do not qualify for the FCL but that have sound policies in place and do not require as extensive policy reforms as are included in the Fund's traditional arrangements.

The upside of the FCL and PCL is that they make the IMF more responsive to rapidly escalating crises and can as such help reinstate market confidence. Instead of the *ex-ante* deliberation and heavy *ex-post* conditionality that mark the Fund's regular programs, the new windows are predicated on the rigor of the prequalification criteria. That at least in theory could propel a policy race to the top as countries should have incentives to climb from the regular basket to the PCL group and further to the FCL basket, and to avoid being demoted from these categories.

At the same time, such a carrot is but one part of the great many factors that drive national economic policies. The new windows could also exacerbate moral hazard, if a country's qualifying to a PCL or FCL basket were interpreted as a path to automatic rescues. There is an argument to be made that limits to, and ambiguity about, the IMF's lending would be more effective at keeping economies on an even keel. There are also first-mover problems in activating the new instruments: an ailing nation could be hesitant to draw on them, particularly if it were the first one to do so, for fears that resorting to the Fund would make markets turn against it. And better tools will not abolish the stigma attached to the Fund in Asia and Latin America. Indeed, Mexico's becoming the first Latin American nation to draw on the FCL was hailed as an act of courage in light of the Fund's image problem in the region.

It is not clear where the line between responsiveness and moral hazard should be drawn. True, the IMF has to evolve into a faster and more agile responder to flickers of instability. However, also clear is that the Fund's strings should not be loosened simply because there exist alternative lenders, such as regional schemes or swap lines. The Fund should not be an automatic loan dispenser: that would inspire moral hazard and undercut the power of conditionality. Substantially looser strings would also be objectionable to the US Congress, which is bound to, and has a right to, insist that bailouts have a price, and that wants to see guarantees that the beneficiary government is able to repay its loans. The long-standing American impetus to reward good governance and sanction bad will not change.

At a minimum, flexibility in lending practices places a premium on sturdy surveillance. Particularly pressing is stronger financial sector surveillance. Also needed is adherence to clear parameters for placing IMF members in the baskets of distinct conditions. Ideally, the Fund would take a more difficult path of preventing crises altogether. But that will require a change in its decades-long modus operandi.

Shifting the Paradigm

The fourth reform area is the IMF's mission. For most of its lifespan, the Fund has served as a tool for global economic surveillance and crisis insurance. The core business is important, and it will remain. But it is also the case that the world has changed. On the one hand, financial markets dwarf governments, and the frequency, cruelty, and global reach of crises are greater. On the other, regional and national insurance instances have proliferated, private capital markets have ballooned, and each successive crisis has delivered new lessons on ways to prevent and end financial turmoil. Surveillance mechanisms and economic forecasts are also now more sophisticated. In light of these challenges and opportunities, the Fund's operational paradigm could be reformed in three ways.

The first is to focus the IMF more keenly on systemic risks, cross-border issues, and the world's main economies, advanced and emerging, rather than on small, poor, developing nations. Developing nations are first and foremost the purview of the World Bank. Besides, small nations would be the biggest beneficiaries of a world free of global financial crises. Nations such as East Timor or Mozambique do not originate global crises but are affected by them. The Fund is the only entity in the world that credibly serves as a systemic overseer and, to the extent possible for a body that referees its shareholders, an objective analyst of national economic policies. The Fund's judging of the economic policies of its main shareholders is politically sensitive, including in Washington. But reserving the Fund's resources for assessing and attacking the adversary of global financial instability, rather than battling its effects or dealing with peripheral issues such as small nations, is fundamentally in the interest of all economies.

Second, rather than a preeminently reactionary body that springs to work when crises hit, the IMF should focus more on preventing crises by rewarding good behavior. One way to do that is provide tangible rewards, such as technical assistance and support for countries' international lending operations, for national policies conducive to financial stability.[89] Such good policies include not only good rules and sound economic management but also greater financial openness, a handmaiden of financial development.[90]

While decidedly political, such a reward system could inspire good behavior around the world and preempt moral hazard, and potentially even induce a race to the top in the standards and services offered by regional funds. The optimal policies for a given country are not easy to identify or prescribe, and instability is notoriously difficult to predict. The IMF has been criticized, including by its own Independent Evaluation Office, for its failure to foresee the Great Crisis.[91] But that does not mean the Fund should not work harder on surveillance and mechanisms for countries to adopt sound policies. The price of doing so is limited when compared to the costs of managing crises.

Bad behaviors could, of course, entail punishments. A drastic punishment might be expulsion of some kind. However, in a world of multiple potential funding sources, a punishment regime, unless globally applied, could only drive a crisis-torn nation to "conditions shop" and opt for a lender that exacts the least punishment. Such considerations accentuate the need for coordination among the various funding instances.[92]

Third, regardless of how the bilateral, regional, and global financial arrangements are configured, governmental resources may still fall short when crises hit. The responses to the Great Crisis were extraordinary, but they still failed to prevent the Great Recession. Against this backdrop, the IMF should be made into a bridge between private and public insurance markets. A number of reasons have kept private markets from insuring sovereigns. There are moral hazard concerns; difficulties in pricing country risk that stem from the spread of crises to seemingly healthy, innocent bystander economies; assumption of adverse selection, whereby only the most prone to fail buy insurance; and counterparty risks, such as difficulties in diversifying sovereign risks.

The IMF is in a unique position to overcome such market failures and develop crisis insurance markets against major systemic shocks. A group of IMF staff has proposed that the Fund perform rigorous surveillance on country risk, including any one country's susceptibility to external shocks, to inform private markets.[93] The Fund could also pool country-specific risks in a diversified portfolio, reducing pricing and creating economies of scale that lower underwriting costs. It could readily provide advice to its members on ways to use the hedging instruments employed in private markets. Such fresh insurance strategies would not only keep the Fund relevant without placing heavy demands on its lending capacities; they could also help depoliticize the Fund and future rescues, and even make reserve hoarding less palatable.

Conclusion

In 1998 then-Federal Reserve Chairman Alan Greenspan called for strong US engagement in fighting financial crises in emerging markets, arguing that the United States could not remain "an oasis of prosperity" if the rest of the world descended into financial chaos.[94] Even if unable to do away with crises, the IMF has helped safeguard the American oasis. Serving as the global credit agency, it has helped stabilize US trade and investment partners, served America's foreign policy goals, and economized international rescues. The IMF staff has issued world-class, even if not flawless, policy advice congruent with America's economic ideals. Whether the Fund can help safeguard US interests in the twenty-first century is a matter of policy.

Changing the IMF's governance, connecting it with emerging regional schemes, and enhancing its responsiveness are no guarantees for keeping Asians engaged, the Fund's advice relevant, or global crises at bay. Nor will it preempt China's mercenary finance. Countries will look to the Fund only if it helps them solve their problems and reach their goals better and more cheaply than conceivable alternatives would. While global recovery could relegate the Fund to the sidelines, governments' memories of the Great Crisis are unlikely to fade quickly. The case for insurance will persist, even in better times; whether the Fund will be seen as the key insurer is another matter.

Policy choices in the IMF's future entail trade-offs that have to be managed. Expanding the Fund further would give the United States greater levers to respond to crises and power over other countries' economic policies, but it would also inspire moral hazard around the world, making crises all the likelier. Refusing bailouts would help preempt moral hazard and play well in domestic politics, but it could let contagious crises spread right to US shores and drive countries to alternative sources of funding with dubious standards. Encouraging regional funds could reduce claims to the Fund, but it also entails the loss of American influence over economic policies abroad, as in Asia. Partnering with regional funds could drag the Fund and America into crises whose resolution ultimately lies with regional authorities, as in Europe.

The IMF will not and should not become an all-powerful insurance agency able to respond to all crises. Nor should America have to sort out other countries' messes. However, the Fund's reach across regions and its multilateral surveillance are as unique as they are uniquely useful. In a globalized world economy, no single government or region will be able to deliver the world from instability. Even if global competition forced countries to manage their economies well and regional institutions excelled in surveillance of their members' policies, the world would still need a chief economist to opine on hidden perils in the global economy. And such a surveyor would still need a purse to have influence. The premise of White and Keynes remains: a global economy requires global institutions.

In the absence of a strong global crisis management regime, the familiar scene where the United States is expected to spring to the rescue while others free ride could reappear. America has always summoned the resolve and funds to act, but it now runs short on both.

The IMF is a readily available global police officer that patrols the treacherous neighborhoods of finance. It is also a fire alarm that alerts the world to approaching dangers when the world is asleep. It will now need to adapt to twenty-first-century challenges. It requires a laser-like analytical focus on the range of risks that can converge into global crises, a system for rewarding members for policies that promote stability, and new ways to use its first-rate technical expertise to bridge public and private insurance markets.

Part of the Fund's future agenda needs to center on building consistency and complementarities among its own instruments and bilateral and regional facilities. As political as such efforts are, countries need to keep their eye on the ball. Just as the World Bank's goal, imprinted above its doors, is a world free of poverty, the aspiration of the IMF must be a world economy free of financial crises.

3 Ruling Out Crises—or Deglobalizing Finance?

> We need to recognize that risk does not respect national borders. We need to prevent national competition to reduce standards and encourage a race to higher standards. . . . To match the increasing global markets, we must ensure that global standards for financial regulation are consistent with the high standards we will be implementing in the United States.
>
> —US Treasury Secretary Timothy Geithner, congressional testimony,
> 26 March 2009

I N HIS LANDMARK BOOK *MANIAS, PANICS AND DEPRESSIONS*, first published in 1978, Charles Kindleberger concluded that financial crises are "hardy perennials" in the world economy. The Great Crisis bolstered efforts around the world to make that remark history. With the crisis hastily traced to shortcomings in financial regulations and their enforcement, regulatory reform emerged as Washington's main means to placate taxpayers enraged by costly bank bailouts. The political backlash required culprits; lined up were Wall Street bankers and their Washington regulators.

The result of the greatest financial regulatory reform since the Great Depression, the 2,319-page Dodd–Frank Act creates an oversight council to monitor the entire financial sector, regulates newer market players such as hedge funds and private equity firms, and establishes a process for unwinding floundering banks in a more orderly fashion. It also seeks to tame "too-big-to-fail" banks, curb bankers' bonuses, and bar credit-default swaps, once called by Warren Buffett "financial weapons of mass destruction."

The reforms should be judged both by the degree to which they meet their objectives—prevent future crises and extricate the taxpayer from the burden to bail out banks when crises do occur—and by their potential for promoting open, competitive, and globalized financial markets, something the United

States has championed for decades. By both standards, the reforms have serious flaws. Yes, improved oversight and supervision are long overdue. But the reforms over-empower regulatory agencies, increase moral hazard among the largest banks, and risk raising the costs of financial services to consumers. Such outcomes are bad for the taxpayer, the United States, and the world.

While too much may be done domestically, too little is accomplished internationally. Free global financial markets and international regulatory coordination are critical for the United States to ensure unfettered flow of capital and a level playing field for US banks and financial markets, particularly at a time when several emerging markets aspire to replace New York as the leading global financial center. But national disagreements over the reach and content of regulations have stunted progress. What needs to be done—and undone?

Mostly Political

The story of American and international financial regulations is one of interest group politics and inertia. Reforms to regulations, when they have been made, have been triggered by economic turmoil and innovations that have undermined old interests and given rise to new demands.

Go back a hundred years. In the early twentieth century, the US banking sector was stunningly fragmented, to a large extent because of laws restricting bank branching and consolidation across state lines. By the early 1920s, there were close to 30,000 banks in the nation, one for every 3,444 people.[1] Geographic limits benefited unit bankers and landowning farmers, powerful interest groups that had prevailed in the nineteenth-century political battles against the integrationist forces. The cost of local bank monopolies was steep. Unable to pool risk, banks were prone to panics—events where hordes of debtors of multiple banks simultaneously sought to withdraw their deposits.[2] The result was repeated bank panics in the decades prior to World War I, in 1863–1913.

The Great Depression cut into the clout of rural interests, but small unit bankers held their sway. Their geographic dispersion was a political asset—many a Congressional representative had a prominent unit bank in his or her district—and helped ensure the passage of the historic 1933 Glass–Steagall Act. By creating the Federal Deposit Insurance Corporation (FDIC) as the government agency in charge of insuring deposits, the act rectified not the cause but the symptom of bank panics. With bank panics preempted, retail deposits would become a more stable source of financing for banks.

While larger banks opposed the act as making them subsidize the insurance of their smaller, unstable counterparts, they were denigrated by the small banks and were anyway too concentrated in hubs such as New York to garner sufficient votes in Congress. Small banks secured another morsel: Glass–Steagall prevented commercial, bread-and-butter banks from engaging in the riskier securities business. The provision, presumably made to lower risks to depositors, was passed despite the fact that banks with securities affiliates in 1930–1933 had been much less likely to fail than banks without them.[3] The fragmentation of American banking by geography became coupled with fragmentation by risk.

Hearings on Glass–Steagall, stacked in favor of its sponsors, overlooked many of the act's flaws.[4] Backed by the small banks and congresspeople favoring them, the enterprising Congressman Henry Steagall overcame objections to the law from the Roosevelt administration and regulatory agencies. The bill was the first to pass of the 150 deposit insurance bills Congress had considered in 1886–1933.[5] The 1956 Bank Holding Company Act followed the lineage, prohibiting bank holding companies—large firms that owned two or more banks—from engaging in nonfinancial commercial activities.

An End to Firewalls

By the 1970s, larger banks, pressured by bouts of inflation and stiffening international competition, had found loopholes in Glass–Steagall and launched a bid to relax the straitjacketing rules.[6] Technological changes strengthened their hand against small state banks. ATMs eroded geographic divisions between customers and banks, checkable money market mutual funds allowed for banking by mail and phone across state lines, and declining transportation and communication costs lowered the costs for customers to use more distant banks.[7] The increasing sophistication of credit-scoring techniques and new, large credit databases put an end to local bankers' monopoly of information about their customers.

Starting in the 1970s, state governments, the Federal Reserve, courts, and the Office of the Comptroller of the Currency (OCC) spearheaded a spree of bank deregulation.[8] The wave unfolded from states with fewer and/or financially weak small banks, and with several small firms dependent on banking services.[9] In 1975 Maine pioneered legislation that permitted out-of-state bank holding companies to acquire in-state banks.[10] Commissions charged by securities companies were also liberalized. The public warmed to deregulation, as well, and the 1980s savings and loan crisis, which resulted in massive taxpayer bailouts, became widely interpreted as caused by the restrictions on bank activities.[11]

After practically all states deregulated bank branching, Congress inscribed the changes in federal legislation. Several European countries, including France, Spain, Italy, Austria, Norway, and Sweden, also phased out bank branching restrictions. The 1994 Riegle–Neal Act eliminated all barriers to interstate banking and branching, and various further legal reforms reduced banks' reserve requirements and approved new investment vehicles.

The firewall between different types of banking operations—commercial banking and the riskier financial services—came down fully in 1999, when the Fed and banks persuaded Congress to repeal Glass–Steagall.[12] The Gramm–Leach–Bliley Act of 1999 allowed more-extensive affiliations between commercial banks, on the one hand, and investment banks, broker-dealers, merchant banks, and other such nonbanking financial firms, on the other. The ultimate winners from deregulation were large banks—especially money center banks, large regional banks, banks with subsidiaries that engaged in underwriting in a limited fashion, and small firms dependent on credit; small banks and rival insurance firms lost.[13]

The Great Opening

By international standards, the United States has been open to foreign banks and investors practically throughout the postwar era. Only amid the Vietnam War, a time of fixed exchange rates that complicated maintaining an open capital account, did the United States temporarily limit capital outflows. Abroad, however, banking deregulation was coupled with cross-border liberalization. Starting with Japan, Canada, Australia, New Zealand, Sweden, Norway, and Finland, by the 1980s and 1990s various nations opened their markets to foreign banks, generally from nations that reciprocated with access to their markets.[14] In 1993 the European Union opened intra-regional banking.

Developed nations also progressed on financial liberalization, freeing bank transactions within and across borders. Securities markets were liberalized, starting with the UK's "Big Bang" in 1986, followed by Canada, Australia, New Zealand, Ireland, Sweden, and Finland, as well as continental Europe, Japan, and Mexico. Capital-account liberalization unfolded from France and

Germany to the other Western European nations and further to Japan, which in 1984 began a staged liberalization at US prodding. American officials sought to open Japan's capital account to strengthen the yen and cut America's trade deficit with the Asian dragon.[15]

Multilateral bodies such as the G7, OECD, and the Financial Stability Forum (FSF) served as meeting grounds for representatives of national central banks and supervisory authorities to open markets further, deregulate banking systems, and converge rules. The United States also held bilateral dialogues with Japan, China, the European Union, and many other economics. Covering the world's largest financial theater, the US–EU forum worked on common principles for financial regulations, accounting, and auditing.

A Level Playing Field

While loosening their grip, Congress and regulators did not relinquish control over banks. Rather, new instruments were devised to control risk taking.[16] Increasing capital requirements was one such measure; sturdier supervision of individual banks was another.[17] Banks were also expected to strengthen their internal risk-management systems.

With banking globalizing, capital requirements would have to be multilateralized in order for US banks to remain competitive with their German and Japanese counterparts, which enjoyed lower requirements. Along with London, by 1988 Washington managed to persuade the G10 advanced nations to adopt the Basel I Accord, which required international banks to hold capital equal to 8 percent of their risk-weighted assets. In the wake of the savings and loan crisis, Congress instructed federal banking agencies to pursue "prompt corrective action" if bank capital ratios dropped below certain levels.[18] Some of the spirit was enshrined in the Basel II accord, promoted by the Federal Reserve and US regulatory agencies, which in 2004 mandated more comprehensive risk and capital management.

Capital requirements notwithstanding, governments in advanced nations became more, not less, involved in insuring banks against failure. Basel capital requirements were a far cry from the 25-percent equity buffers that banks in the United States held as a share of their assets in the late nineteenth century. In the twentieth century the United States and other governments provided progressively greater liquidity support, deposit insurance, and lender of last resort facilities.[19] Government insurance was put to use in a series of banking crises—Spain in 1977, the United States in 1988, Finland, Norway, and Sweden in the late 1980s and early 1990s, and Japan in 1997—and domestic and

IMF lending was deployed to counter the emerging-market crises of the 1980s and 1990s.

The costs of the bailouts were significant: even the most conservative estimates range from a low of 2 percent of GDP in Norway to 2.7 percent in the United States, 8 percent in Japan, and a high of 29 percent in Chile in 1981.[20] Carmen Reinhart and Kenneth Rogoff calculate that the total costs of responses to various banking crises—bailout of the banking sector, shortfall in revenue, and fiscal stimulus packages—since year 1800 increased central government debts on average by 86 percent in the three years after a crisis.[21]

The explicit or implicit promise of public insurance nonetheless persisted, perhaps because near-death crises did not recur in most developed countries. Government rescues were also not necessarily always seen in a bad light. One of the brighter cases was Sweden's rescue of its banking system in 1992 at the tail end of a property boom. The bailout cost the equivalent of 4 percent of GDP, but, as the government received solid returns when it later took the banks public, it ended up costing "only" 2 percent of GDP. The incentives of banks aligned accordingly: with taxpayers cushioning against a fall, banks became uninterested in holding any more capital than required by Basel I.[22] The implementation of Basel II was delayed; for example, US banks were scheduled to start adopting it only in 2010.

Good Riddance

Regulatory reforms and new technologies had dramatic implications on the economics of banking. Thanks to deregulation and liberalization, as well as computerization, securitization, and sheer global economic growth, cross-border financial flows soared from less than a trillion dollars in 1980 and $1.5 trillion in 1990 to more than $11 trillion in 2007.[23] Total global financial assets, foreign and domestic, topped almost $200 trillion that year, or 3.5 times world GDP. US financial assets rose from $39 trillion in 1999 to $62 trillion in 2007. The economic turmoil of the 1980s and the end of the ring fencing of banks led to a wave of bank consolidation across America. The number of banking and thrift organizations was almost halved, from 15,084 in 1984 to 7,842 in 2004.[24]

These effects coincided with banking and financial crises and, except for a brief calm in 2004–2006, increased volatility in world financial markets.[25] Some commentators falsely connected the instability to the spree of financial deregulation and liberalization.[26] However, financial deregulation, when accompanied by good institutions and independent and accountable supervision, *reduces* the likelihood of crises.[27] Excessive regulation is found only to undercut the incentives for banks to introduce new services and products, limiting banks' capacities to hedge against risk.[28]

In the United States, the end of Glass–Steagall was good riddance. George Mason University's Carlos Ramírez finds that the law's separation of commercial and investment banking increased the cost of external finance.[29] According to the Fed's Randall Kroszner and the University of Chicago's Raghuram Rajan, securities issued by unified commercial and investment banks are of higher quality that those issued by stand-alone investment banks.[30] The effect of de-restricting branching across state lines was also unequivocally positive. It increased the availability of banking services (especially in rural areas), increased competition, lowered the cost of credit, and reduced the odds of bank panics.[31]

Financial liberalization has been similarly beneficial, inspiring financial development and entrepreneurship the world over. Surveying numerous studies, William Cline concludes that financial openness boosts growth by about 1 percent annually for industrial countries and 0.5 percent annually for emerging countries.[32] Further studies have found that stock market liberalization leads to a 15-percent appreciation in firms' equity values—and to sales growth, investment, and profitability—and raises the annual compensation of manufacturing workers by 25 percent.[33] Cash-strapped firms in emerging economies have particularly benefited from access to the global pool of investors.

It is these benefits that inspired advanced economies to free financial flows in the 1970s and 1980s, and emerging markets to follow suit some decade later. True, openness does expose countries to outside forces and shocks. There is some evidence that financial liberalization encourages risk taking, likely because it loosens the domestic credit constraint.[34] However, developed-country banking crises were largely national in scope, propelled by inadequate supervision and high, largely domestic debt.[35] And a long line of research shows that emerging-market financial crises were caused not by capital-account liberalization but by such factors as over-leverage, poor macroeconomic management, corruption, and fragile regulatory and supervisory systems. While some analysts have advocated capital controls to reduce volatility, a large body of research shows that capital controls have proven ineffective, counterproductive, and destabilizing.[36]

If deregulation and liberalization have great benefits, capital requirements have their costs, and have also proved ineffective. In the short run,
they reduce individual bank lending and increase loan rates as banks adjust
to new rules.[37] In the long run, banks learn to go around capital requirements
through securitization and other innovations, a finding based on 130 studies
compiled by the Bank of International Settlements, the cradle of the Basel
Accords.[38] With governments implicitly promising to serve as lenders of last
resort, banks have tended to hold fewer liquid assets on their balance sheets
and opted for short-term borrowing, the cheaper yet riskier form of credit.[39]
US banks, reacting to Basel I, reduced commercial loans and increased their
Treasury holdings.[40]

New Rules of the Game

The end of Glass–Steagall and the wave of banking deregulation unfolding
across America inspired similar reforms in countless of nations. Countries
around the world also followed the US lead in liberalizing their financial markets to foreign banks. Good economics followed, from lowered costs of credit
to higher-quality securities issuances, greater availability of banking services,
especially in rural areas, and wealth creation and entrepreneurship the world
over. But a dark cloud above the integrating world was frequent volatility.
Devastating banking and financial crises, while not caused by deregulation,
amounted to more than Black Swan events. And when banks failed, it was the
public that often bore the cost. Though a beneficiary of the expansion of financial services as a consumer, the taxpayer seemed less likely to be in charge
and more likely to become a casualty.

In the wake of the Great Crisis, the Obama White House and congressional Democrats set out to turn the situation on its head—to make the taxpayer
the guardian rather than the casualty of banks by tightening the government's
grip on Wall Street while reducing its implicit insurance to banks. The reforms were tantamount to reengineering the relationship between governments and financial markets. As such, they created a broader contest, both
intellectual and political, between those arguing that markets need to be regulated lest they create socially undesired effects and those who see regulations
as distorting markets, and thus again creating public undesirables.

Signed by the president on 21 July 2010, more than a year after it was introduced, the Dodd–Frank Wall Street Reform and Consumer Protection Act was

hailed as the third major win for the White House after the $862-billion stimulus package in 2009 and the health care overhaul in March 2010. Infused with voter fury about the bailouts and the dismal state of the economy, the passing of the mammoth law was a familiar story of populist pressures to get even with financial tycoons, industry resistance, and turf wars among regulators. Countless Washington bodies wrangled over the outcome, from consumer lobbies such as Americans for Financial Reform, their labor allies such as the AFL–CIO, industry groups from the US Chamber of Commerce, to the Financial Services Roundtable and American Bankers Association, the Treasury, the White House, and the leading Washington financial agencies, SEC, FDIC, and the Federal Reserve, with both houses of Congress squeezed in between.

The thrust of the final outcome approximated the Obama administration's initial proposal. In a major structural change, Dodd–Frank established the Financial Stability Oversight Council to advise the president and the Congress on "macro-prudential" systemic risks in the US financial system. The Council is led by the Treasury Secretary, and it comprises ten voting members, including the heads of the Federal Reserve, the Federal Deposit Insurance Corporation, and the Office of the Comptroller of the Currency. The law also created a Bureau of Consumer Financial Protection (CFPB) to oversee such products as mortgages and credit cards. And it empowered a triumvirate— the Federal Reserve, the Treasury, and the FDIC—to unwind ailing nondepository financial institutions such as AIG and Lehman Brothers, adding their prior powers to resolve commercial and savings banks such as Washington Mutual, IndyMac, and Wachovia.[41]

Market players and instruments were also regulated. Banks and nonbanking entities that have assets of more than $50 billion became subject to more stringent disclosure requirements than were their smaller counterparts.[42] Dodd–Frank designated all commercial banking groups with $50 billion or more in assets as "systemically important financial institutions" (SIFIs), those whose failure would have drastic negative implications for the US financial system and real economy, and it empowered the oversight council to decide which nonbank financial institutions should receive the SIFI designation. Hedge funds and private equity firms overseeing $150 million or more in capital were made to register with the SEC and disclose information about their trades and portfolios. Most derivatives that were previously traded dealer to dealer were brought to public exchanges, presumably to lower the risk that one dealer's failures would bring down others.

The act's most controversial part was the Volcker rule, named after Paul Volcker, the imposing 6-foot-8 early backer of President Obama, Chairman of the President's Economic Recovery Advisory Board, and the legendary Chairman of the Federal Reserve during the turbulent 1980s. The Volcker rule was aimed at making "too big to fail" commercial banks less risky by prohibiting them from engaging in proprietary trading. Commercial banks were also barred from sponsoring hedge or private equity funds—although the very final version of the rule did allow banks to invest up to 3 percent of their Tier 1 capital (capital paid in by shareholders, such as retained earnings) in such funds, the equivalent of some $3–4 billion for the largest banks.

Another controversial, last-minute addition to the law was the Lincoln rule, named after Democratic Senator Blanche Lincoln, the chairman of the Senate Agriculture Committee, which holds jurisdiction on derivatives. The final version of the Lincoln rule forces banks to pass the presumably risky commodity, equity, and noninvestment-grade credit contracts into separate affiliates with higher capital costs. However, it does allow banks to continue engaging in foreign-exchange, interest-rate, and high-quality credit swap dealings, which make up the bulk of the derivatives market. As a result, US banks will likely have to move some 10 percent of their $218-trillion combined derivatives holdings.[43]

An Icy Reception

The reforms were premised on two main notions—that weak or lacking regulation had encouraged "excessive" risk taking on Wall Street and that the results of such risk taking had created the very crisis. Ergo, expanding the government's regulatory reach in the doings of financial institutions would prevent crises and extricate taxpayers from the burden of bailing out banks. As the regulatory bill cleared the House, Speaker Nancy Pelosi argued that "[n]o longer will recklessness on Wall Street cause joblessness on Main Street. . . . No longer will the risky behavior of a few threaten the economy of the whole."[44] Upon signing the Dodd–Frank Act, President Obama declared that "[b]ecause of this law, the American people will never again be asked to foot the bill for Wall Street's mistakes. . . . There will be no more taxpayer-funded bailouts. Period."

The mood in the nation did not match the euphoria in Washington. In a poll, nearly 80 percent of Americans reported "just a little" or "no" confidence that the law would prevent or significantly soften a future crisis.[45] Almost one-half, 47 percent, saw the act as doing more to protect the financial industry than consumers, while 38 percent said consumers would benefit more. Industry groups criticized the law on different grounds, as stifling business and raising the cost of credit. The American Bankers Association stated that the law "contains a tsunami of new rules and restrictions for traditional banks that had nothing to do with causing the financial crisis in the first place."[46] The US Chamber of Commerce opposed the bill "because it would fail to fix effectively the outdated, broken financial regulatory system, would unnecessarily affect companies that had nothing to do with the financial crisis, and would not create the efficient, liquid, and transparent capital markets America needs to fuel long-term economic growth and job creation."[47]

All assessments missed one mark: the ultimate effect of the regulations remains far in the horizon. The Treasury and regulators were left to craft 243 implementing rules for the new regulations, as well as to conduct 67 studies and issue 22 periodic reports.[48] At no time in US history has there been such a number of regulatory requirements placed on agencies. The manpower required for implementation is telling: 5,000 additional people spanning eight agencies, including 1,225 hires at the Consumer Financial Protection Bureau.

Such a massive process offers regulators, policy entrepreneurs, and lobbies as well as interested congressional leaders several angles to shape the outcomes and slow the process. For example, a year after Dodd–Frank was signed, politicking kept the consumer bureau without a leader. Requiring new investments, the reform process has also been burdened by budgetary shortfalls and wrangling among the regulatory agencies. For instance, getting the oversight council members to share information and work well together is difficult when each prioritizes the workloads of his or her respective agency.

By September 2011, only a quarter of the up to 400 regulations in the act had been written, and even fewer approved. And once the rules are in place, banks will need to implement them. The ultimate effects thus will be unclear for a long time. The Volcker rule will take effect only in July 2012, after which banks will have two years to divest any investments that violate the rule—or apply for additional three years of extensions. Capital requirements will take even longer: countries are expected to have adopted Basel III capital standards, approved in September 2010, only by late 2012, and each country has its own implementation schedule. The new leverage ratio, the cap on the amount of borrowing that an institution can do, will go into effect in 2018.

The dilemma facing regulators is that the tougher the new rules are, the more reluctantly they will be implemented. Industry resistance is legitimate: there will be costs to the banks and the US economy. Most estimates place the costs of tied-up capital, fee reductions, and higher compliance costs created by Dodd–Frank to 5–20 percent of the largest banks' total profits by 2013.[49] Whether financial institutions shoulder them or pass them to their customers, the costs are economy-wide, and they can be significant. The Institute for International Finance (IIF), the financial services industry's global association, projects that the cumulative impact of the implementation of the reform package is a reduction of an annual average of 0.5 percentage points from the path of real US GDP growth over 2011–2015, the heaviest implementation period, and an 0.3-percentage-point shave-off from growth in 2011–2020.[50] As result, some 4.8 million fewer jobs would be created in 2010–2015. The United States falls between Europe, which will incur a toll of 0.9 percentage points in 2011–2015, and Japan, at 0.4 points.

Are the reforms worth their cost? Will they preempt crises and end taxpayer liability for bailing out banks? And will they do so while honing unbridled competition in US financial markets and securing an open, fair, and integrated world financial market?

Will They Work?

Many of the flagship items in the reform agenda, such as sharpened macroprudential oversight, stauncher supervision, comprehensive oversight of financial conglomerates, and smarter risk management regimes had received broad-based academic support years before the Great Crisis.[51] In principle, such aims are worthy in today's world of massive and hugely complex financial markets and banks with assets that dwarf many national economies. But despite the jubilant arguments of Washington Democrats, Dodd–Frank will not make America free of crises. Rather, it can make America worse off. The act is subject to the law of unintended consequences—namely that an intervention in a complex system creates unanticipated and undesirable outcomes. In the case of Dodd–Frank, such unintended consequences may include increased moral hazard, stifled competition and innovation, and countermeasures by financial institutions that create new blind sides for regulators. Let's examine these in turn.

More Moral Hazard

The government's implicit or explicit promise to rescue flailing financial institutions fuels the moral hazard that Dodd–Frank's authors wanted to curb. One reason is that the law does not address deposit insurance that allows banks to take tail risks—such as become heavily exposed to toxic real estate assets—without fear of losing their customers. With their savings fully insured, depositors are indifferent about banks' activities, and banks can finance their activities at below-market rates, taking on risk. In July 2010 the FDIC extended its deposit insurance through 2013 after raising the threshold for qualifying accounts to $250,000 from $100,000 in October 2008.

While deposit insurance has arguably helped stem the kinds of bank runs that the United States experienced in the nineteenth century, it also shields banks from market discipline.[52] The counterargument—that market discipline is synonymous with bank panics—appears outdated because of two factors: money-market funds invested in Treasury bills that have equally good insurance as bank CDs do, and technological advances, such as real-time gross-settlement payments, that allow for protecting payment systems from the failure of any payer.[53] However, because bank CDs tend to increase with the deposit insurance, increasing deposit insurance makes good politics for shoring up the banking system.[54] The result is bad public policy: risk is externalized, not internalized.

Dodd–Frank's vesting the Financial Stability Oversight Council with extensive powers also contributes to moral hazard. The council and, through it, the Federal Reserve, will be able to regulate and supervise practically any financial institution in the United States if it "determines that material financial distress at the US nonbank financial company, or the nature, scope, size, scale, concentration, interconnectedness, or mix of the activities of the US nonbank financial company, could pose a threat to the financial stability of the United States." More stringent rules apply to SIFIs. And if a large financial firm is failing, the Treasury has the power to assign a conservator or receiver to "stabilize" it. The council can also impose tougher disclosure rules and regulations on smaller financial firms—insurance companies, securities broker-dealers, and a variety of asset-management firms and funds with assets less than $50 billion—if it deems them systemically important.

Such an expansive mandate means that the council will be able and encouraged not only to clamp down on banks, but also to promptly preempt the failure of any major financial institution. After all, because the failure of an institution would bring the blame to the council's doorstep, its first instinct is to fear the worst.[55] Blamed for being asleep at the wheel as the crisis unfolded, regulators are bound to be on a particularly high alert. In the council's extensive authority may thus lie a tacit commitment to bail out financial firms, particularly the larger ones that regulators are to watch with a sterner eye. If large financial companies believe this to be the case, moral hazard could only increase, not decrease as intended.

Similar problems arise from the government's new authority to resolve a failing financial institution. A resolution authority is positive in that it ends the regulators' dilemma to either bail out a company and its creditors or let it go bankrupt. The idea of bringing order to an otherwise unruly and prolonged death of an institution is also appealing, as a chaotic unwinding all too easily perpetrates the downfall of other institutions connected to the dying entity. But any rule that provides for an orderly unwinding can create an expectation that unwinding will be effected. If firms believe that a bailout is likely—an impression that the repeated bailouts during the Great Crisis have all but solidified—they will have fewer incentives to assess their risks or insure against counterparty failure.

The most immediate implication of moral hazard is that institutions will have incentives to drive without a seat belt—make bets whose costs they don't have to internalize and that can have high negative externalities. Another consequence of moral hazard is financial Darwinism: if large institutions enjoy an implicit government guarantee to bail them out, they can borrow more cheaply than their smaller competitors and thus crowd out the latter.[56] As such, Dodd–Frank may subsidize large institutions—and help the big get bigger. A recent study shows that the borrowing costs for larger banks have become 0.78 less than those for small ones, up from 0.29 in 2000–2007.[57]

Creative Destruction, Destroyed?

The reform drive was premised on the notion that a deregulated market would always be prone to instability because of the risk taking it encourages, so risk would have to be reined in. But just as the only athlete safe from sport injuries is one that does not play sports, the only safe financial system is one that does not allow for risk. A safe financial system is also stagnant: there is no competition, no innovation, and no growth.

Aiming at stability by managing risk taking, Dodd–Frank can end up undermining innovation and competition in America's financial markets, the twentieth century's global envy. Consider the incentives flowing from the law. Peter Wallison, regulatory scholar at the American Enterprise Institute, argues that the Dodd–Frank supercharges the oversight council to a point where financial institutions, large and small, may decide to focus on appeasing Washington more than engaging in the kinds of disruptive innovations and investments that are the essence of America's hard-knuckled market capitalism.[58] Industry, in short, would craft strategies to meet regulations instead of the business objective of maximizing profit. A one-size-fits-all regulation for SIFIs would exacerbate the chilling effect. SIFIs are hugely diverse, with different product types and distinct ways of doing business. Requiring the government to approve each and every new product of the different SIFIs against standardized guidelines would freeze innovation.

The mere costs of uncertainty created by the oversight council's expansive regulatory fiat can offset any supposed benefits of federal oversight. Consulting firm McKinsey argues that the new rules entail an "increase in the cost of liquidity and net reduction in liquidity credit lines," and "higher rates and reduced access to credit."[59] Generally sympathetic to Dodd–Frank, Douglas Elliott and Robert Litan of the Brookings Institution warn that the regulatory uncertainty is real and should be priced out across transactions.[60] Equity investors would demand higher expected returns to compensate for the added risk, debt holders would increase their demanded interest rates or opt to invest in other industries, and creditors might charge borrowers more to compensate for the operational uncertainty.

Regulatory heat is already felt: both banks and businesses see regulatory pressures as the leading cause of banks' risk aversion and declined small business loans.[61] In a 2011 survey, nearly 80 percent of banks argued that pressure from regulators had caused them to avoid making risky loans, and 60 percent agreed that regulatory pressure was the cause of declined small business loans.[62] Republican presidential hopefuls' claim that Dodd–Frank hurts small banks and businesses is not just political theater.

The resolution authority could make financial institutions engage in counterproductive self-censorship, as those empowered to use it might employ it more easily merely because it exists. A hammer sees nails that aren't there because it is hardwired to do so. Once the resolution process gets on the way, institutions have very limited time to resist or react—so limited, in fact, that due process may be violated.[63] Would financial institutions want to reach such a point or rather tie their own hands?

The consumer protection bureau can also have unintended effects. Appointees to the agency, which will have a robust budget of $550 million by 2012, have pledged to crack down on any apparent misbehavior by Wall Street firms in such areas as mortgages, student loans, and credit cards. Such greater enforcement and investigation of lenders is likely, for better or for worse, to limit the means they can employ to make profits. But it can also end up being self-defeating. Although the bureau is to work towards "fairness" and "improved access" to financial products, it can make lenders more risk-averse, inducing them to screen borrowers and credit card holders—which, in turn, can restrict the access of lower-middle-class consumers to credit even if such borrowers are in a condition to repay.[64] Granted, the market could be skewed in the other direction: the fairness goal could end up encouraging riskier loans akin to sub-prime mortgages.[65]

Boomerang Effects

Dodd–Frank can make financial institutions assume new risks, or self-censor, or lose efficiencies. But institutions are unlikely to sit and watch passively. No rule is ironclad: the creativity of the regulated trumps thousands of detailed regulations. Governments face the familiar "bloodhounds and greyhounds" problem: bloodhound regulators will perennially lag behind their regulated greyhounds.[66] The likeliest scenario is one where the greyhounds—large financial institutions—work to outmaneuver the bloodhound regulators.

Take the added costs of a SIFI designation. The designation could induce financial institutions to do what they have practically always done in response to inconvenient government regulations: step up financial engineering. Most financial innovations provide great efficiencies and expand consumers' access to credit. But innovations crafted in efforts to circumvent regulators are probably likelier to be obscure securities or transactions that only appear to mitigate risk—the story of the defamed structured investment vehicles.[67]

In general, making financial institutions shed an activity deemed "risky" can make them compensate for the lost high-risk/high-reward activity by finding another one. For example, institutions can circumvent the Volcker rule by shifting proprietary traders onto desks dealing with clients, a safe haven for conducting the same business as before.[68] Or they can find a way out of the resizing altogether. As the Volcker rule was debated, Goldman Sachs became eager to resume its previous status as a nonbank financial institution lest it fall subject to the Volcker rule and thus lose its hedge fund, a profit center.

US institutions cannot be blamed: the Volcker rule places them in a competitive disadvantage. Banks with US operations that are European based, such as Credit Suisse, are not implementing the rule, nor are banks such as UBS, whose hedge funds and private equity operations run on outside, non-US capital. European finance ministers and regulators have argued that applying the Volcker rule would violate the EU's universal bank laws applicable to such banks as Deutsche Bank.

Of course, Washington's newly empowered regulators have an incentive to, and to an extent can, counter institutions' craftiness to circumvent rules. But institutions hold a potent trump card: in a world of manifold financial hubs, they can quite plausibly threaten to exit the US market should rules and their enforcement, from the Volcker rule to capital standards and rules on SIFIs, prove too rigid. Whether and when regulators would blink remains a question mark.

No Silver Bullets

With large financial institutions continuing to enjoy a tacit government guarantee, a plausible future in American financial markets is increased moral hazard among large financial institutions, crowding out of smaller ones, and politicized, ad hoc reactions by the new Washington regulators. University of Pennsylvania law professor David Skeel suggests that the setting could devolve into a corporativist-style bargaining between institutions and regulators over the implementation of the regulations.[69] That, in turn, could lead to the "capture" of regulators by their regulated and encourage regulators to drive political rather than economic goals in their interaction with banks.

Countless policy makers and analysts have argued that such an outcome would be remedied by breaking up big banks. With too-big-to-fail banks obliterated, the argument goes, there would be no moral hazard, nor would the losing game that bloodhounds play against greyhounds be as consequential. The "big-is-bad" notion motivated the Volcker rule, and it has received staunch support from the former IMF Chief Economist Simon Johnson and Columbia's Nobel Laureate Joseph Stiglitz. Some Wall Street elders such as George Soros, former Treasury Secretary Nicholas Brady, and former Citigroup Co-Chairman John Reed have also appeared sympathetic.[70]

The Volcker rule is unsatisfactory to the big-is-bad school. The exception for Tier 1 capital blunted its bite on supposedly risky operations. It means, for example, that JPMorgan Chase can keep its Highbridge hedge fund because it invests only clients' money. To be sure, the rule will have tangible effects on such firms as Goldman Sachs, which derives a tenth of its revenue from proprietary trading. Also, Morgan Stanley needs to offload its proprietary-trading operation PDT, which accounts for 2 percent of group revenue.

The Volcker rule is no Glass–Steagall resurrected, but it does set a precedent for the government to curtail bank operations. But the argument for slicing up banks is problematic, both for its diagnosis and its proposed remedy. Take the remedy first. One of the most damning parts of the Volcker rule is that it focuses on financial institutions that serve as commercial banks, and does not apply to firms of the kind of Lehman Brothers or AIG, which were at the heart of the crisis yet which do not engage in commercial banking activities.[71] Volcker himself argued the proposal would affect only 4–5 US banks— in his words, those "placing bank capital at risk in the search of speculative profit rather than in response to customer needs"—and 25–30 banks globally.[72]

This speaks to the difficulty of designing a too-big-to-fail rule. The Volcker rule categorizes financial firms by type (hedge fund, private equity firm, commercial bank, and so forth), even though riskiness does not vary by type. Some hedge funds act more like banks, while some banks act more like insurance firms, and so forth.[73] A better differentiation would be made by riskiness of bank operations, but future riskiness is notoriously hard to predict. Federal Reserve Chairman Ben Bernanke has pointed out that separating risky and less risky activities would unlikely contain crises, as both showed weaknesses in the crisis.[74] Basing a too-big-to-fail rule on the degree of "interconnectedness" or "complexity" of an institution is equally thorny. Measuring such terms is hard, technically and politically, and legislating size limits is even harder.

An institution's assets are an easier albeit imperfect yardstick. Three main methods have been proposed to discourage size: taxing it, imposing a surcharge on it, or simply cutting it down. While the tax idea has withered, the G20 has called for a surcharge, along with tougher supervision, for SIFIs above and beyond Basel III capital requirements. The 29 banks designated as global SIFIs (G-SIFIs), among them 8 American banks, face even more onerous requirements, including an additional 2.5-percent capital requirement and tighter monitoring after 2016. National authorities are to ensure that

SIFIs, and the G-SIFIs in particular, will have extra "loss absorbency," which may be met through capital surcharges, contingent capital, or bail-in debt.

The premise of the SIFI rule is that imposing additional supervision and capital requirements on large banks would prevent bank failures and taxpayer bailouts, and perhaps even discourage financial institutions from mushrooming. The international political economy may work: the term "loss absorbency" is broad enough to be acceptable to such nations as Germany, France, and Japan that are opposed to additional surcharges on their banks.[75]

However, the rule has downsides. It cements the perception of an implicit promise of a government rescue of the firms designated "systemically important." Or the extra requirements can end up being so onerous as to be destabilizing. A number of factors pressure even those banks that are equipped to deal with added rules, such as debt that is due in the coming years, central banks' winding down support measures, and competition from governments' debt issuance. These troubles not only squeeze lending capacity, but also encourage institutions to shift select activities to the unregulated and less-transparent shadow banking sector—or threaten they will exit to jurisdictions with less-burdensome regulations.

The Resizing Folly   The idea of imposing an explicit cap on the size of financial institutions is also foolish. Acidic critic of Wall Street Simon Johnson identifies six US banks as too big to fail and thus needing to be broken up— Bank of America, Citigroup, Goldman Sachs, JPMorgan Chase, Morgan Stanley, and Wells Fargo. With coauthor James Kwak, he also advocates a hard cap on bank assets as a share of national GDP.[76] But consider four problems.

The first is the level of the cap. Johnson and Kwak call for a cap of 4 percent of US GDP for all banks and 2 percent of GDP for investment banks as the optimal cutoff points that reconcile the aims of safety and efficiency. They argue that "draconian size limitations could introduce unintended consequences if, for example, investment banks are no longer able to maintain sufficient trading volume in global markets."[77] But calibrating the percentage to avert such a "draconian" cut is hard technically—already because the evolution of banks and finance limits the usefulness of past data for the exercise—and all but impossible politically.

Second, any cutoff point would elicit strategic counterreactions from banks, such as entice them to conceal activities to off-balance sheet hideouts or to exit the US market. A global cap is highly unlikely, as also Johnson and

Kwak recognize. In most nations, banks make up a much larger share of national GDP than they do in the United States. For example, while the largest bank in the United States, Bank of America, and in the UK, HSBC, have the same level of total adjusted assets, BofA assets represent only 15 percent of US GDP, while HSBC's assets constitute 96 percent of UK GDP.[78] Almost three dozen banks in Europe similarly exceed the 15-percent threshold. "Small enough not to rescue" in one country is unlikely that in another. China, whose government-owned mega-banks now top the list of the world's largest banks, is unlikely to agree to any resizing.[79] As such, slicing up US banks could dent their competitiveness with their emerging rivals, and it would also be futile: even if US institutions were small enough to fail, Americans would continue to be exposed to the repercussions of the failures of foreign mega-banks.

Third, limiting bank size and activities have economic trade-offs, as revealed by the experience with Glass–Steagall. Limits undermine the economies of scale and scope that allow customers to enjoy a greater variety of banking services at lower costs. True, evidence on economies of scale and scope benefits in banking—cost savings stemming from larger size and combining different activities, respectively—is somewhat mixed.[80] But banks themselves certainly think that they matter, engaging, since the repeal of Glass–Steagall, in mergers and acquisition precisely *in order to* realize scale and scope economies.[81]

Scope benefits are particularly important. Peterson Institute's Ted Truman argues that breaking up banks prevents consumers from benefiting from the cross-subsidies in universal banks.[82] Adair Turner, the head of the UK's Financial Services Authority (FSA), notes that between narrow banking and pure proprietary trading fall a wide range of functions essential to providing credit to corporations, lubricating global capital flows, and managing the risks of exchange and interest rate and commodity price fluctuations.[83] Integrating rather than cutting financial services firms helps facilitate complex treasury and market-making activities.

Are larger banks more prone to fail? No. There is robust evidence that systemic banking crises are *less* likely in countries with concentrated banking systems.[84] There is some, albeit mixed, empirical evidence that larger banks and concentrated *and* noncompetitive banking sectors might be more prone to instability.[85]

Be that as it may, market structure is not the central issue for considering too big to fail. Rather, the issue is whether an implicit promise of a public rescue, predicated on an institution's importance to the financial system, produces moral hazard that will make bank failure and, subsequently, its public rescue likelier. The issue is also, or at least should be, about the trade-offs of limiting bank size. The advocates of size limits ignore the trade-offs, and they do not necessarily get at moral hazard. This is because of a flaw in the big-is-bad premise: that smaller institutions are inherently less systemically risky. Herein lies the fourth problem with a size cap: a multiplicity of small banks can be equally prone to moral hazard and be as systemically damaging when failing as one large one. Bank panics in nineteenth-century America and the savings and loan crisis of the 1980s engulfed (and were partly caused by) large numbers of small banks. If herd behaviors and interconnectedness of firms persist, the same stresses and losses can inflict the sector regardless of the size of firms. Too big to fail could conceivably become too many to fail.

A Precarious Shield

Financial regulations cannot escape the law of unintended consequences. They also cannot fill all holes that need to be filled to prevent the next debacle. Dodd–Frank has one critical omission: it does not address the mortgage giants Freddie Mac and Fannie Mae, which paved the way to the sub-prime lending spree by guaranteeing almost all newly originated mortgages.[86]

One administration and Congress after the next have prodded Fannie and Freddie to support mortgages to low-income Americans. Half of all mortgages in 2008 were sub-prime or otherwise risky loans.[87] Revealingly, some 90 percent of loans originated by Countrywide, the largest sub-prime lender, were either sold to Fannie Mae or backed by the government corporation Ginnie Mae. As sub-prime lending commenced, the government giants did not adjust for the higher risk, their regulators were too meek and oblivious to the coming storm, and their friends in Congress resisted changes—an unrivaled setting for loan originators and brokers. The mortgage market epitomized a situation of private profit made on the back of public risk. And as the crisis grew, the government's role in housing finance ballooned. By the summer of 2010, Fannie and Freddie, along with the Federal Housing Administration (FHA), backed more than 95 percent of new mortgages in America.[88]

False Confidence   The overarching reason why regulatory reform will not prevent future crises is its method—the myopic focus on regulations. Systemic financial instability tends to result from a confluence of factors in and outside the financial sector. The Great Crisis also had many hypothesized mothers, from high leverage to rampant sub-prime lending helped by the government's affordable housing policies, obscure and massive securitization of mortgages on Wall Street, lax monetary policy, and loosened credit constraint due to foreign financing. In the quest for systemic stability, regulation is inherently but a sliver of the solution: regulators cut some trees but never the entire forest.

Regulators also face a time-inconsistency problem: they devise rules looking in the rearview mirror, but the new known unknowns and unknown unknowns are always ahead. Systemic risks seldom announce themselves as such. What risk is real, and what is not? How do we know—and how do we know we know? Even more difficult is predicting the timing of an impending crisis: regulators are not like meteorologists who can forecast the hour of a storm's arrival. Yet the new regulations place enormous confidence in the oversight bodies to recognize that US financial stability is at risk, identify the instance that is triggering the risk, be able to act on their vision, and all along outsmart their regulated. At their best, regulations are a perpetually imperfect remedy. Washington's faith in the regulators provides false confidence.

Private Gain, Public Pain

If regulations cannot prevent crises, can they reduce taxpayer liability for bank failures when they occur?

The chosen tool for cushioning the taxpayer against the next crisis was increased capital requirements. Basel III seeks to rectify three problems with Basel II. First, Basel II, along with value at risk (VaR) measures, is inherently pro-cyclical: capital requirements do not rise in the asset boom as risks burgeon or fall in sour times when credit is scarce. The highs are truly high, but the lows are really low. Second, Basel II employs a blanket approach, failing to segment banks according to the creditworthiness of their borrowers. Third, Basel focuses on bank capital at the expense of attention to liquidity. The Great Crisis was primarily a liquidity crisis: some Western banks' core capital hovered at 3 percent or less of their assets, and less than a tenth of these assets were liquid. Banks like Bear Stearns failed not because they ran out of assets, but because they accumulated liabilities and because their lenders stopped lending. Lehman Brothers and many other major investment banks had leverage ratios of up to 30 to 1 before the crisis.[89]

Basel III corrects many problems, and its prompt unveiling instilled certainty in the financial sector at a critical time. It is countercyclical and gives pride of place to liquidity. Banks are to hold a minimum of 3 percent of Tier I capital of their total nonrisk-weighted assets, below the 5-percent leverage limit to which US banks were subject in the past. Tier 2 capital must be raise to a minimum of 10.5 percent of risk-weighted assets, up from the current 8 percent. Of the 10.5 percent, 7 percent must be in common equities, rather than the more obscure hybrid debt securities and other such instruments, well above the prior mandates of 2–3 percent and America's 4-percent requirement for large banks. The 7 percent consists of a 4.5-percent floor and an additional 2.5-percent "conservation buffer." Banks will be allowed to have a lower buffer, but if they do so, they will also have to keep down compensation and withhold dividends until the buffer is restored.

These ratios are more lenient than was expected. So is the implementation timeline. Financial institutions will have until 2018 to comply, and the largest US institutions—Bank of America, JPMorgan Chase, and Citigroup—by and large already meet the new requirements. It is European banks that need to raise new capital. Germany's Commerzbank and Spain's Banca MPS are estimated to take six years to meet the regulation, and France's Credit Agricole could need four years. Allied Irish Banks needs two years to reach the Tier I capital threshold, while its cousin Bank of Ireland needs two years.[90]

To be sure, banks can argue that they are hard-pressed to meet the new goalpost as long as growth is lackluster—and that growth cannot be revived to begin with should they be saddled with demanding capital rules. As the 2010 deadline for US banks to implement the 2004 Basel II approached, such banks as Citigroup, JPMorgan Chase, and Wells Fargo asked US regulators for a reprieve, arguing that Basel would crowd out lending in the credit-strapped economy.

Banks have a point: when implemented, capital requirements need to be dynamic; buffers need to be put in place in good times when capital is cheaper. Raising capital ratios should boost confidence that banks can pay off depositors and thus prevent bank runs. But capital requirements are an imperfect insurance, and, like other regulations, they can defeat their purpose. Consider three reasons.

First, the optimal capital ratio is unknown and likely does not exist. One common estimate is above 7 percent, at 8–9 percent: banks tend to need a floor of at least 4 percent so as not to lose the confidence of their depositors, creditors, and counterparties, and a 4–5-percent buffer against losses in crises. Postcrisis stress tests in the United States suggested that the big banks ate up capital worth about 4 percent of their risk-adjusted assets; in the banking crises of Japan, Finland, Norway, and Sweden, the average bank used 4.5 percent.[91] There is a notable variation: for example, Citigroup, HBOS, and Belgium's KBC lost 6–8 percent of risk-adjusted assets, UBS lost 13 percent, and Merrill Lynch lost as much as 19 percent.[92]

This also means that even very high capital ratios may not give the market much confidence in banks or suffice to prevent a bank failure. Indeed, Wharton Business School professor Richard Herring notes that the five largest US financial institutions subject to Basel II that failed or were forced into government-assisted mergers in 2008—Bear Stearns, Washington Mutual, Lehman Brothers, Wachovia, and Merrill Lynch—had regulatory capital ratios between 12.3 and 16.1 percent in their last quarterly disclosure before they were shut down.[93] Not only did their capital exceed the minimum regulated levels, but it was well above it and those many peer institutions, yet with seemingly little effect. Besides, capital requirements inherently focus on the losses a bank may incur, not on the losses it may impose on others in the system, so systemic risk is a function of the weakest link in the web of interconnected banks.

Second, capital ratios can produce perverse incentives. By reducing risk, the new rules also reduce reward. As such, they can drive institutions to take greater risk, as occurred in response to Basel I, in order to compensate for the investments they could have made with the now-latent capital. High capital requirements can also make short-term debt undesirable—although short-term debt can be good cholesterol as it disciplines management and makes banks more productive.[94]

Moreover, faced with higher requirements, financial institutions can also shift to unregulated entities, just like they did in creating structured investment vehicles and conduits.[95] Asset risk weights determine how capital requirements are adjusted to any one bank's portfolio, but Basel III is vague on them. Under Basel II, banks could use their own weights and ended up relying on credit ratings—thus loading up among other things on AAA-rated sub-prime mortgage securities. Granted, regulators are hard-pressed to determine the riskiness of assets and may end up offering loopholes that encourage banks to load up on suspect assets. Michael Casey of the *Wall Street Journal* notes that the fact that Basel left the definition to the signatory nations could result in regulatory arbitrage.[96] The choice could be one between riskier assets and lower capital requirements.

Third, capital requirements have direct costs. To be sure, many analysts have considered the costs bearable. A 2009 Brookings study argues that higher capital requirements would likely entail only small changes in the loan volumes of US banks and not markedly discourage customers to opt for other credit suppliers.[97] FSB and Bank of International Settlement studies hold that even if there could be initial economy-wide costs (whether carried by banks or passed to consumers), they would fade away within a few years of implementation.[98] Bank of Canada, on the basis of the Basel Committee study, forecasts that the combination of new liquidity standards and a 2-percentage point increase in bank capital ratios would reduce the frequency of crises, yielding a positive net GDP effects of the order of 1.8 percent in the implementing economies.[99]

However, the industry sees costs. According to an IIF study issued a few months prior to the final Basel package, assuming a 2-percentage point increase in the minimum Tier 1 and overall regulatory capital ratios to 6 and 10 percent, respectively, US banks will need to raise an estimated $247 billion in new common equity by 2015, slightly less than Europe at $273 billion and more than Japan at $156 billion.[100] A German banking association echoes these results, estimating the costs of Basel III for German banks at $135 billion. The head of Germany's supervisory authority has argued that Basel III hurts smaller and weaker banks that are harder-pressed to raise the capital required to comply with the new rules than large firms are.[101] But as discussed above, SIFIs subject to additional capital charges are hardly home free either.

A Third Way

Dodd–Frank can blunt the benefits of America's financial deregulation and liberalization in the past four decades. In crafting and applying the impending rules, regulators have a chance to avert such an outcome. Zealous oversight and capricious enforcement will entice US financial institutions to gaze offshore and dent New York's edge as the world's leading financial hub. Using their new powers judiciously, with the incentives and countermeasures of the regulated in mind, regulators can nurture transparent and vibrant US financial markets.

That will be politically difficult. The regulatory reform process has foolishly been cast as a battle of Main Street versus Wall Street. Not only is fashioning good policy difficult against a politically charged backdrop; a politicized process produces counterproductive regulations that will be resisted by the regulated and create heavy trade-offs. Dodd–Frank is no exception. Get-tough rules seldom work as intended. Sarbanes–Oxley, even if not without positive effects, illustrated the effects of a threat of heavy punishments: expensive reporting and new constraints on American corporations and competitiveness in the global economy.[102] Public policy will not necessarily be served by expanding the scope of legal obligations.

More fundamentally, conceptualizing regulations as a public–private dichotomy precludes opportunities to build on the public's and banks' common interest in a dynamic and solvent financial system. There are at least five policy areas where joint interests could be harnessed without distorting the economics of banking or making Washington captive to Wall Street.

First, regulators and financial institutions share an interest in assessing systemic risks. One such area of mutual interest is data on the on- and off-balance-sheet assets and liabilities of financial institutions. Such data would allow for measuring the leverage and liquidity in the banking system, and analyzing correlations of asset prices and sensitivity of bank portfolios to changes in economic conditions.[103] Banks and the public also share an interest in analyzing the burden imposed by the new regulations on the regulated and the economy. The financial sector is critical for US and global growth, and everyone wins if banks are innovative, well-capitalized, and self-sustaining. Similarly, banks and authorities have an interest in assessing the banking sectors' exposure to challenging economic and policy scenarios, from a hike in US interest rates to downgrades in global bond markets.

Yet America's oversight council, the Treasury's new Office of Financial Research, and the new European Systemic Risk Council are public bodies staffed by regulators. Anne Sibert of the London School of Economics proposes a useful hybrid organizational model: a five-member committee composed of a macroeconomist, microeconomist, financial engineer, research accountant, and practitioner.[104] Such a committee would be able to assess risks from distinct angles, and it would escape the problem of large and homogeneous committees—free riding, group-think, and reluctance to criticize co-members.

It could be particularly useful if shadowed by a "sounding board" group tasked to criticize, second-guess, comment on its analyses, and galvanize policy opinions about problems in the financial system.

Second, the government and financial sector should work together to fashion countercyclical strategies against crises. Basel III recognizes the problems of pro-cyclicality in Basel II. But the pro-cyclicality problem is far broader: firms' risk assessment and overall prudential regulation contribute to it.[105] Financial firms, fearful of getting burned, restrict credit, while regulators, worried about being criticized, clamp down on banks when banks least need it, contracting credit further. Even if banks were to blame, getting tough is a bad remedy when times turn sour. A good option amid crises, proposed by Alex Pollock, former CEO of Federal Home Loan Bank of Chicago, is to encourage the creation of new banks as lenders that are not hampered by past losses.[106]

Third, financial institutions and regulators can work jointly to manage crises. The resolution authority risks creating more problems than it solves: it practically guarantees that the management of an ailing financial institution will be ousted once the authority is invoked. That gives managers few incentives to prepare for a default and keeps them from voicing their private, superior knowledge of the workings of the ailing institution.[107] A few bankruptcy reforms for financial institutions to initiate voluntary bankruptcy proceedings could remedy the situation.

Living wills would do the job as well. A living will is a corporate estate plan that would preserve an ailing bank as a going concern and continue its financial infrastructure services—or in the case of a meltdown, resolve it in an orderly fashion. Dodd–Frank includes a living-will provision for systemically important institutions, which the FDIC and the Federal Reserve are to implement. Also, the G20 has called for all systemically important firms to draft a living will, and the UK has piloted the idea with several big banks. It is time to institutionalize it.

To be sure, banks are pushing back, but mainly because regulators are vested with powers to layer a bank with new capital and liquidity requirements should its living will prove subpar. Regulators must grasp that living wills are a waste of time and resources if banks are asked to imagine countless outlandish scenarios and draft responses to them. They will be a nonstarter if the data that banks supply are leaked. But if designed to respond to a handful of plausible problem scenarios, such as the failure of a major institution that a bank is intricately connected to, living wills would benefit banks and the public alike. Besides, even if unappealing to banks, the process of preparing living wills can have positive effects. Making banks collect standardized, regularly updated data on their operations, living wills help assess micro- and macro-prudential risks, and at least in theory curb moral hazard by making bankers to imagine failure and their creditors to picture loss. Banks too would benefit: by forcing a financial institution to prove it can fail without costing the public, living wills can mollify zealous regulators.

Another useful self-insurance tool for financial institutions is the contingent convertible bond (CoCo), debt that is converted into equity when regulators announce the presence of a systemic crisis and the bank's capital ratio falls under a predefined limit. A variant would be to require systemically important financial institutions to buy fully collateralized insurance policies from unlevered institutions, foreigners, or the government that can be tapped in the face of imminent failure.[108]

CoCos offer a faster and cheaper way to raise capital than issuing stock does, impose market discipline on banks, and provide regulators a sense of the market's appraisal of risks in the financial system.[109] And by calibrating the cost of insurance by the riskiness of banks and by making financial institutions place "skin in the game," they can reduce moral hazard. Leading policy makers and analysts, including Ben Bernanke and Canada's finance minister, Jim Flaherty, have applauded CoCos. They would be especially useful for banks designated as SIFIs for meeting the extra loss-absorbency cushion. Among others, Lloyds Banking Group, Rabobank Nederland, and Credit Suisse have all issued CoCos. The challenge is setting the trigger for conversion, as a conversion perceived negatively by the markets would produce a liquidity squeeze.[110]

Fourth, regulators and banks share an interest in improved corporate governance. Duly chastened, banks took early measures to self-regulate, including hiring risk managers in bulk and adopting the IIF's 2008 best practices on risk management, valuation, and ratings.[111] While Dodd–Frank pressures boards to implement one-size-fits-all governance reforms, financial firms and regulators need to bear in mind the different starting points of firms and to keep their eye on the ball: improve board oversight, foster integrity, and promote focus on long-term results.[112] Board oversight has to be independent and sturdier, CEOs need to be barred from chairing boards and become more engaged in risk management, and risk officers have to be elevated to the top of the organizational hierarchy. Public disclosure needs to be fuller in the shadow banking system—firms' off-balance-sheet contingent liabilities, including credit-default swaps and "structured investment vehicles," the defamed parking spot for mortgage-backed securities.

The Mortgage Issue

The US mortgage market escaped Dodd–Frank and lives as an elephant in Washington lawmakers' chambers. It is yet another arena where encouraging the private sector to play ball would produce sounder economic outcomes.

There is no good reason why universal home ownership should be prized if a mortgage drowns the presumed beneficiary in a sea of debt. There certainly is no good reason for a government policy that encourages the mass origination of mortgages that will default and place the US economy at risk. And there is no compelling rationale for government intervention in the mortgage business: it is not required to correct a market failure in the largest mortgage segment, prime middle-class loans. Some 85 percent of US homeowners would qualify for a prime loan, but private investment has been lacking in the sector because it has not been able to compete with the government-granted advantages and subsidies.[113] The system has persisted even though lower barriers to entry and strong competition would encourage innovation and lower costs.

Many policy makers agree on the need to reform America's mortgage regime. The policy challenge is getting over the hump—handling the $5 trillion in mortgage debts currently in Fannie and Freddie's books. Private buyers would not materialize for purchasing nonguaranteed, often junk-rated mortgages. Some 6 percent of Fannie and Freddie-backed mortgages are delinquent or in foreclosure. Another problem is handling the losses to Fannie and Freddie related to the financial crisis, estimated to cost taxpayers some $305 billion.[114] Moreover, government withdrawal could not be abrupt as that would increase mortgage rates and hurt the economic recovery. The transition will have to be gradual, and it will take years. Many officials and some investors such as Bill Gross, founder and co-chief investment officer of bond giant PIMCO, have argued that the $5 trillion should be folded in the federal budget.[115]

There are a number of more constructive options for transitioning to a private-sector-driven model. In a 2011 report, the departments of the Treasury and Housing and Urban Development offer a menu of options culminating in an unwinding of Fannie and Freddie. Main courses: increasing the guarantees that Fannie and Freddie charge in order to enable private guarantors to compete, requiring the mortgage giants to obtain more private capital to cover credit losses, and reducing the size of mortgages that qualify for their guarantees.

Georgetown professors Donald Marron and Philip Swagel take a slightly different tack. They propose converting Fannie and Freddie into agencies that package conforming loans into securities eligible for government backing.[116] As private firms would be able to compete by securitizing conforming loans and purchasing the government guarantee, the twins might eventually be driven out by competition.

Alex Pollock proposes perhaps the most politically feasible plan, a "Julius Caesar" strategy whereby Fannie and Freddie would be divided into three parts, with the first one composed of two liquidating trusts that will bear the twin's deadweight losses now borne by the taxpayers, the second made up of private prime mortgage loan securitization and investing businesses, and the third a government entity that provides some housing subsidies and financing of risky loans.[117]

Any unwinding of Fannie and Freddie would take at least half a decade. It is also politically elusive. Although the administration's plan notes that a transition would still allow for social programs to assist low-income borrowers who can pay their mortgages, various marriages of convenience resist change. For example, the Mortgage Bankers Association, the Financial Services Roundtable, the NAACP, and numerous liberal groups such as the Center for American Progress, among others, advocate retaining the federal government's role as the backstop for the mortgage industry. As a result, numerous members of Congress from both parties are hesitant to move on the issue—even if it is win–win for home buyers and taxpayers alike.

Sovereign Vestiges

The globalization of banking and crises alike has made internationally coordinated rule making increasingly important. Opening the Pandora's box of financial mercantilism, protectionism, and politically divisive arbitrage, the postcrisis reform spree has raised the premium of global regulatory coordination. In the wake of the crisis, Germany, France, China, Thailand, Korea, India, and others sensed an opportunity to dethrone the United States and UK as the world's premier financial centers and fashion new rules favorable to their domestic banks. Even if rather subdued, discord has been rampant.

UK and France have locked horns on regulations on hedge funds; transatlantic disagreements have flared over accounting standards and rules on hedge funds, derivatives, and registration of fund managers; and emerging markets, many with flimsy regulations, have resisted the politicized regulatory prescriptions drafted in Washington and Brussels.

The United States has sought to coordinate reforms both across the Atlantic and at the global level. Of the 47 action items on the agenda of the first-ever G20 Summit in November 2008 in Washington, 39 focused on financial regulation.[118] The G20 agreed to pursue common approaches on bankers' pay, systemically important hedge funds, credit rating agencies, tax havens and offshore banking, and processing of credit-default swaps through a regulated centralized counterparty.[119] At its London Summit in April 2009, the G20 also launched the Financial Stability Board as the new incarnation of the Financial Stability Forum (FSF). The Basel-based entity would serve as the coordinator of financial regulations and global standard setting, contingency planner against cross-border crises, and the IMF's partner in conducting early warning exercises on macroeconomic and financial risks, among many other duties.[120] The enterprise had ambition: Treasury Secretary Timothy Geithner envisioned the FSB as the "fourth pillar" of global economic governance, right alongside the IMF, World Bank, and the WTO.

Multispeed Regulatory World   Pledges to coordinate notwithstanding, national governments have remained firmly in the driver's seat, and meaningful coordination is proving difficult. The economic and legal starting points differ too much: the sophistication of regulations and the overall level of financial development of emerging and developing nations lag well behind those of the United States and Europe. In addition, in many emerging economies, finance is already quite tightly regulated, and there are often state-owned banks. In Asia, governments also had already fashioned extensive financial regulatory reforms in the wake of the 1997–1998 financial crisis. The region's various macro-prudential mechanisms, such as loan-to-value ratios, were sturdier at the time of the crisis than they were in the United States and Europe. That arguably shielded Asia from the gale of 2008–2009— and contributed to the region's disdain for revising its rules to match US and European regulations.

Political imperatives also pull countries away from the global table. Beholden to their respective taxpayers and industry lobbies, all countries want to hold on to the prerogative to set their own rules and proceed at their own pace. If Washington's reform politics took a year to align, Europe's legalistic multi-country reform process would last even longer, and is at the time of writing still in progress. Emerging nations such as China and India are jealous of their rule-making powers and want to steer clear of US and European politicized regulatory zeal. If the United States was the twentieth-century wayfarer in reforming financial regulations, its new regulations have less global appeal. The French think Dodd–Frank is too lenient; the Indians see it as too large and complex.

Emerging nations have all the fewer reasons to play along because their banks scored relative gains in the crisis: the share of emerging markets of the total market capitalization of the world's 100 largest banks soared from less than 5 percent in 2004 to above 30 percent in 2010.[121] At the same time, the share of US banks of the global banking pie shrank from more than 50 percent to less than 30 percent, and the share of European banks dropped near 20 percent. China led the emerging-market pack after the initial public offerings of its banks in 2005–2006, with its largely state-owned banks ascending to the pinnacle of global banking after US conglomerates crumbled.[122]

Regulatory coordination is also stifled by the intensifying competition among advanced and emerging nations for a position as global financial centers. In Europe, Paris and Frankfurt vie to unseat London as the continent's financial hub; in Asia, the legendary Hong Kong, the vibrant Singapore, and the aspirant Shanghai, Seoul, and Bangkok elbow for an advantage and dream of dethroning New York. Mumbai is staging an offensive from India, and Chinese cities Shanghai, Beijing, Shenzhen, Guangzhou, and Zhuhai are all working to growing into financial centers.[123] In the race are also some more established centers such as Chicago, Tokyo, Zurich, Geneva, Toronto, Milan, Sydney, and Dubai.

Shifts are unfolding. Although New York, London, Hong Kong, and Singapore are still the world's financial strongholds, holding 79 percent of global equity trading, emerging-market hubs are squeezing especially European financial hubs. Beijing, Seoul, Shenzhen, Shanghai, Mumbai, and Dubai have improved their global competitiveness strongly since 2007, largely at the expense of Frankfurt, Paris, Madrid, Milan, and Amsterdam.[124] The change reflects an ages-old theory and practice: the main determinant of financial kingship is proximity to centers of economic activity.[125]

With manifold economic and political obstacles to coordination, the G20 has backtracked from many of its prior commitments. Basel III survived the wreckage because common capital standards already existed, because some nations like China already apply capital ratios well above those of Basel III, and because implementation was left to the participating governments. With other issues taking the center stage on the G20 agenda, the arcane financial regulatory issues will be left to the Basel-based talk shops.

De-Globalizing Finance?

Differences in national regulations are not necessarily negative. Global finance has soared in the past two decades even in the presence of distinct rules, and countries have not waged wars over financial arbitrage. Completely harmonizing financial regulations would be enormously time-consuming and futile, resulting in watered down rules ineffective and ill-suited for countries' idiosyncratic purposes. It certainly would not fly in or be good for America. In the world of finance, one size does not fit all. Allowing for distinct regulatory models could even lead to the discovery of better practices. And in some areas, the breakdown of international coordination can be welcome. One example is the European and US effort to impose a global bank tax, which died in the G20 Toronto Summit in the face of opposition from countries that did not have a banking crisis—host nation Canada, Australia, and most emerging nations.

However, it is also the case that markets are more global than ever before, volatility persists, rules are in flux, and new players with their idiosyncratic and immature rules, especially from Asia, are entering the fray.[126] The bite of any country's rules is blunted by the fact that while rules are national, finance is global. Suspect decisions in one part of the world will have repercussions in others just as quickly as instruments issued in a bank in Hong Kong find their way to counterparts in New York and Frankfurt. Actions in one country can drain the flow of money to others: even if Washington and Brussels agreed on a universal approach to regulating derivatives, laxer rules in, say, Singapore or Seoul could result in global regulatory arbitrage, as traders switch to more convenient Asian venues. Coordination in such key areas as derivatives is firmly in US interests. Three scenarios would arise in its absence.

Regulatory fragmentation. The first scenario is uncoordinated re-regulation of finance. With all countries fashioning their own rules and financial nationalism raising its head, differences are bound to be several and great. Even if mercantilism was subdued, the ensuing regulatory fragmentation could increase the compliance costs of doing global business and hold back the potential of global capital markets. Take the over-the-counter derivatives market. Differences in supervision and clearance of derivatives would quickly fragment the $605-trillion derivatives market along geographical or currency lines. Europe's planned regulations for derivatives clearing clash in many areas with the new US law, and Asians remain undecided on ways to handle clearing and trade reporting, as many regional banks carry out the trades in Europe or the United States. Similarly, differences in accounting standards create another cost center for global companies.

Fortress Europe. The second scenario is a discriminatory world of renationalized banking systems, with favoritism to locals over foreigners. Protectionist impulses have set in on numerous occasions, particularly in Europe. In March 2010 the European Commission issued plans to force EU-based private equity and hedge funds to use only locally based banks as custodians and depositaries, and make non-EU funds comply with the new rules if they wish to market themselves in the EU. The rule was contested by the US Treasury as discriminatory against US groups, and such concerns persist among American fund managers.[127] In addition, the commission proposed rules for all investment fund managers, even if operating outside Europe, to register there—meaning they would have to establish a physical presence on the continent, a costly enterprise for outsiders.[128] Europe also unveiled ambitious proposals to crack down on derivatives trading to end what EU Commissioner Michel Barnier, in charge of financial regulatory issues, has called "Wild West territory." One of the plans is to prohibit those investors from speculative trading of credit-default swaps who do not own the underlying debt of the country in question.[129] Even if Europeans converged to a reasonable set of rules, it is not difficult to imagine how the growing competitive pressures from foreign institutions and financial hubs, especially now that European banks and financial markets are in disarray, would result in demands for protectionism and favoritism.

Arbitraging Asia. The third scenario is one of intensifying competition among financial centers that results in all-out financial arbitrage, or "regulatory dumping." Such a regulatory race to the bottom could result, for example, from the aspiring Asian financial centers' application of laxer rules, enforcement, and supervisory standards than are being applied by the United States or Europe in order to woo financial firms and their clients. Facing stiffer global competition and having a greater number of vibrant financial venues to choose from, global banks and businesses are increasingly factoring financial regulations into their decisions. However, it is also the case that cutting corners is not a way to victory for any nation: companies are first and foremost interested in venues that offer clear and stable rules and good macroeconomic conditions. Also, tax evasion and off-shore activities of companies are increasingly scrutinized at the international level, leaving governments fewer tools to attract companies. Besides, governments themselves will, as a result of the Asian financial crisis and the latest Great Crisis, disfavor loose rules. The Asian financial crisis, after all, was in part caused by poor regulation of Asia's newly licensed banks. Competition among governments may take the form of a race to the top, not to the bottom.

What are implications of these scenarios for the United States? The fragmentation scenario can be neutral (if differences in rules are not economically significant) or negative (if they are), but the discriminatory scenario will never work for the better: it is a world that deprives US financial institutions of opportunities and denies the potential of globalized financial markets to produce wealth. Competition among financial hubs can raise all boats and benefit US companies and American financial centers. But if devolving into a regulatory race to the bottom, it could run counter to US interests. Each scenario can invite political conflict.

The Comeback of Capital Controls   As worrisome as regulatory fragmentation is the resurgence of capital controls across the emerging world. Emerging markets, particularly those in Latin America that had traveled the rocky road of debt crisis in the early 1980s, adopted the tenets of Washington Consensus in the late 1980s and sharply relaxed capital controls in the 1990s. Emerging East Asian nations also became forceful advocates of liberalization. Although there were numerous episodes of backsliding in the 1990s and 2000s from Russia to Brazil to India and emerging East Asia, most emerging countries had liberalized capital accounts at the dawn of the twenty-first century. This is for a good reason: freeing capital flows gives a higher rate of return on people's savings in advanced countries and reduces the cost of capital, increases growth, spurs employment, and increases incomes in developing ones.[130] The resulting financial integration aids the transfer of technological and managerial know-how and propels competition in domestic financial markets.

But shielding against "hot money" from abroad is becoming fashionable among Asian and Latin American emerging nations worried about credit bubbles and currency appreciation now that low interest rates in the advanced economies are pushing capital outward. The IMF has broken with its uniform rejection of capital controls, with a few staff papers issued in 2011 proposing a set of criteria when controls could be permitted. The US Treasury is also said to be reexamining its long-standing stance against controls. However, the IMF's cautious nod was not well founded, based on the latest crisis episode and a handful of Baltic nations. The fact remains: the trade-offs of capital controls outweigh their presumed benefits, for at least five reasons.

First, capital controls obstruct trade. An open trade regime generally requires an open financial regime because exporters and importers need access to international financial markets. By the end of the twentieth century, three-quarters of countries that had liberalized trade had also liberalized financial flows.[131] The growth in intra-regional trade was a key reason for Europeans to dismantle capital controls in the 1980s.

Second, in practice it is hard to distinguish between "hot" portfolio flows and more stable foreign direct investment because operating companies (such as GE Capital) can serve as conduits for large flows to unrelated companies and because foreign subsidiaries can buy and sell portfolio instruments. Rigid controls on portfolio finance can curtail FDI, narrowing a proven channel for technology transfer. Granted, there are by now some 5,900 international investment agreements such as bilateral investment treaties and double taxation treaties—such deals were signed at a rate of four per week in 2009—that provide legal certainty to cross-border investments. But more than one-half of OECD members have lists of sectors closed to foreign investment, many with elusive connections to national security, and the share of national regulatory changes that restrict, not liberalize, FDI has steadily climbed to a third of the total reforms in 2010 from a mere 2 percent in 2000 and 20 percent in 2006.[132] Barriers to investment all too easily ricochet around the world in the form of retaliatory barriers. Their effect would only be compounded by capital controls.

Third, research finds no clear relationship between capital controls and success at avoiding contagion and crisis. During the 1970s and 1980s economic duress, Latin America was unable to contain capital outflows despite pervasive controls. Brazilian controls in the 1990s were largely ineffective. In more complex financial markets, investors are quite able to circumvent capital controls.

Further leakage comes from the corruption that capital controls are found to breed among their enforcers. In the meantime, some African countries have enjoyed only minimal inflows despite the absence of restrictions on capital.

Fourth, advocates of capital controls argue that controls further stability, which, in turn, translates into superior economic growth. But the translation mechanism is not proven. Compare Thailand, a liberalized economy that has gone through the roller coaster of booms and busts, with India, the nonliberalized economy that has been on something resembling a steady train ride. India's GDP per capita grew by 99 percent between 1980 and 2001, but Thailand's grew by 148 percent—despite the 1997–1998 Asian financial crisis that originated in Bangkok.

Fifth, at the global level, one country's controls are another country's headache. Blocked from one market, money will find its way to the next. Worse, the prevalent use of controls in nations with current-account surpluses and undervalued exchange rates, such as China, will only exacerbate global imbalances, generating worldwide pressures for trade protectionism. Even the more enthusiastic IMF researchers, and certainly its board, recognize these challenges.

The first-best policies to weather volatility and translate the benefits of financial flows to real economic development are macroeconomic tightening— something emerging markets now avoid because of concerns about lackluster growth in the advanced economies—and good macroeconomic management and better supervised and regulated financial markets. The benefits of capital-account liberalization have been greatest in advanced countries, which not only have the most open capital accounts but also the strongest institutions. Emerging markets need more rather than less financial integration, but they also need to do their homework on managing money. Relying on hard capital controls can discourage macro tightening and domestic reform.

The problem is that the horse is out of the barn: a number of emerging nations have already imposed capital controls, and the odds of some kind of binding framework on when controls can and cannot be used are slim: many emerging economies have rejected the IMF's proposed guidelines on permitted controls (which implicitly bar the controls not on the list). And even if adopted, a framework would be ineffective unless married with an enforcement mechanism akin to the WTO's dispute-settlement mechanism, whereby aggrieved parties could challenge wrongdoers. The use of controls is unlikely to dissipate, and it can entail more volatility than it is meant to stem.

A World Free of Friction

Capital controls aside, could the global regulatory overhaul bring about seamless global integration and amicable regional division of labor among financial centers? After all, a variant of this model has been in place for three decades: London, New York, and Tokyo as supercenters, with tremendous scale advantages in foreign exchange, international bonds, and depth of capital markets, and a rise of an increasing number of smaller regional financial centers across Asia-Pacific, from Sydney to Singapore and now also Seoul.

Centralization is theorized to result from the tendency of "clustering" of financial services in single locations for economies of scope. Meanwhile, decentralization is thought to be caused by the demand for brokers between the centralized services and businesses in the "hinterlands" in the global financial value chain.[133] For example, Singapore and Hong Kong have developed specialized knowledge of Chinese businesses in both mainland China and throughout Southeast Asia that New York and Tokyo can tap. Regional centers have also benefited as outsourcers of low-value-added services. Communications technologies have aided the process.

But geographic economies of scale and scope are becoming obsolete with instant communications. Financial institutions are indifferent to time and place, as are many of their clients. Division of labor between financial centers is unlikely in a world where business is global and under serious cost pressures, aiming at the best service for the lowest cost. Gone are the days where companies would want to issue IPOs in their region of origin or want to bank in the same time zone as the corporate headquarters. Instead of physical environments, banks and businesses are more interested in regulations and institutions. Regulating a regional division of labor would be foolish and practically impossible.

At the end of the day, the effects of the regulatory reform on the United States will depend on the United States itself—the way in which Dodd–Frank ends up being implemented and how financial services are treated overall. In enforcing the new rules at home, Washington regulators must be mindful of the world beyond US shores. But work also needs to be done abroad. The best outcome would be a frictionless global financial market and competition among institutions and financial centers. However, this will require coordination. What needs to be done?

A Hollow Center

The costs of a collision between global finance and national rules do not need to be, but can be, very high. However, the tools to avoid it are hollow.

In 2009 the Treasury began sponsoring the FSB a means to propel a global regulatory "race to the top."[134] Whereas in the past the United States had been lukewarm about the FSF, the American intent now was to reduce the odds of systemic crises and ensure a level playing field for US banks. After all, nearly a quarter of American banking revenues come from outside the United States, more than for Japan or for Western European nations.[135] Regulatory coordination would be needed, it was thought, as regulations were in flux in Europe, an important region for American banks, and as Asian nations, many with incomplete financial regulatory regimes, were vying to become global financial hubs.

Before the FSB was launched, Berkeley's Barry Eichengreen proposed a World Financial Organization as the financial equivalent to the World Trade Organization, a body with binding rules and credible dispute settlement and enforcement.[136] However, the WTO is hard to replicate in the world of finance because the properties of finance and trade are distinct. Finance changes fast, uncertainties abound, and flexibility to adjust quickly is required in lieu of rigid binding rules; trade is about locking in practices and leveling the playing field among 150-plus members, and gradually achieving deeper liberalization together. Finance is like an obstacle course charted by individual nations, trade a marathon run by a team. Financial regulations also go to the heart of national governments' fiscal and regulatory prerogatives; trade policy, at least the at-the-border reductions in trade barriers, is less so. There is a reason why trade rules on areas affecting domestic regulations, like government procurement and competition policy, have not prospered at the global level.

Most difficult, the theoretical underpinnings of financial activities that should be permissible and those that should not are not as cut-and-dried as they are in trade. Even in trade policy, the effects of so-called "behind-the-border" activities such as subsidies are much more difficult to judge than those of tariffs. Besides, much of financial regulations, unlike trade policy, deals with extreme events, which are not only hard to forecast but whose effects are nearly impossible to analyze. As such, financial matters often end up being considered on a case-by-case, country-by-country basis. A further problem in building a coherent theory of regulatory practice is the potential scale of the losses associated with extreme events.

In its November 2011 Summit in Cannes, the G20 agreed to give the FSB formal legal status and greater resources. Granted, in principle the idea of a technocratic shepherd is very sound in a setting where 20-plus countries seek to coordinate their most jealously guarded policies. Stéphane Rottier of the National Bank of Belgium and Nicolas Véron of the Bruegel Institute show that the G20's proposed common regulatory principles that the group has delegated to international organizations to manage—the IMF and the specialized bodies under the FSB umbrella, the Basel Committee on Banking Supervision, the International Organization of Securities Commissions (IOSCO), and the International Accounting Standards Board (IASB)—have fared much better than the rules that governments have decided to negotiate with one another outside an institutional setting. Of course, this may mean that governments delegated the easiest rules to international bodies. But more likely, it speaks to the difficulties in meshing different country positions.

Rottier and Véron's analysis shows that the success of the FSB has been superior to that of the intergovernmental processes but lagged far behind that of the IMF and the older institutions. This is no surprise. The FSB reflects the supremacy of national regulators. Made up of national governments and coordinating standard setters such as the Basel Committee on Banking Supervision and the International Accounting Standards Board and housing a lean staff, the FSB has scant independent analytical capacity or political heft. The staff can be built up, but the FSB would still face the problem of all clearinghouses: members will unlikely share with it anything they would not share with one another, let alone take on binding rules. The FSF knew that and preempted itself. For instance, its April 2009 principles for cross-border cooperation on crisis management ran a total of two pages of suggestions for voluntary cooperation, largely information sharing.[137] With a larger and more diverse membership and a plethora of demands, can the FSB be any different from the FSF?

It will not be and does not have to be a super-regulator. Besides, an FSB with supra-national powers is unfeasible and not in America's interests. Instead, the FSB should become a reliable analytical air traffic controller among global regulatory agencies and governments. Besides coordinating rules and proposals, it has a huge niche to fill in the monitoring of the global financial system and regulatory frictions. Governments are perennially hungry for impartial technical information for holding civilized conversations about vexing issues. All countries would benefit from an FSB that had analytical horsepower and staff resources for monitoring national rules and best practices, vigorously assessing their implementation and economic impact, and proposing improvements.

The FSB's new peer review mechanism is one answer; its Implementation Monitoring Network (IMN), made up of experts and international organizations, including the IMF, is another. Because the IMF also has financial monitoring and surveillance functions, the two institutions need to build on their respective comparative advantages and mutual complementarities. The FSB's advantages are regulations as well as linkages between the financial sector, real economy, and cross-border matters; the IMF's advantages are surveillance of macro-financial issues and the global monetary system.

Peer reviews offer one opportunity. The FSB's reviews will need to be sequenced not to coincide with the IMF's Financial Sector Assessment Program (FSAP) studies, which are issued every five years per each member country. Of course, the FSB covers a narrower set of countries than the Fund does and usefully focuses on inherently systemically important nations. The FSB should work to make systematic comparisons between national regulations spillovers of one country's rules to others. It should also seek to streamline these findings to its other lines of work, something that has been the challenge for the FSAP in the past at the IMF.[138] The FSB's thematic reviews of such issues as executive compensation or bank resolution practices should be integrated in the IMF's national and global surveillance.

The FSB's (and IMF's) analytical work is worthy, and it gives Washington a useful bird's-eye perspective on regulatory policies and practices around the world. The challenge is taking action on the information. The FSB's studies should be candid about any unfair or risky rules and practices of the members and flag particular regulatory weaknesses. The membership should provide technical assistance for regulatory reforms where needed. Much harder is to craft mechanisms for taking effective action against destabilizing practices and noncompliance with common principles. For now, the main task is to pave the way for agreements in principles on areas that are key for financial globalization and stability. What should be on Washington's global regulatory agenda?

The Pending Agenda

Washington's international regulatory agenda needs to center on ensuring open capital markets, improving information, and preparing better for the worst. The priorities should include Basel III and its implementation, derivatives clearing, converging accounting and auditing rules, and, importantly, coordinating approaches to the failures of multinational banks, something that epitomizes the unhealthy discord between rules that are national and banking that is global.

The supervision of derivatives trading needs to be better coordinated. At the minimum, US supervisors should have information held by other nations' supervisors and vice versa so that everyone can be better able to assess systemic risks. Integrating clearance is politically very complicated, not only because of different standards and Europe's more heavy-handed reporting requirements of derivatives trades, but also because of money—apportioning national responsibilities in the event that the central counterparties fail.

Accounting and auditing standards need to be more integrated for US investors to have access to good and comparable financial reporting on firms around the world, and for all parts of US financial institutions with subsidiaries abroad to be assessed by the same standard. The main blueprints are US Generally Acceptable Accounting Principles (GAAP) and International Financial Reporting Standards (IFRS), used in Europe and applied in most countries. The two sides seeking to find common ground—the US Financial Accounting Standards Board and the International Accounting Standards Board—have been unable to resolve differences by deadlines. New York Mayor Michael Bloomberg has long argued the United States should recognize the IFRS without requiring foreign companies listing in the United States to report by GAAP.[139] The proposal would be good for New York and America as the world's financial hub. Common accounting rules are also critical for defining capital in calculating Basel III capital standards.

Auditing firms are still regulated at the national level, even though the firms they audit are global. Better coordination of auditing would help make auditing firms more streamlined, and lower auditing costs to globally operating US companies. American firms should also have an interest in being assessed by similar standards as their peers, and US investors would have access to comparable evaluations of US and non-US firms. Sarbanes–Oxley took a step in that direction, seeking to grant US auditors an extraterritorial mandate, but other nations resisted. More recently, negotiations between US and Chinese regulators toward a bilateral agreement on cross-border auditing regulations have been delayed, reportedly because the US insisted on supervising US-listed Chinese companies. The main coordinator, the International Forum of Independent Audit Regulators (IFIAR), created after Enron's collapse, does not even have a secretariat.

Still another and a particularly important area in the world of globalized banking is to craft common principles for resolving failing multinational banks. Done right, such coordination is in America's interest. How to accomplish it?

Funeral Expenses

Bank of England Governor Mervyn King's quip "banks are global in life but national in death" has become a cliché. Banking is global; bank resolution rules are not. Although cross-border banks hold 75 percent of European continental banking assets, the EU is only now defining common bank-unwinding procedures.[140]

In the Great Crisis, countries acted in an uncoordinated, ad hoc fashion in recapitalizing banks with public funds, expanding lender of last resort facilities, and protecting creditors and depositors. Common responses to failures—such as those of UK's Northern Rock in 2006 and Belgian–Dutch consortium Fortis in 2008—were improvised at best. In the Fortis case, for instance, friendly neighbors Belgium, Luxembourg, and the Netherlands did aspire to manage the debacle together, but cooperation collapsed as each national supervisor saw the situation differently. Markets and depositors lost confidence, and Fortis's operations were split along national lines.

What exactly happens when a bank fails? The host country regulator starts a cumbersome process of extracting supervisory, regulatory, and enforcement information from the home country regulators. The dance among regulators gets complex quickly. Sorting out the assets of modern financial entities—sprawls of interconnected branches and subsidiaries dispersed across countries—is hugely complicated. Before its fall, the Lehman Brothers alone consisted of 2,985 legal entities operating in 50 countries. Financial conglomerates that combine banking, securities, and insurance activities, such as Allianz in Germany, ING and Fortis in the Netherlands, Credit Suisse in Switzerland, and America's Citigroup, are particularly thorny, as countries tend to have separate regulators for each area.

The main problem is power and money. Tensions rise when host nation authorities, pressured to protect domestic depositors and taxpayers, collide with foreign shareholders and depositors. With regulators passing the buck, confidence in the troubled bank erodes, practically guaranteeing its disorderly, costly, and politicized failure. In the event of a bank failure, the host nation might end up discriminating against the foreign bank's clients in favor of the domestic ones. Not inconceivable, countries can be enticed to seal themselves off from cross-border finance to shield their taxpayers from the failures of foreign banks.

Many countries are too small to unwind their global banks alone. The case of Iceland is as emblematic as it is infamous. In the years leading up to the crisis, the country's leading banks, Kaupthing, Glitnir, and Landsbanki, joined the ranks of the world's fastest-growing financial institutions.[141] The exuberance ended in October 2008, when all three banks fell within a week. The wreckage was spectacular: the assets of the three banks ran at more than ten times Icelandic GDP, and their foreign clients numbered more than Iceland's population. In expanding, the Icelandic conglomerate banks had simply outpaced the country's supervisors, becoming too big to save and inflicting multiple nations. But larger economies are also exposed: a good dozen banks in Europe that are relatively larger than Bank of America have assets greater than 15 percent of the GDPs of their home nations.

Chaotic bank failures risk contagion among interlinked banks—and tempt barriers against foreign banks that would jeopardize the benefits of globalized banking. Yet success is possible: as Dexia became troubled in October 2008, Belgium, France, and Luxembourg concluded an agreement on a joint guarantee mechanism to improve Dexia's access to financing.[142] Of the total, 60.5 percent was covered by Belgium, 36.5 percent by France, and 3 percent by Luxembourg, burdens proportional to the ownership by institutional investors and public authorities in the three countries.

Failing Well   Absent common rules, national authorities continue vying to maximize the interests of national stakeholders, small fires can flare into bonfires, everyone with accounts in foreign banks faces the fate of foreign account holders in Iceland, and protectionism looms. Such outcomes are not in America's interests—fluid cross-border operations are. What needs to be done?

There are worse and better options. Ideas to ring-fence banks into national companies or axing them into "small-enough-to-fail" entities are bad.[143] Neither can be implemented internationally; both would increase risk taking and the cost of credit, just like Glass–Steagall did in America. Candidate banks would doubtless resist them. Ideas for a common unwinding fund, a supra-national agency to scrutinize the major international banks, or detailed burden-sharing rules would face taxpayer resistance, be prone to moral hazard, and take years to negotiate.[144]

An innovative option would be a "debtor selection system" proposed by Peter Wallison, whereby each financial institution would select the national insolvency system under which it would be resolved in the event of a bankruptcy.[145] As such, no country would have to change its insolvency laws, but all countries become encouraged to adopt insolvency rules attractive to both debtors and creditors, and have efficient court systems. Such a rule would also absolve authorities of the need to privilege either debtors or creditors.

The FSB's proposed resolution regime is to go into effect in 2013. It calls for global standards and institution-specific cooperation agreements by which all regulators would have to comply in the event of the failure of a large systemic bank. The FSB has also devised a tool kit of procedures tailored for different circumstances.

The FSB's proposal is perhaps politically the most feasible one. Its premise is right: the harmonization of national rules is also unfeasible and unnecessary; what is needed is better coordination. In the short run, low-hanging fruit like mutual recognition can be picked in such areas as through intra-group transfers of assets from an ailing arm to a healthy one, a measure that would protect taxpayers without hurting shareholders and creditors. Living wills of multinational banks also need to consider precisely such intra-group measures when crises hit.

Beyond Basel

Forging globally accepted principles and processes may require governance reforms at the FSB. The institution lacks cachet with emerging nations, particularly China, which sees it much like it sees other global governance institutions, a Western-dominated construct. While each country has one vote, the United States and Europe dominate the FSB's working committees.

Emerging economies are also rather poorly represented in related institutions, the Bank for International Settlements (BIS) and the IASB. But, much like in other areas of global governance, emerging nations must be ready to abide by common rules of the game as a quid pro quo for a greater say.

The FSB is only one tool to drive US interests, for two reasons. First, relying on the FSB would be regulatory myopia, only at the global level. Regulatory coordination has to be complemented with credible warnings about financial instability; part of the task can be passed to the IMF. Second, the FSB has no powers to punish countries that discriminate against US interests. Bilateral and regional agreements are required. Transatlantic coordination, formal and informal, is already strong and needs to be extended: the transatlantic arena is still home to most US overseas bank activity, and Europeans share US interests in transparency and good regulations in emerging markets. Transatlantic cooperation is inherently required for global coordination in such areas as accounting rules. In Asia, Washington needs to further regulatory coordination by working both through regional mechanisms and bilateral negotiations.

Conclusion

Starting in the 1970s, regulations in America and across the developed world were revised to enable financial markets to grow, globalize, and generate wealth. The trouble in the integrating world was frequent volatility. As the Great Crisis unfolded, financial regulations were presumed guilty as charged and subjected to a historic overhaul. The technocratic aim for improved oversight and transparency is of course sound. But the supposed remedy, the Dodd–Frank Act, is flawed—and mostly so because of its ulterior political motives to shift blame from Washington to Wall Street. Its makers vilified risk taking, though that is the essence of capitalism and impetus for innovation. Many of the law's purported remedies, such as the consumer protection agency and the oversight council, are good politics—grand and visible organizational innovations that are easy to explain to the public—but that ultimately can produce bad economics that create perverse incentives and can make America worse off.

There is an opportunity to avoid such an outcome. The impact of the new rules will depend on their implementation and Washington's wielding of regulatory authority. Regulators need to prioritize strong analysis and management of systemic risks over zealous regulations and politicized attempts to reengineer banks. Adaptability is of essence: new rules are untested, and America and other nations must be prepared to change course if and when they backfire, such as hurting small businesses, as is already the case. At the global level, regulatory coordination should not be pursued as an end in itself, but as a means to preempt discrimination against US interests and to foster multinational responses to global crises. The unwavering aim must be free and globalized financial markets.

The process can also be better. In the wake of the crisis, the antagonism between the public and financial institutions has been inevitable. But insulating policy makers is impossible and impractical: Washington needs Wall Street for a front-row view of the markets and for implementing the new rules. There are also several areas of shared interests that should be tapped, including risk assessment and management. The test for the regulators is to see that their regulated have incentives to play along.

4 Endangered Reign?

Dollar's Dilemma

Geopolitical power depends on financial power, each of which supports the other. To ignore the real benefits of controlling the international currency system is [unfortunate]. . . . The death of the dollar order will drastically increase the price of the American dream while simultaneously shattering American global influence.

—*Historian Diane B. Kunz,* Foreign Affairs, *1995*

CREATING A SUDDEN SENSE OF GLOOM ABOUT THE FUTURE of the US economy, the Great Crisis triggered widespread doubts about the future of the US dollar as the world's reserve currency. Days before the April 2009 G20 Summit, in London, China's central bank governor, Zhou Xiaochuan, slighted Washington, arguing that financial crises resulted from a clash between the domestic imperatives of the country issuing a reserve currency and international needs for stability. Zhou called for a super-sovereign reserve currency managed by a global institution, a reference to the International Monetary Fund's special drawing rights (SDRs).

Since then, the dollar has been fair game in world affairs. Countless analysts have argued that the United States is in a net debtor position similar to Britain after World War I, a declining nation soon to lose its standing as the issuer of the reserve currency.[1] Sensing an opportunity to openly criticize the United States, Russian President Dmitry Medvedev argued that a mix of regional currencies, including the ruble, would be required to help steady the world economy. The IMF was also enthused, with the First Deputy Managing Director John Lipsky arguing that SDRs could be used as the basis for a "revolutionary" step of creating a new global reserve currency that would gradually replace the dollar.[2] Also, the euro was raised as a currency contender. Among others, World Bank President Robert Zoellick argued that if the dollar weakens in the face of US budget deficits, the euro might be a "respectable alternative."[3] If deciding to convert its dollar holdings into the euro, China could emerge as the power broker between the two leading currencies.

The dollar's resilience has been questioned on several occasions since the 1940s, when it unseated the sterling as the leading global currency. Yet the greenback has always rebounded in a reflection of America's continued prominence in the world economy, the liquidity and stability of US financial markets, and the scale benefits that the dollar provides its users in global transactions. But the dollar's central role has been a mixed blessing for the United States. Issuing the global reserve currency allows Americans to borrow at low cost and escape balance-of-payments shortfalls, but it also practically guarantees that the United States will run steep trade deficits, which could ultimately undermine confidence in the dollar. The world's growing demand for fresh resources and America's gaping fiscal deficit amplify the dilemma.

A co-currency of some kind would ease America's burdens. But no other currency enjoys the economic prowess and financial market liquidity that underpin the US dollar. The alternatives—the SDR, the yen, the sterling, the RMB, and even the most viable one, the euro—are poor. That the dollar remains the principal reserve currency reflects this fact. Are the dollar doubts blown out of proportion? And how to ensure a global currency order that will buttress American and global growth and stability in the coming decades?

Global Public Good

The dollar's prominence is indisputable. It is employed in nine of every ten transactions, makes up over 60 percent of global reserves, and serves as a currency peg for 89 nations and as a reference for the managed floats of 8 nations.[4] In contrast, a quarter of global reserves are in euros, and slightly less than 5 percent are in each of the two other stalwart currencies, the yen and the pound; the small remaining share is divided among the Hong Kong dollar, the New Zealand dollar, the Swiss franc, the Norwegian krone, the Australian dollar, the Swedish krona, the Polish zloty, the Chinese RMB, and the Indian rupee. The dollar turnover makes up 85 percent of the global foreign-exchange market turnover, well above that of the runner-up, the euro (19 percent).[5]

Global debt markets primarily run on the dollar. According to Linda Goldberg of the New York Federal Reserve, 39 percent of all debt securities issued anywhere in the world are denominated in dollars, about the same as 42 percent in 1999, and above 32 percent for euro-denominated issues.[6] The dollar is especially prominent among issuers in the Middle East, Latin America, and Asia-Pacific, while issuers in new EU member states, Scandinavian countries, the UK, and Africa tend to split evenly between dollar- and euro-denominated bonds. And great amounts of dollars are also held in cash overseas: almost 60 percent of 20- and 50-dollar notes and more than 70 percent of 100-dollar notes are abroad.[7]

The dollar dethroned the previous currency hegemon, the British pound, in 1945. A number of reasons prompted the switch. The first and perhaps most important one was America's liquid and sophisticated financial markets. In the 1940s New York offered a wide range of financial facilities for short-term investments of reserve funds and for large purchases and sales of liquid financial assets.[8] The dollar was gradually adopted as the global vehicle currency for interbank transactions, and the 1945 Bretton Woods agreement sealed its primacy. Every country pegged to the dollar, and the United States tied the dollar's value to gold.

The second key reason for the global switch to the dollar was the size of the US economy, the world's largest since 1872. Economic prowess undergirds currency dominance. Barry Eichengreen and Jeffrey Frankel have found that a rise of 1 percentage point in the currency country's share of world economic output is associated with a 1.33-percentage-point rise in that currency's share of central bank reserves around the world.[9] Third, US weight in global commerce also boosted the dollar: the United States had emerged as the largest exporter in 1915, and the dollar's use in world trade and finance surged further with America's postwar export boom.[10] By the time of the Bretton Woods conferences, the United States produced half of the world's manufactured goods and held half of its reserves.

Nations around the world benefit from a single, dominant currency. For one, the dollar provides network benefits: the more it is used in global transactions, the greater the benefits of using it. The dollar is much like the English language: because just about everyone uses English in international business, there are much greater benefits to speaking it as opposed to, say, Hungarian.

Second, the dollar economizes transacting. Were foreign-exchange dealers trying to trade across each pair of currencies—Swedish krone against Australian dollar, Korean won against Japanese yen, and so forth—they would in a world of 150 currencies have to operate a total of 11,175 bilateral relationships.[11] Setting up a foreign-exchange trading desk for every currency would be costly, so banks choose to employ one vehicle currency and trade and exchange against it.

Third, the greenback helps ensure global financial stability. Providing for liquid debt markets and being backed by the Federal Reserve, it enables central banks to intervene in foreign-exchange markets to smooth out fluctuations in currency values. For countries with frequent economic instability, the dollar has served as a substitute for transactions in domestic currency. European nations grappling with hyperinflation in the 1920s used the dollar, as did Latin American nations amid the 1980s debt crisis and the former Soviet Republics upon the collapse of communism.[12] Seven countries have either implemented a currency board pegged to the dollar or permanently dollarized their economies in order to escape exchange risk.[13]

The Privileged Debtor

Issuing the global reserve currency provides the United States a number of benefits that other nations do not obtain. First, it allows Americans to borrow at low cost. Foreign residents hold US currency in large quantities that Americans can borrow. With the dollar so widely held and demanded globally, Treasury yields are low, and the United States gets a "liquidity discount"— it is better able to finance larger deficits for longer and at lower interest rates than other nations. At 25–60 basis points, the discount is estimated to amount to some $90 billion in annual savings.[14]

Second, except for the Europeans, other countries cannot lend to the United States in their own currencies. The foreign-exchange risk is thus borne by the creditor countries, a setting that the French Finance Minister and Premier of the 1960s, Valéry Giscard d'Estaing, famously called America's "exorbitant privilege." Indeed, the United States is still the only nation that can go deeply into debt to the rest of the world in its own currency. Borrowing in dollars gives the United States a capital gain when the dollar depreciates; in 2002–2007, the net capital gain was more than $1 trillion.[15]

Contrast that to being on the opposite side and in dire straits. An extreme example is Argentina at the turn of the millennium. Unable to issue debt in its own currency, the Argentine government pegged its peso to the dollar and issued billions of dollars of debt. As the economy deteriorated as a result of poor fiscal and economic management, Argentina quit the currency board, investors took flight, and the peso plummeted to a third of its value—which tripled Argentina's massive dollar-denominated debt, causing Buenos Aires to default.

Third, the United States benefits from the dollar in global trade. Because America purchases imports in its own currency, in theory it should never run into balance-of-payments crises—shortages of foreign exchange—that have often battered developing countries. The assets and liabilities of US banks are denominated in the same currency, which means that the dollar can fluctuate against other currencies without provoking a banking or currency crisis in the United States. In addition, because international commodities, including oil, are priced in dollars, a fall in the dollar's value does not lead to a rise in commodity import prices.

Fourth, the dollar also provides the United States with seigniorage: government's profit from issuing coinage at cost of minting that is much below the face value of the coinage. Coins and notes are practically costless to produce, enabling the United States to acquire vast amounts of goods, services, and assets from the rest of the world at little sacrifice. The benefits of seigniorage are estimated at some $10–20 billion annually.[16]

A Mixed Blessing

In 1964 economist Robert Aliber wrote that "the advantage of additional flexibility in financing the US payments deficit appears to have outweighed the various costs which can be attributed to the US reserve currency role. While the additional income advantage has not been insignificant by some standards, it appears extremely unlikely that it is anywhere near large."[17]

America's exorbitant privilege is a mixed blessing, for two reasons. First, the United States is nearly guaranteed to be mired in the Triffin dilemma, after the Belgian–American economist Robert Triffin. On the one hand, the dilemma says, the United States needs to supply the world with its currency to meet the global demand for reserves. On the other hand, the more dollars are supplied, say, through US trade deficits, the likelier it is that confidence in the dollar will erode—which, in turn, jeopardizes the dollar's role as a reserve currency. Escaping the trap is practically impossible without another currency.

The corollary of the dilemma is that because the United States runs current-account deficits and foreigners invest in America, the dollar tends to be consistently overvalued. The situation is exacerbated by Asia's devalued currencies, and it hurts US exports, worsens the trade gap, and sparks

anti-trade sentiments in Congress. McKinsey Global Institute estimates that
the dollar is overvalued by 5–10 percent, undermining US exports and domestic goods that compete with imports on the order of $30–60 billion annu-
ally.[18] As such, the net benefit for the United States from serving as the reserve
currency issuer is about $40–70 billion, or 0.3 to 0.5 percent of US GDP. The
exorbitant privilege is, in short, a hard-earned one.

The second problem, even if a more manageable one for the issuer of the
global currency, is a weakened constraint on economic policy making and
increased temptation to borrow. This is not unlike what happened in the slide
to the Great Crisis. In Washington unprecedented fiscal deficits compelled
borrowing from abroad to sustain domestic investment. Like East Asians who
are trapped by their economic growth model into buying dollars, the United
States also risks being trapped, only by its exorbitant privilege.[19]

The political benefits from the dollar are similarly mixed. "Great powers
have great currencies," argued Nobel Prize winner Robert Mundell.[20] Political
scientist Benjamin Cohen has equated the geographic domain of a currency
to the issuing nation's effective political power.[21] Financial Times columnist
Wolfgang Münchau argues that "losing the dollar as the world's leading international currency not only leads to a loss of political power. It constitutes
loss of power."[22]

In theory, the currency hegemon is insulated from outside pressure in
formulating and implementing monetary policy, while being able to exercise
influence over others.[23] However, the translation of a global currency into
international political influence is far from automatic. Asian nations' reactionary exchange-rate policies illustrate how others can dent the powers of
the monetary hegemon. Rather than currency per se, the same factors that
enable a country to become the issuer of a reserve currency, such as economic
size and prowess, are also the ones driving political power. Rather than prodding each other, currency leadership and political leadership are caused by the
same factors. If the fundamentals are lost, both currency and political clout
will be, as well.

Empty Doubts

In a 2004 lecture, banker Avinash Persaud reminded his audience that "reserve currencies come and go. They don't last forever. International currencies in the past have included the Chinese Liang and Greek drachma, coined

in the fifth century B.C., the silver punch-marked coins of fourth century India, the Roman denari, the Byzantine solidus and Islamic dinar of the middle-ages, the Venetian ducato of the Renaissance, the seventeenth century Dutch guilder and of course, more recently, sterling and the dollar."[24] Will the dollar also fade?

There have been many waves of questioning of the dollar. The first one swelled in the 1960s, a time when the global economy ran on a system of fixed exchange rates. By the early part of the decade, many countries began to view their official dollar holdings as excessive and risking foreign-exchange losses if the United States, then running out of gold and facing inflation, decided to devalue the dollar.[25] The Triffin dilemma, first conceptualized in 1960, became prescient. The problem was not one of liquidity, but of ways to substitute for both dollars and gold.[26] Some countries, led by France, sought to replace the dollar with a super-sovereign reserve currency; the SDR emerged as the solution.[27]

Upon its launch, the SDR was hailed as the future principal reserve asset. In 1967 the IMF forecast that the SDR would account for over half of total world reserves before the end of the twentieth century.[28] US Assistant Secretary of the Treasury Merlyn Trued extolled the SDR as a "breakthrough on the world's monetary front comparable perhaps on the scientific front to that first orbit of a capsule in outer space."[29] However, the SDR never caught on, and the problems stemming from the fixed exchange rates were defused when President Nixon broke the gold peg in the fall of 1971. By March 1973, the leading economies had allowed their currencies to float against the dollar, in theory ending the need for dollar reserves.

Another wave of dollar doubts crested with the rise of Japan in the 1980s. Propelled by the Japanese miracle economy, trade and financial flows grew in Asia to the point that leading academics predicted the rise of a regional yen bloc.[30] Although the Japanese economy was at its largest (only one-half of America's), and its capital markets were underdeveloped, the yen was predicted to become the next global currency. But politics undid the momentum: despite gradually opening up its capital markets, Japan resisted the Reagan administration's calls to open its capital markets and internationalize the yen, as that would have raised the yen's value and dented Japan's export edge—precisely what the United States sought to accomplish.[31] The debate wound down in the 1990s, as the Japanese economy imploded and the US economy recovered.

It was the third wave of dollar doubts that would become the most substantive one. In 1999 the German mark was folded into the euro. A continental currency used by twelve nations, the euro was to a good extent an initiative of Germany itself. Here was an experiment that the dollar would have to reckon with.

Optimum Currency?

Academic debate about a common European currency commenced decades before the first euro coins and bills bewildered shoppers from Berlin to Barcelona. In the 1960s Robert Mundell issued his theory of "optimum currency areas," regions where national economies could be integrated into a single monetary system for shared welfare gain. The notion provided the theoretical basis for the European experiment 30 years later and earned Mundell a Nobel Prize in 1999, the year the euro was launched. By then, academics had used his framework to illustrate that Europe indeed approximated an optimum currency area. Forecasts deemed the economic benefits of the single currency sizable, also fueling Asian nations' aspirations for regional financial integration.[32]

With US economic problems of the 1980s prompting claims about the "dollar's last lap,"[33] the forthcoming European single currency was thought to replace the greenback. However, most American observers saw the euro as a weak rival to the dollar.[34] Then-Deputy Treasury Secretary Lawrence Summers argued that "the dollar will remain the primary reserve currency for the foreseeable future. . . . We expect the impact of the euro on the monetary system to be quite limited initially and to occur only gradually."[35] His fellow Harvard economist Jeffrey Frankel agreed that "there is little likelihood that some other currency will supplant the dollar as the world's premier reserve currency by 2020. One national currency or another must occupy the number-one position, and there is simply no plausible alternative."[36]

London School of Economics scholars countered that the euro "will become 'plausible' [as a global reserve currency] long before 2020 . . . the 'number-one position' could actually be shared, and this might be the most likely outcome."[37] The arguments about the euro's coming were not ludicrous, for three reasons.

First, trends in the preceding 30 years seemed to augur poorly for the dollar. In 1973–1981, America went through a period of high inflation. US economy and productivity grew sluggishly for some two decades from the early

1970s through the beginning of the 1990s. The United States also ran growing external deficits, especially in 1982–1987 and 1998–2000, emerging as the
world's leading debtor. The dollar's global market share eroded in the late
1970s and early 1980s.

Second, at 74 percent of the US GDP in 1999, the Eurozone economy was
large.[38] There were reasons to believe that economic size would entail a prominent currency. After all, the Deutsche mark, the world's second key currency
for most of the postwar period, had a market share that was one-fourth of the
share of the dollar, precisely the size of the German economy relative to the
US economy.[39]

Third, the euro made a solid debut. During its first year, it became the
most widely used currency for international bond flotations.[40] Euros accounted for 75 percent of all corporate bonds issued by euro-area borrowers
and 20 percent of bonds of companies outside the euro area. In contrast, in
1990–1998, before the euro was introduced, these figures were only 10 and 2
percent, respectively, among the to-be Eurozone currencies.[41] Fred Bergsten,
the American who did see the euro as a credible co-currency, argued that even
if the international monetary system was not genuinely bipolar, international
financial markets were.[42]

The Hardy Greenback

The euro gained prominence in the following decade, largely thanks to economic fundamentals. By the Great Crisis, the by-then sixteen-member Eurozone was almost at a par with the size of the US economy. The EU's GDP was
three-quarters of US GDP at purchasing parity rates, and its extra-regional
imports amounted to 86 percent of US imports in 2007. Notwithstanding the
size of the Eurozone economy and the euro's early success, the euro has notably trailed the dollar both as a vehicle and reserve currency. This has three
causes.

First, the dollar proved more resilient than expected. The US economic
rebound and productivity surge in the 1990s made America the darling of investors and a safe haven amid bouts of instability in the emerging markets.
Paradoxically, the euro's introduction also helped: losing the opportunity to
diversify their holdings across Europe's multiple national currencies, investors bought dollars to rebalance their portfolios.

Second, the US government securities market is large, fluid, and liquid,
one where a federal fiscal authority issues homogenous debt instruments.

In contrast, the European bond market, while also large, is fragmented—divided into many parts with vastly different risk characteristics, which makes the various markets imperfect substitutes for one another.[43] National bond markets are not particularly attractive. Among the main euro-denominated government securities are those issued by the Italian government, but Italy's fiscal policies have inspired few central banks to hold its securities.[44] German government bonds tend to be more stable, but they are also not liquid as institutional investors tend to hold them to maturity. European bonds are also not considered as infallible as US government securities. In the United States, a single authority, the Federal Reserve, backs government-issued securities, but the ECB does not unquestionably guarantee European bonds—thus not acting as the "Big Bazooka" that investors would have wanted it to amid the Eurozone's sovereign debt crisis.[45] Rather, national central banks are to act as lenders of last resort.

Third, past is prologue in monetary matters. There are strong incumbency advantages, as countries are uncertain about the benefits of a new leading currency versus those of the existing one and as a result are reluctant to switch. For instance, once Japan dropped exchange controls and the yen became viewed as a plausible, even if distant, global reserve currency, the dollar was already the network currency, and there were few incentives to move away from it.[46] That the dollar is used as the reference currency for exchange-traded goods, such as most commodities, further entrenches it. In the dollar-centric world, being the first-mover away from the greenback could be risky. What if the others did not follow?

The Elusive Tipping Point

Historical transitions from one currency to the next have been erratic rather than smooth and linear, and governments play a limited role in the process. How change happens is bottom-up, with a sufficient number of adoptions in international transactions so that a tipping point is reached where inertia is broken and everyone starts to move in the same direction. At the turn of the millennium, there were no good reasons for such a moment.

Even the Great Crisis could not force a tipping point. It was predicted to result in a loss of confidence in the United States, followed by capital flight and the dollar's decline, but no such hard landing occurred. America's investment position deteriorated much less than expected, and once the crisis globalized, the worldwide flight to safety favored US Treasuries. A home bias set in, as well, and an important stock of dollar-funded portfolio investments abroad returned to America, strengthening the dollar. The irony did not go unnoticed: after all, the United States was blamed as the main culprit in the crisis. Europe's debt crises and political turmoil in the Middle East reemphasized the US role as the world's safe haven, a status unshaken even by America's deficit travails and credit-rating downgrade in the fall of 2011. But a happy ending was elusive, as the ballooning US fiscal deficit and rise of China shrouded the dollar in doubt.

Renminbi's Rise?

What are the RMB's long-term prospects on the global stage? Judging by the size of the Chinese economy, strong. Economic historian Angus Maddison predicts that China's economy will surpass that of the United States prior to 2020 in purchasing power parity terms.[47] Goldman Sachs has famously predicted that the Chinese economy would grow larger than that of the United States in 2030, and be nearly twice as large by 2050.[48] OECD research director Helmut Reisen argues that the RMB could replace the dollar as a reserve currency around 2050.[49] Nouriel Roubini has argued that the dollar's decline may take "more than a decade" from 2009, but it could also be hastened by continued US fiscal deficits.[50]

The April 2009 comments by Chinese central banker Zhou Xiaochuan about the need for an international reserve currency triggered, as probably intended by Beijing, a global debate on the future of the dollar. The currency issue epitomized the economically interconnected and politically complicated relationship between the United States and China. Treasury Secretary Timothy Geithner, into only his third month in office and still widely viewed as lacking the gravitas required for it, argued that the Chinese proposal merited consideration. As the dollar fell in reaction, the White House quickly stated that the dollar would continue as the global reserve currency. President Obama provided further assurances, stating that the dollar was "extraordinarily strong" thanks to America's economic prospects.[51] Former Federal Reserve Chairman Paul Volcker criticized the Chinese for taking on the United States, all the while themselves holding dollar assets.[52] Across the Atlantic, ECB President Jean Claude Trichet buttressed Washington, arguing that the euro was not designed to be a global reserve currency and that a strong dollar was critical for global economic stability.[53]

Why Now?   In China the central banker's comments were doubtless popular. One of the country's best-selling books is Song Hongbing's *Currency Wars.*[54] Reportedly widely read in government circles, the volume posits that Western countries and central banks are controlled by a clique of international bankers who accumulate wealth by engaging in currency manipulation—lending dollars to hapless developing nations, followed by shorting their currencies. But what motivated the Chinese comments about the dollar?

It is unlikely that Beijing sees the SDR as a viable alternative to the dollar. Even with the G20 commitment to expand SDRs by $250 billion, SDRs make up no more than 4 percent of global reserves, a far cry from the $12 *trillion* of American Treasury bonds. It would take years for the SDR to be widely accepted.

More likely, Beijing sought to accomplish two objectives. First, it wanted to convey the depth of Chinese concern about the US fiscal deficit. Holding a massive portfolio of US government bonds, China would be the first to incur losses should the dollar's value decline. According to Arvind Subramanian, a 20-percent capital loss for the Chinese resulting from a dollar decline and consequent appreciation in the RMB's value would be tantamount to $400 billion, roughly 10 percent of Chinese GDP.[55]

Second, China floated a trial balloon to gauge the global opinion on the viability of the RMB as a leading currency in the world economy. Beijing has taken manifold steps in recent years to start internationalizing its currency. Right when the central banker was airing his views, Beijing established a series of currency swaps with Argentina, Hong Kong, Indonesia, Malaysia, and South Korea, followed by Russia and Belarus. The swaps were to supply the RMB to the partner-country central banks to use in their trade with China in lieu of the dollar. Brazil and China also agreed to use each other's currencies in their bilateral trade. The swap schemes totaled $120 billion combined. Also in 2009, China authorized the Hong Kong-based HSBC Holdings and Bank of East Asia to sell RMB-denominated bonds. In July 2010 the government allowed limited RMB trading outside the mainland, in Hong Kong. Beijing also promoted its trade and currency ties in Southeast Asia through a China–Asean free trade agreement that began in January 2010.

Beijing also announced a major expansion of a 2009 pilot program to allow local Chinese entities and multinational corporations to settle merchandise trades in RMB with counterparties globally and enjoy tax rebates. The expanded list included some 67,000 companies, up from some 400 in the past.

The Chinese central bank began allowing foreign central banks or monetary authorities, RMB clearing banks in Hong Kong and Macau, and overseas banks participating in cross-border trade settlements in RMB to invest with RMB in the on-shore interbank bond, a move that is expected to make more RMB to flow back to China. In the run-up to Chinese President Hu Jintao's January 2011 visit to the United States, the Bank of China was also allowed to offer RMB-denominated bank accounts and currency-conversion services in New York. And in a particularly significant move to internationalize the RMB, China permitted banks and enterprises based in certain pilot cities to start making overseas direct investments (ODI) in the Chinese currency to set up subsidiaries, buy foreign equity stakes, and make project investments.

Some multinationals looking to expand operations in China seized the moment, starting to offer invoicing to Chinese customers in RMB and borrowing with bonds denominated in RMB in Hong Kong. In August 2010 McDonald's sold RMB 200 million, or $29 million, of 3-percent notes due in September 2013. Caterpillar issued a RMB 1-billion bond offering three months later. In January 2011 the World Bank issued its first RMB bonds, valued at $79 billion, following the RMB issuances of its affiliate, the International Finance Corporation, as well as the Asian Development Bank. Unilever followed with RMB 300 million, becoming the first European multinational to issue offshore RMB bonds.

By August 2011, the restrictions on exporters were lifted, enabling any exporter in China to settle cross-border trade transactions in RMB. China also instituted the so-called qualified foreign limited partner program (QFLP), whereby certain foreign investors would be allowed to invest in RMB funds in Shanghai. In November 2011, JPMorgan Asset Management secured permission from the Beijing city government to create a $1-billion RMB fund under the program, a third of Beijing city's FLP allotment, becoming the largest foreign manager of an RMB-denominated fund. Blackstone Group and Carlyle Group each proceeded to raise 5-billion-RMB funds.

RMB internationalization is a pillar in China's twelfth Five-Year Plan (2011–2015). As an offshore market, Hong Kong has been a focal point in the latter strategy by allowing China to build up a market for the RMB without having to open its capital account. The strategy succeeded: RMB deposits in accounts in Hong Kong surged rapidly, from slightly over RMB 100 billion in July 2010 to RMB 622 billion by September 2011, and offshore bond issuances in Hong Kong multiplied.

China also issued plans to bolster Shanghai, a city that aspires to become a global financial center of the stature of London and New York by 2020, as the onshore RMB market, including allowing foreign companies to list there. Beijing may also allow private equity funds to raise RMB abroad and invest it in long-term projects onshore.[56] Hong Kong will meanwhile likely see the rise of various RMB-denominated financial products in the offshore RMB market, such as insurance, securities, fund products, and other financial derivatives.

Out of Options

China has been moving on many fronts to internationalize the RMB. The efforts will create greater flexibilities in payments, collection, and investments for companies and investors operating, expanding into, or working with Chinese counterparts. But there are many reasons not to be bullish about the Chinese currency. It starts from a low base: it is hardly used as a reserve currency, and its circulation outside China is very limited. The RMB makes up well less than 1 percent of the turnover in the foreign-exchange market, about an eighth of the turnover of the Hong Kong dollar.[57] Daily offshore trading in RMB doubled to $1 billion between 2010 and 2011, but the figure is still small relative to the daily $4-trillion foreign-exchange market. The Chinese bilateral swap agreements are shallow: US–China trade alone amounts to almost four times their value. And although China's fiscal policy is conservative, the country has a sizable amount of public debt. According to one thorough calculation, China's total public debt may be as much as $5.8 trillion by the end of 2011, or $4–4.5 trillion more than the government figures reveal and about the same size as the country's GDP.[58] Whether foreign firms that receive Chinese ODI would accept RMB will be one indicator of the viability of the Chinese currency in world markets.

As the experience with the euro has demonstrated, economic size and prominence in world trade are only two of the determinants of currency dominance. Liquidity of financial markets and convertibility of the currency are *sine qua non* for a global currency, but China has neither. Nor are its financial markets transparent, which undermines foreign investor confidence.

The main hurdle to RMB internationalization is politics. In order for the Chinese currency to be convertible, its value would have to be dictated by the market, with traders, investors, governments, and companies around the world free to buy and sell it. This, in turn, would require a flexible exchange rate and appreciate the RMB, torpedoing the Chinese government's export-led growth paradigm—not unlike the problem Japan faced in the past. With a less competitive exchange rate, growth would have to come from domestic consumption. Full convertibility would also diminish the government's control over the economy and politics, an inconceivable outcome for the Chinese leadership.

Even if the political hurdles were somehow cleared, there would be practical challenges to spurring domestic growth and reducing savings. Keen China observer Michael Pettis notes that one way to reduce the high savings is to increase investment, yet Beijing wants to reduce the economy's dependence on high investment levels, which risk overcapacity and inflation.[59] Another way to reduce savings is to considerably increase the share of consumption of the economy. But that is bound to be difficult to effect quickly given the immensely low share of household consumption of the GDP.

Thus far, the Chinese government has kept intervening in the foreign-exchange markets and employing strict foreign-exchange controls on cross-border transfers of capital and direct investment. Only some 100 foreign financial institutions have been able to invest in China's domestic bond and stock markets and do so on a limited quota basis. China worries about the entry of "hot money" run by hedge funds that could destabilize the financial system. Beijing's willingness to allow foreign corporations to issue bonds in the mainland is also questionable, for that would interfere with the government's efforts to channel savings to Chinese industry. Chinese leadership has reiterated the need for gradualness in liberalizing the capital account and internationalizing the RMB. The drive by Shanghai, the 1920s "Pearl of the Orient," to become the leading global financial center will take years, if not decades.

Tenuous SDRs   In 2009 a UN expert commission led by Joseph Stiglitz called for a "greatly expanded SDR" system.[60] SDRs might be the quickest way to add to global liquidity and enable credit-strapped emerging markets to increase domestic spending. However, the SDR is a tenuous option for a prominent currency.[61] Making it the principal reserve asset today would require a tremendous amount of fresh SDRs—close to $3 trillion, more than the GDP of France—and the IMF would have to be authorized as a world central bank able to print money.

Politics stands in the way. Issuing new SDRs would require the agreement of 85 percent of the 186 IMF members, a decision over which the United States holds a veto, as do Europeans if voting as a block. The United States is not enthusiastic about such an arrangement, as even hints about it could hurt the dollar. Diversifying the composition of SDRs to include, say, major emerging-market currencies would also pose political problems because Brazil, China, Russia, and India would want their respective currencies (but not necessarily one another's currencies) represented—in addition to the four main currencies, the dollar, the euro, the yen, and the pound. Economists would likely argue that the basket SDRs should also include Australian, Canadian, Chilean, and Norwegian currencies to link SDRs to commodity price cycles.[62] For now, the issue is moot: in the fall of 2011, the IMF's board decided not to alter the criteria for including a currency in the SDR basket, which left the composition of the basket unchanged.

Even if the SDR composition was agreed upon, the governance of the SDR system would be fiercely contested. The larger the pool of SDRs, the more political the SDR would become. In addition, when growth resumes in the world economy, issuing additional SDRs could be akin to the infamous image of tossing money from a helicopter, and it would generate inflationary pressures. Even if all nations agreed to expand the role of the SDR, the adoption of the new construct would have to occur across global transactions—from invoicing international transactions to denominating private international capital flows in the forms of loans, bonds, and deposits.

China has been interested in SDR bonds as a means to reduce its dollar exposure. However, for it to truly elevate SDRs to a reserve-currency status, Beijing would need to create a liquid market in SDRs—issue its own SDR-denominated bonds, rather than buying them from the IMF.[63] After all, the bonds bought from the Fund cannot be traded and thus would not provide liquidity. If using SDRs, China would also have to have a counterpart, something unlikely to materialize. There is no foreign exchange for SDRs: members cannot use SDRs to intervene in foreign-exchange markets or in other transactions with market participants. The first SDR liabilities would thus be in a competitive disadvantage against the dollar- and euro-denominated assets. The SDR, in short, has properties that seriously constrain its expansion much beyond its infamous "funny money" status.[64]

The Uncertain Euro   The euro is a far more plausible currency contender than any other, but the odds for it to unseat the dollar are slim. The familiar obstacles persist: the fragmented Eurobond market and Europe's inverted age pyramid and lackluster growth. Long-term confidence in the euro may have been hurt by the reluctance of European leaders to fully and promptly commit to countercyclical policies when the 2008–2009 crisis hit. The euro was not widely adopted even as America contracted; rather, investors opted for dollar-denominated assets in lieu of euro-denominated ones.[65] Europeans' procrastination amid the debt crisis raised further questions about the future stewardship of Eurozone affairs. Even though Europeans are much more resolute in defending the euro than foreigners would expect, the allure of the common currency has been replaced by talk about the burdens it imposes on its members. Europe's debt problems may also be thornier to solve than those of the United States, and they will persist for a longer time. Part of the US debt will vanish when financial assets acquired by the government in the crisis increase in value.

Positively, the 2010 financial turmoil in Europe sparked a debate about issuing Eurozone bonds collectively backed by the euro-area nations. The European Stability Mechanism (ESM), the system of tough conditions and debt restructuring for Eurozone countries that cannot repay their loans that are due in mid-2013, can, if institutionalized, help rein in moral hazard in the region. But Berlin and other northern European governments, exasperated by southern profligacy, have scant incentives to move toward anything akin to fiscal federalism. Germany's reluctance to adopt the idea of E-Bonds, or Europe-wide sovereign bonds issued by a sovereign European-wide issuer and backed by the ECB or the Eurozone governments, speaks to the limits of integration.

Europeans, and Germans in particular, would also be unlikely to want a more prominent role for the euro in the global economy should that entail the euro's appreciation, which would undermine Europe's extra-regional exports. If the euro rose to equal the dollar in global markets by 2020, European exports would be reduced by an estimated 10 percent, and the continent's GDP would decline by 0.1 percentage points.[66]

The yen is a long shot for the leading global currency. The problems of Europe and China meet in Japan: the Japanese government has a large amount of debt outstanding, but the yield of Japanese short-term securities is very low, below 1 percent. The government also discriminates against foreigners in the Japanese market. And, much like in the 1980s, it resists internationalizing the yen, for that would blunt Japan's competitiveness and industrial policy.

Into Turbulence

Managed yuanization in East Asia and organic euronization elsewhere, if proceeding, are unlikely to dislodge the dollar from its predominant position in the world economy. The economics of holding dollar reserves remain compelling because of the US prominence in the world, because of the liquidity of the US financial markets, because of the dollar's network externalities, and because it simply makes sense for countries to hold reserves in the same currency in which they denominate foreign debt and conduct foreign trade.[67] In order for the surplus nations to meet the world's reserve needs, they would need to engineer macroeconomic policies conducive to current-account deficits. Given the absence of good alternatives, the dollar would likely tower over others even if the US recovery was slow. Today's situation is in many ways no different than the prior episodes of gloom about the future of the dollar.

However, two problems cast a shadow on the dollar. The first is that future demand for fresh reserves in the world economy may be overwhelming US capacity to supply them without damage to the American economy. Hufbauer and Suominen calculate that just to keep up with global import growth—which at least in the previous years was almost 10 percent annually—official global reserves should grow by another $13 trillion by 2020.[68] Assuming a responsible creation of $4.5 trillion of new dollar reserves over the next decade, the global reserve gap would be $8.5 trillion. But running high current-account deficits to supply reserves would imply heavy foreign borrowing, which, per the Triffin dilemma, could end up hurting the dollar. Such an outcome is not as far-fetched as it was in the past because of America's twin deficit, a current-account deficit coupled with a deep budget deficit.

The second problem is the US fiscal deficit. The US ability to pay up is being questioned, and there are concerns that America is choosing to inflate its debts down. The calls from Congress for the Fed to purchase public debt and the efforts to curb Fed's independence will only fan worries about US economic policies. It was debt and inflation that dethroned the sterling. The British inflation rate was thrice that of the United States over the first three-quarters of the twentieth century, and repeated devaluations against the dollar gradually dethroned the sterling as the reserve currency.[69] By 2010, the dollar had had a 35-year history of trend depreciation and particularly rapid depreciation since 2004.

The precarious fiscal situations in the United States, along with the two other major currency issuers, Japan and Europe, risk exchange-rate volatility. That would be more consequential than in the past: global reserves have nearly tripled in the past five years, to 10 trillion, and carry trade moves enormous sums and can significantly move exchange rates in the blink of an eye.[70] Swings in exchange rates would increase uncertainties of firms about future profits and investment choices. In a 2006 Deutsche Bank survey, exchange-rate risk ranked as the top strategic issue facing executives, above market risk, commercial risk, and others, and in a 2009 McKinsey survey, 29 percent of global executives reported that exchange rates have "extremely" or "very" significant effects on company profits.[71] In a 2011 PricewaterhouseCoopers survey, as many as 54 percent of CEOs worried about the threat of exchange-rate volatility.[72] Exchange-rate volatility can also stunt growth, especially in countries with underdeveloped financial markets. Such effects would entice governments, now holding record reserves, to intervene in currency markets—something that has already occurred rather widely, including across Asia, in reaction to the depreciating dollar. Political controversy could follow.

In Defense of the Dollar

The adequacy of international liquidity was a leading topic in international economics and dominated intergovernmental meetings in the 1920s and early 1930s.[73] It was central to the IMF's founding and surged again in the 1960s as Washington got mired in the Triffin dilemma. The issue, all but gone in the 1990s, is back with a vengeance. However, options are limited.

A central role for the SDR in the global economy is highly unlikely; a complementary and limited role is feasible, and such a role is in fact inscribed in the Bretton Woods-era IMF Articles of Agreement.[74] The SDR could be employed in two ways on a more modest scale to fuel trade and provide for reserve diversification.

First, the SDR could be privileged in trade invoicing, like the Chinese swap arrangements but on a grander scale. Second, creating an "SDR substitution account" would allow countries that want to reduce their dollar holdings to convert dollars into SDRs.[75] This could help overcome the thorny question of how countries might transfer from dollars to use SDRs in the existing stock of foreign-exchange reserves. If the conversion occurred outside the market, it would not hurt the value of the dollar. However, the exchange risk would persist to an extent, as the SDR substitution account would likely hold mostly dollars as assets.

Although stopping short of endorsing a gold standard, Robert Zoellick provoked a global uproar by suggesting in the fall of 2010 that gold be used as an international "reference point of market expectations" about the future of currency values.[76] Could gold be employed as a new reserve currency? The G20 countries collectively hold about one billion ounces of gold in their central banks. Valued at the "official price" of around $42/ounce, these holdings are worth less than $50 billion. If the central banks agreed to a new official price near today's market price, around $1,000/ounce, they could create reserves worth about $1 trillion.[77] To make a real difference, gold would have to be massively revalued from the current market price of about $1,000/ounce, say to $5,000/ounce. Such a measure would overnight create $5 trillion of new official reserves, even if distributed in a very lopsided manner among countries, with the United States, Germany, Italy, France, and China gaining the largest shares.[78]

No Banking on Bancor

A much more distant idea is a single global currency—a means of exchange akin to the euro but global, managed by a global central bank and operating within a global monetary bloc. Various permutations of the idea have been raised since Keynes's Bretton Woods-era calls for a common currency, the bancor. Keynes envisioned a global bank called the International Clearing Union that would issue bancor. The bancor, in turn, would be based on the value of 30 representative commodities, including gold, and it would be, like the dollar came to be, exchangeable against national currencies at fixed rates. Countries would maintain bancor accounts and have an overdraft allowance from the ICU when experiencing balance-of-payment turmoil.

Robert Mundell has advocated a world currency since discussing it in a congressional hearing in 1968.[79] Like many other proposals, his is not one for a single global currency, but for a setting where each country exchanges its respective currency at par with the world unit that he calls "intor."[80] Various opinion leaders have stoked this debate. In 1998 former Clinton administration Undersecretary of Commerce Jeffrey Garten called for a "Fed for the World," and he has revisited the idea a number of times since.[81]

In his March 2009 comments, China's central banker, Zhou Xiaochuan, conjectured that Keynes's approach based on the bancor "may have been more farsighted" than the US-sponsored order that came into being.[82] The 2009 UN Commission's call for an expanded SDR system is rather akin to the bancor-based system. In a staff paper, an IMF team also discussed a modified version of bancor, a global reserve currency (GRC) that would be accepted as an international legal tender by the member countries of the international monetary institution (IMI) that backs it.[83] Unlike the bancor, the GRC would not be based on commodity values. The IMI, an independent central bank with an unrivaled AAAA rating, would issue the GRC. The member states in turn could issue financial instruments such as bonds denominated in GRC, and choose the value of their currencies in relation to the GRC.

Such schemes would provide exchange-rate stability, provide worldwide network effects and scale economies, and be "fair" in the sense that no nation would enjoy exorbitant privilege. They would also practically undo the transactions costs involved in trading across borders in a multicurrency world, which in one estimate amount to $400 billion each year.[84] At the same time, as their advocates tend to acknowledge, many of the proposals presume that the dedicated global central bank would have impeccable judgment and balance sheet, and be able to reconcile political independence with accountability to the member nations. Bluntly, a single global currency or even a Mundellian world currency are too difficult to implement and nonstarters politically to matter in today's policy debate.

Co-Currency World?

Perhaps the most feasible means to alleviate the Triffin dilemma is a system of co-currencies. The dollar is still the unquestionable *primus inter pares*, but the rise of the euro has brought the world closer to a bipolar currency system. A world of co-currencies would not be new.[85] There have been frequent episodes, especially before 1914, when several currencies have shared the role of the global reserve currency. While a multicurrency system is arguably costlier than the status quo, some level of diversity could produce healthy competition: with central banks and other international investors having strong alternatives, policy makers could be encouraged to engage in a policy race to the top to foster investor confidence.[86]

To the extent that it also alleviated the US burden to act as the consumer of last resort *and* provided greater stability than the present system did *while also not* disrupting the network benefits, a co-currency system could be favorable to America and the world. With growth and stability, diversification could occur all the while the *value* of dollar holdings continued to rise. As such, a co-currency system could at least in theory emerge as the global equilibrium.[87]

Three factors could help further the rise of a more genuinely co-currency world.

The first is technology: financial innovation could reduce the costs of converting currencies, lowering incentives to hold reserves in a single currency.[88]

Second, long-term developments in Europe—financial integration, issuance of E-bonds commonly backed by the Eurozone nations, and Frankfurt's continued development as a financial hub—could make the euro more prominent. Simulations by Harvard's Menzie Chinn and Jeffrey Frankel show that British accession to the Eurozone, while a highly unlikely prospect, would be a tipping point in light of London's large and liquid financial markets, and make the euro into the world's premier currency.[89]

Third, if world trade continues to regionalize, major economies in Asia and Europe would grow even more connected to one another and perhaps become somewhat less connected to the US economy. The euro, already covering the bulk of intra-EU transactions, could in such a setting be a stronger complement to the dollar. As countries around the EU, such as the former Soviet Republics, develop stronger ties with the Old Continent, they may be induced to hold euros—provided, of course, that the Europeans manage to overcome their economic crisis and save the euro. Russia increased the share of euros in its reserves from 42 percent to 47.5 percent in 2008–2009, while in a mirror image reducing the share of dollars from 47 percent to below 42 percent.[90] Similar developments could take place in Asia around China if and when the regional financial markets become liberalized. Intra-regional trade integration in Asia, if continuing, could even encourage the region to move toward monetary integration, as suggested by dozens of observers, including Mundell just two years following the launch of the euro.[91]

Perhaps the likeliest long-term outcome is some currency diversification at the regional levels alongside the global dollar. If such equilibrium provided global network benefits and was not trade diverting—favoring trade within any one currency bloc over trade between the blocs—it could be beneficial for world trade and economy.

Trade diversion in a world of currency blocs can and must be avoided. Studying the 1930s, Barry Eichengreen and Douglas Irwin find that the odds of trade diversion depend on the policies adopted by the currency bloc members.[92] The sterling bloc promoted intra-group trade without diverting trade away with nonmembers. In contrast, exchange controls and bilateral clearing arrangements implemented by Germany and Central and Eastern European countries reduced trade with nonmembers. Even formal currency unions, if well designed, do not need to be trade diverting. The bulk of studies on the Eurozone find no evidence of trade diversion but, rather, that the euro has helped increase trade between the Eurozone and nonmembers.[93] The odds of trade diversion will be diminished by full convertibility and free trade between the blocs.

Conclusion

All countries benefit from a stable global currency and the network and growth benefits that it confers. The dollar order has provided such public goods to the world and benefited America, and it has prevailed through thick and thin. The great advantages of the United States—a huge economy, vibrant and liquid financial markets, and gold standard institutions—make holding dollars attractive as long as the US economy is large and strong. But the US budget deficit, in 2011 again above $1 trillion, now risks undermining confidence in the US economy, the dollar, and America's enjoyment of its exorbitant privilege. The issues at hand have gnawed since the end of World War I; they are now acute as the demand for fresh reserves could eclipse the US capacity to supply them without negative repercussions to the US economy.

America can continue trapped in overseas borrowing and risk a situation where the dollar becomes an untenable option for foreigners, or it can reduce its debts and continue enjoying the benefits that its currency confers. Whether a pariah America or a safe-haven America will result is a matter of policy. Size, growth, liquidity, and faith of investors in an even better tomorrow are what matters in monetary matters, but they do not come for free. Reinstating confidence means fiscal discipline, transparent financial regulations, refusal to inflate away any debt overhang, guarantees of central bank independence, and investments in human capital.

To be sure, the fate of the dollar is contingent on the behaviors of other nations. Martin Wolf points out that if the US private sector deleverages and other countries accumulate dollar-denominated assets as reserves, the US government would reemerge as the borrower of last resort.[94] In such a case, fiscal solvency and central bank independence might not suffice to shield the greenback; rather, international coordination would be required. The G20 effort to curb global financial imbalances is one such means; reducing Asian reserve hoarding is another.

An unmanaged reserve currency system would serve no one. At the same time, the reserve currency regime is not a zero-sum, winner-take-all game: there is room at the top. But mandating a switch to another currency or a co-currency system is impossible: Washington would and should oppose dislodging the dollar, and China, Japan, and Europe would each surely resist seeing the others' currencies being assigned as the next global medium of exchange. Rather, the global currency regime will evolve in a bottom-up fashion, led by market forces rather than grand designs of central bankers. Markets have thus far gone long on America. Notwithstanding the burdens of the exorbitant privilege, the benefits that the United States has scored from the global vote of confidence in the US economy have been immense, from economic advantages to soft power in world affairs. The dollar is still the best bet. Sound policies in Washington can keep it so.

5 Central Banking at a Crossroads

The money powers prey on the nation in times of peace and conspire against it in times of adversity. The banking powers are more despotic than monarchy, more insolent than autocracy, more selfish than bureaucracy. They denounce as public enemies all who question their methods or throw light upon their crimes.

—*President Abraham Lincoln speaking on the third attempt to establish a central bank in America, 1862*

It is said that Government could not be safely entrusted with the power of issuing paper money; that it would most certainly abuse it. . . . There would, I confess, be great danger of this, if Government—that is to say, the ministers—were themselves to be entrusted with the power of issuing paper money.

—*David Ricardo, in "Plan for the Establishment of a National Bank," 1846*

T HE GREAT CRISIS SHOOK THE POSTWAR BALANCE BETWEEN governments and markets. Rescuing banks and auto companies, issuing major stimulus programs, and re-regulating financial markets, governments became heavily involved in managing economies. This compounded precrisis concerns about the rise of "state capitalism" and "new mercantilism," a world where governments would play an outsized role in regulating, owning, and prodding swaths of economic life previously the purview of the private sector. The profit motive, it was feared, would be replaced by political motivations.

The role of central banks was perhaps most novel and controversial. Monetary mavens were blamed for excessively loose monetary policy in the run-up to the crisis. Spearheaded by the US Federal Reserve, central banks aroused passions after joining the rescue effort with historic monetary expansion and credit infusions to ailing banks, emerging as kingmakers on Wall Street. The act itself was less worrisome than its repercussions. Some in Congress sought to take advantage of the Fed's credit window for political ends, while others accused the Fed of overreach and sought to curb its room to maneuver.

Both moves jeopardized central bank independence, the crowning achievement of twentieth-century economic policy making, which has tamed inflation and safeguarded financial stability the world over. A dilemma arose: while releasing liquidity in the economy amid crises may be necessary for the Fed to forestall a depression, the implications of such a measure for independent monetary policy making can be hugely negative and lasting. Yet a failure to act would subject the Fed to political wrath should the economy turn sour—and give rise to accusations that the Fed was failing to serve its dual mandate, price stability *and* full employment.

In the United States, the dilemma is enormously consequential. The Fed's policies not only reverberate around the world; political constraints on it can as easily be emulated abroad as its independence has been. Central bank actions during the crisis aroused passions not only in smaller economies but also in such advanced nations as the UK, Japan, and Germany.

How to best keep central bankers above politics and accountable to the public, and acting in the interest of price stability and growth?

The Fed's New World: Boring, No More

Industrialized nations experienced spells of double-digit inflation in the 1970s and 1980s, while developing and transition economies were ravaged by episodes of hyperinflation through the mid-1990s.[1] Since then, inflation has been subdued around the world. The global inflation rate declined from an annual average of nearly 15 percent in 1980–1984 to 3.8 percent in 2005,[2] and the "Great Inflation" of the 1970s was replaced by the "Great Moderation," a 25-year period of price stability accompanied by low unemployment. In the steadier nations, central banking at the end of the twentieth century was almost dull.

There are a number of hypotheses for the Great Moderation. One is the famous "good luck" hypothesis, which attributes the low inflation to a lucky streak. Another links the diminished volatility to factors that have improved flexibilities in the economy, such as freer trade and improved inventory management. Still another is a "good policy" hypothesis, whereby improved macroeconomic and monetary policies caused the Great Moderation.

Better monetary policy can be enacted because of central bank independence. Such independence can be measured in many ways—such as the length of central bank governors' appointments, the frequency of central banks' contacts with the executive, and an explicit mentioning of the price stability objective in central bank statutes. In 1993 Alberto Alesina and Larry Summers famously showed that advances in central bank independence lowered both the level and volatility of inflation.[3] Many others have confirmed the finding. Independent central banks have delivered greater price stability than their less independent counterparts, and done so without compromising growth.[4] When the Bank of England gained its independence in 1997, yields on UK Treasury bonds fell sharply, reflecting expectations of lower risk, and studies ascertained great stability in UK inflation expectations.[5] Research has also established that price stability, in turn, helps further financial stability.[6] Apolitical and credible central bankers can also act as immensely useful and influential independent commentators about general economic matters. For example, both of the two most recent Fed chairmen, Alan Greenspan and Ben Bernanke, have used their bully pulpit to preach virtues of fiscal discipline.

The reason for central bank independence is simple and good. Monetary policy is best managed by an entity that has a long time horizon and economy-wide concerns at heart. Legislators do not fit the mold: they tend to have short time horizons and focus on the particularistic needs of their electoral districts.[7] The very reason for congressional representatives to delegate monetary policy to the Fed by way of the 1913 Federal Reserve Act was to protect monetary policy making from their own narrow incentives in the interest of the national economy. Interest group politics played a role: the act reflected the aims of New York bankers for efficient and depoliticized monetary policy making. Politics was purged further in 1935, when Congress removed the Secretary of the Treasury and the Comptroller of the Currency from the Fed's seven-member Board of Governors.[8]

The Fed's ability to set interest rates was suspended during World War II, but the 1951 Treasury–Federal Reserve Accord reestablished the power, albeit requiring active consultation with the Treasury. The amendment of the Federal Reserve Act in 1977 at last set the current objectives of maximum employment and price stability. After the war, Germany also established an independent central bank as a lock on 1920s-style hyperinflation, and the Bundesbank did prove impervious to political pressure over the years.[9] Similar measures followed around the world. Global inflationary pressures in the 1970s compelled several other advanced nations to cement central bank independence. The Bank of Japan gained independence at the same time as the Bank of England did, in 1997. The independence of the European Central Bank (ECB), established in 1998, was codified in the Maastricht Treaty, which can be altered only by unanimity among its signatories. With the collapse of communism and the advance of the 1990s Washington Consensus, independent central banking took hold also in the transition economies and emerging markets.[10] The Great Moderation set in, and a positive feedback loop developed: low inflation helped buttress central bank independence, as politicians had few reasons to interfere with central bankers' work.[11]

Checked Independence

The US Federal Reserve is the world's most powerful monetary authority. Its decisions affect the fortunes of the world economy and the actions of central bankers in other nations. But the Fed is not almighty: Congress has delegated but not abdicated power to it. The Fed's independence is not absolute, unconditional, or unchecked, nor is it as complete as that of the Supreme Court, by Constitution the third power in the federal government and one whose justices are appointed for life. In contrast, the president appoints and the Senate confirms the seven members of the Board of Governors for fourteen-year terms, and two Governors as Chairman and Vice Chairman of the Board for four-year terms.[12]

The Fed's objectives, price stability and full employment, are also set by Congress. Like the Supreme Court, the Fed enjoys "instrument independence," meaning that it can freely choose among its tools (open market operations, discount window, and bank reserve requirements) to pursue its mission. But unlike the justices, monetary policy makers do not necessarily enjoy "goal independence." That the Fed's dual objectives are in tension with each other also conditions its policy making. Its full employment mandate also makes the Fed more accountable to the public than most of its foreign counterparts. Most other major central banks have only one tool and one target—interest rate and price stability.

The Fed's independence is checked by its day-to-day operation amid Washington bureaucracies. The Fed does not operate in a cocoon, but is in constant tension and dialogue with the Treasury, Congress, White House, and the public.[13] Because its policies interact with those of Congress and economic agencies, the Fed has to work in the context of the government's economic policy paradigm and coordinate its actions particularly closely with the Treasury in order to meet America's broad economic goals. In addition, because the Fed's actions have distributional implications and can make or break political fortunes, Congress has an inherent interest in monitoring the Fed.[14] Inflationary policies boost growth and create jobs, benefit debtors and those holding fixed income assets, and hurt creditors, while deflationary policies do the opposite.

Neither above the rest of government nor perfectly insulated from politics yet with tremendous economic sway, the Fed tempts usury by enterprising policy makers. The government stepped on the Fed's terrain both during the Great Depression and World War II, when the Fed was called to keep interest rates low to help finance the war effort.[15] The Johnson, Nixon, and Carter administrations subjected the Fed to the interests of the White House in expanding employment and stemming inflation.[16] Examining historical records, Alan Meltzer argues that only part of Paul Volcker's chairmanship in 1979–1987, during which interest rates were raised drastically (above 16 percent in 1981) to end inflation, has approximated textbook Fed independence.[17]

At the turn of the millennium, the Fed's independence was strong by global and historical standards. The Fed was left alone because it succeeded at responding to public moods, to the needs of different administrations, and to changes on Wall Street and in economic thought.[18] However, even Alan Greenspan, serving as Fed chairman in 1987–2006 and considered a skillful Washington navigator and powerful central banker, recalled in his April 2010 testimony, "I sat through meeting after meeting in which the pressures on the Federal Reserve and all the other regulatory agencies to enhance lending were remarkable."[19]

The Lender of First Resort

The Great Crisis forced central banks to depart from their measured ways. The Fed's first response was to pull the familiar monetary policy lever. On 8 October, it lowered the policy rate to 1.50 percent, down dramatically from 5.25 percent in September 2007 and well below the 4.25 percent in effect still through 21 January 2008; rates were pulled to 1 percent three weeks later and further to a target range of 0–0.25 percent on 16 December of that year, the lowest on record. The Fed coordinated with other major central banks, such as those of the UK, China, Canada, Sweden, and Switzerland, and the

European Central Bank (ECB). The generally hawkish ECB cut its key policy rate from 4.25 percent to 1 percent between October 2008 and June 2009.

Monetary loosening could not stop the evaporation of credit and erosion of trust among banks. Along with some other central banks, the Fed filled the gap by opening its credit window wide open.[20] In normal times using credit to merely grease the banking system, the Fed now bought government debt to boost credit and the money supply, and, most historically, set out to rescue failing banks.

In March 2008 the Fed extended a $29-billion loan to help bridge the JPMorgan Chase acquisition of Bear Stearns. Six months later, in September, the black month of the crisis, the Fed lent $85 billion to the American International Group (AIG), one of the world's largest insurers.[21] In October, it announced $900 billion in short-term cash loans to banks, made a $1.3-trillion emergency loan to nonfinancial companies, and bought $540 billion worth of short-term debt from money market mutual funds, which had reduced lending to banks and contributed to the credit freeze in interbank markets. In March 2009 the Fed performed its first round of quantitative easing, buying government bonds and mortgage-related securities issued by housing finance giants Fannie Mae and Freddie Mac for a total of $1.25 trillion.

By the end of 2010, the Fed had made more than $3.3 trillion in loans to financial institutions, companies, and foreign central banks during the crisis, and its balance sheet had expanded to $2.37 trillion from just over $800 billion in the summer of 2007, with mortgage-backed securities making up the bulk of the total. The initial results proved cost-effective—in 2009 the Fed made a record $46.1 billion on its lending programs. But with unemployment stagnating, the Fed performed a second round of quantitative easing, or QE2, worth $600 billion in November 2010. As markets sagged in August 2011 with lackluster US deficit-reduction plans, Bernanke pledged no interest rate hikes through mid-2013. In September the Fed issued the "twist," selling short-term bonds and buying long-term bonds with the aim at reducing long-term interest rates. These unprecedented measures created a firestorm debate on the future role and powers of central banks.

Operation Bernanke   The two defining schools of macroeconomics of the twentieth century—Keynesians, inspired by the legendary British economist John Maynard Keynes and monetarists, following Milton Friedman and

Anna Schwartz—disagree on the role of markets. Examining the Great Depression, Keynes saw markets as having failed and requiring rescuing by the government, while Friedman and Schwartz argued that monetary policies had constrained markets from operating properly. The policy recommendations thus differed: Keynesians advocated countercyclical fiscal spending (or cutting taxes) in the event of a downturn, while monetarists preferred the money supply as the lever of economic policy making and monetary expansion as the response.

Despite their fundamental disagreement, the two streams converged on one point: that a decline in aggregate demand, whether caused by cuts in government spending or in money supply, was what made a recession into the Great Depression. This view went squarely against that of the Depression-era Hoover administration, which believed that restoring growth would require rooting out underperforming companies. Treasury Secretary Andrew Mellon famously encapsulated the mantra by stating, "[L]iquidate labor, liquidate stocks, liquidate the farmers, liquidate real estate. It will purge the rottenness out of the system." Fiscal and monetary policies were tightened, and recovery was painfully delayed. Bad apples did get thrown out, but so did good ones. The lessons of the 1930s were reiterated six decades later in the aftermath of Japan's real estate collapse. Failing to provide adequate and timely liquidity, policy makers in Tokyo set the stage for years of economic stagnation.

The point of convergence between Keynesians and monetarists helped shape fiscal and monetary policy making in the Great Crisis. The key architect of the government's response was Ben Bernanke, the even-keeled and cryptic Princeton professor who in 2005 had replaced Alan Greenspan as the Fed chairman. Propitiously a lifelong scholar of the Great Depression, or a self-ascribed "Great Depression buff," Bernanke was keen to release liquidity in the economy. One of his own seminal works links the Great Depression to the financial shocks of 1930–1933. By undermining the efficiency of credit allocation, the shocks made credit more expensive, which, in turn, lowered aggregate demand and turned a recession into the Great Depression.[22]

In 1996 Bernanke, Mark Gertler, and Simon Gilchrist termed the mechanism by which such financial shocks and even smaller disturbances are amplified and result in major economic problems the "financial accelerator." Simplifying the elaborate theory, the accelerator starts when a shock like an implosion of an asset bubble reduces asset prices, which, in turn, lowers the creditworthiness of potential firms that would use their assets as collateral.

As credit is curbed, investment diminishes, and firms' output declines. Decreased output reduces asset prices further. A vicious cycle results—not unlike what happened in the Great Crisis. To be sure, the accelerator can also be positive: an increase in productivity that improves the cash flow and balance sheets of firms leads to lower borrowing costs and furthers investment, which adds to productivity.

The theory has immediate policy implications. Governments can put a brake on the accelerator—stabilize economic activity and help restore asset values—by buying bank shares and credit instruments at the bottom of the economic cycle and selling them at the top.[23] Such a measure could have further advantages: the rescue funds, if wisely employed, can be recovered, and central banks' subsequent sale of the acquired assets can help moderate what could be the next asset bubble. Amid the Asian financial crisis, the Hong Kong Monetary Authority purchased Hong Kong equities shorted by speculators. It sold the equities when the crisis subsided for a $14-billion profit.

Bernanke's liquidity response in the crisis was aimed at braking the financial accelerator. It became widely hailed as having delivered the world from the brink of a meltdown. In the *Financial Times*, Niall Ferguson argued that Bernanke should get a gold medal for his work, and *Time* magazine declared Bernanke 2009 Person of Year. In August 2009, President Obama nominated Bernanke for a second term.

While highly esteemed in academia and among his government colleagues, Bernanke would not escape controversy, particularly not on Capitol Hill. Some argued that he helped perpetrate the crisis by having favored, like Greenspan, loose monetary policy; others claimed he had squandered the crisis management. Bernanke weathered the egos and critics with an authoritative, professorial approach and the self-deprecating demeanor that inspired President George W. Bush to appoint him in the first place.[24] But the issue transcended the individual and inflicted the institution.

Guard or Prisoner?

For the Fed, there was little delight in the rescues. Bernanke knew perfectly well the dilemma he was facing: while releasing liquidity in the economy was all but necessary, it would also corner the Fed into breaching its delicate balancing act with the rest of the government. By taking measures of distributive consequences, the Fed would risk exposing itself to usury and accusations of overreach. Besides politics, from the time they enter the fray to the time they exit, central bankers would also have to engage in guesswork about the future state of individual banks and the overall economy, in and of itself a complicated exercise. Yet refusal to act would make politicians blame the Fed for any future economic problems.[25]

Is the need for Fed involvement in crises worth the risk to its independence? There are at least three arguments for why it is not.

The first is that by opening the credit window, the Fed risks making itself captive to politicians and bankers. At its face value, the close coordination between the Treasury and the Fed during the crisis seemed positive.[26] However, as fiscal expenditures soared, analysts worried the Treasury and Congress would pressure the Fed to play the role of fiscal policy makers and stimulate the flailing economy.[27] Equally worrisome, anticipating such an outcome, the Fed could be inclined to run loose monetary policy to deflect political attempts on its credit policy.[28] The consequences could be dire: a large fiscal debt and a central bank serving as government's printing press have been the two ingredients for every hyperinflation in history.[29]

These concerns were not unfounded. Amid the crisis, Senate Banking Committee Chairman Christopher Dodd and Congressman Paul Kanjorski of Pennsylvania asked the Fed to aid car companies and provide more credit to commercial real estate, measures that Bernanke declined to take. In December 2008, Dodd asked Bernanke in a letter "whether there is anything in your statute that prevents you from lending to any of these domestic auto-manufacturing companies." Bernanke replied that "questions of industrial policy are best resolved by Congress."[30]

The Fed's close daily interaction with Wall Street became a further source of concern and conspiracy theories. Critics saw the liquidity strategy as confirming long-standing suspicions that the Fed and the Treasury are captive to financial titans rather than serving the public interest. In a scathing and widely cited article, former IMF Chief Economist Simon Johnson argued that the heavy presence of former bankers in the upper echelons of the Treasury had made Washington agencies and Wall Street too intertwined.[31] The public agreed, even if with reservations. In a December 2009 poll, 47 percent of respondents said Bernanke cared more about Wall Street than Main Street, 20 percent thought he cared more about Main Street, and 33 percent were not certain.[32] Another poll found that only 21 percent believed the president should reappoint Bernanke to another term, while 39 percent were uncertain.[33]

A year later, 39 percent of Americans said they believed that Fed independence should be reduced, and another 16 percent argued for abolishing the Fed altogether.[34] And in October 2011, only 40 percent of Americans trusted the ideas of Bernanke to create jobs, below the 43 percent for congressional Republicans and 44 percent for Democrats.[35]

The second reservation against the Fed's involvement in crises centers on its accountability to the public. Even though making decisions of major redistributive consequence, central bankers are at the end of the day unelected technocrats exempted from the appropriations process and have few of the immediate restraints or responsibilities of politicians.[36] Amid the crisis, a slew of commentators from defenders of free markets to conspiracy theorists produced images of an all-mighty Fed that would concentrate economic power in the nation's capital.[37] The debate echoed and was compounded by the concurrent, divisive health care reform battle, where the opposing sides voiced concerns about a power transfer to Washington bureaucrats. The Treasury's unpopular idea to make the Fed the nation's macro-prudential authority sharpened the criticism.[38]

Fears of the Fed's powers run deep in American history. In 1803 Thomas Jefferson spoke against the first attempt to establish a central bank in America, stating that "the bank of the United States is one of the most deadly hostilities existing against the principles and form of our Constitution. I deem no government safe which is under the vassalage of any self-constituted authorities. . . ."[39] In 1996, a decade before the crisis, 40 percent of the top 200 US business leaders rated the Fed chairman at least as important as the president.[40]

Perhaps more worrisome than a Fed power grab were concerns about a potential conflict between price and financial stability. Critics argued that Fed's credit injections could create inflationary pressures and undermine its price stability objective.[41] In a rather unprecedented statement for a German politician, at the height of the Great Crisis Chancellor Angela Merkel remarked that "I am very skeptical about the extent of the Fed's actions and the way the Bank of England has carved its own little line in Europe. . . . [E]ven the European Central Bank has somewhat bowed to international pressure with its purchase of covered bonds."[42]

The third concern over Fed involvement in crises goes a step further, focusing on the reaction that politicians might have to the Fed's widened sphere of action. Politicians, the argument goes, might think it necessary to take back some of the Fed's independence, which would undermine the celebrated basis of technocratic monetary policy making.

Congress saw in the crisis an opportunity to cater to the deep-seated fears about unaccountable central bankers. A longtime Fed critic and author of a 2009 book *End the Fed*, firebrand Texas Congressman Ron Paul proposed subjecting the Fed's lending programs and policies to auditing by the Government Accountability Office. Usually an outlier, Paul enlisted a staggering 307 House members and 30 senators for the proposal; the House Financial Services Committee endorsed the idea with a 43–26 vote in November 2009 over Chairman Frank's objections.[43] For his part, Senate Banking Committee Chairman Christopher Dodd, headed for his toughest reelection battle yet, recommended that the Fed be stripped of most of its powers to supervise banks and recommended giving the Senate the power to select the twelve regional Fed presidents.[44] Richard Shelby of Alabama, senior Republican on the Senate Banking Committee, seconded calls to limit the Fed's regulatory role.[45] Fed's QE2 in late 2010 sparked another wave of criticism from Congress as producing inflation and weakening the dollar, with legislators calling for an end to the Fed's full employment mandate.

The Fed countered these initiatives head-on. In testimony, Fed Vice Chairman Donald L. Kohn warned Congress against destabilizing the Fed's decision making and risking high long-term interest rates resulting from hedging by investors against future inflation.[46] Bernanke was forced to defend the Fed's independence only a few weeks short of his reappointment hearing, and a year later he justified the controversial QE2 by writing an editorial and making a second *60 Minutes* appearance. Bernanke also repeatedly stood in opposition to proposals to limit the Fed's oversight functions to but the largest banks, arguing that its oversight of America's 5,000 bank holding companies and 850 smaller state banks is necessary for understanding the entire range of potential financial risks.

In January 2010 the Senate confirmed Bernanke by 70 to 30, the closest margin of any central banker in modern history. However, the issue lingered, and it assumed center stage after an April 2010 fraud case involving Goldman Sachs, one of the recipients of the Fed's rescue funding. A month later, the Senate voted 96–0 to authorize the Government Accountability Office to perform an audit of the Fed's rescues during the crisis and to require the Fed to post on its website all recipients of emergency funding.[47] A compromise struck by Bernanke ensured that the audit would not investigate or question the Fed's monetary policy decisions.

Elusive Exits

The dilemmas and politics of central bank entry in a crisis are magnified by the challenges of exiting it. The first issue is timing. Granted, the Fed is required by law to cease "unusual and exigent" credit operations when normal times emerge. However, the question is when the economy is "normal" enough. In the crisis analysts tended to agree that the "new normal" would not be the buoyant normal of the past.[48] In late 2008 the IMF ominously argued that "there is no expectation that markets will return to their pre-crisis mode of operation soon, if ever."[49]

The optimistic hypothesis was that those central banks that had been particularly active in the rescue process, the Fed and the Bank of England, would also have the most compelling incentives to unwind their positions quickly. However, uncertainties about the future state of the economy clouded judgments as the Fed weighed a major dilemma.

On the one hand, a premature unwinding could hurt the recovery and only require a reintroduction of the interventions. In 1979–1982 Fed Chairman Volcker raised interest rates as the best of the bad options to end inflation, and by so doing produced a deep recession. In Japan the central bank's hasty withdrawal in 1997 helped precipitate a double-dip recession. When exiting, the Fed would need to be certain that if it withdraws—stops supporting banks, buying mortgages, and so forth—that there will be private capital as a substitute. After the Great Crisis, a sudden withdrawal of the hundreds of billions the Fed had injected in the economy could make interest rates spike and perpetuate or even deepen the recession.

On the other hand, a delayed exit could undermine markets' ability to run on their own and possibly require a larger interest rate adjustment to tame inflation as recovery takes hold.[50] For example, Japan's interbank market shriveled when the Bank of Japan became the primary supplier of overnight funds to banks in the early 2000s. Delayed exit, in short, postpones but increases the ultimate pain. Erring on the side of caution is feasible when the economy is expected to strengthen and thus more able to weather the rate adjustment. But the Fed's lack of goal independence shapes the decision: especially in its less independent years, the Fed had incentives to delay rate increases much too long in order to stoke employment.[51] With unemployment persisting also after the Great Crisis, the Fed remained hesitant to raise rates.

Much like central banks, finance ministries also have to time their exits well. They will want to avoid replaying the experience of 1937, when fiscal support was withdrawn too quickly. But they will also want to avert prolonged fiscal spending that only deepens fiscal deficits, which, in turn, can crowd out private investment and require foreign borrowing. However, for the fiscal guardians, the exit options narrow when voters lose heart with steep deficits. For central bankers, the choice is more amorphous.

Even if the timing was right, the correct exit strategy would need to be identified. One question centers on the sequencing of the unwinding of the Fed's respective instruments—near-zero interest rates and extensive financial support. One could be unwound without the other, or some mix of the two could be used. A further choice to be made is between the various government interventions—support to the banking sector and individual banks, general monetary stimulus, and budgetary stimulus. That, in turn, requires a clear definition of the exact expenditures that fall into these various areas. For instance, it is not clear whether support to banks is different from overall monetary stimulus.[52]

The Fed's exit would also need to be choreographed to fit the plays of other actors.[53] For example, in January 2010 President Obama proposed a 0.15-percent fee from large banks to repay for the bailouts. Because the fee added to banks' funding concerns, it was seen as hindering the Fed's plans to exit and raise short-term interest rates. Similarly, Senator John Thune's initiative to end the Treasury Department's Troubled Asset Relief Program (TARP) would have withdrawn a sizable sum from the economy, again complicating the Fed's exit. The bill fell just seven votes short. Also, international coordination is required to ensure adequate liquidity in the markets if and when all governments deem it time to exit.[54] Few appeared to be in a hurry. In the summer of 2009, arguing for a prompt exit, the ECB delayed its plans as the Greek crisis unfolded in 2010.

Capitol Hill's timing also matters. Even if calling on the Fed to exit, congressional incumbents hoped that it would keep buttressing employment, housing markets, and credit programs for small businesses and consumers in the run-up to elections.

The events surrounding the crisis epitomized the difficulties for timing the exit. The Fed halted its tentative exit as the Greek crisis came to a head, clouding global economic prospects. And as the Eurozone crisis cast a lengthening shadow on the world economy and America's unemployment rates prevailed in near-double digits, the Fed reengaged with QE2 and the twist.

A Global Challenge

Politicians in other nations also took bolder actions to influence monetary policy and limit or take advantage of central banks. The Bank of England, which gained independence in 1997, raised controversy after essentially printing money to spend $295 billion on government bond purchases. The passions about the BOE's measures grew in the run-up to the June 2010 general elections. As the Eurozone crisis escalated, the ECB became widely seen as run by Berlin, which resisted the idea that the ECB become the "big bazooka" that would backstop the Eurozone bond markets. In Japan the Liberal Democratic Party has barely recognized central bank independence gained in 1997. The Democratic Party of Japan, a longtime defender of BOJ independence, all but changed its approach after rising to power in the fall of 2009, with the finance minister explicitly hoping that the BOJ would engage to save the fiscally strapped nation from a double-dip recession.

Similar pressures built up in the emerging world. In South Korea the government sent a political official to a central bank policy meeting for the first time in a decade. In Argentina a standoff over policy made the Argentine president fire the central bank chief, who was reinstated the following day by a court order. The relations between the Argentine government and the country's central bank had soured already in 2001, when Argentina defaulted on its external debts. In India pressures mounted on the role and independence of the Reserve Bank of India in financial regulatory matters.[55]

The worries about central bank independence grew to the point where Ben Bernanke believed that he needed to stress the importance of independence in a long speech titled "Central Bank Independence, Transparency, and Accountability" during a visit to Japan in May 2010.[56] Granted, there were critics. Populist scholars like Joseph Stiglitz hinted, albeit without any good empirical basis, that central bank independence might be less beneficial than its advocates argued. [57]

Avoiding Meddling

Is the Fed growing all-powerful? Unlikely. Congress can withdraw its powers at any time, and Fed officials have no interest in engaging in politics or

encroaching on fiscal policy makers' territory precisely because of the perilous repercussions that would have on their independence. Having spent the
latter part of the twentieth century weaning themselves off politics, central
bankers cherish and take pride in their technocratic trade and are reluctant to
do anything to jeopardize it.

A much greater risk is political interference with Fed's independence, its
prized faculty behind the low inflation of the past three decades. Of course,
such a risk may be short-lived: the hazards of inflation are well known and
accepted, as are the benefits of central bank independence. Strong economic
growth and a drop in unemployment figures would silence many a critic. But
the strong reaction by the Fed and academia to political initiatives to stymie
Fed independence amid the financial crisis attest to the depth of concerns
about politicized central banking. Even if Fed intervention was brief, reactions to it could be long-lasting and consequential.

Pressures on Fed independence could grow in the coming years not only
in the face of instabilities, but also as it assumes a visible and prominent role
in financial supervision as a leading member of the new financial oversight
council. The Fed's actions will be watched closely in Europe, where the ECB
president will be the first leader of the new European Systemic Risk Board. Yet
the Fed's legal independence is precarious: it does not derive from the Constitution like those of the Supreme Court and federal judiciary do; rather, it
is codified in a statute, alterable by Congress at any time. Does it now require
buttressing and, if so, how?

Cover for the Fed: Credit Accord

Should the Fed be designated as the lender of last resort? The immediate reaction is to argue no, for four reasons. First, any major Fed lending program is
a political minefield, from entry to exit. Sustained credit expansion is ultimately incongruous with central bank independence. Second, whenever the
central bank is caught in a situation where it lends when it had not done so
before, the probabilities that it will lend again will be revised upward, and
the chances for risk taking and moral hazard grow.[58] Third, by becoming involved, the Fed runs the risk of intertwining its fate with the whims of the
economy. Should the economy, for whatever reason, sour after the Fed gets
involved, the Fed would incur a political backlash and see its credibility, and
likely its independence, seriously damaged. Fourth, exiting the marketplace
is not only politically challenging; it is also difficult on technical grounds.

The decision to enter markets will have to be weighed against the elusiveness of exit.

At the same time, major credit injections amid devastating crises may be the best of bad options. The Great Depression revealed the high costs of failing to act; future economic historians may find that the Great Crisis reiterated or, more likely, qualified that lesson. But if a rescue is enacted, the Fed is likely the most qualified for the task: it is technocratic, holds the best information on banks, and has a built-in aversion to playing politics. Besides, the Fed is in a catch-22: while intervention creates a host of problems, standing in the sidelines would likely produce, and would certainly in the Great Crisis have produced, criticism that the Fed was replicating the errors of the pre-Depression monetary policy makers.

Because Fed intervention may be warranted and Congress has a claim on the Fed's independence, the questions are, first, how to reduce the odds of Fed involvement in the first place, and, second, how to enhance the odds that when the Fed does act, its actions will not prompt politicians to curb its independence.

The simple answer to the first question is financial regulations and corporate governance reforms that make crises less frequent. Another answer that gets at both questions at once is an accord on Fed credit policy proposed by Marvin Goodfriend.[59] Such an accord would specify rules of engagement for the Fed when crises hit: that the Treasury and Fed cooperate in letting Fed credit programs expire promptly, that credit policy not be allowed to undermine price stability, and that the Fed adhere to a "Treasuries only" asset acquisition policy, except for limited discount window lending to banks deemed solvent. The accord could also specify something advocated by James Hamilton of the University of California, San Diego: that if the Fed intervenes, it should buy only assets that will deliver unquestionable return above inflationary expectations.[60]

Such an accord would limit unnerving, politically motivated entreaties to the Fed, prevent the Fed's credit from being misallocated for fiscal purposes, and cement the Fed's price stability objective. It would also further the Fed's transparency and accountability to the public, a necessity in any democracy. The accord would essentially be a sequel to the one-paragraph 1951 accord between the Treasury and the Fed that reasserted Fed independence by restoring its instrument independence, and thus allowed the Fed to end the wartime commitment to an interest rate peg. And it would save politicians from themselves: allowing the Fed to work for the broader good of price and financial stability instead of subjecting monetary policy to the particularistic demands of congressional representatives. Precisely that realization made Congress adopt a statute on central bank independence in 1913.

Advantages of Ambiguity   Guidelines for Fed actions once it gets involved should *not* come with rules specifying *when* the Fed ought to become involved. The Fed will remain a lender of last resort as long as there are systemic risks. Only its role should not be codified as such, both in order to distance it from politics and to avoid moral hazard. Ambiguity is in the interest of both central bank independence and healthy risk aversion in financial markets. Making the Fed anything like a bank bankruptcy court would certainly compromise its independence.[61]

To be sure, randomized lending policy is not sufficient for curbing moral hazard: if done for the sole purpose of retaining a sense of ambiguity, rather than on the grounds of the facts of each case, it might never be credibly applied.[62] In other words, the announcement of ambiguity does not necessarily alter the incentives of too-big-to-fail institutions. The air of ambiguity can also be obliterated by behavior, as the Fed's past behavior conditions market expectations about its future behavior. The horse may be too far out of the barn: taking extensive actions in the Great Crisis, central banks may have created, in the worlds of Paul Volcker, "an implied promise of similar actions in times of future turmoil."[63] Precedence is as powerful as blind faith in randomized lending is foolish. This reality should make crisis prevention a policy priority.

Bursting Bubbles?

Central banks could, of course, use monetary policy to detonate asset build-ups before they flare into crises. The Federal Reserve has been criticized for not countering the housing bubble with an interest rate hike. However, such preemptive policy poses philosophical, political, and technical questions.

The philosophical question is whether the Fed ought to be in the business of determining asset values. If so, then the political question is which bubble exactly—speculative bubble, "carbon" bubble, or something else—that the Fed should attack. Not all bubbles are the same, but come in various risk profiles. The IT bubble damaged the real economy much less than the housing bubble, arguably because the latter, by affecting consumer credit, reaches deep into the middle and lower classes.[64]

The technical questions are numerous. The first is whether a bubble exists. For example, some argue that oil prices are too high because of speculation, while others argue they are too low because markets fail to price the negative externalities of carbon emissions. It is also not clear which exact indicator the Fed should use to determine that a bubble exists to begin with. Should an overall housing market, stock market, or perhaps oil market index be used?[65] If a veritable bubble were identified, bursting it with interest rates can be ineffective and counterproductive: rates are a blunt instrument for fighting specific bubbles, yet hugely consequential for the overall economy.

There could also be negative effects on the targeted sector: had the Fed undone the housing bubble early, it could have triggered a fall in housing prices and a wave of defaults and foreclosures, and possibly now be blamed for perpetrating a recession. An interest rate increase would also have hurt growth and asset prices outside the real estate industry, as corporations were still working to weather the aftershocks of the dot.com boom.[66] Besides, the Fed's policy in the 2002–2005 boom years had few critics, and it was reasonable for the times. After all, the Fed was resolved to bring down the persistently high unemployment rates in those years' jobless recovery. By keeping interest rates low, it was simply seeking to fulfill its second mandate. Because it also managed to keep inflation down, policy makers and academics saw few reasons to worry.

Even if the Fed had acted, it still might not have prevented the crisis. The creator of the "Taylor rule"—a formula that shows how much the central bank should change the nominal interest rate in response to divergence of actual inflation rates from target inflation rates—Stanford economist John Taylor argues that the low interest rates in 2003 and 2004 as compared with the Taylor rule contributed to the boom in housing starts and may have boosted house prices, lowered delinquency and foreclosure rates, expanded credit, and led to higher demand for housing.[67]

But the evidence about the contributions of monetary policy to housing price increase is contested. Fed officials, including Bernanke, argue that there is no meaningful relationship.[68] A St. Louis Federal Reserve study strikes the middle ground, showing rather convincingly that monetary policy did have a significant effect on housing investment and prices and that easy monetary policy in 2002–2004 contributed to the boom in the housing market in 2004–2005.[69] However, the study also finds that the effect on the overall economy was rather limited: without such policies, inflation would have been only 25 basis points lower at the end of 2006. The lesson from these studies is that while loose monetary policy can contribute to asset bubbles, it may not drive economies into crises—and undoing it could also have heavy trade-offs.

An Impossible Mandate?

Scrutiny on the role and policies of central banks, and the Fed in particular, is bound to only grow in good times and bad now that they are receiving stupendous regulatory powers. Should the Fed's dual mandate be dropped? And should the Fed engage in inflation targeting to preempt critics and provide greater transparency?

The dual mandate is a remnant of the 1970s, when stagflation caused politicians to call on the Fed to propel employment. The 1978 Full Employment and Balanced Growth Act, or the Humphrey–Hawkins Act, set off by now three decades of challenges to the Fed's dual mandate. The dual mandate is operationalized in the Fed's analyses by the "output gap," which postulates that inflation cannot rise as long as there is unused capacity in the economy. Unemployment is one measure of the output gap.

Opponents to the dual mandate charge that the Fed's drive to boost job creation by printing money in the late 1970s caused the inflationary pressures and eventually a recession in the 1980s—an experience that made the Europeans charge the ECB with a single mandate upon its founding in 1998. The dual mandate is argued to be so ingrained in the Fed's decision making that it persuaded Greenspan and Bernanke to keep interest rates low even in the face of the commodity and housing booms.[70]

In the wake of the crisis, conservative congressional representatives introduced several bills that would strip the Fed of its employment mandate and focus it exclusively on price stability. The concerns about the implications of the dual mandate are appropriate. The dual mandate is flawed for several reasons.

First, it inherently politicizes monetary policy making. The Fed's playing the role of a benevolent engineer of labor market performance risks the ire of politicians who in turn might interfere with the Fed's independence. Second, the Fed is hard-pressed to ever fulfill its mandate, as the level of employment in the long run depends on the natural rate of employment rather than being affected by monetary policy.[71] Third, the dual mandate could force the Fed to pursue social policy objectives perhaps at the expense of its price stability objective—even though a moderate level of inflation is costly because it complicates long-term planning, such as firms' capital allocations and individuals' savings decisions.[72]

The theoretical justifications for the dual mandate are rather tenuous. For example, defenders argue that the economic and social costs of unemployment are higher than those of moderate inflation, so supply shocks such as the Great Crisis require the Fed to allow prices to increase to avoid mass unemployment.[73] Or, they say, the dual mandate has helped the United States to have lower unemployment than nations where central bankers focus solely on inflation, and also enjoy comparable levels of inflation. Or that because central bankers tend to be inflation-averse, the Fed should be expected not to prod employment at the expense of inflation, nor should it expected to interpret the goal of maximum employment literally. Still another defense of the dual mandate is that it gives the Fed degrees of operational freedom to deviate momentarily from the goal of long-run price stability, which helps the United States attain superior economic outcomes, such as faster economic recoveries, than is the case for nations with a single mandate.[74]

However, the empirical studies on any of these theories seldom go beyond crude correlations between the dual mandate and economic outcomes, and they are inherently based on only a few observations. It is hardly clear that the relative price stability and solid economic performance in the several years before the 2008–2009 crisis owe to the Fed's dual mandate—let alone whether economic performance might have been the same had the Fed pursued a single mandate of price stability.

But the opponents of the dual mandate also face an empirical challenge: it is not clear that the dual mandate has resulted in inflationary bias in monetary policy making.[75] US experience during the Great Moderation could be taken to mean that noninflationary monetary policy can be accompanied by strong macroeconomic performance and employment levels, and relatively mild recessions compared to other nations. Whether Greenspan and Bernanke should have taken the punch bowl away sooner to burst the housing bubble is also debatable, as discussed above. And there is little evidence of trade-offs between the objectives—that very low unemployment would necessarily be inflationary.

Rather, an argument can be made that the dual objectives are complementary, as high inflation could require central bankers to raise interest rates at the risk of perpetrating a job-killing recession, as in the 1980s. In addition, the Fed's focus is not dominated by one goal or the other, but it is rather found to alternate between its two objectives over time. For example, the Fed prioritized low inflation in the first decade of Greenspan's term, and in 1998 it turned to employment.[76] Greenspan himself has argued that modest and stable inflation fuels employment—and that in practice the dual mandate is implemented as a single one.[77]

In short, it is not clear that the dual mandate has led to adverse economic outcomes—the bills opposing it have likely failed to prosper for that very reason—or that a single mandate would have led to better economic outcomes. But it is also not clear that the impact of the dual mandate has been superior to what a Fed vested with a single mandate might have produced.

Thus far, debate on the long-run effect of the Fed's policies and the usefulness of the dual mandate boil down to one question: whether the central bank should be responsible for anything beyond price stability, particularly if that jeopardizes its independence to pursue the price stability objective. The political repercussions of the mandate—the pressure it brings on the Fed's independence both by inflation hawks and by officials keen on spurring employment—are the main and most important objection to it. Of course, it is conceivable that the Fed would be criticized for its policies even in the counterfactual case—i.e., even if it had had a single mandate. However, what is clear is that a single mandate would take away political pressure on the Fed to serve as a "fast-track" substitute for other means to propel employment. However, politics does not favor the opponents of the dual mandate: the Obama White House, struggling with persistently high unemployment, has balked at proposals to shed the full employment goal.

Targeted Inflation

While at Princeton, Federal Reserve Chairman Ben Bernanke coedited a book titled *Inflation Targeting*, in which his own chapter carefully argues that "the experience of inflation targeting countries," today Australia, Canada, Chile, the Eurozone, New Zealand, Norway, Iceland, Poland, Sweden, South Africa, Turkey, and the United Kingdom, "appears to be sufficiently positive to warrant close examination of this new approach to monetary policy."[78]

One argument for the Fed to set an inflation target and specify a time to get to the goal is that the costs of even moderate inflation merit a hard target of some kind, and inflation targeting provides just such an anchor; another is that the dual mandate, if not revoked, is inflationary and as such requires an inflation target. There is some recent evidence on the benefits of inflation targeting. An IMF study shows that since August 2008, countries that practice inflation targeting lowered nominal policy rates by more than those that did not, and that the loosening translated into a large differential in real interest rates relative to other countries.[79] The targeting nations were less likely to have deflationary concerns and saw sharper real depreciations. Although the study is based on correlations and does not establish causality between targeting and economic outcomes, it notes that the nations practicing inflation targeting experienced less unemployment and stronger industrial production than those that did not.

After taking office in 2006, Bernanke tested Washington's receptivity to inflation targeting. But as the Great Crisis erupted, the Fed appreciated its room to maneuver. Indeed, inflation targeting sounds better than it is in practice. One of the main hurdles is choosing the underlying measure, such as the consumer price index (CPI). Such a measure, like others of its kind, may not accurately gauge the growth of the money supply and thus handcuffs central bankers into suboptimal policies. Another thorny question is policy design itself, including determining the target and the time horizons to get to it. And there is no compelling evidence that the use of yardsticks yields superior outcomes.[80] Besides, explicit inflation targeting could prove incompatible with the Fed's dual mandate, so shedding the full employment goal—or loosening adherence to it—might be necessary for inflation targeting.

Conclusion

The role of public bodies in financial markets is rightly controversial. However, the positions assumed by the Federal Reserve are temporary. More worrisome than the investments themselves are politicians' reactions to them. This is not the time to overreact and limit the Fed's independence. There simply is no evidence to warrant such measures. The trade-offs could be very high: political interference would destabilize the Fed's day-to-day monetary policy management and send a worrisome signal to other nations wrestling with similar issues, and even give other nations a license to expand the role of politicians in managing economies. The proposed cure would be worse than the presumed disease.

Instead, safeguards should be put in place. A Fed–Treasury accord on the specific measures that the Fed can and cannot take in a crisis should be struck as a means to preempt political pressures on the Fed to allocate credit for fiscal purposes, all the while ensuring the Fed's accountability to the public. Solutions to bubbles lie more outside the Federal Reserve than within it: if bubbles cannot easily be tamed or randomized lending credibly implemented, the premium on preemptive regulation rises. The new and coming regulations will need to be matched by clear commitments from the Treasury and Congress to keep the Fed above politics.

The broader questions about state capitalism in the twenty-first-century world economy, including public ownership of major companies in such nations as Russia or China, are beyond the scope of this book. But free markets and market capitalism are far from dead. Rather than subverted and subordinated to political ends, private property, the essence of capitalism, lives on. If the lessons of the crisis are learned and the rules on the role of public actors in private markets sharpened, the twenty-first century promises to be a century not of state capitalism, but of smarter capitalism.

6 The Myth of America's Decline

[O]ur economic power and military might have grown beyond anything that our forefathers could have imagined. But that power and might can only be sustained and renewed if we can regain our authority with the world, the authority not simply of a large and wealthy nation but of the American idea. If we can live up to that idea, if we can exercise our power wisely and well, we can make America great again.

—*US senator and candidate for Democratic Party presidential nominee Hillary Clinton*, Foreign Affairs, *November 2007*

THIS BOOK OPENED BY DISCUSSING THE CONTRIBUTIONS of the US-led world economic order—the postwar framework of global governance built on rules-based institutions and free and open markets—to global prosperity in the past six decades. It went on to discuss the challenges to that global economic instability and the divergent demands that the leading economies pose to the American order. It then argued that there are no substitutes for the institutions and ideals of the American order, just as there are no conceivable alternative paradigms for global governance, but also that this peerless order must now be revitalized. The American order made anew is necessary for a world where growth and globalization are accompanied by sustained stability.

This book has proposed that rather than by way of watershed events, stability, just like growth, needs to be pursued with persistence and as a process. Rather than pitting policy makers against market makers, the process needs to align interests. Rather than each nation futilely fending for itself, the common aspiration for growth and stability takes coordination.

Such approaches are difficult, for they are political. While nations share an interest in a thriving world economy, they disagree on the means to that end. National interests, shaped by domestic political economy constraints, clash. Within countries, the preferences of politicians, beholden to the particularistic demands of their respective constituencies, also often diverge. Disagreements among and within nations over pathways to prosperity threaten mutual economic gains.

This is where leadership comes in.

Reforms and regimes are not automatic. They cannot be wished into being. Someone has to coordinate the play: the field needs a quarterback. The cast of characters on the global stage may have grown, but leadership runs thin. This book has held that no nation is as able to shoulder the responsibility of leadership, with its rights and its responsibilities, as the United States. US leadership, I have argued, is required because of America's unique aptness to lead and because global economic problems cannot be solved without America. The United States should not be a global sheriff brokering the world's collective action problems, but in the economic arena, it must. Once centrifugal forces—of protectionism against the foreign, favoritism of locals, exclusive nationalism and regionalism—defeat centripetal ones, globalization collapses, pulling growth and stability in its wake.

At this critical hour, an isolationist America would be a tragedy for the world and the United States. The United States must uphold its order, and only it can. Leadership is America's price of global prosperity.

Yet America's ability and willingness to lead are questioned. Commentators, some outright gleefully, have declared the end of *Pax Americana* in the face of the ascent of Asia, Washington's deficit spending, and postcrisis disillusionment with US-style capitalism. To many observers, the United States can no longer be expected to provide growth, liquidity, and stability in the global economy, let alone continue setting the tempo in international relations. Even if willing, America is said to be unable. It is, critics say, an inexorably declining nation with diminishing leverage in world affairs.

Is America eclipsing? Will the American order be recalled as an interlude short of a century in world affairs, just like the Cold War was an episode of a few decades in world politics? What can and should US economic and foreign policies be in the twenty-first century?

A Perpetual Myth

Talk about American decline is much what Charles Kindleberger has argued global financial crises to be: a hardy perennial. In the 1970s, the oil shocks, the war in Vietnam, and the Iranian Revolution were considered to condemn

America to economic stagnation and prematurely terminate the American Century. The tripling of imported petroleum prices and the mass flight of industries from the Rust Belt left Americans disillusioned with their economic future; the endless war and the Watergate sagas stripped their faith in their government. Competitors from Japan to France were supposedly catching up with the US lead in the world economy. Demoralized, the nation took pains to clutch at the American Dream. Gazing at the global stage, at the turn of the decade Singapore's Foreign Minister R. S. Rajaratnam inquired in the *Wall Street Journal*, "Who Will Be Number One?"[1]

Taking over in Washington in 1981, the Reagan administration saw the 1970s as an era of economic and spiritual decline, both domestically and inter nationally.[2] Behind the descent, argued the new White House, was not some structural deficiency but, rather, political leadership especially of the Carter years: the driver, not the vehicle, was at fault. Elevated by inspirational, high-integrity leadership, America would reemerge as the shining city upon a hill.

Reagan's unflinching optimism could not silence a cadre of naysayers feeding off the recession and deficits. Countless accounts in the 1980s and 1990s predicted a steady erosion of American power and the rise of Asia.[3] Best-selling books such as Paul Kennedy's *The Rise and Fall of the Great Powers* predicted that America's "imperial overstretch" would trigger the nation's decline; former Reagan administration official Clyde Prestowitz's *Trading Places: How We Allowed Japan to Take the Lead* bellowed about America's waning competitiveness and gaping trade deficits.[4] In *Mortal Splendor*, Walter Russell Mead criticized the economic policies of conservative and liberal administrations alike, arguing that America's decline would need to be accompanied by a new global social contract.[5]

Few objected, but some did. In 1990 George Washington University Professor Henry Nau's *The Myth of America's Decline* elegantly argued that mainstream arguments about American decline were overly structuralist—that they attributed outcomes to economic and demographic transformations while discounting the power of policy in shaping nations' destinies.[6] *The Myth* posited that fatalistic, structuralist determinism would any day lose out to good policy aimed at bringing America back at the helm of the world economy.

Nau would prove to be right. Policy made a difference. While US policy makers succeeded at taming inflation, ending deficits, and reviving growth, their Japanese counterparts failed to contain the implosion of the miracle economy. As the Berlin Wall fell, the flaws not only of policy but an entire political paradigm antithetical to America's became devastatingly glaring. The end of communism was caused by a cascade of failures of a political regime that suffocated the most profound of human aspirations, individual freedom. Perfected in America, the very same quest produced a new wave of technological advances and a surge of productivity that discredited the remaining Malthusians. Francis Fukuyama's 1992 book *The End of History and the Last Man* famously saw the two paradigms championed by the United States, capitalism and democracy, as universally triumphant.[7]

In the 1990s the United States was uncontested on the world stage. It was the unquestioned superpower, the most innovative economy, the nation that had defied predictions and beat the odds. Its calls for capitalism and open markets the world over paved the way to a new wave of globalization. As Deputy Secretary of State Robert Zoellick wrote, "[I]n 2000, the world is again in an era of rapid change, reminiscent of a century ago. The vitality of America's private economy, the preeminence of its military power, and the appeal of the country's ideas are unparalleled."[8]

But history had yet to author its end. Commentary about America's decline began to reemerge in the early 2000s, as the United States came under an attack of terrorism and set out to wage a war against a nebulous enemy. Criticism swelled to a gale after the prolongation of the Iraq war, which by 2008 consumed even by a conservative estimate a stunning $275 million per day and brought to the surface residual grudges that America's friends and enemies held against Washington.[9]

Gloom hung heavy. *Newsweek's* Michael Hirsh argued that America's clout was waning and that the nation itself bore the blame.[10] Retired Army Colonel Andrew Bacevich's 2008 book *The Limits of Power: The End of American Exceptionalism* bitterly excoriated America's consumerism as freedom disfigured in search of self-gratification.[11] In a tenuous argument, he attributed America's expansive foreign policy, pursued even at the expense of war, to the nation's consumption craze. David Walker, former head of the US Government Accountability Office, argued that with its wars and burgeoning domestic challenges from fiscal deficits to health care, education, energy, environment, and immigration, America resembled the Roman Empire prior to its fall.[12] Foreign media, all too easily given to *Schadenfreude*, interjected with such patronizing claims as "Americans are so optimistic that they often blur the line between optimism and naivete."[13]

The logic of most such criticisms followed that of Nau: compounded policy mistakes as drivers of troubles. A parallel "whither America?" debate was more structuralist, grounded on economic transformations. Dozens of authors painted the world as being on the cusp of an epic, West versus East struggle, a battle of the old transatlantic world against the ascendant Asia-Pacific. Niall Ferguson became a spokesperson, writing that the twentieth century ended with the "the descent of the West" and "a reorientation of the world" toward the East.[14] Fareed Zakaria's 2008 book *Post-American World* argued that America would be sidelined by the emerging Asian nations. And as in the 1980s, there was commentary about the rise of Europe. Charles Kupchan's 2007 *The End of the American Era* maintained that the biggest challenge to the United States would not come from Asia, but from the increasingly unified Europe.[15] The euro was said to await in the wings as the dollar took its last lap.

Among the most influential were predictions from within the US government. In its 2009 report, the US National Intelligence Council, Washington's official national security think tank, argued that the international system as constructed after World War II would be "unrecognizable" by 2025 thanks to globalization, the rise of emerging powers, and a "historic transfer of relative wealth and economic power from west to east." [16] It warned that "the next 20 years of transition to a new system are fraught with risks. . . . [S]trategic rivalries are most likely to revolve around trade, investments and technological innovation and acquisition, but we cannot rule out a nineteenth-century scenario of arms races, territorial expansion, and military rivalries."

While many writers were resigned to an inevitability of American decline, some called for policy reversals to wean the United States off the perilous path. Zakaria put forth a positive domestic economic policy agenda for the United States to continue as a great power.[17] Mead argued for humble and pragmatic foreign policy of ends proportionate to America's means.[18] Robert Kagan's book *The Return of History and the End of Dreams* called for a combination of neoconservatism with neorealism in US foreign policy—balancing with other democracies against the authoritarian China and Russia.[19]

Flawed Premises
The Great Crisis amplified the pessimist voices. It was quickly interpreted as a tipping point that would unleash simmering mega-trends deemed to undercut America's economic primacy: the ascent of Asia, the withering of the

West, and the erosion of American capitalism. America's economic decline, in turn, was said to lead to the end of US global political leadership. The hegemon might be willing, the argument went, but it would be unable. The mantle bearer, the global consensus went, would be China.

Will the twenty-first century be remembered as an Asian century, just like the twentieth century was an American century? Not necessarily. Much like in Nau's time, the recent arguments about American decline have three flaws.

The first is a zero-sum premise of the world economy, when global economics is all about mutual gains. In both finance and trade, others' gain is not America's loss. Economists have since Adam Smith and David Ricardo shown that the world economy is a win–win setting where everyone does best by specializing and engaging in free exchange. Lost in much of the commentary is that economic success in Asia and Europe would only buoy America's economy, just like downturns elsewhere would hurt the United States. As China rises, so does the United States; if China falls, America will also be hurt. Also unmentioned in the talk about American decline is that today's world economy is a global factory where the cogs need one another in order for the wheel to spin. The crisis refuted the theories of "decoupling" of emerging markets from advanced nations, validating the intricate dependence of nations on one another's fortunes.

Second, arguments about America's decline (and Asia's rise) are astoundingly linear, expecting America to continue a steady slide while Asia gradually climbs on its foreordained path. But history tends to be more capricious than that, largely evolving in a nonlinear and even chaotic fashion.[20] Among the many shocks that have obliterated neat economic projections are pandemics, oil price hikes, wars, democratization, use of nuclear weapons, and disruptive technologies from the combustion engine to containerization, the Internet, and, possibly now, worldwide electrification of transportation and space transportation. Weren't forecasts of Japan's inevitable rise proven wrong by the 1990s? Didn't the Cold War end against all expectations? Weren't the recent political shakeups from Tunisia to Egypt, Libya, and Syria unforeseen by most observers? Indeed, wasn't the very Great Crisis a shock that discredited theses about the world's having reached a new, heady growth frontier? The marveled housing boom turned into an epic economic bottoming, sub-prime mortgages were renamed toxic assets, and the scorned prophets of the calamity such as Nouriel Roubini took the stage as clairvoyant celebrities.

Third and perhaps most importantly, many accounts about American decline are inherently structuralist—attributing outcomes to tectonic shifts in demographics, economic size, productivity, and the like, while discounting the power of policy and leadership in shaping nations' destinies. And yet, Nobel prizes have for decades been dealt to men and women who have discredited such structuralist scholars as Karl Marx, Max Weber, and Emile Durkheim by showing that policy makers and the institutions they operate in critically shape structural trends, rather than only being shaped by them. Henry Nau's argument—that structuralist determinism would be trumped by savvy policies—was proven right in the 1990s, and it rings even truer today. That problems exist in America—and they do, from the fiscal deficit to gaping unemployment, flailing economic growth, and subpar schools and infrastructure—does not mean that they cannot and will not be fixed. The future is not preordained.

Economic Remake

Still another problem with the talk about American decline is the conjecture that the rise of other economies will inevitably erode US leadership in the world. Yet economic power does not make leadership alone: policy, diplomacy, and the appeal of timeless values also affect balance of power in the global polity. But although not sufficient, economic strength is a necessary element of power. US economic prowess is also critical for solving global challenges, for they are unsolvable without America. Economic strength is imperative for America's global engagement, for discontent at home all too easily translates into disengagement abroad. And good economic policy is crucial for the credibility of US leadership. A nation that squanders its own economy will not be granted the authority to lead.

How, then, will the US economy perform in the twenty-first century? And what are America's main challenges and the policies to tackle them?

In 2007 Goldman Sachs famously predicted that the Chinese economy would surpass that of the United States in 2030 and grow nearly twice as large by 2050.[21] Postcrisis projections by the Carnegie Endowment for International Peace forecast that the Chinese economy will grow larger than the US economy in 2032, a point of time when India will have surpassed Japan as the third-largest economy. Between 2010 and 2050, the US economy will grow at

2.7 percent per year, twice as fast as most G7 economies, even if behind the 5.6-percent annual growth in China and 6.2 percent in India.[22] Americans will continue as the wealthiest people. Goldman puts US average annual per capita income in 2050 at $92,000 and Korea's at $90,000. Chinese incomes will soar to $50,000 in 2050, slightly above the US per capita income in 2010. The other G7 economies and Russia fall between China and Korea. Carnegie reaches rather different figures, placing the US per capita income at $88,000 in 2050 and the UK's at $78,000. China's per capita would be $32,000 and Korea's $65,000.

Projections are educated guesses. They are based on great many variables that may or may not bear out. However, what is clear is that America's economic potential is stifled, for two reasons.

The first is the US fiscal deficit, something this book has highlighted on several occasions. The debt is not only a drag on the economy and investments required for increasing productivity; it also perpetuates global imbalances, fuels protectionist sentiments, and undermines foreign creditors' confidence in the US economy. Spending needs to be curbed and entitlements reformed. The issue is simple, solutions hard—yet critical for the future of America and the US role in the world.

The second constraint on growth is America's flagging productivity. Economic growth is a function of productivity. Economists like to say that productivity is not everything—except in the long run, when it is. Projecting on the basis of figures dating back to 1891, Robert Gordon of Northwestern University argues that in 2007–2027, labor productivity in the US economy is bound to grow 1.7 percent per year, slower than the 2.02 percent in 2000–2007 or the 1.79 percent for 1987–2007, even if faster than the 1.25 percent for 1972–1995.[23] That entails a 2.4-percent annual GDP growth for 2007–2027, same as in 2000–2007 and at a par with other projections. GDP growth in turn translates into a per capital income gain of 1.5 percent per annum, much below the 2.17 percent attained in 1929–2007 and representing, Gordon states, "the slowest growth of the measured American standard of living over any two-decade interval recorded since the inauguration of George Washington."

Productivity has many drivers. New technologies and innovation, infrastructures and education, specialization and division of labor, openness to trade, good institutions, even such intangibles as trust among people have all been argued to affect it.[24] It is well-known that America faces challenges in a number of these areas—primary and secondary education, infrastructure, and innovation.

In 2009 OECD rankings, the latest available, American teenagers ranked 27th in the world in mathematics aptitude, below such nations as Czech Republic and Hungary, barely above Greece and Portugal, and far behind their peers in nations that have service-based economies comparable to the US economy, such as Korea, Canada, Australia, and the Netherlands.[25] American students' attainment had not improved from past rankings. In science, US students rank 20th, which is toward the bottom among advanced economies. Consulting firm McKinsey estimates that had the United States closed the gap between its educational achievement levels and those of better-performing nations such as Finland and Korea, US GDP in 2008 would have been $1.3 trillion to $2.3 trillion greater, 9–16 percent higher.[26] The level of learning has been too stagnant, and it is particularly poor among African Americans and Hispanics. Yet education is perhaps the best shot America has for equality of opportunity. Tapping America's latent talents and breaking the poisonous politics of rising inequality, across-the-board quality education makes for good economics and politics.

Population growth and increase in international trade in the next decades will pressure infrastructures particularly in Southern California, the Dallas and Atlanta metropolitan regions, and the corridor connecting the northeastern and mid-Atlantic states. Road infrastructure is illustrative. In 1982–2008 road congestion cost 2.9 billion gallons of fuel annually, and in 2008 the average commuter spent 40 hours in gridlock each year, or three times the amount of 1982 and equivalent to $78 billion in annual lost productivity. Between 2008 and 2018, the hours of delay are estimated to grow by more than 170 percent.[27] Maintaining even the most essential physical infrastructure will require an estimated $2.2 trillion, more than the annual output of the state of California, in the period 2010–2014.[28]

The United States became the leading global economic power in good part thanks to innovation and application of new technologies in agriculture, transportation, communication, and manufacturing, followed by health care and information technology. Technological leaps are produced by several factors—patent rights, education, market structures are just some of the determinants. But one of the key drivers is spending on research and development (R&D), which has increased almost annually in the postwar years and is forecast to continue rising. However, the share of government R&D—widely seen as catalytic of private R&D—has declined drastically.[29] Also, the share of defense R&D outlays, which have greater positive spillover effects to other sectors, has declined.[30] And while state governments' R&D incentives have proliferated since the mid-1980s, the fact that strong incentives in one state merely draw innovation from other states limits the net national gains in innovation.[31]

Private sector is the driver of productivity. America's six million employment-providing small businesses are hubs of innovation and jobs creation. They are both highly dynamic and fickle, with nearly as many deaths as births. The survivors serve genuine market needs, and they need to be buttressed. Yet they are hamstrung by taxes, regulations, and lack of financing, as venture capital migrates to more mature and safer bets.

Big business is also good for America. Large companies are the leading investors in research and development; they account for more than 70 percent of US exports, a job and growth driver; and they pay some 50 percent more and provide 10 percent more working hours per week than small companies.[32] They have economies of scale and scope, which fuel competitiveness and reduce costs. Walmart is a case in point: the arrival of a Walmart Supercenter in a neighborhood leads to a 25-percent decrease in local residents' grocery bills.[33]

Granted, there is much more to these select drivers of productivity. The quality of education is not the only factor behind labor productivity; on-the-job training and entrepreneurship, two areas where the United States excels, are another. Physical infrastructure is only one part of productivity in the information technology era. And innovation transcends borders: new technologies abroad can be imported to America just as R&D can be outsourced overseas and used by US companies operating in and outside America. Private R&D has public good benefits: by their massive R&D spending, US businesses from Google to GE produce positive externalities that benefit not only them and their customers, but also the public at large.

Spending more on any productivity driver is not the only or necessarily even the best solution. An education overhaul will not be accomplished as much with money as through a fundamental political change. With teachers' unions obstructing change, charter schools and vouchers must be on top of the policy menu, right alongside merit-based pay and promotion for teachers. Piling R&D incentives on large companies can encourage spending on projects that would have but scant commercial value; giving a tax credit to small business to innovate can be more effective. Reforming the migration regime for the highly skilled would allow America to tap some of the most productive and entrepreneurial people on the planet. There are additional good programs that can be bolstered. For example, the revised EB-2 visa extends a green card to foreign entrepreneurs whose ventures are in US national interests, and the EB-5 visa gives foreign entrepreneurs a green card if they invest $500,000 in an American project that generates at least ten jobs. Embracing such self-starters is a deal for America in the short run and long run alike.

At the same time, America can and must do better. Investments, public and especially private, in the economy's backbones are not only necessary for fueling US productivity; they are also critical for enabling future generations to reach their fullest potential. The public deficit obstructs closing the investment deficit.

Unacknowledged Fundamentals

The challenges facing the United States are serious, but they do not spell disaster. The keen focus in the past few years on America's Achilles heels has eclipsed attention to its strengths, just as the attention to the strengths of China has masked its many weaknesses. Presidential candidate John McCain risked ridicule amid the 2008 recession when declaring American economic fundamentals strong, but he was not wrong.

Consider some facts. The United States is the home of a larger share (133) of the world's leading companies on the Fortune Global 500 list than any other country, thrice as many as Germany and also more than China and Japan *combined*. The US military is still overwhelming in reach and has multiples of the equipment, sophistication, and projection of those of the closest competitors. American universities, incubators of more Nobel Laureates than other nations combined, are still the global leaders in higher education.

Now consider fundamentals and trends. Although America fell three places in the World Economic Forum's perceptions-based ranking of most competitive nations in 2011, it is still fifth, behind Switzerland, Singapore, Sweden, and Finland, while such juggernauts as China and Korea trail far behind (at 26th and 24th).[34] Reported US competitive advantages range from technological readiness to labor and goods market efficiencies, innovation, strength of investor protections, and certain aspects of higher education, such as use of IT and tertiary enrollment. Unsurprisingly, infrastructure, quality of mathematics and science, primary education, the macroeconomic situation, certain health indicators, and wasteful government spending and burdens of government regulation are ranked as America's competitive disadvantages.

The United States also has the greatest potential for pushing the frontiers of innovation. The "2010 Global R&D Funding Forecast" expects the United States, which makes up over a third of global R&D spending, to maintain technology leadership in specific, high-growth areas over the next decade, including health care and medicine, basic energy research, carbon dioxide sequestration, and security and defense.[35]

The United States is also by global standards hospitable to business. It is fourth in World Bank's Doing Business rankings, along with Singapore, New Zealand, and Hong Kong, while Germany is 19th, China is 91st, and India is 132nd. America tops the list with Singapore and Australia on labor market dynamism and flexibility. It is fourth in availability of credit and fifth in investor protections. In a world where garage entrepreneurs have a chance to build global companies with a fraction of the cash needed for a start-up just a decade ago, America outperforms most nations: starting a company in the United States takes only 6 days, as opposed to 15 days in Germany, 29 in India, 38 in China, and 119 in Brazil.[36] Trading goods across borders in the United States takes 5–6 days, compared to 7 days in Germany and 21–24 days in China.

International trade obliterates resource constraints that autarkies would have to consider. But energy is different. Even the most level-headed analysts raise concerns about the future availability and cost of energy, and its impact on business costs and economic growth. However, trends indicate that the United States is not running out of gas. In contrast to Europe, Japan, China, or even India, the United States has a wealthy resource base: it has not only the most arable land and is the largest food exporter in the world, but also has extensive domestic sources of energy. The Great Plains and Appalachian regions hold massive reservoirs of natural gas, and America's Midwest is famously labeled the Saudi Arabia of wind power.[37] According to the US Department of Energy, America's net imports of energy will decline as a share of US energy consumption from 24 percent in 2009 to 18 percent in 2035 owing to increased use of biofuels and shale gas produced in the United States, rapid improvements in the efficiency of appliances, and higher energy prices.[38] Also, the much-discussed dependence on foreign oil is dissipating: in 2035 the foreign share of the US liquid energy supply will have dropped to less than one-half, or 42 percent, of the total from a peak of 60 percent in 2006.

What of demographics? The United States is aging like the other main economies, but it is also the only major advanced country with a persistent population increase—and thus more likely to produce, build businesses, contribute tax revenues, and sustain aging retirees than Europe or Japan is.[39] The US median age will be 42 in 2050, only slightly above the 37 in 2010. Americans 65 and over will make up 22 percent of the US population in 2050, above the 13 percent in 2010, but far below figures in many other leading economies.[40] The European, Japanese, and Korean median age is in the fifties by 2050, and a third of these nations' populations will be 65 or older. China is also aging rapidly. Its population growth will turn negative by 2035, and, at 45 years in 2050, its median age will be higher than that of the United States and well above the 34 in 2010. The share of Chinese over 65 will be 23 percent of the population in 2050, higher than the share of Americans in the 65-plus category, and markedly up from the 8 percent in 2010. And entitlement reforms as well as innovations in health care, labor market, and migration regime can reduce the pressure that aging populations have on the US budget. Americans are likely to work longer, full and part time; stories about American retirees who start businesses are bound to proliferate.

How Others Struggle   Much has been said about China's strengths that have provided the bases for the projections: its huge pool of labor, its massive reserves, its privileged location at the heart of the integrated Asian economy. China's positives are also positive for America: a productive and growing China serves US economic and national security interests. At the same time, the Chinese have their battles, from the ghost of inflation to a cascade of bad loans in the banking system, overcapacity spurred by overinvestment, mega-infrastructure and real estate developments devoid of sound standards, and intensifying bouts of political instability. Beijing faces broader problems of an aging population, a lack of national cohesion, an opaque regulatory system, and environmental degradation. It is addressing these concerns. But leading China cannot be easy; it is harder than leading America.

Much is at stake for Beijing's mandarins. Unlike in America, where lackluster growth entails a change in power, in China it could undo the very political regime. In her 2007 book *China: Fragile Superpower*, Susan Shirk, a Clinton administration official and global authority on Chinese politics, reveals a catch-22 facing the Chinese leadership.[41] While relying on economic growth for political stability, Beijing is feeling more threatened by its own citizens the more prosperous they become. Today, wealthy Chinese are voting on their feet, purchasing entry into the US by way of the EB5 program, both to hedge against government scrutiny on the ways their wealth was created and to educate their children in US universities. But such an escape valve is available only to a handful of the growing middle and upper classes. Will China dare go far enough to reinvent itself?

Europe is an unlikely global leader. The European integration process, now encompassing 27 nations with a common currency among 17, gives the continental economy tremendous scale and a basis for intra-regional trade and investment. The European infrastructure is sound, and its workers are increasingly well educated and cosmopolitan, with younger generations speaking flawless English among other languages and sporting a borderless mind-set conducive to global business. But the prolonged Eurozone crisis has dealt a blow to the continent's growth prospects and raised questions about the European economy and the viability of integration process. In the longer run, the European penchant for generous welfare states and rigid labor regimes holds the continent's dynamism hostage, as does the structural challenge of large aging populations. A policy status quo will perpetuate the steady state of economic affairs. Demographic constraints may at last convince the continent to revise its social contract or migration regimes, but such changes would likely be minor and slow. Similar issues now confront Japan, the feared dragon of the 1980s.

The Institutions Issue

In his 1982 book *Rise and Decline of Nations,* Mancur Olson theorized that countries start declining when special interests aiming at securing private benefits, such as trade protectionism or particular regulations, grow too entrenched for political systems to serve public economic interests.[42]

Much has been said about the arrival of such a point in America. Government of the people is argued to be dishonored by callous K Street, defiled by calcified Congress, and gone awry in over-representative California. There is no question that a great economy requires gold standard institutions. It is also clear that American politics is divided and troubled. The Founding Fathers did intend the moderating effect produced by the checks and balances, and the frequent deadlocks and frustratingly slow decision-making process that they entail. But they unlikely wished for career politicians with a vested interest in wasteful pork, taxing and spending for their own sake, and gerrymandering their electoral districts so as to choose their constituents. But by global standards the US political system is a vibrant marketplace of ideas, where interests from all sides and policy entrepreneurs with vastly different convictions deliver highly specialized expert knowledge to decision makers. There is arguably too much money in the system, but money is not the only tool of persuasion, nor is it channeled from or to one side only. American democracy, while requiring self-corrections to encourage independents to run rather than relent, politicians to propose instead of routinely opposing, and leaders to focus on governing not fundraising, is not subverted. And it is a democracy, the public equivalent of capitalism's creative destruction.

Much has also been made about the ease with which authoritarian regimes appear to engineer their economies and mobilize their populations. The undertone of the debate is disquieting. Authoritarianism is nothing to envy or esteem: authoritarian governments, like all others, do not operate in a political vacuum but have numerous demanding constituents to please. They also have to produce pork, often more than democracies do. Decisions by authoritarian regimes that may seem straightforward and technocratic, based on a clean economic cost–benefit calculus, are the products of clientelism and political calculi just as they can be elsewhere, often even worse. China has many bridges to nowhere.[43] The media in authoritarian nations do not vigorously debate or critique misallocations and channels of influence, for they are not allowed to. Nor does creative political destruction occur, at least not for the same reasons or by the same method as it does in democracies.

The long-run record of authoritarian nations in producing prosperity lags behind that of democracies.[44] There is a very good reason why political scientists see checks and balances as requisite to prosperity. Time will tell whether Chinese-style authoritarianism and China's system of "reciprocal accountability," a unique relationship between party leaders and subordinate officials, provide sufficient checks.[45]

At the same time, America can have better politics. Economic policy is inherently hostage to politics. There is a perennial tension between good politics and sound economics, between policy makers and market makers. For many in Washington, good politics demands a crackdown on Wall Street; sound economics calls for rules that ensure financial innovation and unfettered capital flows. For many, good politics means tariffs against an influx of imports; sound economics counsels adherence to free trade. And for many, good politics tempts usury of central banks as governments' printing presses, when sound economics requires cementing central bank independence. Granted, policy cannot be kept above politics, but arbitrariness follows when politics permeates each decision. When populism and particularistic interests dictate public policy, the benefits of markets will be lost. Political cycles are short in democracies, giving both credit and slack to politicians for economic policies that prove rotten only with a time lag. The dilemma is that economic policy of any kind, good or bad, cannot be effected without political power.

There are ways to defuse the dilemma. Washington needs to pursue reforms that lock in good policies and depoliticize decisions affecting America's long-term economic future. An example of such a solution is central bank independence. As discussed in Chapter 5, an accord that predefines the Federal Reserve's role after it opens its liquidity taps amid crises would help spare the Fed from accusations of overreach during crises and from attempts to take advantage of its resources for political gain. It would hold the Fed accountable to the public and keep politicians from meddling with monetary policy—for their own good. Bigger fixes to complete: establishing an independent redistricting process in the 36 states where there is not one, and a constitutional balanced budget amendment.

Back in the Saddle

Comparisons can blind the analyst to their implications. Yes, other nations are reaping some of the US share in the world economy and trade. But what are the implications? Would US national security be at risk, or might it be bolstered? Would other nations, better equipped, necessarily be hostile to America, or would they take off some of the US burden to safeguard global peace and stability? Would living standards in America be undercut, or would they improve? Would US influence on the actions of others be less, or might it be more? And would *Pax Americana* end, or might it thrive?

America itself can and must provide the answers. The United States has never bought into fatalism. Rather, it thrives in tough moments—key junctures, eras of flux and change, bright-line moments of history that belie prediction—because of America's unrivaled capacity for self-reinvention. It is well-known, and no accident, that some of the greatest companies in America have been created amid recessions—General Electric amid the Panic of 1873; Hewlett Packard, RCA, DuPont, and IBM after the Great Depression; Hyatt and Burger King during the Eisenhower recession; Microsoft and Apple amid the turbulence of the 1970s; CNN and MTV in the 1980s; and Wikipedia during the dot.com crash in 2001.[46] From the pool of unemployed created by the Great Crisis has also emerged entrepreneurship; from the set of new firms can again come global companies.

What certainly is no accident is what America always does after crises strike: explore policies that point the way back.[47] While its defeats are thoroughly analyzed—recall the post-9/11 "why do they hate us?" debates and the countless columns on the causes of the financial crisis—the nation does not wallow in its predicament, but promptly moves to address it. That trait has been critical in refuting the waves of claims about American decline. The deliberative body politic may be raucous, but it equips the nation to deal with critical junctures and quirks of history—to find a way out, back, and to better things. It is again needed: the premium on good policy peaks in times like these.

This book has argued that the principles that guided the construction of America's world economic order in the twentieth century are also critical for driving US economic interests in the twenty-first. America's foreign policy makers no longer enjoy the clarity that the dichotomy of the Cold War gave their counterparts in the past century. The hallmark of the new century is ambiguity. In this more complex world, the United States needs to work even harder to earn the loyalties of others by the merits of its actions and the outcomes of its order. At the same time, only America has the ability to steer the world in a positive direction. Rising powers have yet to match their nascent economic prowess with a sense of direction and responsibility for the world economy. There are no alternative leaders on the horizon, just as there are no substitutes for the American world economic order. The United States must be engaged. It cannot dominate, but it also mustn't withdraw. It must lead.

Global economic policy leadership has been a tenet of America's postwar primacy. It is even more critical today. The weight of the Treasury Department in the making of America's foreign policy toward China, India, East Asia, and European nations has increased dramatically in the past two decades. The importance that Secretary of State Hillary Clinton is wisely attaching to "economic statecraft" similarly reflects the power that economic globalization has in shaping strategic and political outcomes. The successive international financial crises of the past three decades have also driven home the importance of international economic policies. The Great Crisis was an exclamation mark for that story.

American leadership in the international economy is imperative lest the United States lose its grip in world affairs. This book has called for strategic multilateralism for organizing America's foreign economic policy in the twenty-first century: working through multilateral instances and with pivotal powers to manage economic instability and further integrate the world economy. A great deal of work remains to be done, from managing global imbalances to improving crisis response and prevention, crafting a level playing field in global financial markets, and at last concluding the decade-long Doha Trade Round. Each arena awaits political agreements among leading nations.

This book has also argued that America must reform at home to lead abroad. The US economy is at a difficult juncture. Frustratingly but also encouragingly, the constraints to America's economic vitality are known and removable. The fixes are clear, but they are politically difficult. There are no surprises, but also no shortcuts. America's future depends on investing in and harnessing the productivity of its newcomers and next generations. Needed are fiscal discipline, ironclad central bank independence, an education overhaul that challenges the smartest and rewards excellence in teaching, an end to taxes and regulations stifling US companies, migration reforms to encourage the world's brightest to join forces in America, a bipartisan commitment to hone institutions, and incentives for the private sector to innovate, export, turn around schools, and take the lead in rebuilding infrastructures. US leadership is wide ranging, and America can continue leading also by the strength of its economy—but Washington must be resolved to make it so.

A Council on Global Economic Strategy

The United States also needs a bridge between global and domestic economic policies. In no other time has the line between the two spheres been as amorphous and irrelevant. At the same time, there are sharp divisions between parties and between the Congress and the executive across all the areas discussed in this volume. Congress and the White House, much like Democrats and Republicans, battle over ways to deal with imbalances, the shape of financial regulations, the need for bailouts to foreign nations, the powers of central bankers, the tone America should strike with China, and fiscal and economic priorities. Discord all too often obstructs America's global projection.

Spirited debate must replace deadlock. What is needed is a bipartisan Council on Global Economic Strategy that would assemble representatives from the executive agencies, Congress, the private sector, and academia to regularly discuss, define, and integrate US domestic and foreign economic policies in the interest of America's prosperity in the twenty-first-century world economy. The issues interlink, affect all sides, and are critical for the future of America, yet they are by default dealt with in silos. They must be treated as a coherent whole among players with a regard for the nation's future.

The Purview of Presidents

Arguing that America can no longer lead presupposes that leadership is inadaptable to changes in circumstance, when it is not. The United States needs constructive strategies in line with the ways of the world and America's means. Success will not be sudden or serendipitous. As Henry Kissinger states in his visionary book *Diplomacy*, "[T]he fulfillment of America's ideals [in the twenty-first century] will have to be sought in the patient accumulation of partial successes."[48]

The United States must treasure its idealism, for it lends America power and the providence to see where others yet can't. Americans have had chances to succumb to sarcasm in the face of Pearl Harbor and Hitler's advance in the 1940s; amid the oil shocks and Vietnam in the 1970s; during the stagflation and savings and loans crisis of the 1980s; in the slowdown of the early 1990s; certainly again on September 11, 2001; and amid the latest, job-killing recession. Optimism has floundered of late in the face of the jobless recovery and fears about an end to America's economic mobility. It mustn't be let to lapse. The claim to renewed opportunity is what upholds American idealism, dynamism, and enduring global appeal.

Idealism risks self-righteousness, but when blended with a sober assessment of the constraints and priorities of the new era, it will enable America to accomplish more than others can. The benchmark for US foreign policy should not be unchallengeable hegemony; it should be sustained global growth and stability. The American world economic order has been based on this notion. It now needs to be refurbished to meet twenty-first-century global challenges. Its institutions need to be actively managed and maintained as agents of globalization, precisely in order to do what institutions are meant to do: encourage and aid long-term cooperation among actors with divergent preferences. Its ideals of free markets and good governance are not free, but must be worked for. This volume has focused on impending improvements rather than the long term, but the latter must follow the former. The world economy does not cease to hurl out challenges, nor are the key players' interests likely to converge. Rather than an occasional pursuit, institutions and ideals are the lifestyle of leaders.

Ideals are advocated by presidents, carried by citizens, and adopted by adherents. America's influence transcends guns and butter and even Joseph Nye's soft power and Max Weber's charismatic authority. It is more fundamental and innately American. It is based on, and draws on, the values of open markets, private property, and democracy on which America was founded, which de Tocqueville discovered, and which Washington has striven to bring to others and others have sought to emulate. The American order draws on these ideals, and it has prevailed. It is a benign order that provides mutual economic gains to its members and is open to all. Its core nation and institutions, while necessary for the world economy, are now tested.

Tests to nations are passed with good policy, domestic and foreign. And policy needs good leadership to fly. While history is much more than the great man theory, leaders make a difference. Franklin Delano Roosevelt summoned a profoundly isolationist nation secure between two oceans to the fatal yet critical contest on the old continent. Harry Truman's vision of the world governed by global institutions made America the world's benign beacon. John F. Kennedy's resolve to undo the standoff in Cuban waters correctly gauged the motives of the Soviet leadership. Ronald Reagan persisted in his calls to tear down the Berlin Wall against his disbelieving administration and, with Margaret Thatcher, shattered the prevailing paradigm of the relationship between the state and the market. George H. W. Bush stepped up upon the fall of the Berlin Wall and the implosion of the Soviet Union, setting out to unleash the potential of capitalism across the communist bloc and engaging the garrulous Russia. Bill Clinton balanced the budget and freed trade against his reluctant party, revitalizing US economic leadership. George W. Bush stormed against the incredulous world, bringing Iraqis and Afghans to polling booths and all the while opening new markets to American business.

Barack Obama seized the *Zeitgeist* and orchestrated an electoral feat that overnight altered the world's expectations about American foreign policy. The tireless Secretary of State Hillary Clinton has projected American power and benevolence on the world stage. But President Obama's own imprint on the world and America's role in it remains ambiguous.

Conclusion

What would the world economy be today without America's vision to build a globalized economy buttressed by good institutions and free markets? What would economies around the world look like without America's espousal of democracy, private property, open markets, and capitalism that enable self-made men and women to soar? Where else would migrants look for a chance beyond making ends meet, a chance to make the most of themselves? What would the world be like without America's impatient optimism, can-do spirit, and perpetual capacity for self-reinvention?

Critics would respond that America's pursuit of happiness has become equated to capacity for consumption and subverted into self-righteous crusading to convert other nations into America's image. True, the United States is prone to what others might call excess, for it scorns what other nations prize as reasonable or rational. Americans respect history but are unburdened by a need to be bound by it. The trait has innate beauty, and it holds keen practical application in entrepreneurship. It is a tenet of America's exceptionalism. And it has shaped America's foreign policy. The creed of manifest destiny moved the nation to fight for California and Texas; its conviction about universal values led it to wage a long Cold War; its innocence, shielded by seas and shocked by a rare attack on US soil, induced it to give a free rein to its leaders.

When things go wrong, America self-corrects, at the kitchen table and at the ballot box. Another day of reckoning has recently been reached: a quick buck is as elusive as victory by virtual war. The moment marks yet another swing in the American pendulum between heady optimism and sober pragmatism, between booms and busts at home, triumphs and tragedies abroad. The frustrations have been and will be brought to the political arena to change policies previously deemed commonsensical and crucial.

Will history judge the twenty-first century as one where the postwar institutions and free-market economics lost out to national rivalries and protectionist politics? Or will twenty-second-century historians look back to a hundred years of a global economic order that mediated and managed competing national claims in the interest of global prosperity? The former is not an American century; the latter could be.

Policy will arbitrate the outcome. At home, correction is required. President Bill Clinton's "there is nothing wrong in America that cannot be fixed with what is right in America" finds an echo in this century. Abroad, American leadership is critical. The global economic order requires champions to prosper. Asking whether new power contenders will have economic bases for global leadership is inadequate. The question should be whether the other powers, even if economically ascendant, will be willing to lead, whether they are capable of leadership, and whether they have the temperament that garners loyalty and admiration—or even the grudging respect—of their peers. The question should be whether they have the economic prowess and moral authority to show the way and the farsightedness to know the right way. And the question is whether America still does. It can.

NOTES AND INDEX

Notes

Introduction

1. Per Robert Mundell's useful definition, *order* here refers to "laws, conventions, regulations and mores that establish the setting of the system and the understanding of the environment by the participants in it." For example, a "[m]onetary order is to a monetary system somewhat like a constitution is to a political or electoral system." Mundell, Robert A. 1972. "The Future of the International Financial System." In A. Acheson, J. Chant, and M. Prachowny, eds. *Bretton Woods Revisited*. Toronto: University of Toronto Press, 91–104. *Institutions* here refers broadly to "rules and roles" by which nations and their actors play. For the definition, see, for instance, Muller, Wolfgang C., and Kaare Strom. 1999. *Policy, Office or Votes? How Political Parties in Western Europe Make Hard Decisions*. Cambridge: Cambridge University Press. The institutions addressed here are central to the postwar global economy.

2. Helene Cooper, "G20 Summit Review: Strength in Unity," *Times*, 4 April 2009. See also Paul Taylor, "G20 Ends Anglo-Saxon Era," *Reuters*, 2 April 2009.

3. For a sweeping account of the Argentine episode, see Blustein, Paul. 2005. *And the Money Kept Rolling In (and Out): Wall Street, the IMF, and the Bankrupting of Argentina*. New York: PublicAffairs.

4. For a summary of studies, see Reinhardt, Carmen, and Kenneth Rogoff. "Banking Crises: An Equal Opportunity Menace." CEPR Discussion Paper No. 7131.

5. Ibid.

6. See, for example, "If G7 Didn't Meet, No One Would Notice," *Toronto Star*, 10 May 1998; "Outlook: G7's Band Aid Solution Won't Work," *The Independent*, 17 September 1998.

7. See, for example, Rogoff, Kenneth. 1999. "International Institutions for Reducing Global Financial Instability." *Journal of Economic Perspectives* 13.4 (Autumn):

21–42; Eichengreen, Barry. 1999. *Toward a New International Financial Architecture: A Practical Post-Asia Agenda.* Washington: Institute for International Economics; Jeffrey Garten, "In This Economic Chaos, a Global Central Bank Can Help," *International Herald Tribune*, 25 September 1998; Paul Krugman, "Saving Asia: It's Time to Get Radical," *Fortune*, 7 September 1998; Paul Krugman, "Heresy Time," 28 September 1998 <web.mit.edu/krugman/www/heresy.html>; Sachs, Jeffrey. 1998. "Fixing the IMF Remedy." *Banker* 148 (February): 1618; and Soros, George. 1998. *The Crisis of Global Capitalism.* New York: PublicAffairs.

8. Lane, Philip, and Gian Maria Milesi-Ferretti. 1998. "Drivers of Financial Globalization." Institute for International Integration Studies Discussion Paper 238 (January) <www.ecb.int/events/pdf/conferences/ecbcfs_cmfi2/Philip_Lane_paper.pdf?39 7f060a275b897cb229619c49b9793d>.

9. Globalization stimulated growth, which the World Bank long ago showed has a direct, one-to-one relationship with poverty reduction. See Dollar, David, and Aart Kraay. 2002. "Trade, Growth, and Poverty." World Bank Policy Research Working Paper 2615. Also, Fischer, Stanley. 1998. "Capital-Account Liberalization and the Role of the IMF." *Princeton Essays in International Finance* 207 (May): 1–10; and Summers, Lawrence H. 2006. "International Financial Crises: Causes, Prevention, and Cures." *American Economic Review* 90.2 (May): 1–16. See also Ranciere, Romain, Aaron Tornell, and Frank Westermann. 2006. "Decomposing the Effects of Financial Liberalization: Crises vs. Growth." *Journal of Banking and Finance* 30 (December): 3331–3348; Henry, Peter Blair. 2003. "Capital-Account Liberalization, the Cost of Capital, and Economic Growth." *American Economic Review* 93.2 (May): 91–96; and Bekaert, Geert, Campbell Harvey, and Christian Lundblad. "Does Financial Liberalization Spur Growth?" *Journal of Financial Economics* 77.1 (July): 3–55. For the effect on firms, see Chari, Anusha, and Peter Blair Henry. 2008. "Firm-Specific Information and the Efficiency of Investment." *Journal of Financial Economics*, 87.3 (March): 636–655; and Mitton, Todd. 2008. "Stock Market Liberalization and Operating Performances at the Firm Level." *Journal of Financial Economics* 81.3 (September): 625–647. For the effects on worker output, see Henry, Peter Blair, and Diego Sasson. 2009. "Capital Market Integration and Wages." NBER Working Paper 15204 (July). For a review, see Hufbauer, Gary Claude, and Kati Suominen. 2010. *Globalization at Risk: Challenges to Finance and Trade.* New Haven: Yale University Press.

10. East Asian growth dropped to 2 percent in 1998 but rebounded to an annual average of 8.5 percent in 2000–2005, with China leading the pack. Middle-income economies, while at 3 percent growth in 1998–1999, surpassed 6-percent average growth in 2000–2005. Latin American and Caribbean growth plunged to zero in 2000–2001 but recovered to almost 6 percent in 2003–2007, as did Middle Eastern nations when oil prices soared in 2004–2008. The United States grew at 3–4 percent in 2003–2006 after 1–2-percent growth in 2001–2002. Turkey rebounded forcefully in 2002. Data are based on World Bank's World Development Indicators.

11. Data from the Bureau of Economic Analysis, US Department of Commerce.

12. Goldman Sachs. 2007. "BRICs and Beyond." New York: Goldman Sachs <www2.goldmansachs.com/ideas/brics/BRICs-and-Beyond.html>.

13. Frieden, Jeffrey. 2007. "Global Inequality: Trends and Remedies." *Harvard College Economics Review* (Spring): 48–49.

14. For the term, see Dooley, Michael P., Dieter Folkerts-Landau, and Peter Garber. 2004. "The Revised Bretton Woods System." *International Journal of Finance and Economics* 9.4 (October): 307–313.

15. By 2007, most of the 86 middle-income countries (with per capita income between $826 and $10,065 per year) had credit ratings; 20 were investment grade. See "Help Where It's Not Needed?" *Washington Post*, 21 September 2007.

16. Eichengreen, Barry. "The IMF Adrift on a Sea of Liquidity." In Edwin M. Truman, ed. *Reforming the IMF for the 21st Century.* Washington, DC: Peterson Institute for International Economics.

17. For a description, see Julian Cribb, "The Coming Famine," *New York Times*, 24 August 2010.

18. See, for instance, "Washington Summit: Converting G8 into G20?" *Rianovosti* (Russia), 19 November 2008; Nitin Sethi, "G8 Doing Little on Climate Change," *Economic Times* (India), 9 July 2008; Deep K. Datta-Ray, "G8 Needs an Overhaul," *Times of India*, 15 July 2008.

19. Wessel, David. 2009. *In Fed We Trust: Ben Bernanke's War on the Great Panic.* New York: Crown Business.

20. See Lake, David A. "America's Imperial Dilemma: Political Order v. Global Insurgency." Draft under review. September 2009 <http://weber.ucsd.edu/~dlake/documents/LakeImperialDilemma.pdf>.

21. Reinhart, Carmen, and Kenneth Rogoff. "Banking Crises: An Equal Opportunity Menace." CEPR Discussion Paper No. 7131; and Reinhart, Carmen, and Kenneth Rogoff. 2009. *This Time Is Different: Eight Centuries of Financial Folly.* Princeton: Princeton University Press.

22. Allen, William A., and Geoffrey Wood. 2005. "Defining and Achieving Financial Stability." LSE Financial Markets Group Special Paper 160 (April) <www2.lse.ac.uk/fmg/documents/specialPapers/2005/sp160.pdf>. Just as defining war is easier by defining peace, financial instability is easier to capture by its opposite, financial stability: a situation where there are no financial crises or, if there are, they do not affect the economic and financial behaviors of consumers and businesses. See Foot, Michael. 2003. "Protecting Financial Stability—How Good Are We at It?" Financial Services Authority, 6 June 2003 <www.fsa.gov.uk/Pages/Library/Communication/Speeches/2003/sp133.shtml>.

23. Kindleberger, Charles P. 2005. *Manias, Panics, and Crashes: A History of Financial Crises.* New York: Wiley.

24. Roubini, Nouriel, and Stephen Shim. *Crisis Economics: A Crash Course in the Future of Finance.* New York: Penguin.

25. See Bernanke, Ben S. 1983. "Non-Monetary Effects of the Financial Crisis in the Propagation of the Great Depression." *American Economic Review* 73 (June), 257–276; and Bernanke, Ben S., Mark Gertler, and Simon Gilchrist. 1996. "The Financial Accelerator and Flight to Quality." *Review of Economics and Statistics* 78.1 (February): 1–15.

26. Bordo, Michael D., Barry Eichengreen, D. Klingebiel, and M. S. Martinez-Peria. 2001. "Is the Crisis Problem Growing More Severe?" *Economic Policy* 16 (April): 51–82.

27. See interview as reported in Bob Willis and Thomas R. Keene, "Europe's Debt Crisis Increases Risk of 'Double-Dip' Recession, Roach Says," Bloomberg, 10 May 2010.

28. See, for instance, Fischer Private Investment Funds, "Presenting Total Bank Assets as a Percentage of Host Countries' GDP," 19 February 2010, on the basis of JP Morgan data.

29. For causes of contagion or global spread of crises, see such studies as Kaminsky, Graciela L., and Carmen M. Reinhart. 2000. "On Crises, Contagion, and Confusion." *Journal of International Economics* 51: 145–68; and Corsetti, Giancarlo, Marcello Pericoli, and Massimo Sbracia. 2002. "Some Contagion, Some Interdependence: More Pitfalls in Tests of Financial Contagion." Centre for Economic Policy Research Discussion Paper 3310 (April).

30. Liaquat Ahadem, "Did Lehman's Fall Matter?" *Newsweek*, 18 May 2009.

31. United Nations. 2009. "Meeting of the Committee of Experts of the 2nd Joint Annual Meetings of the AU Conference of Ministers of Economy and Finance and ECA Conference of Ministers of Finance, Planning and Economic Development," Cairo, Egypt, 2–5 June.

32. Schwartz, Anna J. 1986. "Real and Pseudo-Financial Crises." In F. Capie and Geoffrey Wood, eds. *Financial Crises and the World Banking System*. London: MacMillan.

33. See Deutsche Bank. 2006. "The Theory and Practice of Corporate Risk Management Policy" (February). In a McKinsey survey at the end of 2009, 29 percent of global executives reported that exchange rates have an "extremely" or "very" significant effect on company profits, and 28 percent say the impact is "somewhat" significant. Only a quarter did not see any major effects. In total, 44 percent reported increased pertinence of exchange-rate issues in their decision making in the past two years, and 21 percent said exchange-rate uncertainty has reduced their planned investment over the next two years. The latter number soars much further, to nearly 40 percent, for companies in countries outside the United States and the Eurozone, such as China and India, and is particularly steep for manufacturing firms. McKinsey Global Institute, "An Exorbitant Privilege? Implications of Reserve Currencies for Competitiveness," December 2009 <www.mckinsey.com/mgi/reports/pdfs/reserve_curren cies/reserve_currencies_full_discussion_paper.pdf>.

34. McKinsey Global Institute, "An Exorbitant Privilege?"

35. Bibow, Jörg. 2010. "The Global Crisis and the Future of the Dollar: Toward Bretton Woods III?" Working Paper No. 584, Levy Economics Institute of Bard College and Skidmore College (February) <www.levyinstitute.org/pubs/wp_584.pdf>.

36. Jeremy Seigel and Jeremy Schwartz, "The Great American Bond Bubble," *Wall Street Journal*, 18 August 2010.

37. See, for example, Crockett, Andrew. 1997. "Why Is Financial Stability a Goal of Public Policy?" In Federal Reserve Bank of Kansas City, *Maintaining Financial Stability in a Global Economy*, Kansas City. Wyplosz, Charles. 1999. "International

Financial Instability." In Inge Kaul, Isabelle Grunberg, and Marc A. Stern, eds. *Global Public Goods*. New York: Oxford University Press, 152–189. Also, Bank of International Settlements. 1997. "Financial Stability in Emerging Market Economies." Report of the Working Party on Financial Stability in Emerging Market Economies (April); and Hufbauer, Gary Clyde, and Wendy Dobson. 2001. *World Capital Markets: Challenge to the G10*. Washington, DC: Institute for International Economics.

38. For the latter, see Easterly, William, Roumeen Islam, and Joseph Stiglitz. 2001. "Shaken and Stirred: Explaining Growth Volatility." In Boris Pleskovič and Nicholas Stern, eds. *Annual World Bank Conference on Development Economics*. Washington, DC: World Bank.

39. Ranciere, Romain, Aaron Tornell, and Frank Westermann. 2008. "Systemic Crises and Growth." *Quarterly Journal of Economics* 123.1: 359–406.

40. See, for example, Tom Braithwaite, "Lehman Could Not Be Saved, Insists Bernanke," *Financial Times*, 3 September 2010.

41. For excellent reviews, see Elizabeth Economy, "Leadership Gap in China," *Washington Post*, 1 December 2008; Gill, Bates. 2001. "United States, China, and the World Order." Remarks presented before the U.S.–China Security Review Commission (3 August) <www.brookings.edu/views/testimony/gill/20010803.pdf>.

42. David Shambaugh, "Beijing: A Global Leader with 'China First' Policy," Yale-Global, 29 June 2010 <http://yaleglobal.yale.edu/content/beijing-global-leader-china-first-policy>.

43. There are some Beijing analysts who see the global order as a reasonable construct through which China can exercise its interests; others see it as something to be remodeled completely in order for China to drive its interests. See Adcock Kaufman, Alison. 2010. "The 'Century of Humiliation,' Then and Now: Chinese Perceptions of the International Order." *Pacific Focus* 25.1 (April): 1–33 <http://onlinelibrary.wiley.com/doi/10.1111/j.1976-5118.2010.01039.x/full>.

44. As Charles Krauthammer correctly stated on *Fox News* in April 2009, "Obama says, 'In America there is a failure to appreciate Europe's leading role in the world.' Well, maybe that's because when there was a civil war on Europe's doorstep in the Balkans, and genocide, it didn't lift a finger until America led. Maybe it's because when there was an invasion of Kuwait, it didn't lift a finger until America led. Maybe it's because with America spending over half a trillion a year, keeping open the sea lanes in defending the world, Europe is spending pennies on defense. It's hard to appreciate an entity's leading role in the world when it's been sucking on your tit for 60 years" <www.realclearpolitics.com/video/2009/04/03/krauthammer_europes_been_sucking_on_americas_tit_for_60_years.html>.

45. International Monetary Fund. 2010. *World Economic Outlook: Rebalancing Growth*. Washington, DC: IMF (April).

46. Kagan, Robert. 2008. *The Return of History and the End of Dreams*. New York: Vintage.

47. Lake, David A. 1999. *Entangling Relations: American Foreign Policy in Its Century*. Princeton, NJ: Princeton University Press.

48. There are varying degrees of hierarchy, and a system of no hierarchy is anarchy. See Lake, David A. 2009. *Hierarchy in International Relations.* Cornell: Cornell University Press; and Lake, David A. 1999. *Entangling Relations.*

49. Pew Research Center for the People & the Press. 2009. "U.S. Seen as Less Important, China as More Powerful." Survey Report (3 December) <http://people-press.org/report/569/americas-place-in-the-world>.

50. Pew Research Center for the People & the Press. 2011. "China Seen Overtaking U.S. as Global Superpower." Survey Report (13 July) <http://pewglobal.org/2011/07/13/china-seen-overtaking-us-as-global-superpowerr>. Interestingly, yet befittingly for a nation with a huge number of poor people, the reverse is true for China: 50 percent of Chinese believe the United States is the leading economy, and only 26 percent think China is. This view holds across the world, though not in Europe.

51. See Paul, Ron. 2010. *End the Fed.* New York: Grand Central.

52. Ryan Lizza, "The Consequentialist," *New Yorker,* 2 May 2011.

53. See, for example, Crockett, Andrew. 1997. "Why Is Financial Stability a Goal of Public Policy?"; Wyplosz, Charles. 1999. "International Financial Instability"; Bank of International Settlements. 1997. "Financial Stability in Emerging Market Economies"; and Hufbauer, Gary Clyde, and Wendy Dobson. 2001. *World Capital Markets: Challenge to the G10.*

54. Lake, David A. 2009. "America's Imperial Dilemma: Political Order v. Global Insurgency." Draft under review (September) <http://weber.ucsd.edu/~dlake/documents/LakeImperialDilemma.pdf>.

55. Naim, Moises. 2009. "Minilateralism: The Magic Number to Get Real International Action." *Foreign Policy,* July/August; and Graham Allison's many-lateralism in Katrin Bennhold and Alison Smale, "In Davos, Signs of Shift in Global Power," *New York Times,* 27 January 2010.

56. Shambaugh, David. 2011. "Coping with a Conflicted China." *Washington Quarterly* 34.1: 7–27.

57. Economy, Elizabeth C., and Adam Segal. "The G-2 Mirage: Why the United States and China Are Not Ready to Upgrade Ties," *Foreign Affairs,* May/June 2009.

58. Cited in Suri, Jeremy. 2007. *Henry Kissinger and the American Century.* Cambridge, MA: Harvard University Press.

59. Henry A. Kissinger, "Rebalancing Relations with China," *Washington Post,* 19 August 2009.

60. Elizabeth Economy, "Leadership Gap in China," *Washington Post,* 1 December 2008.

61. Michael Green and Daniel Twining, "Why Aren't We Working with Japan and India?" *Washington Post,* 18 July 2011.

Chapter 1

1. Comments respectively from International Monetary Fund. 2011. *World Economic Outlook: Tensions from the Two-Speed Recovery.* Washington, D.C.: IMF

(April); and International Monetary Fund. 2010. "G-20 Mutual Assessment Process—IMF Staff Assessment of G-20 Policies." Prepared for G-20 Summit of Leaders, 11–12 November, Seoul, Korea <www.imf.org/external/np/g20/pdf/111210.pdf>.

2. European Central Bank. 2010. "Prospects for Real and Financial Imbalances and a Global Rebalancing." *ECB Monthly Bulletin* (April) <www.ecb.int/pub/pdf/other/art3_mb201004en_pp91-100en.pdf>.

3. See Engel, Charles, and John H. Rogers. 2006. "The U.S. Current Account Deficit and the Expected Share of World Output." Board of Governors of the Federal Reserve System International Finance Discussion Papers 856 (March) <www.federalreserve.gov/Pubs/Ifdp/2006/856/ifdp856.htm>.

4. For a similar argument, see Eichengreen, Barry. 2000. "From Benign Neglect to Malignant Preoccupation: U.S. Balance of Payments Policy in the 1960s." NBER Working Paper 7630 (March).

5. Ibid.

6. Ibid. Original title used in Paul Samuelson, "From Benign Neglect to Malignant Preoccupation," *Newsweek*, April 1971.

7. See Destler, I. M. 1995. *American Trade Politics*. Washington, D.C.: Peterson Institute for International Economics.

8. Meyer, Laurence H., Brian M. Doyle, Joseph E. Gagnon, and Dale W. Henderson. 2002. "International Coordination of Macroeconomic Policies: Still Alive in the New Millennium?" International Finance Discussion Paper Number 723, Board of Governors of the Federal Reserve System (April). See also Bergsten, Fred C. "Should G7 Policy Coordination Be Revived?" *International Economy*, 24 November 2003.

9. See, for example, Sobel, Mark, and Louellen Stedman. 2006. "The Evolution of the G7 and Economic Policy Coordination." Occasional Paper 3, Department of the Treasury, Office of International Affairs (July).

10. Gilpin, Robert. 1987. *The Political Economy of International Relations*. Princeton: Princeton University Press.

11. Fallows, James. 1989. "Containing Japan." *Atlantic* (May).

12. See Henning, C. Randall, and I. M. Destler. 1988. "From Neglect to Activism: American Politics and the 1985 Plaza Accord." *Journal of Public Policy* 8.3/4 (July–December): 317–333.

13. Ibid.

14. Funabashi, Yoichi. 1989. *Managing the Dollar: From the Plaza to the Louvre*. Washington, D.C.: Institute for International Economics.

15. Cline, William R. 2005. "The Case for a New Plaza Agreement." IIE Policy Brief 05-4 (December). According to Cline, the German mark, which had appreciated against the dollar by 19 percent from end-February to end-August, appreciated another 13 percent by end-December. The Japanese yen, which had risen 9.4 percent against the dollar from end-February to end-August, appreciated by another 18.3 percent by end-December. See also Funabashi, Yoichi. 1989. *Managing the Dollar;* and Meyer, Laurence H., Brian M. Doyle, Joseph E. Gagnon, and Dale W. Henderson. 2002. "International Coordination of Macroeconomic Policies: Still Alive in the New Millennium?"

16. Henning, Randall. 1994. *Currencies and Politics in the United States, Germany, and Japan*. Washington, D.C.: International Institute of Economics; and Sperling, James C. 1990. "West German Foreign Economic Policy During the Reagan Administration." *German Studies Review* 13.1 (February): 85–109.

17. Economists have shown that it was indeed Plaza rather than some other factor that compelled governments to adopt policies that changed trade balances. See Klein, Michael, Bruce Mizrach, and Robert G. Murphy. 1991. "Managing the Dollar: Has the Plaza Agreement Mattered?" *Journal of Money, Credit and Banking* 23.4 (November): 742–751.

18. The United States agreed to reduce its fiscal 1988 deficit to 2.3 percent of GDP from 3.9 percent in 1987, and France agreed to cut its budget deficit by 1 percent of GDP by 1988 and reduce taxes. Japan would reduce its trade surplus and cut interest rates; the UK would cut public expenditures and reduce taxes; and Germany would lower public spending, cut taxes for individuals and corporations, and commit to low interest rates.

19. Aiding the rebalancing were America's foreign transfer payments resulting from the First Gulf War.

20. Sobel, Mark, and Louellen Stedman. 2006. "The Evolution of the G7 and Economic Policy Coordination."

21. See, for instance, Gallup Poll 1992–2009 answers to these questions: "What do you think foreign trade means for America? Do you see foreign trade more as an opportunity for economic growth through increased U.S. exports or a threat to the economy from foreign imports?" <www.pollingreport.com/trade.htm>. See also Marjorie Connelly, "Poll Preview: Trade," *New York Times*, 6 April 2009 <http://thecaucus.blogs.nytimes.com/2009/04/06/poll-preview-trade>.

22. See Sobel, Mark, and Louellen Stedman. 2006. "The Evolution of the G7 and Economic Policy Coordination."

23. "Goodbye G7, Hello G20," *Economist*, 20 November 2008.

24. Sobel, Mark, and Louellen Stedman. 2006. "The Evolution of the G7 and Economic Policy Coordination."

25. Just for the most affected three countries in Asia, total lending by the IMF, multilateral agencies, and national governments reached $118 billion. IMF Factsheet, "The IMF's Response to the Asian Crisis," January 1999 <www.imf.org/external/np/exr/facts/asia.HTM>.

26. America's overall trade soared, as well—it rose to some 20 percent of US GDP at the end of the 1990s, as opposed to just 10 percent in the 1960s. For trade, see Findlay, Ronald, and Kevin H. O'Rourke. 2007. *Power and Plenty: Trade, War, and the Global Economy in the Second Millennium*. Princeton, NJ: Princeton University Press. For FDI, see United Nations Conference on Trade and Development (UNCTAD). 1999. *World Investment Report 1999: Foreign Direct Investment and the Challenge of Development*. Geneva: United Nations Conference on Trade and Development.

27. See, for example, Bradford, Colin I., Jr., and Johannes F. Linn. 2004. "Global Economic Governance at a Crossroads: Replacing the G7 with the G20." Brookings Institution Policy Brief (April), and other works by the authors.

28. An estimated two-thirds of the reserve hoarding is because of insurance motivations. See Obstfeld, Maurice, Jay Shambaugh, and Alan M. Taylor. 2009. "Financial Stability, the Trilemma, and International Reserves." *American Economic Journal,* forthcoming <http://elsa.berkeley.edu/~obstfeld/OSTreservesupdate.pdf>.

29. See McKinnon, Ronald. 2005. "Trapped by the International Dollar Standard." Working paper (March). See also Jagannathan, Ravi, Mudit Kapoor, and Ernst Schaumburg. 2010. "Why Are We in a Recession? The Financial Crisis Is the Symptom Not the Disease!" NBER Working Paper 15404.

30. For the various explanations of the imbalances, see, for instance, Feldstein, Martin. 1999. "A Self-Help Guide for Emerging Markets." *Foreign Affairs* 78.2: 93–109; Yongding, Yu. 2007. "Global Imbalances: China's Perspective." Paper prepared for International Conference on Global Imbalances, Organized by the Institute for International Economics, Washington, D.C., 8 February 2007; Ben Bernanke, "Global Saving Glut and the U.S. Current Account Deficit," Sandridge Lecture, Virginia Association of Economists, Richmond, Virginia, 14 April 2005; Rachel Lomax, "Global Financial Imbalances," speech, Chatham House Conference on Global Financial Imbalances, London, 24 January 2006; Roubini, Nouriel, and Brad Setser. 2004. "The US as a Net Debtor: The Sustainability of the US External Imbalances." Working paper <http://pages.stern.nyu.edu/~nroubini/papers/Roubini-Setser-US-External-Imbalances.pdf>. See also Bibow, Jörg. 2008. "The International Monetary (Non-)order and the 'Global Capital Flows Paradox.'" In Eckhard Hein, Peter Spahn, Torsten Niechoj, and Achim Truger, eds. *Finance-Led Capitalism?* London: Metropolis; Mann, Catherine L. 2000. "Is the U.S. Current Account Deficit Sustainable?" *Finance and Development* 37.1 (March); Martin Neil Baily, "How Large a Dollar Adjustment to Reduce the US Imbalance?" Paper presented at the Joint Bruegel, KIIEP, and Peterson Institute Workshop on Adjusting Global Imbalances, Washington, D.C., 8–9 February 2007.

31. See Wolf, Martin. 2008. *Fixing Global Finance.* Baltimore: Johns Hopkins University Press; Ben Bernanke, "Global Saving Glut and the U.S. Current Account Deficit"; and "Bernanke's Speech to Council on Foreign Relations," Reuters, 10 March 2009.

32. Ben Bernanke, "Global Saving Glut and the U.S. Current Account Deficit."

33. See, for example, Bibow, Jörg. 2008. "The International Monetary (Non-)Order and the 'Global Capital Flows Paradox.'" See also International Monetary Fund. 2008. *Global Financial Stability Report: Containing Systemic Risks and Restoring Financial Soundness* (April); and Simon Johnson and James Kwak, "Don't Blame China," *Washington Post,* 6 October 2009.

34. Scheve, Kenneth F., and Matthew J. Slaughter. 2007. "A New Deal for Globalization." *Foreign Affairs* 86.4 (July/August). In May 2007 US House members sought to file a Section 301 petition to request the USTR to investigate undervaluation of the RMB.

35. Stephen Roach, "Are US Protectionist Threats About to Become Reality?" *MoneyWeek,* 12 April 2009.

36. Obstfeld, Maurice, and Kenneth Rogoff. 2005. "The Unsustainable US Current Account Position Revisited." Draft (30 November) <http://elsa.berkeley.edu/~obstfeld/NBER_final.pdf>.

37. See Eichengreen, Barry, and Douglas A. Irwin. 2007. "The Bush Legacy for America's International Economic Policy." Paper prepared for the conference American Foreign Policy After the Bush Doctrine, Miller Center, University of Virginia, 7–8 June 2007 <www.econ.berkeley.edu/~eichengr/bush_legacy.pdf>.

38. Obstfeld, Maurice, Jay C. Shambaugh, and Alan M. Taylor. 2008. "Financial Stability, the Trilemma, and International Reserves." NBER Working Paper 14217.

39. The Federal Reserve's first QE to shore up the economy in March 2009—a massive $1.2 trillion in asset purchases—depreciated the dollar by 6.5 percent, while the Bank of England's QE resulted in a 4-percent depreciation of the pound.

40. See International Monetary Fund. 2010. "Global Economic Prospects and Policy Challenges." Document for the Meeting of G-20 Finance Ministers and Central Bank Governors, 21–23 October 2010, Gyeongju, Korea; and Cline, William R., and John Williamson. 2010. "Currency Wars?" Policy Brief 10–26, Peterson Institute for International Economics <www.iie.com/publications/pb/pb10-26.pdf>.

41. Cline, William R., and John Williamson. 2010. "Currency Wars?"

42. There is no necessary link between budget deficit and current-account deficits: the United States had a deepening current-account deficit while running a budget surplus in 1996–2000, and some other countries deep in arrears, like Japan and Germany, run current-account surpluses. However, most of recent American and international economic history has shown that by causing total national savings to decline, budget deficits tend to increase borrowing from abroad.

43. Congressional Budget Office. 2010. *The Long-Term Budget Outlook*. Washington, D.C.: CBO (revised version, August) <www.cbo.gov/ftpdocs/115xx/doc11579/06-30-LTBO.pdf>.

44. Office of Management and Budget. 2010. *Historical Tables: Budget of the U.S. Government, Fiscal Year 2011*. Washington, D.C.: OMB <www.whitehouse.gov/omb/budget/Historicals>.

45. Bartolini, Leonardo, and Amartya Lahiri. 2006. "Twin Deficits, Twenty Years Later." *Current Issues in Economics and Finance* 12.7 (October), Federal Reserve of New York. The authors find that even if the federal fiscal deficit (in 2006 at 2 percent of GDP) were fully erased, the US current-account deficit would improve by only a fraction of its current 7 percent of GDP. Also see Chinn, Menzie D. 2005. "Getting Serious About the Twin Deficits." *CSR* 10 (September), Council on Foreign Relations.

46. International Monetary Fund. 2011. *World Economic Outlook 2011: Slowing Growth, Rising Risks*. Washington, D.C.: IMF (September).

47. Cline, William. 2009. "Long-Term Fiscal Imbalances, US External Liabilities, and Future Living Standards." In C. Fred Bergsten, ed. *The Long-Term International Economic Position of the United States*. Washington, D.C.: Peterson Institute for International Economics.

48. Most analyses corroborate IMF's forecast of the direction of imbalances, but many also predict deeper imbalances. For example, Gagnon argues imbalances among the G20 will in 2011–2015 widen to, and even exceed, their precrisis levels, substantially more than predicted by the IMF. One of the IMF's critical assumptions is

that real exchange rates will remain constant over the next five years, Under different assumptions, the scenarios are dramatically different. Gagnon, Joseph E. 2011. "Current Account Imbalances Coming Back." Peterson Institute Working Paper 11–1 (January). The OECD argues that the magnitude of global imbalances through 2025 varies widely depending on the success of fiscal consolidation and structural reforms in the leading economies. See OECD. 2010. *OECD Economic Outlook,* issue 1. Paris: OECD.

49. See, for example, Blanchard, Olivier, and Gian Maria Milesi-Ferretti. 2009. IMF Staff Position Note 09/29, December 22. Donald L. Kohn. 2010. "Global Imbalances," speech at the High-Level Conference on the International Monetary System, Zurich, Switzerland, 11 May <www.federalreserve.gov/newsevents/speech/kohn20100511a.htm>.

50. *NBC News/Wall Street Journal* survey of 1,000 adults, 22–26 September 2010.

51. Blanchard, Olivier, and Gian Maria Milesi Ferretti. 2009. IMF Staff Position Note 09/29.

52. The EU has been the worst offender, followed by Russia, Argentina, and India. See Evenett, Simon. 2010. *Tensions Contained . . . for Now: The 8th GTA Report* <www.globaltradealert.org/tensions_contained_8th_gta_report?upad>.

53. See, for example, Roubini, Nouriel, and Brad Setser. 2004. "The US as a Net Debtor: The Sustainability of the US External Imbalances." Working paper <http://pages.stern.nyu.edu/~nroubini/papers/Roubini-Setser-US-External-Imbalances.pdf>; and Martin Wolf, "America on the Comfortable Path to Ruin," *Financial Times,* 17 August 2004. See also Rubin, Robert, Peter R. Orszag, and Allen Sinai. 2004. "Sustained Budget Deficits: Longer-Run U.S. Economic Performance and the Risk of Financial and Fiscal Disarray." Brookings Institution paper (January); Obstfeld, Maurice, and Kenneth Rogoff. 2004. "The Unsustainable US Current Account Position Revisited." NBER Working Paper 10869 (November); and Peterson, Peter. 2004. *Running on Empty: How the Democratic and Republican Parties Are Bankrupting Our Future and What Americans Can Do About It.* New York: Farrar, Straus and Giroux. For the view that imbalances contributed significantly to the crisis, see, for example, Ben S. Bernanke, "Remarks on the Economic Outlook," International Monetary Conference, Barcelona, Spain, 3 June 2008; Wolf, Martin. 2008. *Fixing Global Finance.* Baltimore: Johns Hopkins University Press; and Brad Setser, "Bretton Woods 2 and the Current Crisis: Any Link?" <http://blogs.cfr.org/setser/2008>. For opposing views, see, for instance, Dooley, Michael P., David Folkerts-Landau, and Peter M. Garber. 2009. "Bretton Woods II Still Defines the International Monetary System," NBER Working Paper 14731 (February); and Obstfeld, Maurice, and Kenneth Rogoff. 2009. "Global Imbalances and the Financial Crisis: Products of Common Causes" (November) <www.econ.berkeley.edu/~obstfeld/santabarbara.pdf>.

54. Obstfeld, Maurice, and Kenneth Rogoff. 2005. "The Unsustainable US Current Account Revisited."

55. Obstfeld, Maurice and Kenneth Rogoff. 2004. "The Unsustainable US Current Account Position Revisited"; and Obstfeld, Maurice, and Kenneth Rogoff. 2000. "Perspectives on OECD Capital Market Integration: Implications for U.S. Current

Account Adjustment." In Federal Reserve Bank of Kansas City, *Global Economic Integration: Opportunities and Challenges* (March), 169–208.

56. Timothy F. Geithner, "Policy Implications of Global Imbalances." Remarks at the Global Financial Imbalances Conference at Chatham House, London, 23 January 2006.

57. Freund, Caroline, and Frank Warnock. 2007 "Current Account Deficits in Industrial Countries: The Bigger They Are, the Harder They Fall?" In Richard H. Clarida, ed. *G7 Current Account Imbalances: Sustainability and Adjustment.* Chicago: University of Chicago Press. See also Freund, Caroline L. 2000. "Current Account Adjustment in Industrialized Countries," International Finance Discussion Papers 692, Board of Governors of the Federal Reserve System (December).

58. Dooley, Michael P., David Folkerts-Landau, and Peter M. Garber. 2004. "The Revived Bretton Woods System," *International Journal of Finance and Economics* 9: 307–313 <http://web.ku.edu/~intecon/Read/Dooley04.pdf>.

59. Greenspan, Alan. 2004. "The Evolving U.S. Payments Imbalance and Its Impact on Europe and the Rest of the World." *Cato Journal* 24 (Spring–Summer): 1–11. The comments echoed the view that improvements in international financial intermediation permitted larger current-account imbalances than could have been run in the past: savings in one country could increasingly be used to finance investment in others, and home bias was becoming moot.

60. Croke, Hilary, Steven B. Kamin, and Sylvain Leduc. 2005. "Financial Market Developments and Economic Activity During Current Account Adjustments in Industrial Economies," International Finance Discussion Paper 827, Board of Governors of the Federal Reserve System.

61. Rather, the measure should factor in consumer durables, education, and investment in and expenditure on research and development. Such an encompassing measure would bring the additional US savings to about 19 percent of GDP. Cooper, Richard. 2005. "Living with Global Imbalances: A Contrarian View." Peterson Institute Policy Brief 05–3 (November) <www.iie.com/publications/pb/pb05-3.pdf>. However, Cline argued that this would not cover the widening US external deficit going forward. Cline, William R. 2005. *The United States as a Debtor Nation.* Washington, D.C.: Institute for International Economics & Center for Global Development.

62. Hausmann, Ricardo, and Federico Sturzenegger. 2005. "U.S. and Global Imbalances: Can Dark Matter Prevent a Big Bang?" Working Paper, Kennedy School of Government, November.

63. See Carmen M. Reinhart and Vincent Reinhart, "Is the US Too Big to Fail?" VoxEU.com, 17 November 2008. The effects of current-account deficits also vary widely across countries, making comparisons somewhat futile. See Eichengreen, Barry, and Muge Adalet. 2005. "Current Account Reversals: Always a Problem?" NBER Working Paper 11634.

64. To be sure, recent research has revealed the limits of this argument. See Curcuru, Stephanie E., Charles P. Thomas, and Francis E. Warnock. 2008. "Current Account Sustainability and Relative Reliability." International Finance Discussion Paper 947, Board of Governors of the Federal Reserve System (September).

65. For a review, see Suominen, Kati. 2010. "Did Global Imbalances Cause the Crisis?" VoxEU.org, 14 June. For an assessment of America's attractions for investment, see Forbes, Kristin J. 2009. "Why Do Foreigners Invest in the United States?" MIT Sloan Research Paper 4701–08 (16 June).

66. See Catherine Rampell, "Lax Oversight Caused Crisis, Bernanke Says," *New York Times*, 4 January 2010; Freund, Caroline L. 2000. "Current Account Adjustment in Industrialized Countries"; Edwards, Sebastian. 2004. "Thirty Years of Current Account Imbalances, Current Account Reversals, and Sudden Stops." IMF Staff Papers 51, special issue <www.imf.org/external/pubs/ft/staffp/2003/00-00/e.pdf>.

67. Bibow, Jörg. 2010. "The Global Crisis and the Future of the Dollar: Toward Bretton Woods III?" Working Paper No. 584, Levy Economics Institute of Bard College and Skidmore College (February) <www.levyinstitute.org/pubs/wp_584.pdf>.

68. Mann, Catherine L. 1999. *Is the U.S. Trade Deficit Sustainable?* Washington, D.C.: Institute for International Economics; and Mann, Catherine L. "Is the U.S. Current Account Deficit Sustainable?" *Finance and Development* 37.1 (March) <www.imf .org/external/pubs/ft/fandd/2000/03/mann.htm>. See also Mann, Catherine. 2009. "International Capital Flows and the Sustainability of the US Current Account Deficit." In C. Fred Bergsten, ed. *The Long-Term International Economic Position of the United States*. Washington, D.C.: Peterson Institute for International Economics; and Martin Feldstein, "America's Saving Rate and the Dollar's Future," *International Business Review*, 6 August 2009.

69. See Bergsten, C. Fred. 2009. "The Dollar and the Deficits: What Washington Must Do to Prevent the Next Crisis." *Foreign Affairs* 6.88 (November/December).

70. Gilpin, Robert. 1987. *The Political Economy of International Relations*. Princeton: Princeton University Press. See also Funabashi, Yoichi. 1988. *Managing the Dollar: From Plaza to the Louvre;* and Cooper, William H. 1989. "U.S. Trade Policy Towards Japan: Where Do We Go from Here?" Congressional Research Service, 8 May.

71. Under one estimate, a 27.5-percent tariff on China, as threatened by Congress in 2003, would have caused a nearly 30-percent drop in Chinese US-bound durables and a 37-percent drop in nondurables, and a 3-percent drop in China's real GDP. McKibbin, Warwick, and Andrew Stoeckel. 2005. "What If the US Imposes a Tariff on China's Exports to Force a Revaluation?" *Economic Scenarios* 11 <www.economicsce narios.com/public/pdfredir_sample.asp?issueNo=11>.

72. Ferguson, Niall, and Moritz Schularick. 2009. "The End of Chimerica." Harvard Business School Working Paper 10–037 (October) <www.hbs.edu/research/ pdf/10-037.pdf>.

73. American Chamber of Commerce in Shanghai. 2011. *The 2010–2011 China Business Report*.

74. As China expert Nick Lardy summarized in 2007, "[T]he evidence to date suggests that the transition to more consumption-driven growth is off to a slow start." Lardy, Nicholas R. 2007. "China: Rebalancing Economic Growth." In *The China Balance Sheet in 2007 and Beyond*, Center for Strategic and International Studies and the Peterson Institute for International Economics. See also Lardy, Nicolas R. 2006. "China: Toward a Consumption-Driven Growth Path." Peterson Institute Policy Brief

06–6 (October) <www.iie.com/publications/pb/pb06-6.pdf>. See also Derek Scissors, "Deng Undone," press commentary, Heritage Foundation, 29 April 2009; and C. Fred Bergsten, testimony before the Subcommittee on Asia, the Pacific and the Global Environment, Committee on Foreign Affairs, US House of Representatives, 10 September 2009.

75. In 2008 gross exports were almost 40 percent of GDP, and the US was the largest trading partner, absorbing some 18 percent of China's exports, followed by Hong Kong, Japan, and South Korea. In contrast, only some 2 percent of US exports went to China. By a purely value-added calculation, exports came only to 10 percent. See "An Old Chinese Myth," *Economist*, 3 January 2008.

76. See summary in Nicholas R. Lardy, "China's Role in the Origins of and Response to the Global Recession," testimony at the hearing before the US–China Economic and Security Review Commission, 17 February 2009.

77. IMF. 2009. *Regional Economic Outlook*. Washington, D.C.: International Monetary Fund (October); Huang, Yiping. 2010. "What Caused China's Current Account Surplus?" In Simon Evenett, ed. *The US–Sino Currency Dispute: New Insights from Economics, Politics and Law*. London: Centre for Economic Policy Research <www.voxeu.org/reports/currency_dispute.pdf>.

78. Lardy, Nicolas R. 2006. "China: Toward a Consumption-Driven Growth Path."

79. See Pei, Minxin. 2006. *China's Trapped Transition: Limits of Developmental Autocracy*. Cambridge: Harvard University Press. See also Pei, Minxin. 2006. "The Dark Side of China's Rise." *Foreign Policy* (March/April) <www.carnegieendowment.org/publications/index.cfm?fa=view&id=18110>.

80. See Dennis Scissors, "The Fall and Rise of Chinese State-Owned Enterprises," testimony before the US–China Economic and Security Review Commission, 30 March 2011.

81. McKinsey Global Institute. 2009. "If You've Got It, Spend it: Unleashing the Chinese Consumer" (August) <www.mckinsey.com/mgi/reports/pdfs/unleashing_chinese_consumer/MGI_Unleashing_Chinese_Consumer_full_report.pdf>.

82. Bergsten, C. Fred. Testimony, "Correcting the Chinese Exchange Rate: An Action Plan," US House Ways and Means Committee Hearing on China's Exchange Rate Policy, 24 March 2010.

83. For a review of an unreleased paper by Victor Shih and David Steinberg on the topic, see "RMB X-Rate: The Power of China's Export Lobby," *China Track*, 6 April 2010.

84. During President Obama's visit to China in November 2009, the Chinese argued they had done enough to propel global growth. "A RMB-Sided Argument," *Economist*, 19 November 2009.

85. Cline, William, and John Williamson. 2009. "Equilibrium Exchange Rates," VoxEU.org, 18 June; and Ferguson, Niall, and Moritz Schularick. 2009. "The End of Chimerica." See also C. Fred Bergsten. 2007. "The Global Imbalances and the US Economy," testimony before the Subcommittees on Trade, Ways and Means Committee: Commerce, Trade and Consumer Protection, Energy and Commerce Committee;

and Domestic and International Monetary Policy, Trade and Technology, Financial Services Committee of the House of Representatives, 9 May 2007.

86. C. Fred Bergsten, "Correcting the Chinese Exchange Rate: An Action Plan," testimony, US House Ways and Means Committee Hearing on China's Exchange Rate Policy, 24 March 2010; and Cline, William R., and John Williamson. 2009. "Estimates of Fundamental Equilibrium Exchange Rates," Peterson Institute for International Economics Policy Brief 09–10.

87. Dani Rodrik, *Financial Times* blog. Rodrik argues that currency appreciation would pose "a tragedy for the world's most potent poverty reduction engine" and risk instability in China.

88. IMF has studied 28 policy-driven reversals—those caused by exchange-rate change or macroeconomic stimulus—in the past 50 years, finding that only policy-driven reversals were effective and, on average, the surplus narrowed by 5.1 percentage points of GDP and, on average, the current-account balance was afterward a relatively small 0.4 percent of GDP. On average, growth did not suffer after the reversal but remained unchanged, although there was a wide range of growth outcomes, from −5.1 percentage points to 9.4 percentage points. Current-account adjustments also resulted in gains in employment and capital, and significant reductions in savings (2.1 percentage points of GDP) and a sharp increase in investment (3 percentage points of GDP). Imports rose by some 4.2 percentage points of GDP, while exports remained unchanged. International Monetary Fund. 2010. *World Economic Outlook: Rebalancing Growth*. Washington, D.C.: IMF (April).

89. Chinn, Menzie. 2004. "Incomes, Exchange Rates and the U.S. Trade Deficit, Once Again." *International Finance* 7.3: 451–469; Chinn, Menzie, and Shang-Jin Wei. 2008. "A Faith-Based Initiative: Does a Flexible Exchange Rate Regime Really Facilitate Current Account Adjustment?" NBER Working Paper 14420 (October); Hooper, Peter, Karen Johnson, and Jaime Marquez. 2000. "Trade Elasticities for G7 Countries." *Princeton Studies in International Economics* 87; and Lee, Jaewoo, and Menzie Chinn. 2006. "Current Account and Real Exchange Rate Dynamics in the G7 Countries." *Journal of International Money and Finance* 25.2: 257–274; Broda, Christian. 2004. "Terms of Trade and Exchange Rate Regimes in Developing Countries." *Journal of International Economics* 63: 31–58; Engel, Charles. 2009. "Exchange Rate Policies." Federal Reserve Bank of Dallas Staff Paper 8 (November); and Staiger, Robert W., and Alan O. Sykes. 2008. "Currency Manipulation and World Trade." NBER Working Paper 14600.

90. See Helmut Reisen, "On the Renminbi and Economic Convergence," VoxEU .com, 17 December 2009.

91. "Rebalancing the World Economy: Japan—Stuck in Neutral," *Economist*, 13 August 2009.

92. David E. Sanger, "For U.S.–Japan Trade Pact, Less at Stake," *New York Times*, 5 August 1996.

93. "Rebalancing the World Economy: Japan—Stuck in Neutral."

94. Ibid.

95. Germany cut manufacturing costs and wages to restore its export competitiveness both in the 1970s, when the Deutschemark surged with the end of fixed exchange rates, and in the 1990s, when devaluations by Germany's trading partners increased relative wage costs. "Rebalancing the World Economy: Germany—The Lives of Others," *Economist*, 6 August 2009.

96. Ibid.

97. OECD data <www.oecd.org/dataoecd/5/48/2483858.xls>.

98. Carlo Bastasin, "Is It Wise or Productive for the United States to Press Germany to Abandon Its Export-Driven Economy?" Peterson Institute blog, 25 September 2009.

99. Ted Truman raises the idea of a semi-enforcement regime in the IMF that would inherently apply also to imbalances. Truman, Edwin M. 2010. "Strengthening IMF Surveillance: A Comprehensive Proposal." Peterson Institute Policy Brief 10−29 (December) <www.iie.com/publications/interstitial.cfm?ResearchID=1730>.

100. Cline, William R., and John Williamson. 2010. "Currency Wars?" Policy Brief 10−26, Peterson Institute for International Economics <www.iie.com/publications/pb/pb10-26.pdf>.

101. Germany is 84th out of 183 economies in the ease-of-starting-a-business variable of the World Bank's 2010 Doing Business database. For example, it takes 18 days to start a business, as opposed to 7 in France and 6 in the United States <www.doingbusiness.org/ExploreTopics/StartingBusiness/?direction=Asc&sort=4>.

102. See Thorbecke, Willem, and Gordon Smith. 2010. "How Would an Appreciation of the Renminbi and Other East Asian Currencies Affect China's Exports?" *Review of International Economics* 18.1: 95–108.

103. C. Fred Bergsten, "We Can Fight Fire with Fire on the Renminbi," *Financial Times*, 4 October 2010.

104. Gary Hufbauer, "Patience and the Currency Wars," *National Interest*, 27 October 2010.

105. C. Fred Bergsten, "Correcting the Chinese Exchange Rate: An Action Plan." For a similar proposal, see Arvind Subramanian, "The Weak Renminbi Is Not Just America's Problem," *Financial Times*, 17 March 2010. For methodology, see Robert W. Staiger and Alan O. Sykes, "Currency 'Manipulation' and World Trade: A Caution," VoxEU.com, 30 January 2009.

106. Paul Krugman, "Taking On China," *New York Times*, 14 March 2010.

107. Morrison, Wayne M., and Marc Labonte. 2008. "China's Currency: Economic Issues and Options for U.S. Trade Policy." Congressional Research Service, 9 January 2008.

108. See Lau, Lawrence J., Xikang Chen, Leonard K. Cheng, K. C. Fung, Jiansuo Pei, Yun-Wing Sung, Zhipeng Tang, Yanyan Xiong, Cuihong Yang, and Kunfu Zhu. 2006. "The Estimation of Domestic Value-Added and Employment Generated by U.S.–China Trade." Working Paper No. 2, Institute of Economics, the Chinese University of Hong Kong. See also Daniel Ikenson, "China Trade and American Jobs," *Wall Street Journal*, 2 April 2010; and Koopman, Robert, Zhi Wang, and Shang-Jin

Wei. 2008. "How Much of Chinese Exports Is Really Made in China? Assessing Domestic Value-Added When Processing Trade Is Pervasive." NBER Working Paper 14109.

109. Beijing retaliated against the US anti-dumping tariffs on Chinese tires in September 2009 with a 36-percent tariff on US nylon products, followed by preliminary anti-dumping duties of up to 105 percent on US broiler chicken.

110. See Hufbauer, Gary Clyde, and Jeffrey Schott. 2009. "Buy American: Bad for Jobs, Worse for Reputation." Peterson Institute for International Economics Policy Brief 09–2.

111. Jamil Anderlini, "US Companies Find China Less Welcoming," *Financial Times*, 22 March 2010 <www.ft.com/cms/s/0/66958052-355c-11df-9cfb-00144feabdc0 .html>.

112. For a similar argument, see Philip I. Levy, "U.S. Policy Options in Response to Chinese Currency Practices," testimony, US House Ways and Means Committee Hearing on China's Exchange Rate Policy, 24 March 2010.

113. Elizabeth Economy, "Leadership Gap in China," *Washington Post*, 1 December 2008.

114. Without a relative weakening of the dollar that would help America increase net exports, higher savings (and lower consumption) could translate into a recession.

115. Guidolin, Massimo, and Elizabeth A. La Jeunesse. 2007. "The Decline in the U.S. Personal Saving Rate: Is It Real and Is It a Puzzle?" *Federal Reserve Bank of St. Louis Review* 89.6 (November/December): 491–514.

116. Thornton, Daniel L. 2009. "Personal Saving and Economic Growth." *Economic Synopses* 46, Federal Reserve Bank of St. Louis <http://research.stlouisfed.org/ publications/es/09/ES0946.pdf>.

117. For a discussion on optimal taxation, see Mankiw, N. Gregory, Matthew Weinzierl, and Danny Yagan. 2009. "Optimal Taxation in Theory and Practice." NBER Working Paper 15071 (June).

118. Alesina, Alberto F., and Silvia Ardagna. 2009. "Large Changes in Fiscal Policy: Taxes Versus Spending." NBER Working Paper 15438.

Chapter 2

1. For an excellent overview, see Boughton, James M. 2002. "Why White, Not Keynes? Inventing the Post-War International Monetary System." IMF Working Paper 02/52 (1 March) <www.imf.org/external/pubs/ft/wp/2002/wp0252.pdf>.

2. See "International Monetary Fund and World Bank," Encyclopedia of American Foreign Relations <www.americanforeignrelations.com/index.html>.

3. For studies on ways in which the United States exercises its role in the IMF, see, for example, Randall W. Stone, "The Scope of IMF Conditionality," working paper, March 2007; and James Raymond Vreeland, "The International and Domestic Politics of IMF Programs," working paper, October 2005.

4. Argentina subsequently defaulted on $100 billion in private debt. For a sweeping account of the Argentine episode, see Blustein, Paul. 2005. *And the Money Kept Rolling In (and Out): Wall Street, the IMF, and the Bankrupting of Argentina*. New York: PublicAffairs.

5. See Elliott, Kimberly, and Gary Clyde Hufbauer. 2002. "Ambivalent Multilateralism and the Emerging Backlash: The IMF and the WTO." In Stewart Patrick and Shepard Forman, eds. *Multilateralism and US Foreign Policy*. Boulder: Lynne Rienner.

6. Richard Medley quipped that Russia was an "Indonesia with nukes." Paul Blustein and Sandra Sugawara, "Two Crises Shake Foreign Stock Markets," *Washington Post*, 28 May 1998.

7. Joseph Kahn, "U.S. Backs Aid to Turkey Tied to Economic Overhaul," *New York Times*, 21 April 2001.

8. See Frankel, Jeffrey. 2004. "Bush's Spectacular Failure." *International Economy* (Spring) <www.international-economy.com/TIE_SP04_Frankel.pdf>.

9. Dreher, Axel, Jan-Egbert Sturme, and James Raymond Vreeland. 2009 "Global Horse Trading: IMF Loans for Votes in the United Nations Security Council," *European Economic Review* 53.7 (October): 742–757.

10. Stone, Randall W. 2004. "The Political Economy of IMF Lending in Africa." *American Political Science Review* 98 (December): 577–592.

11. Broz, J. Lawrence, and Michael Brewster Hawes. 2006. "Congressional Politics of Financing the International Monetary Fund." *International Organization* 60.1: 367–399.

12. For insights, see Henning, C. Randall. 2009. "US Interests and the International Monetary Fund." Peterson Institute Policy Brief 09–12, June 2009.

13. For a review, see Ul Haque, N., and M. S. Khan. 1998. "Do IMF-Supported Programs Work? A Survey of the Cross-Country Empirical Evidence." IMF Working Paper 169; and Dreher, Axel. 2006. "IMF and Economic Growth: The Effects of Programs, Loans, and Compliance with Conditionality." *World Development* 34.5 (May): 769–788. See also Joyce, J. P. 2003. "Promises Made, Promises Broken: A Model of IMF Program Implementation." Wellesley College Department of Economics Working Paper 2003–03; and Mussa, Michael, and M. Savastano. 1999. "The IMF Approach to Economic Stabilization." IMF Working Paper 108.

14. For instance, an IMF program decreases the risk of a currency crisis and increases the likelihood that the exchange rate will be adjusted once a crisis is under way. See Dreher, Axel, and Stefanie Walter. 2010. "Does the IMF Help or Hurt? The Effect of IMF Programs on the Likelihood and Outcome of Currency Crises." *World Development* 38.1 (January): 1–18.

15. Henning, C. Randall. 2009. "US Interests and the International Monetary Fund."

16. Henning, C. Randall. 2009. "America the Deadbeat?" *Foreign Policy*, 2 June 2009.

17. For a similar review, see Hufbauer, Gary, and Kati Suominen. 2010. *Globalization at Risk: Challenges to Finance and Trade*. New Haven: Yale University Press.

18. Loan conditions are not devised by the IMF alone, as commonly believed, but represent the confluence of the interests of the IMF and a range of supplementary financiers such as creditor states, private banks, and other multilateral organizations, all of which have a stake in the success of the loan. See Gould, Erica R. 2003. "Money Talks: Supplementary Financiers and International Monetary Fund Conditionality." *International Organization* 57 (Summer): 551–586.

19. Independent Evaluation Office of the IMF. 2005. "Issues Paper for an Evaluation of Structural Conditionality in IMF-Supported Programs." IMF (18 May) <www.ieo-imf.org/eval/ongoing/051805.pdf>.

20. Stiglitz, Joseph E. 2002. *Globalization and Its Discontents.* London: Allen, Penguin Press; and Radelet, Steven, and Jeffrey Sachs. 1998. "The East Asian Financial Crisis: Diagnosis, Remedies, and Prospects," *Brookings Papers on Economic Activity,* no. 1. For a less scathing yet still critical assessment, see Feldstein, Martin. 1998. "Refocusing the IMF." *Foreign Affairs*, March/April. Also, Wolf, Martin. *Why Globalization Works.* New Haven: Yale University Press, 2004. Another authoritative account is Kenen, Peter. 2001. *The International Financial Architecture: What's New? What's Missing?* Washington, DC: Institute for International Economics. For an outstanding recent overview of various issues at stake, see Hillman, Jennifer. 2010. "Saving Multilateralism." *German Marshall Fund Brussels Forum Paper Series* (22 March).

21. For IMF commentary on the US housing market, see, for example, IMF. 2006. *Global Financial Stability Report.* Washington, DC: IMF (September) <www.imf.org/external/pubs/ft/GFSR/2006/02/index.htm>.

22. Walter Pincus and Joby Warrick, "Financial Crisis Called Top Security Threat to US," *Washington Post*, 13 February 2009.

23. Swap lines extended were with the central banks of Australia, Brazil, Canada, Denmark, Britain, South Korea, Mexico, New Zealand, Norway, Singapore, Sweden, and Switzerland, along with the European Central Bank. The swap lines had positive effects for quelling the crisis. See Joshua Aizenman and Gurnain Kaur Pasricha. 2009. "Selective Swap Arrangements and the Global Financial Crisis: Analysis and Interpretation." NBER Working Paper 14821 (March).

24. See Bob Davis, "IMF Gets New Role of Serving the G20," *Wall Street Journal*, 5 October 2009.

25. See, for example, "DSK Sets Out His Vision for the IMF," *Euronews*, 1 October 2007.

26. See "The International Monetary Fund: Back from the Dead," *Economist*, 17 September 2009.

27. This sum includes direct spending, loans, and guarantees by the London G20 Summit to arrest the financial crisis. The funds were provided by the FDIC as well as the Treasury and the Federal Reserve. See Congressional Oversight Panel, "Assessing TARP Strategy," Washington, DC, 7 April 2009 <http://cop.senate.gov/documents/cop-040709-report.pdf>.

28. Hufbauer, Gary, and Kati Suominen. 2010. *Globalization at Risk.*

29. See Dominique Strauss-Kahn, "Making the Most of an Historic Opportunity: Three Principles for Reshaping the Global Economic and Financial Framework," Speech, Istanbul, 2 October 2009.

30. Simon Johnson, "Shadow Agenda for the G20 Summit: More Money for the IMF," *Peterson Institute Real Time Economic Issues Watch,* 6 November 2008 <www.petersoninstitute.org/realtime/?p=222>; and Guillermo Calvo, "Lender of Last Resort: Put It on the Agenda!" VoxEU.com, 23 March 2009. Kenen argues persuasively that the IMF is not the lender of last resort as properly defined by the inventor of the term, nineteenth-century *Economist* editor Bagehot, but rather a "credit union," where lenders and borrowers have reciprocal rights. See Kenen, Peter B. 1986. *Financing, Adjustment, and the International Monetary Fund.* Washington, DC: Brookings Institution; and Kenen, Peter B. 2001. *The International Financial Architecture: What's New? What's Missing?* Washington, DC: Institute for International Economics.

31. House Speaker Newt Gingrich (R–GA), pledging Republican support, summarized the sentiment as "we have zero choice in this." See Humphrey, Brett M. 2000. "The Post-NAFTA Mexican Peso Crisis: Bailout or Aid? Isolationism or Globalization?" *Hinckley Journal of Politics* (Spring): 33–40. For an analysis of congressional politics, see also Broz, J. Lawrence. 2005. "Congressional Politics of International Financial Rescues." *American Journal of Political Science* 49.3 (July): 479–496.

32. For the uses of the ESF, see Henning, C. Randall. 1999. *The Exchange Stabilization Fund: Slush Money or War Chest? Policy Analyses in International Economics.* Washington, DC: Institute for International Economics.

33. For a discussion, see Broz, J. Lawrence. 2002. "The Domestic Politics of International Bailouts: Congressional Voting on Bailout Legislation in the 1990s." Draft (March) <www.nyu.edu/gsas/dept/politics/seminars/broz.pdf>.

34. See Eric Schmitt, "Republicans Step Up Attack on Clinton's Russia Policy," *New York Times,* 15 September 1999; and Ariel Cohen, "Reasons to Oppose New IMF Credits to Russia," Heritage Foundation Executive Memorandum 597, 18 May 1999.

35. "Report of the International Financial Institution Advisory Committee," US House of Representatives, March 2000 <www.house.gov/jec/imf/meltzer.pdf>.

36. Quoted in "Skepticism on IMF Lending to Argentina Gains Congressional Support," US Congress Joint Economic Committee Press Release 107–57, 14 December 2001.

37. See Council on Foreign Relations Task Force. 1999. *Safeguarding Prosperity in a Global Financial System: The Future International Financial Architecture.* New York: Council on Foreign Relations Press.

38. See Lee, Jong Wha, and Kwanho Shin. 2008. "IMF Bailouts and Moral Hazard." *Journal of International Money and Finance* 27.5 (September): 816–830; and Dreher, Axel. 2009. "Does the IMF Cause Moral Hazard? A Critical Review of the Evidence." IVS discussion paper series 598, Institut für Volkswirtschaft und Statistik (IVS), University of Mannheim. There is substantial repetition in defaults: countries that have defaulted on their secured loans are quite likely to default again.

39. For an overview, see Haldane, Andrew, and Ashley Taylor. 2003. "Moral Hazard: How Does IMF Lending Affect Debtor and Creditor Incentives?" *Bank of England Financial Stability Review* 14.6 (June) <www.bankofengland.co.uk/publications/fsr/2003/fsr14art6.pdf>. For a conceptual discussion on moral hazard and other challenges facing the IMF, see Obstfeld, Maurice. 2009. "Lenders of Last Resort in a Globalized World." CEPR Discussion Paper 7355 (July).

40. See Dell' Ariccia, Giovanni, Isabel Schnabel, and Jeromin Zettelmeyer. 2002. "Moral Hazard and International Crisis Lending: A Test." IMF Working Paper No. 02/181 (October).

41. Taylor, John B. 2007. *Global Financial Warriors: The Untold Story of International Finance in the Post-9/11 World.* New York: Norton. See also Eichengreen, Barry, and Douglas A. Irwin. 2007. "The Bush Legacy for America's International Economic Policy." Draft (August) <www.econ.berkeley.edu/~eichengr/bush_legacy.pdf>.

42. Joseph Kahn, "From No Aid to a Bailout," *New York Times,* 23 August 2001.

43. "Reforming the IMF: Is Bigger Better? And Who Should Get More Say?" Panel with Anne D. Krueger and Allan H. Meltzer, Council on Foreign Relations, 22 May 2009.

44. The $106-billion emergency bill included commitments to the wars in Afghanistan and Iraq, funding for battling swine flu, and $5 billion to approve of the US $108-billion loan to the IMF. The Senate approved the legislation June 18 on a vote of 91–5; it passed the House 226–202 on June 16.

45. S. A. Miller, "Senate Upholds IMF Contribution," *Washington Times,* 22 May 2009. See also Brian Faler, "U.S. House Approves War-Spending Bill Amid Dispute Over IMF Share Business," *Bloomberg,* 17 June 2009. House Majority leader Steny Hoyer called the bill "an insurance policy for the global economy." See "Hoyer Statement on Supplemental Appropriations Bill," press release, Majority Leader's Office, 16 June 2009.

46. Henning, C. Randall. 2009. "US Interests and the International Monetary Fund."

47. Ibid.

48. Broz, J. Lawrence. 2005. "Congressional Politics of International Financial Rescues." *American Journal of Political Science* 49.3 (July): 479–496.

49. Henning, C. Randall. 2009. "US Interests and the International Monetary Fund."

50. Four top Democrats, including chairman of the House Financial Services Committee, Barney Frank, stated that further aid may not be available next time for the IMF and other international institutions if the White House ignores the conditions set in the law. Lesley Wroughton, "Top Democrats Warn Obama on IMF Funding Qualifier," *Reuters,* 21 July 2009.

51. Truman, Edwin, ed. 2006. *Reforming the IMF for the 21st Century.* Special Report 19. Washington, DC: Peterson Institute for the International Economy.

52. "President Hu Jintao's Attendance at the Second Financial Summit of G20 Leaders Achieves Major Outcomes," Chinese Foreign Ministry, 4 April 2009 <www.chinaembassy.org.in/eng/zgbd/t556460.htm>.

53. Lipscy, Phillip Y. 2008. "Japan's Shifting Role in International Organizations." In Masaru Kohno and Frances Rosenbluth, eds. *Japan and the World: Japan's Contemporary Geopolitical Challenges*. New Haven: Council on East Asian Studies at Yale University.

54. "China Wants IMF to Be Tougher with Rich States," *Reuters*, 9 February 2009.

55. Sebastian Mallaby, "Supersize the IMF," *Washington Post*, 13 November 2008.

56. Late-2010 IMF calculations based on the IMF's quota formula and postcrisis economic data indicate that if votes were strictly based on the formula, several Western European nations, such as Germany, UK, France, Netherlands, Belgium, Switzerland, Sweden, Austria, Denmark, Finland, and Italy, would incur cuts. Spain, Ireland, as well as Poland and some other Eastern European nations would score gains. US share would be 16.5 percent, down from 16.7, and Japan's share would shift from 6.2 to 6.1 percent. Saudi Arabia would lose, while China's share would rise to 6 percent and India's to 2.6. Many Asian emerging nations would score gains. Robust growth in emerging markets would entail further gains in the coming years. See IMF. 2010. "Illustration of Proposed Quota and Voting Shares" (December) <www.imf.org/external/np/sec/pr/2010/pdfs/pr10418_table.pdf>.

57. A paper circulated among European capitals by the French EU Presidency in November 2009 argues for emerging powers to take on "increased responsibility" in the IMF. However, the paper also calls for a stronger attention to the imbalances issue and exchange-rate policies. See "EU Mulls Swapping IMF Seat with Chinese Commitments," *EurActiv*, 3 November 2008.

58. Ibid.

59. Ahearne, Alan, and Barry Eichengreen. 2007. "External Monetary and Financial Policy: A Review and a Proposal," In Andre Sapir, ed. *Fragmented Power: Europe and the Global Economy*. Brussels: Bruegel.

60. Europeans have cooperated more closely at the IMF also after the 1998 Vienna European Council meeting, where the member states pledged to collaborate more in international forums. See Bini Smaghi, Lorenzo, "A Single Seat in the IMF?" *Journal of Common Market Studies* 42.2: 229–248; Alan Ahearne and Barry Eichengreen, "Resetting Europe's Place at the Global Financial Table," VoxEU.com, 18 October 2007; and ADS Insight. 2006. "European Coordination at the World Bank and the International Monetary Fund: A Question of Harmony?" (January).

61. Ahearne, Alan, and Barry Eichengreen. 2007. "External Monetary and Financial Policy." Also, Bini Smaghi, Lorenzo, "A Single Seat in the IMF?"

62. Bini Smaghi, Lorenzo. 2006. "Powerless Europe: Why Is the Euro Area Still a Political Dwarf?" *International Finance* 9: 1–19; and Robert Leech. 2005. "Voting Power Implications of a Unified European Representation at the IMF," unpublished manuscript (January). Also, Alan Ahearne and Barry Eichengreen. 2007. "External Monetary and Financial Policy."

63. Malmur Keliat, "Part 1 of 2: Lessons from E. Asian Financial Cooperation," *Jakarta Post*, 26 February 2005. The literature on Asian financial integration is voluminous. See, for example, de Brouwer, G. 1999. *Financial Integration in East Asia*.

Cambridge: Cambridge University Press; Asian Development Bank. 2004. *Monetary and Financial Integration in East Asia: The Way Ahead*. Basingstoke: Palgrave Macmillan; Kenen, Peter B., and Ellen E. Meade. 2007. "Monetary Integration in East Asia: Why East Asia Is Different and Why That Matters." In Peter B. Kenen and Ellen E. Meade, *Regional Monetary Integration*. Cambridge: Cambridge University Press; and Henning, C. Randall. 2002. *East Asian Financial Cooperation*. Policy Analyses in International Economics No. 68. Washington, DC: Institute for International Economics.

64. Joel Rathus, "Japan, the DPJ and Regional Financial Arrangements," *East Asia Forum*, 11 August 2009 <www.eastasiaforum.org/2009/08/11/japan-the-djp-and-regional-financial-arrangements>.

65. See McKay, Julie, Ulrich Volz, and Regine Wölfinger. "Regional Financing Arrangements and the Stability of the International Monetary System." German Development Institute Discussion Paper 13/2010.

66. "Asia Looks to Its Own Financial Stability," *Oxford Analytica*, 27 August 2009.

67. Brookings Workshop, "Financial Regionalism: Lessons and Next Steps," Brookings Institute, Washington, DC, 13–14 October 2010.

68. See, for example, Eichengreen, Barry, and C. P. Yung. 2005. "Financial Liberalization and Capital Market Integration in East Asia." EU Center of the University of California, Berkeley and the Ford Foundation.

69. Blustein, Paul, 2001. *The Chastening: Inside the Crisis That Rocked the Global Financial System and Humbled the IMF*. New York: PublicAffairs.

70. Maria Monica Wihardja, "ASEAN+3 Needs an Independent Regional Surveillance Institution," *East Asia Forum*, 8 October 2009 <www.eastasiaforum.org/2009/10/08/asean3-needs-an-independent-regional-surveillance-institution>.

71. "Japan-China Spat Results in Delay of Sale of Plot for New Chinese Consulate," *Telegraph*, 20 December 2010.

72. Interview with Professor Sung-Hoon Park. Graduate School of International Studies, Korea University, 6 October 2009.

73. Jung, Jee-young. 2008. "Regional Financial Cooperation in Asia: Challenges and Path to Development." In *Regional Financial Integration in Asia: Present and Future*, BIS Papers No. 42 (October) <www.bis.org/publ/bppdf/bispap42.htm>.

74. "Game, Set and Match to Angela," *Economist*, 29 October 2010.

75. "Italy Calls for Euro Bonds, UK Backs Fiscal Union," Reuters, 13 August 2011.

76. See Paolo Manasse, "The Trouble with the European Stability Mechanism," VoxEu.org, 5 April 2011; and Daniel Gros, "Pact for the Euro: Tough Talk, Soft Conditions?" VoxEu.org, 14 March 2011.

77. Dalibor Rocah and Michal Lehuta, "A Fannie Mae for Europe," *Wall Street Journal*, 19 July 2011.

78. For a summary, see Aizenman, Joshua, Yothin Jinjarak, and Donghyun Park. 2010. "International Reserves and Swap Lines: The Recent Experience." Working paper (April) <http://aric.adb.org/grs/papers/Aizenman.pdf>.

79. IMF. 2010. "The Fund's Mandate—Future Financing Needs: Revised Reform Proposals," 29 June.

80. For a thorough study of regional trade agreements, see Estevadeordal, Antoni, and Kati Suominen. 2009. *The Sovereign Remedy: Trade Agreements in the Globalizing World*. Oxford: Oxford University Press.

81. See also Kati Suominen, "Lessons in Regionalism: What Can the WTO Teach the IMF?" VoxEU.org, 3 November 2010.

82. Ted Truman proposes that the IMF charter be modified to allow the IMF to enter into short-term arrangements with national central banks to swap SDR for key national currencies in the global financial system—the US dollar, the euro, the yen, the pound, and the Swiss franc. The currencies would then be used to fund the IMF's short-term lending facility. Like a GSM, such a centralized system would replace the bilateral lending operations of national central banks. Edwin M. Truman, "The G20 and International Financial Institution Reform: Unfinished IMF Reform," Voxeu.com, 28 January 2009.

83. Lipscy, Phillip Y. 2008. "Japan's Shifting Role in International Organizations." In Masaru Kohno and Frances Rosenbluth, eds. *Japan and the World: Japan's Contemporary Geopolitical Challenges*. New Haven: Council on East Asian Studies at Yale University.

84. Brookings Workshop, "Financial Regionalism: Lessons and Next Steps."

85. See, for instance, Bergsten, C. Fred. 2009. "The Dollar and the Deficits: What Washington Must Do to Prevent the Next Crisis." *Foreign Affairs* 88.6 (November/December).

86. Ted Truman proposes that total quotas will be increased in line with the expansion of the global economy, trade, and financial system. See Edwin M. Truman, "The G20 and International Financial Institution Reform: Unfinished IMF Reform." Ralph Bryant has called for a formula based on economic relevance (population or GDP at PPP exchange rates, which favors emerging markets) and capacity to pay (GDP at market exchange rates, which favors the US). See Bryant, Ralph C. 2008. "Reform of Quota and Voting Shares in the International Monetary Fund: 'Nothing' Is Temporarily Preferable to an Inadequate 'Something.'" Draft, Brookings Institution (January) <www.g24.org/bray0308.pdf>.

87. See "The International Monetary Fund: Back from the Dead."

88. Kenen, Peter. 1986. *Financing, Adjustment, and the International Monetary Fund*. Washington, DC: Brookings Institution.

89. Truman makes a rather similar argument. See Edwin M. Truman, "The G20 and International Financial Institution Reform."

90. For a discussion, see Hufbauer, Gary, and Kati Suominen. 2010. *Globalization at Risk: Challenges to Finance and Trade*. New Haven: Yale University Press. See also Fischer, Stanley. 1998. "Capital-Account Liberalization and the Role of the IMF." *Princeton Essays in International Finance* 207 (May): 1–10; and Summers, Lawrence H. 2000. "International Financial Crises: Causes, Prevention, and Cures." *American Economic Review* 90.2: 1–16. Also see Edwin M. Truman, "The G20 and International Financial Institution Reform."

91. Independent Evaluations Office of the IMF. 2011. "IMF Performance in the Run-Up to the Financial and Economic Crisis: IMF Surveillance in 2004–07" (February) <www.ieo-imf.org/eval/complete/eval_01102011.html>.

92. For a discussion, see Helleiner, Eric. 2008. "The Mystery of the Missing Sovereign Debt Restructuring Mechanism." *Contributions to Political Economy* 27.1. Ideally, of course, the provision of finance and adjustment would go hand in hand.

93. For this and an overview review of other proposals, see Mateos y Lago, Isabelle, Rupa Duttagupta, and Rishi Goyal. 2009. "The Debate on the International Monetary System." IMF Staff Position Paper 09/26 (11 November) <www.imf.org/external/pubs/ft/spn/2009/spn0926.pdf>.

94. *The NewsHour with Jim Lehrer*, transcript, 8 September 1998.

Chapter 3

1. Calomiris, Charles W. 2000. *US Banking Deregulation in Historical Perspective*. Cambridge: Cambridge University Press.

2. For an authoritative political economy study, see Calomiris, Charles W. 2000. *US Banking Deregulation in Historical Perspective*. Another key piece of the Glass–Steagall, Regulation Q, prohibited banks from paying any interest on checking accounts.

3. White, Eugene. 1986. "Before the Glass–Steagall Act: An Analysis of the Investment Banking Activities of National Banks." *Explorations in Economic History* 23.1: 33–55.

4. See Benston, George J. 1990. *The Separation of Commercial and Investment Banking: The Glass–Steagall Act Revisited and Reconsidered*. New York: Oxford University Press.

5. Calomiris, Charles W. 2000. *US Banking Deregulation in Historical Perspective*.

6. The law had holes: on the order of their customers, commercial banks could invest in bonds, manage mutual funds, and execute securities trades. Even if they could not underwrite corporate stocks and bonds, they could underwrite government securities.

7. See Kroszner, Randall S., and Philip E. Strahan. 1999. "What Drives Deregulation? Economics and Politics of the Relaxation of Bank Branching Restrictions." *Quarterly Journal of Economics* 114.4: 1437–1467 (November); and Peltzman, Sam. 1976. "Toward a More General Theory of Regulation." *Journal of Law and Economics* 19: 109–148.

8. Calomiris, Charles W. 2000. *US Banking Deregulation in Historical Perspective*.

9. Kroszner, Randall S., and Philip E. Strahan. 1999. "What Drives Deregulation?"

10. Ibid.

11. Kane, Edward J. 1996. "*De Jure* Interstate Banking: Why Only Now?" *Journal of Money, Credit, and Banking* 28: 141–161.

12. Calomiris, Charles W. 2000. *US Banking Deregulation in Historical Perspective.*

13. Kroszner, Randall S., and Philip E. Strahan. 1999. "What Drives Deregulation?"; and Mamun, Abdullah, M. Kabir Hassan, and Neal Maroney. 2005. "The Wealth and Risk Effects of the Gramm–Leach–Bliley Act (GLBA) on the US Banking Industry." *Journal of Business Finance & Accounting* 32.1–2: 351–388.

14. By mid-1995, most OECD countries allowed at least some foreign banks to operate on their soil, usually on a national treatment basis. See Edey, Malcolm, and K. Hviding. 1995. "An Assessment of Financial Reform in OECD Countries." OECD Economics Department Working Papers 154.

15. Following the reforms, and partly because of them, Japan became home to seven of the world's ten largest commercial banks and rose to become a leading financial power and the world's largest international creditor. In late 1986, Japanese banks held over $1 trillion in international assets, a third of total cross-border assets, compared to a fifth held by US banks. See, for example, Funabashi, Yochi. 1999. *Alliance Adrift.* New York: Council on Foreign Relations Press.

16. See Calomiris, Charles W. 2000. *US Banking Deregulation in Historical Perspective.* See also Daniel K. Tarullo, "Financial Regulation in the Wake of the Crisis," speech at the Peterson Institute for International Economics, Washington, D.C., 8 June 2009 <www.federalreserve.gov/newsevents/speech/tarullo20090608a.htm>.

17. See Haubrich, Joseph G., and Paul Wachtel. 1993. "Capital Requirements and Shifts in Commercial Bank Portfolios." *Cleveland Federal Reserve Research Review,* 93.3 <www.clevelandfed.org/research/Review/1993/93-q3-haubrich.pdf>. Capital requirement applies to bank assets; in contrast, reserve requirement applies to liabilities. The latter imposes the amount of reserves a bank must own relative to the demand deposits of its customers.

18. Daniel K. Tarullo, "Financial Regulation in the Wake of the Crisis." Also see Peek, Joe, and Eric S. Rosengren. 1996. "The Use of Capital Ratios to Trigger Intervention in Problem Banks: Too Little, Too Late." *New England Economic Review* (September): 49–58.

19. "Base Camp Basel," *Economist,* 21 January 2010.

20. For a summary of studies, see Reinhardt, Carmen, and Kenneth Rogoff, "Banking Crises: An Equal Opportunity Menace." CEPR Discussion Paper 7131. Governments managed to contain fires in individual institutions, but their record was poor in dealing with large institutions or limiting systemic contagion across economic sectors. Santomero, Anthony M., and Paul Hoffman. 1998 "Problem Bank Resolution: Evaluating the Options." Working paper, Wharton School, University of Pennsylvania (October) <http://fic.wharton.upenn.edu/fic/papers/98/9805.pdf>.

21. Reinhardt, Carmen, and Kenneth Rogoff, "Banking Crises."

22. "Base Camp Basel."

23. See Lane, Philip, and Gian Maria Milesi-Ferretti, 1998. "Drivers of Financial Globalization." Institute for International Integration Studies Dis-

cussion Paper 238 (January) <www.ecb.int/events/pdf/conferences/ecbcfs_cmfi2/Philip_Lane_paper.pdf?397f060a275b897cb229619c49b9793d>.

24. See Jones, Kenneth D., and Tim Critchfield. 2005. "Consolidation in the U.S. Banking Industry: Is the 'Long, Strange Trip' About to End?" *FDIC Banking Review* 17.4 <www.fdic.gov/bank/analytical/banking/2006jan/article2/article2.pdf>.

25. See Bank for International Settlements. 2006. "The Recent Behavior of Financial Market Volatility." BIS Papers 29 (August).

26. For views favorable to capital controls, see, for instance, Stiglitz, Joseph. 2000. "Capital Market Liberalization, Economic Growth, and Instability." *World Development* 28.6 (June): 1075–1086; and Rodrik, Dani. 1998. "Who Needs Capital-Account Convertibility?" *Essays in International Finance* 207 (February).

27. Tanveer Shehzad, Choudhry, and Jakob De Haan. 2009. "Financial Reform and Banking Crises." CESifo Working Paper 2870 (December) <www.ifo.de/pls/guestci/download/CESifo%20Working%20Papers%202009/CESifo%20Working%20Papers%20December%202009/cesifo1_wp2870.pdf>. See also Edey, Malcolm, and K. Hviding. 1995. "An Assessment of Financial Reform in OECD Countries." OECD Economics Department Working Papers 154; and Davies, Howard, and David Green. 2008. *Global Financial Regulation: The Essential Guide.* Cambridge: Polity. Hüpkes, Eva, Marc Quintyn, and Michael W. Taylor. 2006. "Accountability Arrangements for Financial Sector Regulators." *IMF Economic Issues* 39 <www.imf.org/external/pubs/ft/issues/issues39/ei39.pdf>.

28. Tanveer Shehzad, Choudhry, and Jakob De Haan. 2009. "Financial Reform and Banking Crises."

29. Ramírez, Carlos D. 1999. "Did Glass–Steagall Increase the Cost of External Finance for Corporate Investment? Evidence from Bank and Insurance Company Affiliations." *Journal of Economic History* 59.2 (June): 372–396.

30. Kroszner, Randall S., and Raghuram G. Rajan. 1994. "Is the Glass–Steagall Act Justified? A Study of the U.S. Experience with Universal Banking." *American Economic Review* 84.4 (September): 810–832.

31. Calomiris, Charles W. 2000. *US Banking Deregulation in Historical Perspective.*

32. Cline, William R. 2010. *Financial Globalization, Economic Growth, and the Crisis 2007–09.* Washington, D.C.: Peterson Institute for International Economics.

33. For a review, see Hufbauer, Gary, and Kati Suominen. 2010. *Globalization at Risk: Challenges to Finance and Trade.* New Haven: Yale University Press.

34. Kaminsky, Graciela L., and Carmen M. Reinhart. 2000. "On Crises, Contagion, and Confusion." *Journal of International Economics*, 51.1 (June): 145–168; Mehrez, Gil, and Daniel Kaufmann. 2000. "Transparency, Liberalization, and Banking Crisis." Policy Research Working Paper Series 2286, World Bank.

35. Reinhart, Carmen, and Kenneth S. Rogoff. 2009. "Is the 2007 U.S. Subprime Crisis So Different? An International Historical Comparison." *American Economic Review* 98.2 (May 2008): 466–472.

36. For a review, see Hufbauer, Gary, and Kati Suominen. 2010. *Globalization at Risk.*

37. Risk increased relative to capital levels. For a review, see VanHoose, David D. 2008. "Bank Capital Regulation, Economic Stability and Monetary Policy: What Does the Academic Literature Tell Us?" *Atlantic Economic Journal* (March).

38. Working group led by Patricia Jackson. 1999. "Capital Requirements and Bank Behavior: The Impact of the Basel Accord." Basel Committee on Banking Supervision Working Papers 1 (April).

39. "Practical Issues Drive Banking Reform," *Oxford Analytica*, 17 February 2010.

40. Berge, Allen, and Gregory Udell. 1994. "Did Risk-Based Capital Allocate Bank Credit and Cause a 'Credit Crunch' in the U.S.?" Wharton School Center for Financial Institutions Working Paper 94–07.

41. Troutman Sanders LLP, "Treasury Proposes 'Resolution Authority' for Systemically Significant Financial Companies," 31 March 2009.

42. The council may require any such large entity to report on its financial condition, systems for monitoring and controlling risks, transactions with subsidiaries that are regulated banks, and on the extent to which any of the company's activities could disrupt financial markets or the US economy.

43. "Not All on the Same Page," *Economist*, 1 July 2010.

44. Brady Dennis and Jia Lynn Yang, "House Passes Financial Overhaul; Senate Leaders Postpone Vote," *Washington Post*, 1 July 2010.

45. Rich Miller, "Wall Street Fix Seen Ineffectual by Four of Five in U.S.," *Bloomberg*, 13 July 2010.

46. Ross Colvin, "Obama Signs Sweeping Wall Street Overhaul into Law," *Reuters*, 21 July 2010.

47. R. Bruce Josten, "Letter Opposing the Conference Report for H.R. 4173, the 'Dodd–Frank Wall Street Reform and Consumer Protection Act,'" press release, US Chamber of Commerce, 28 June 2010 <www.uschamber.com/issues/letters/2010/letter-opposing-conference-report-hr-4173-dodd-frank-street-reform-and-cons>.

48. Davis Polk. "Summary of the Dodd–Frank Wall Street Reform and Consumer Protection Act" passed by the House of Representatives on June 30, 2010 <www.davispolk.com/files/Publication/7084f9fe-6580-413b-b870-b7c025ed2ecf/Presenta tion/PublicationAttachment/1d4495c7-0be0-4e9a-ba77-f786fb90464a/070910_Financial_Reform_Summary.pdf>.

49. "Not All on the Same Page."

50. Institute of International Finance. 2010. *Interim Report on the Cumulative Impact on the Global Economy of Proposed Changes in the Banking Regulatory Framework* (June) <http://iif.com/press/press+151.php>.

51. For an excellent overview, see Davies, Howard, and David Green. 2008. *Global Financial Regulation: The Essential Guide.* Cambridge: Polity.

52. For the beneficial effects of insurance, see Diamond, Douglas W., and Philip H. Dybvig. 1983. "Bank Runs, Deposit Insurance, and Liquidity." *Journal of Political Economy* 91: 401–419.

53. Rajan Raghuram G. 2010. *Fault Lines: How Hidden Fractures Still Threaten the World Economy.* Princeton: Princeton University Press.

54. Felix Salmon, "The Mess That Is Deposit Insurance," Reuters blog, 16 August 2010.

55. See Wallison, Peter J. 2010. "The Dodd–Frank Act: Creative Destruction, Destroyed." AEI Outlook Series (August) <www.aei.org/outlook/100983>; and Peter J. Wallison, "Why Financial Reform Is Stalled," *Wall Street Journal,* 1 March 2010.

56. Wallison, Peter J. 2009. "Perspectives on Regulation of Systemic Risk in the Financial Services Industry." Testimony, House Financial Services Committee (17 March) <www.aei.org/speech/100024>.

57. Johnson, Simon, and James Kwak. 2010. *13 Bankers: The Wall Street Takeover and the Next Financial Meltdown.* New York: Vintage.

58. See Wallison, Peter J. 2010. "The Dodd–Frank Act: Creative Destruction, Destroyed"; and Richard Posner, "The Financial Regulation Law—Posner's Comment," blog entry, 11 July 2010 <www.becker-posner-blog.com/.../the-financial-regulation-lawposners-comment.html>.

59. McKinsey Co. 2011. "Assessing and Addressing the Implications of New Financial Regulations for the US Banking Industry." McKinsey Working Papers on Risk 25 (March).

60. Elliott, Douglas J., and Robert E. Litan. 2011. "Identifying and Regulating Systemically Important Financial Institutions: The Risks of Under and Over Identification and Regulation." Brookings Policy Brief (16 January)

61. See Kauffmann Foundation. 2011. *Kauffman Firm Survey: Results from 2009 Business Activities*; and Graziadio School of Business, Pepperdine University. 2011. *Pepperdine Private Capital Markets Project Survey June 2011.*

62. Graziadio School of Business, 2011. *Pepperdine Private Capital Markets Project Survey June 2011.*

63. Skeel, David. 2010. *The New Financial Deal: Understanding the Dodd–Frank Act and Its (Unintended) Consequences.* Hoboken, NJ: Wiley.

64. Ibid.

65. Pollock, Alex J. 2010. "Lots of Regulatory Expansion but Little Reform." AEI Online (June).

66. Barry Eichengreen, "Financial Re-Regulation, Yes. But Europe's Cacophony of Ideas Is Counter-productive," *Europe's World,* Summer 2009.

67. Elliott, Douglas J., and Robert E. Litan. 2011. "Identifying and Regulating Systemically Important Financial Institutions."

68. Skeel, David. 2010. *The New Financial Deal.*

69. Ibid.

70. Louis Uchitelle, "Elders of Wall St. Favor More Regulation," *New York Times,* 16 February 2010.

71. Wharton's Jeremy Seigel wrote an excellent summary of why the rule would not work as a preemption tool: "Banking Reform Proposals: Why They Miss the Mark," Knowledge@Wharton, 17 February 2010.

72. Paul Volcker, "How to Reform Our Financial System," *New York Times*, 1 February 2010.

73. See Avinash Persaud, "Too Big to Fail Is No Redemption Song," VoxEU.com, 10 February 2010.

74. Gadi Dechter and Alan Katz, "Regulators Resist Volcker Wandering Warning of Too-Big-to-Fail," *Bloomberg*, 15 December 2009.

75. "Too Big to Fail Banks to Be Determined in Mid-2011—Draghi," Reuters, 23 October 2010. National authorities also have leeway to devise "supplementary prudential and other requirements." See "Leaders' Declaration, the Seoul G20 Summit," 11–12 November 2010.

76. Johnson, Simon, and James Kwak. 2010. *13 Bankers*.

77. Ibid., p. 217.

78. Neil Hume, "Europe and Volcker's Rule," *Financial Times Alphaville Blog*, 27 January 2010.

79. Edwin M. Truman, "Lessons from the Global Economic and Financial Crisis," keynote address at the conference G20 Reform Initiatives: Implications for the Future of Regulation, Institute for Global Economics and the International Monetary Fund, Seoul, Korea, 11 November 2009.

80. For scale economies and mixed results, see "Economies of Scale and Continuing Consolidation of Credit Unions," *Federal Reserve Bank of San Francisco Economic Letter* 2005–29, 4 November 2005. For positive effects, see Allen, Jason, and Ying Liu. 2005. "Efficiency and Economies of Scale of Large Canadian Banks." Bank of Canada Working Paper 2005–13 (May). For scope, see, Calomiris, Charles W. 2000. *US Banking Deregulation in Historical Perspective*; and Nagata, Takahiro, Yasuo Maeda, and Hiroaki Imahigashi. 2004. "Economies of Scope in Financial Conglomerates: Analysis of a Revenue Side." Draft <www.fsa.go.jp/frtc/english/e_nenpou/2004/02.pdf>.

81. See, for example, Jones, Kenneth D., and Tim Critchfield. 2005. "Consolidation in the U.S. Banking Industry."

82. Edwin M. Truman, "Lessons from the Global Economic and Financial Crisis."

83. UK Treasury. 2009. "Banking Crisis: Dealing with the Failure of the UK Banks" (21 April) <www.publications.parliament.uk/pa/cm200809/cmselect/cmtreasy/416/41602.htm>.

84. Beck, Thorsten, Asli Demirguc-Kunt, and Ross Levine. 2003. "Bank Concentration and Crises." NBER Working Paper 9921.

85. For size and bank failure, see review by Calomiris, Charles W. 2000. *US Banking Deregulation in Historical Perspective*; and Wagner, W., 2007. "Diversification at Financial Institutions and Systemic Crises." University of Tilburg Discussion Paper 71. For concentration, see Beck, Thorsten. 2008. "Bank Competition and Financial Stability: Friends or Foes?" World Bank Policy Research Working Paper 4656 (1 June).

86. Some analysts argue that the 1977 Community Reinvestment Act (CRA) caused the crisis by encouraging commercial banks and savings institutions to meet

the credit needs of lower-income borrowers and borrowers in lower-income neighborhoods. The evidence is less convincing. See Bhutta, Neil, and Glenn B. Canner. 2009. "Did the CRA Cause the Mortgage Market Meltdown?" Federal Reserve Bank of Minneapolis (March) <www.minneapolisfed.org/publications_papers/pub_display .cfm?id=4136>.

87. Peter J. Wallison, "A Way Forward for the Mortgage Market," *Wall Street Journal*, 15 February 2011.

88. John Carney, "Too Big Not to Fail," *New York Times*, 11 August 2010.

89. James B. Stewart, "New Bank Rules Good for Everything—Except Bankers' Bonuses," *Wall Street Journal*, 15 September 2010.

90. Michael Corkery, "Basel III: And the Biggest Winners Are . . .," Associated Press, 13 September 2010.

91. "Base Camp Basel."

92. Ibid.

93. Herring, R. J. 2010. "Wind-Down Plans as an Alternative to Bailouts." Pew Financial Reform Project forthcoming Briefing Paper.

94. See Squam Lake Working Group on Financial Regulation. 2009. "Reforming Capital Requirements for Financial Institutions." Squam Lake Working Group Paper, Council on Foreign Relations Press (April) <www.cfr.org/publication/19001/ reforming_capital_requirements_for_financial_institutions.html>.

95. For a thorough discussion, see Raghuram Rajan, "Too Systemic to Fail: Written Statement to the Senate Banking Committee on May 6th 2009" <http://faculty .chicagobooth.edu/raghuram.rajan/research/recent.htm>.

96. Michael Casey, "Basel III's Light Touch Has Its Risks," *Wall Street Journal*, 13 September 2010.

97. Elliott, Douglas J. 2009. "Quantifying the Effects on Lending of Increased Capital Requirements." Briefing Paper 7, Pew Financial Reform Project <www.pewtrusts .org/uploadedFiles/.../Elliott-Capital-final.pdf>. "U.S. Financial Market Regulation, U.S. Economy." Brookings Institution Paper <www.brookings.edu/~/media/Files/rc/ papers/2009/0924_capital_elliott/0924_capital_elliott.pdf>.

98. Macroeconomic Assessment Group Established by the Financial Stability Board and the Basel Committee on Banking Supervision. 2010. *Interim Report: Assessing the Macroeconomic Impact of the Transition to Stronger Capital and Liquidity Requirements* (August) <www.bis.org/publ/othp10.pdf?noframes=1>; and Basel Committee on Banking Supervision. 2010. *An Assessment of the Long-Term Economic Impact of Stronger Capital and Liquidity Requirements* (August) <www.financialsta bilityboard.org/publications/r_100818a.pdf?noframes=1>.

99. Mark Carney, "Bundesbank Lecture 2010: The Economic Consequences of the Reforms," speech, Deutsche Bundesbank, Berlin, 14 September 2010 <www.bankof canada.ca/en/speeches/2010/sp140910.html>.

100. Institute of International Finance. 2010. *Interim Report on the Cumulative Impact on the Global Economy of Proposed Changes in the Banking Regulatory Framework* (June) <http://iif.com/press/press+151.php>.

101. "Basel III Will Cause 'Financial Darwinism': BaFin's Sanio," *Risk Magazine*, 17 January 2011.

102. Leuz, Christian, Alexander Triantis, and Tracy Wan. 2004. "Why Do Firms Go Dark? Causes and Economic Consequences of Voluntary SEC Deregistrations." Working paper, Wharton School (November). In 2006, Russell Reynolds Associates reported that SOX would dissuade 70 percent of the European companies from seeking a US listing. Russell Reynolds Associates, "How CFOs Are Managing Changes in Roles and Expectations," 2006 <www.russellreynolds.com/pdf/thought/How CFOsareManagingChanges_US>. The London Stock Exchange advertised that non-US companies find London a more attractive listing than New York, thanks to SOX. See, for example, Peter J. Wallison, "Escape from New York," *American*, 20 February 2008.

103. Andrew Lo, "Hedge Funds, Systemic Risk, and the Financial Crisis of 2007–2008," written testimony for the House Oversight Committee Hearing on Hedge Funds, 13 November 2008. See also as summarized in Anne Sibert, "A Systemic Risk Warning System," VoxEU.com, 16 January 2010.

104. Anne Sibert, "A Systemic Risk Warning System."

105. Pollock, Alex J. 2010. "Lots of Regulatory Expansion but Little Reform."

106. Ibid.

107. Skeel, David. 2010. *The New Financial Deal.*

108. Raghuram Rajan, "Too Systemic to Fail: Written Statement to the Senate Banking Committee," 6 May 2009.

109. Rajan Raghuram G. 2010. *Fault Lines.*

110. Pazarbasioglu, Ceyla, Jianping Zhou, Vanessa Le Leslé, and Michael Moore. 2011. "Contingent Capital: Economic Rationale and Design Features." IMF Staff Discussion Note SDN/11/01 (25 January) <www.imf.org/external/pubs/ft/sdn/2011/sdn1101.pdf>.

111. Institute for International Finance. 2008. "Final Report of the IIF Committee on Market Best Practices: Principles of Conduct and Best Practice Recommendations" (June) <www.iif.com/press/press+75.php>.

112. Martin Lipton, "Some Thoughts for Boards of Directors in 2011," Harvard Law School Forum on Corporate Governance and Financial Regulation, 18 January 2011. For an excellent set of proposals, see Center for Strategic & International Studies (CSIS) Hills Program on Governance, American Assembly, and the Institute of International Finance. 2010. *Governance of Financial Institutions.* Washington DC: IIF <www.iif.com/press/press+136.php>.

113. Rajan, Raghuram G. 2010. *Fault Lines*; and Alex J. Pollock, "To Overhaul the GSEs, Divide Them into Three Parts," *American Banker*, 26 August 2010.

114. Blinder, Alan S., and Mark Zandi. 2010. "How the Great Recession Was Brought to an End" (27 July) <www.economy.com/mark-zandi/documents/End-of-Great-Recession.pdf>.

115. Chidem Kurdah, "Fannie, Freddie, and the Mortgage Addiction," *Christian Science Monitor*, 26 August 2010.

116. Donald Marron and Phillip Swagel, "Whither Fannie and Freddie? A Proposal for Reforming the Housing GSEs," *Economic Policies for the 21st Century*, 24 May 2010 <http://economics21.org/commentary/whither-fannie-and-freddie-proposal-reforming-housing-gses>.

117. Alex J. Pollock, "To Overhaul the GSEs, Divide Them into Three Parts"; and Marron, Donald, and Phillip Swagel. 2010. "Whither Fannie and Freddie?"

118. Rottier, Stéphane, and Nicola Véron, 2010. "Not All Regulation Is Global," Bruegel Policy Brief 2010/07 (August).

119. See "Leaders' Statement: The Pittsburgh Summit," 24–25 September 2009 <www.pittsburghsummit.gov/mediacenter/129639.htm>. Also see Huw Jones, "Factbox: G20 Progress on Financial Regulation," Reuters, 12 September 2010.

120. See "Financial Stability Board Charter" <www.financialstabilityboard.org/publications/r_090925d.pdfhttp://www.financialstabilityboard.org/publications/r_090925d.pdf>; and "Financial Stability Board Holds Inaugural Meeting in Basel," FSB Press Release 28/2009, 27 June 2009.

121. Rottier, Stephane, and Nicola Verón, 2010. "Not All Regulation Is Global."

122. The state remains the predominant banker, owning controlling stakes in the five largest commercial banks and all of the three policy banks, which together manage 60 percent of Chinese bank assets. The government also owns a high share of the seven main securities firms, which run 40 percent of securities assets, and of the four main insurance firms, which manage 48 percent of China's insurance assets. Krause Bell, Susan, and Howard Chao. 2010. "Financial System in China: Risks and Opportunities Following the Global Financial Crisis." Promontory Financial Group, LLC, and O'Melveny & Myers, LLP (April) <www.promontory.com/assets/0/78/110/202/5186dfdb-cc55-4123-940d-1a372ac441e9.pdf>.

123. See Xiaobin Zhao, Simon. 2010. "The Centennial Competition of Global Financial Centers: Key Determinants and the Rise of China's Financial Centers." International Centre for China Development Studies Working Paper 2010-041, University of Hong Kong (May) <www.regional-studies-assoc.ac.uk/events/2010/may-pecs/papers/Zhao.pdf>.

124. Deutsche Bank Research. 2010. "Global Financial Centres After the Crisis" (2 August) <www.dbresearch.com/PROD/DBR_INTERNET_EN-PROD/PROD0000000000260736.pdf>.

125. Jarvis, D. S. L. 2009. "Race for the Money: International Financial Centres in Asia." Research Paper Series, Lee Kuan Yew School of Public Policy (June).

126. Asia's regulatory frameworks vary as much as development levels do. Japan is the regulatory gold standard; smaller nations such as Vietnam lag behind. Sung Lee, Chee, and Cyn-Young Park. 2009. "Beyond the Crisis: Financial Regulatory Reform in Emerging Asia." ADB Working Paper Series on Regional Economic Integration 34 (September) <http://aric.adb.org/pdf/workingpaper/WP34_Financial_Regulatory_Reform.pdf>.

127. Martin Arnold and Sam Jones, "Geithner Warns of Rift Over Regulation," *Financial Times*, 10 March 2010. See also Stevenson Jacobs, "Financial Reform Efforts Pit US Against Europe," Associated Press, 15 March 2010.

128. Price, Daniel M. 2009. "The New Face of Anti-Globalization: Economic Recovery and Reform Efforts." In *Renewing Globalization and Economic Growth in a Post-Crisis World: The Future of the G20 Agenda*. Report of the Atlantic Council and Carnegie Mellon University (September).

129. The German Chancellor Angela Merkel called on the United States to limit such trades, while US regulators preferred to regulate them.

130. See, for instance, Fischer, Stanley. 1998. "Capital-Account Liberalization and the Role of the IMF," *Princeton Essays in International Finance*, 207 (May): 1–10; and Summers, Lawrence H. 2000. "International Financial Crises: Causes, Prevention, and Cures." *American Economic Review* 90.2: 1–16.

131. For a review, see Hufbauer, Gary Clyde, and Kati Suominen. *Globalization at Risk*.

132. *World Investment Report 2010*. Geneva: UNCTAD.

133. For a review, see Jarvis, Darryl S. L. "Race for the Money: International Financial Centers in Asia." Working paper, Lee Kuan Yew School of Public Policy, National University of Singapore <www.spp.nus.edu.sg/docs/rr/RR6%20Race%20 for%20the%20Money.pdf>. See also Poon, Jessie P. H., Dradley Eldredge, and David Yeung. 2004. "Rank Size Distribution of International Financial Centers." *International Regional Science Review*, 27.4 (October): 411–430.

134. Timothy Geithner, "We Must Keep at the Process of Repair and Reform," *Financial Times*, 23 April 2009.

135. Posen, Adam, and Nicolas Véron. 2009. "A Solution for Europe's Banking Problem." Peterson Institute Policy Brief 09–13 (June) <www.piie.com/publications/ pb/pb09-13.pdf>.

136. Eichengreen, Barry. 2008. "The Global Credit Crisis as History." Draft, University of California, Berkeley (December) <www.econ.berkeley.edu/~eichengr/ global_credit_crisis_history_12-3-08.pdf>.

137. See Financial Stability Forum, "FSF Principles for Cross-border Cooperation on Crisis Management," April 2009 <www.financialstabilityboard.org/publications/ r_0904c.pdf>.

138. Independent Evaluation Office of the IMF. 2006. "Report on the Evaluation of the Financial Sector Assessment Program." 5 January <www.imf.org/External/NP/ ieo/2006/fsap/eng>.

139. Bloomberg, Michael, and Charles Schumer. 2007. "Sustaining New York's and the US' Global Financial Services Leadership" <www.abanet.org/buslaw/committees/ CL116000pub/materials/library/NY_Schumer-Bloomberg_REPORT_FINAL.pdf>.

140. See Stefano Micossi, "Bank Crisis Management in the EU: Overview of the Issues," presentation, Assonime-CEPS-Unicredit Task Force on Banking Crisis Resolution Procedures, Brussels, 17 July 2009 <www.ceps.be/system/files/Micossi _BankCrisisManagementEU.pdf>.

141. See Thráinn Eggertsson and Tryggvi Thor Herbertsson, "System Failure in Iceland and the 2008 Global Financial Crisis," paper presented at the 13th Annual Conference of ISNIE, Walter A. Haas School of Business, University of California at Berkeley, 18–20 June, 2009.

142. Basel Committee on Banking Supervision. 2009. "Report and Recommendations of the Cross-Border Bank Resolution Group" (September). Basel: Bank for International Settlements <www.bis.org/publ/bcbs162.pdf>.

143. Michael Pomerleano, "A Solution to Financial Instability: Ring-Fence Cross-Border Financial Institutions," VoxEU.com, 7 August 2009. For a set of proposals for overcoming to big to fail in the EU-wide context, see CEPS-Assonime Task Force on Bank Crisis Resolution. 2010. "Overcoming Too-Big-to-Fail: A Regulatory Framework to Limit Moral Hazard and Free Riding in the Financial Sector." Report, Center for European Policy Studies (15 March) <www.ceps.eu/book/overcoming-too-big-fail-regulatory-framework-limit-moral-hazard-and-free-riding-financial-secto>.

144. Posen, Adam S., and Nicolas Véron. 2009. "A Solution for Europe's Banking Problem."

145. Peter J. Wallison, "A Global Solution for Cross Border Financial Resolutions," Financial Centres International, 1 July 2010.

Chapter 4

1. See, for example, Helmut Reisen, "Shifting Wealth: Is the US Dollar Empire Falling?" VoxEU.com, 20 June 2009; and Nouriel Roubini, "The Almighty Renminbi?" *New York Times*, 13 May 2009.

2. Alexander Nicholson, "IMF Says New Reserve Currency to Replace Dollar Is Possible," Bloomberg, 6 June 2009.

3. Robert B. Zoellick, "After the Crisis," speech at the Paul H. Nitze School of Advanced International Studies, Johns Hopkins University, Washington, 28 September 2009 <http://web.worldbank.org/WBSITE/EXTERNAL/NEWS/0,,contentMDK:2232 9125~pagePK:34370~piPK:42770~theSitePK:4607,00.html>.

4. For the currency peg calculations, see Linda Goldberg, "What Is the Status of the International Roles of the Dollar?" VoxEU.com, 31 March 2010.

5. Bank of International Settlements. 2010. "Triennial Central Bank Survey of Foreign Exchange and Derivatives Market Activity in April 2010." September <www.bis.org/publ/rpfx10.htm>.

6. Linda Goldberg, "What Is the Status of the International Roles of the Dollar?"; and European Central Bank. 2008. "The International Role of the Euro" (July) <www.ecb.int/pub/pdf/other/euro-international-role200807en.pdf>.

7. For a summary of work, see Linda Goldberg, "What Is the Status of the International Roles of the Dollar?"

8. Chinn, Menzie D., and Jeffrey A. Frankel. 2008. "The Euro May Over the Next 15 Years Surpass the Dollar as Leading International Currency." NBER Working Paper 13909 (April). Liquidity refers to the turnover in a country's foreign-exchange market.

9. Eichengreen, Barry, and Jeffrey Frankel. 1996. "The SDR, Reserve Currencies and the Future of the International Monetary System." In James D. Boughton, Michael Mussa, and Peter Isard, eds. *The Future of the SDR in Light of Changes in the International Financial System*. Washington, D.C.: International Monetary Fund.

10. Chinn, Menzie, and Jeffrey Frankel. 2008. "Why the Euro Will Rival the Dollar." *International Finance* 11.1: 49–73.

11. McKinnon, Ronald I. 2005. "The World Dollar Standard and Globalization: New Rules for the Game?" Draft, Stanford University.

12. Pollard, Patricia S. 2001. "The Creation of the Euro and the Role of the Dollar in International Markets." *Federal Reserve Bank of St. Louis Review* 17 (September/October).

13. For a summary of work, see Linda Goldberg, "What Is the Status of the International Roles of the Dollar?"

14. See McKinsey Global Institute. 2009. "An Exorbitant Privilege? Implications of Reserve Currencies for Competitiveness" (December) <www.mckinsey.com/mgi/reports/pdfs/reserve_currencies/reserve_currencies_full_discussion_paper.pdf>.

15. Richard Clarida, "With Privilege Comes . . . ?" *PIMCO Global Perspectives*, October 2009 <www.pimco.com/LeftNav/Global+Markets/Global+Perspectives/2009/With+Privilege+Comes+Clarida+Oct+2009.htm>.

16. Of course, if the seigniorage revenues result from economic or political instability overseas, the net benefit to United States may be negative. See McKinsey Global Institute, "An Exorbitant Privilege?"; and Blinder, Alan S. 1996. "The Role of the Dollar as an International Currency." *Eastern Economic Journal* 22.2 (Spring): 127–136.

17. Aliber, Robert Z. "The Costs and the Benefits of the US Role as a Reserve Currency Country." *Quarterly Journal of Economics* 78.3 (August): 442–456.

18. McKinsey Global Institute, "An Exorbitant Privilege?" In a crisis year such as 2009, McKinsey argues that the net financial benefit can turn negative (on the order of $5–25 billion) because the dollar appreciated by an additional 10 percent because of its safe-haven status.

19. McKinnon, Ronald I. 2005. "Trapped by the International Dollar Standard." Draft, Stanford University (March). McKinnon even argues that the decline of jobs in US manufacturing owes to this trap: as the US has to borrow from abroad, the dollar appreciates, which, in turn, renders US manufacturing exports less competitive in global markets.

20. Mundell, Robert A. 1993. "EMU and the International Monetary System: A Transatlantic Perspective." Austrian National Bank Working Paper 13.

21. Cohen, Benjamin J. 1998. *The Geography of Money*. Ithaca and London: Cornell University Press.

22. Wolfgang Münchau, "This Crisis Could Bring the Euro Centre-Stage," *Financial Times*, 24 March 2008.

23. For a discussion, see, for example, Cohen, Benjamin J. 1998. *The Geography of Money*. For types of monetary power, see Kirshner, Jonathan. 1997. *Currency and Coercion: The Political Economy of International Monetary Power*. Princeton: Princeton University Press.

24. Persaud, Avinash. 2004. "Why Currency Empires Fall." Gresham Lectures, 7 October 2004 <www.gresham.ac.uk/event.asp?EventId=260&PageId=108>.

25. See Owen F. Humpage, "Will Special Drawing Rights Supplant the Dollar?" Voxeu.com, 8 May 2009.

26. Johnson, Harry G. 1972. "The Link That Chains." *Foreign Policy* 8 (Autumn): 113–120. Johnson wrote that "the only alternatives for the future are between the dollar standard and the SDR standard. (A third possibility should be mentioned—the establishment of a bifocal system based on the dollar on the one hand and a common European currency on the other, with a floating exchange rate between them.)"

27. Owen F. Humpage, "Replacing the Dollar with Special Drawing Rights— Will It Work This Time?" *Cleveland Federal Reserve Economic Commentary,* March 2009.

28. Polak, Jacques J., 1967. "Special Drawing Rights: The Outline of a New Facility in the Fund." *Finance and Development* 4.4: 275–280.

29. Trued, Merlyn N. 1970. "Special Drawing Rights (SDRs) or the Great Escape from Gold." *Financial Analysts Journal* 26.1 (January–February): 67–68.

30. See, for example, Frankel, Jeffrey A. 1995. "Is Japan Creating a Yen Bloc in East Asia and the Pacific?" NBER Working Paper 4050.

31. See Tagaki, Shinji. 2009. "Internationalizing the Yen, 1984–2003: Unfinished Agenda or Mission Impossible?" Paper presented at BoK–BIS seminar on Currency Internationalization: Lessons from the Global Financial Crisis and Prospects for the Future in Asia and the Pacific, 19–20 March 2009, Seoul, Korea; and Frankel, Jeffrey A. 1995. "Is Japan Creating a Yen Bloc in East Asia and the Pacific?"

32. Bergsten, C. Fred. 1997. "The Dollar and the Euro." *Foreign Affairs* 76.4 (July/August): 83–95.

33. See articles on the *Financial Times* in-depth site "American Empire" <www .ft.com/indepth/americanempire>.

34. See articles on the *Financial Times* in-depth site "American Empire" <www .ft.com/indepth/americanempire>. See also Portes, Richard, and Hélène Rey. 1997. "The Emergence of the Euro and an International Currency." Paper, London Business School (December).

35. Lawrence Summers, "Speech to Euromoney Conference," New York, 30 April 1997.

36. Frankel, Jeffrey A. 1995. "Still the Lingua Franca: The Exaggerated Death of the Dollar." *Foreign Affairs* 74.4 (July/August). Cited in Portes, Richard, and Hélène Rey. 1997. "The Emergence of the Euro and an International Currency."

37. Portes, Richard, and Hélène Rey. 1997. "The Emergence of the Euro and an International Currency."

38. Data based on World Bank's World Development Indicators.

39. Bergsten, C. Fred. 2002. "The Euro Versus the Dollar: Will There Be a Struggle for Dominance?" Paper at a roundtable at the Annual Meeting of the American Economic Association, Atlanta, 4 January 2002.

40. Mussa, Michael. 2001. "Reflections on the International Role of the Euro." Remarks before the Euro 50 Group in Washington, D.C. (November).

41. Galati, Gabriele, and Kostas Tsatsaronis. 2001. "The Euro in International Financial Markets: Where Do We Stand?" Paper prepared for a meeting of the Euro 50 Group in Washington, D.C. (November).

42. See Bergsten, C. Fred. 2002. "The Euro Versus the Dollar: Will There Be a Struggle for Dominance?" See also Bergsten, C. Fred. "The Euro and the World Economy." Paper presented at the conference The Eurosystem, the Union and Beyond: The Single Currency and Implications for Governance, an ECB Colloquium Held in Honor of Tommaso Padoa-Schioppa, European Central Bank, Frankfurt am Main, 27 April 2005; and Bersten, C. Fred. 2010. "I Was a Euro Enthusiast." *Econ Journal Watch* 7.1 (January): 53–55 <http://econjwatch.org/articles/i-was-a-euro-enthusiast>.

43. Codogno, Lorenzo, Carlo Favero, Alessandro Missale, Richard Portes, and Marcel Thum. 2003. "Yield Spreads on EMU Government Bonds." *Economic Policy* 18.37 (October): 503–532. Similar fragmentation has occurred in European banking and equity markets, with national rivalries precluding cross-border mergers and acquisitions. See Bergsten, C. Fred. 2002. "The Euro Versus the Dollar: Will There Be a Struggle for Dominance?"

44. Cooper, Richard N. 2009. "The Future of the Dollar." Policy Brief 09–21, Peterson Institute for International Economics (September).

45. Eichengreen, Barry. 2009. "The Crisis and the Euro." Policy Paper, University of California, Berkeley (April) <www.econ.berkeley.edu/~eichengr/crisis_euro_5-1-09.pdf>. See also Cooper, Richard N. 2009. "The Future of the Dollar."

46. For inertia, see, for instance, Chinn, Menzie D., and Jeffrey A. Frankel. 2008. "The Euro May Over the Next 15 Years Surpass the Dollar as Leading International Currency." Also see Krugman, Paul, 1980. "Vehicle Currencies and the Structure of International Exchange." *Journal of Money, Credit and Banking* 12: 513–526. See also, Papaioannou, Elias, and Richard Portes. 2008. "The International Role of the Euro: A Status Report." *European Commission Economic Papers* 317 (April) <http://faculty.london.edu/rportes/International%20role%20-%20EMU@10%20-20Commission%20WP.pdf>. For literature on the rise of vehicle currencies, see Goldberg, Linda S., and Cédric Tille. 2008. "Vehicle Currency Use in International Trade." *Journal of International Economics* 76: 177–192.

47. Maddison, Angus, and Harry X. Wu. 2007. "China's Economic Performance: How Fast Has GDP Grown; How Big Is It Compared with the USA?" Draft (February) <www.ggdc.net/maddison>.

48. Goldman Sachs. 2007. *BRICS and Beyond*. New York: Goldman Sachs <www2.goldmansachs.com/ideas/brics/BRICs-and-Beyond.html>. By 2040, the economies of Russia, Brazil, and India, while trailing far behind the United States and China, will each also be larger than the economies of America's G7 partners Japan, Germany, UK, France, Canada, and Italy; by 2045, Mexico will grow larger than these developed economies. By 2050, Nigeria's economy will be larger than that of France and Korea's almost as large.

49. Helmut Reisen, "Shifting Wealth: Is the US Dollar Empire Falling?" Riesen notes that the RMB is equivalent to a real language like the dollar is equivalent to English; in contrast, SDRs are the equivalent of Esperanto.

50. Nouriel Roubini, "The Almighty Renminbi?" *New York Times*, 13 May 2009.

51. "Obama Sees Dollar Strong, No Single World Currency," Reuters, 25 March 2009.

52. Phil Izzo, "Volcker: China Chose to Buy Dollars," "Real Time Economics," *Wall Street Journal* blog, 24 March 2009.

53. "ECB's Trichet says U.S. Support for Strong Dollar Important," Reuters, 24 April 2009.

54. "China Bestseller Sees Plots and Profit in Financial Crisis," Reuters, 21 September 2009.

55. Arvind Subramanian, "Is China Having It Both Ways?" *Wall Street Journal*, 25 March 2009.

56. Peter Stein, "Time for Next Move on Yuan Liberalization," *Wall Street Journal*, 28 February 2011.

57. Bank of International Settlements. 2010. "Triennial Central Bank Survey of Foreign Exchange and Derivatives Market Activity in April 2010" (September) <www .bis.org/publ/rpfx10.htm>.

58. Gady Epstein, "The China Bubble," *Forbes*, 10 December 2009.

59. Michael Pettis, "The Dollar, The RMB and the Euro?" Seeking Alpha, 13 March 2011.

60. The Commission of Experts of the President of the UN General Assembly on Reforms of the International Monetary and Financial System. 2009. "Recommendations" (19 March) <www.un.org/ga/president/63/letters/recommendation Experts200309.pdf>.

61. See Hufbauer, Gary Clyde, and Kati Suominen. 2010. *Globalization at Risk: Challenges to Finance and Trade*. New Haven: Yale University Press.

62. The four currencies proxy the price fluctuations of copper, iron ore, gold, and oil. See Helmut Reisen, "Shifting Wealth: Is the US Dollar Empire Falling?"

63. Eichengreen, Barry. 2009. "The Dollar Dilemma: The World's Top Currency Faces Competition." *Foreign Affairs* 88.5 (September/October).

64. Aiyar, Swaminathan, and S. Anklesaria. 2009. "An International Monetary Fund Currency to Rival the Dollar?" *Cato Institute Development Policy Analysis* 10 (7 July); Arvind Subramanian, "Is China Having It Both Ways?" John Williamson argues that the issue is much less clear-cut. See Williamson, John. 2009. "Why SDRs Could Rival the Dollar." Peterson Institute Policy Brief 09–20 (September).

65. Jean Pisani-Ferry, and Adam S. Posen, eds. 2009. *The Euro at Ten: The Next Global Currency?* Washington, D.C.: Peterson Institute and Bruegel Institute.

66. McKinsey Global Institute, "An Exorbitant Privilege?"

67. Eichengreen, Barry. 2009. "The Dollar Dilemma."

68. Hufbauer, Gary Clyde, and Kati Suominen. 2010. *Globalization at Risk*.

69. Eichengreen, Barry. 2005. "Sterling's Past, Dollar's Future: Historical Perspective on Reserve Currency Competition." NBER Working Paper 11336 (May).

70. McKinsey Global Institute, "An Exorbitant Privilege?"

71. See Deutsche Bank. 2006. "The Theory and Practice of Corporate Risk Management Policy" (February); and McKinsey Global Institute, "An Exorbitant Privilege?"

72. PricewaterhouseCoopers. 2011. "14th Annual Global CEO Survey" <www.pwc.com/gx/en/ceo-survey>.

73. See Clark, Peter B., and Jacques J. Polak. 2004. "International Liquidity and the Role of the SDR in the International Monetary System." *IMF Staff Papers* 51.1: 49–71.

74. Article XVIII, Allocation and Cancellation of Special Drawing Rights, states that "in all its decisions with respect to the allocation and cancellation of special drawing rights the Fund shall seek to meet the long-term global need, as and when it arises, to supplement existing reserve assets in such manner as will promote the attainment of its purposes and will avoid economic stagnation and deflation as well as excess demand and inflation in the world."

75. Onno Wijnholds, "The Dollar's Last Days?" *Project Syndicate,* May 2009.

76. Robin Knight, "Zoellick Sees 'Elephant,' Not Endorsing Gold Standard," *CNBC News,* 10 November 2010.

77. See discussion in Hufbauer, Gary Clyde, and Kati Suominen. 2010. *Globalization at Risk.* Stiglitz calls for a global reserve system anchored on the IMF's gold reserves. See Stiglitz, Joseph E. 2009. "Death Cometh for the Greenback." *National Interest* (November/December).

78. World Gold Council's Reserve Asset Statistics, December 2009.

79. Robert Mundell, "Plan for a World Currency," testimony in the Joint Economic Committee Subcommittee on International Exchange and Payments, 9 September 1968.

80. See *The Works of Robert A. Mundell* <www.robertmundell.net/Menu/Main.asp?Type=5&Cat=09&ThemeName=World Currency>.

81. Jeffrey E. Garten, "Needed: A Fed for the World," *New York Times,* 23 September 1998.

82. See Zhou Xiaochuan, "Reform the International Monetary System," speech, 23 March 2009 <www.pbc.gov.cn/english/detail.asp?col=6500&id=178>.

83. Mateos y Lago, Isabelle, Rupa Duttagupta, and Rishi Goyal. 2009. "The Debate on the International Monetary System." IMF Staff Position Paper 09/26 (11 November) <www.imf.org/external/pubs/ft/spn/2009/spn0926.pdf>.

84. See Bonpasse, Morrison. 2008. *The Single Global Currency: Common Cents for the World.* Newcastle, ME: Single Global Currency Association.

85. Eichengreen, Barry. 2005. "Sterling's Past, Dollar's Future: Historical Perspective on Reserve Currency Competition"; and Eichengreen, Barry. 2011. *Exorbitant Privilege: The Rise and Fall of the Dollar and the Future of the International Monetary System.* Oxford: Oxford University Press.

86. Eichengreen, Barry. 2009. "The Dollar Dilemma."

87. Genberg, Hans. 2009. "Currency Internationalization: Analytical and Policy Issues," paper prepared for the BoK–BIS Seminar Lessons from the Global Financial Crisis and Prospects for the Future in Asia and the Pacific, 19–20 March 2009, Seoul, Korea.

88. Ibid.

89. Chinn, Menzie D., and Jeffrey A. Frankel. 2008. "The Euro May Over the Next 15 Years Surpass the Dollar as Leading International Currency."

90. "Euro's Share in Reserves Overtakes U.S. Dollar," Reuters, 19 May 2009.

91. Mundell, Robert. 2001. "Currency Area Formation and the Asian Region," paper presented at the Conference on the Monetary Outlook in East Asia in a Changing World Monetary Order, Bangkok, 5–6 September.

92. Eichengreen, Barry, and Douglas A. Irwin. 1993. "Trade Blocs, Currency Blocs and the Disintegration of World Trade in the 1930s." NBER Working Paper 4445 (August).

93. See, for example, Micco, Alejandro, Ernesto Stein, and Guillermo Ordoñez. 2003. "The Currency Union Effect on Trade: Early Evidence from EMU." *Economic Policy* 37: 316–356. For a review of literature, see Baldwin, Richard. 2006. "The Euro's Trade Effects." European Central Bank Working Paper 594 (March) <www.hei.unige .ch/~baldwin/PapersBooks/EuroTradeEffectsBaldwin_ECB_WP594.pdf>.

94. Martin Wolf, "The Rumours of the Dollar's Death Are Much Exaggerated," *Financial Times*, 13 October 2009. The Triffin dilemma stipulates that the international role of the dollar could make it hard for the US to manage its fiscal policy even if it wanted to.

Chapter 5

1. For instance, Bolivia's inflation in 1983–1985 was 23,000 percent, Argentina's surpassed 3,000 percent in 1989, Brazil's reached 2,000 percent in 1994, and a year earlier Russia's climbed to almost 1,000 percent.

2. Anne O. Krueger, "Stability, Growth, and Prosperity: The Global Economy and the IMF," speech, Conference De Montreal, Montreal, Canada, 7 June 2006.

3. Alesina, Alberto, and Lawrence H. Summers. 1993. "Central Bank Independence and Macroeconomic Performance: Some Comparative Evidence." *Journal of Money, Credit and Banking* 25.2 (May): 151–162; Fischer, Stanley. 1995. "Central Bank Independence Revisited," *American Economic Review* 85: 201–206; Cukierman, Alex. 2008. "Central Bank Independence and Monetary Policymaking Institutions: Past, Present and Future." *European Journal of Political Economy* 24.4 (December): 722–736; and Crowe, Christopher, and Ellen E. Meade. 2008. "Central Bank Independence and Transparency: Evolution and Effectiveness." IMF Working Paper 08/119 <www.imf .org/external/pubs/ft/wp/2008/wp08119.pdf>.

4. See, for example, Cukierman, Alex, Geoffrey P. Miller, and Bilin Neyapti. 2002. "Central Bank Reform, Liberalization and Inflation in Transition Economies—An International Perspective." *Journal of Monetary Economics* 49.2: 237–264; Cukierman, Alex, Pantelis Kalaitzidakis, Lawrence H. Summers, and Steven B. Webb 1993. "Central Bank Independence, Growth, Investment, and Real Rates." *Carnegie-Rochester Conference Series on Public Policy* 39.1: 95–140; and Grilli, Vittorio, Donato Masciandaro, and Guido Tabellini. 1991. "Political and Monetary Institutions and Public Finance Policies in the Industrial Countries." *Economic Policy* 6.13: 342–392.

5. Gürkaynak, Refet S., Andrew Levin, and Eric T. Swanson. 2006. "Does Inflation Targeting Anchor Long-Run Inflation Expectations? Evidence from Long-Term Bond Yields in the U.S., U.K., and Sweden." Centre for Economic Policy Research Discussion Paper 5808 (August).

6. See, for instance, Schwartz, Anna J. 1988. "Financial Stability and the Federal Safety Net." In William S. Haraf and Rose Marie Kushneider, eds. *Restructuring Banking and Financial Services in America*. Washington, D.C.: American Enterprise Institute, 34–62. For an affirmation of the "Schwarz hypothesis," see Bordo, Michael, and David Wheelock. 1998. "Price Stability and Financial Stability: The Historical Record." *Federal Reserve Bank of St. Louis Review* (September/October): 41–62. For a thoughtful exploration of the literature, see Otmar Issing, "Monetary and Financial Stability: Is There a Trade-off?" Speech at the Bank for International Settlements Conference Monetary Stability, Financial Stability and the Business Cycle, Basel, Switzerland, 28–29 March 2003.

7. See Blinder, Alan S. 1998. *Central Banking in Theory and Practice*. Cambridge: MIT Press. Discussed in Drazen. Allan. 2002. "Central Bank Independence, Democracy, and Dollarization." *Journal of Applied Economics* 5.1 (May): 1–17. See also Broz, J. Lawrence. 2002. "Political System Transparency and Monetary Commitment Regimes." *International Organization* 56.4: 863–889.

8. See, Meltzer, Allan H. 2003. *A History of the Federal Reserve: 1913–1951*. Chicago: University of Chicago Press.

9. See Maier, Philipp, Jan-Egbert Sturm, and Jakob de Haan. 2002. "Political Pressure on the Bundesbank: An Empirical Investigation Using the Havrilesky Approach." *Journal of Macroeconomics* 24.1 (March): 103–123.

10. For a comprehensive review of central bank independence around the world, see Crowe, Christopher, and Ellen E. Meade 2007. "The Evolution of Central Bank Governance Around the World." *Journal of Economic Perspectives* 21.4: 69–90. For an analysis of the modernization of central banks in emerging markets, see Maxfield, Sylvia. 1997. *Gatekeepers of Growth: The International Political Economy of the Rise of Central Banking in Developing Countries*. Princeton, NJ: Princeton University Press.

11. For statistical analyses, see Crowe, Christopher, and Ellen E. Meade 2007. "The Evolution of Central Bank Governance Around the World."

12. Congress retains ultimate control in case of dire emergency. Blinder, Alan S., 1996. "Central Banking in a Democracy." *Federal Reserve Bank of Richmond Economic Quarterly* 82.4 (Fall). The Fed also has built-in internal checks and balances: the Washington-based board is matched by strong regional representation to avoid groupthink and bring the diverse interests of the nation to the fore.

13. Greenspan, Alan. 2007. *The Age of Turbulence: Adventures in a New World*. New York: Penguin.

14. See Fischer, Stanley. 1995. "Central Bank Independence Revisited."

15. Marvin Goodfriend, "Financial System and Monetary Policy Implementation," paper prepared for the Bank of Japan 2009 International Conference, 27–28 May 2009.

16. Levin, Andrew B., and John B. Taylor. 2009. "Falling Behind the Curve: A Positive Analysis of Stop-Start Monetary Policies and the Great Inflation." Draft (23 December) <www.aeaweb.org/aea/conference/program/retrieve.php?pdfid=269>.

17. Meltzer, Allan H. 2009. "Learning About Policy from Federal Reserve History." Carnegie Mellon University and the American Enterprise Institute (October) <www2.tepper.cmu.edu/afs/andrew/gsia/meltzer/Learn%20about%20policy.pdf>.

18. Megan McArdle of the *Atlantic* noted that "Ben Bernanke isn't on '60 Minutes' because he loves the attention." Megan McArdle, "Democracy and Capitalism," 14 April 2009 <http://meganmcardle.theatlantic.com/archives/2009/04/democracy _and_capitalism.php>.

19. "Greenspan Defends Fed Record in Consumer Protection," Bloomberg, 7 April 2010.

20. See "The Monetary-Policy Maze," *Economist*, 23 April 2009.

21. Fed documents released in December 2010 showed that most of its loans and other aid for US institutions went to Citigroup ($2.2 trillion), Merrill Lynch ($2.1 trillion), Morgan Stanley ($2 trillion), Bear Stearns ($960 billion), Bank of America ($887 billion), Goldman Sachs ($615 billion), JPMorgan Chase ($178 billion), and Wells Fargo ($154 billion). Also, foreign banks benefited, with Swiss bank UBS borrowing more than $165 billion, Deutsche Bank $97 billion, and the Royal Bank of Scotland $92 billion. "Fed Shares Details on Crisis Lending," Associated Press, 2 December 2010.

22. See Bernanke, Ben S. 1983. "Non-Monetary Effects of the Financial Crisis in the Propagation of the Great Depression." *American Economic Review* 73 (June): 257–276; and Bernanke, Ben S., Mark Gertler, and Simon Gilchrist. 1996. "The Financial Accelerator and Flight to Quality." *Review of Economics and Statistics* 78: 1–15.

23. John N. Muellbauer, "Time for Unorthodox Monetary Policy," VoxEU.com, 27 November 2008.

24. As the president in the job interview inquired Bernanke about previous official duties, the future chairman deadpanned, "representative on Montgomery Township's school board." Wessel, David. 2009. *In Fed We Trust: Ben Bernanke's War on the Great Panic.* New York: Crown Business. Bernanke's credibility encouraged Treasury Secretary Paulson to ask him to join Paulson in critical meetings with congressional leaders and other appearances.

25. Goodfriend, Marvin, and Jeffrey M. Lacker. 1999. "Limited Commitment and Central Bank Lending." Federal Reserve Bank of Richmond Working Paper 99–2 (26 January). <www.clevelandfed.org/research/conferences/1999/december/wp99-2.pdf>.

26. Wessel, David. 2009. *In Fed We Trust.*

27. Goodfriend, Marvin. 2009. "Financial System and Monetary Policy Implementation."

28. Ibid.

29. Hamilton, James D. 2009. "Concerns About the Fed's New Balance Sheet." In John D. Ciorchiari and John B. Taylor, eds. *The Road Ahead for the Fed.* Stanford, California: Hoover.

30. Craig Torres, "Bernanke Housing Plan May Prompt Calls to Extend Aid," *Bloomberg*, 3 November 2009.

31. Simon Johnson, "The Quiet Coup," *Atlantic Online,* May 2009 <www.the atlantic.com/doc/print/200905/imf>. Similar concerns emerged in the UK, where *The Economist* called the British banking supervisor, the FSA, as prone to the Stockholm syndrome after the FSA exempted Northern Rock from regular examination and allowed the Royal Bank of Scotland to buy ABN AMRO. See "Rulers of Last Resort," *Economist*, 23 July 2009.

32. Research 2000 National Poll, 11–13 December 2009 <http://act.boldprogres sives.org/cms/sign/natpollresults>.

33. Rasmussen, "Just 21% Favor Bernanke's Reappointment as Fed Chairman," 2 December 2009 <www.rasmussenreports.com/public_content/business/general _business/november_2009/just_21_favor_bernanke_s_reappointment_as_fed _chairman>.

34. Joshua Zumbrun, "Majority of Americans Say Fed Should Be Reined in or Abolished, Poll Shows," *Bloomberg*, 9 December 2010.

35. Frank Newport, "Americans Trust Small-Business Owners Most on Job Creation," *Gallup*, 3 November 2011.

36. See, for example, Tom Braithwaite, "Coalition to Attack Plan for Fed Powers," *Financial Times*, 15 July 2009; and Axel Leijonhufvud, "Central Banking Doctrine in Light of the Crisis," VoxEU.com, 13 May 2008.

37. See, for instance, www.populistamerica.com/how_the_federal_reserve_runs _the_us___part_iii.

38. World Bank President and former US Deputy Secretary of State Robert Zoellick pointed out that the American public has historically been skeptical of granting greater powers to the Federal Reserve and its "independent and powerful technocrats." Peter Whoriskey, "World Bank Chief Suggests Treasury as Prime Financial Regulator," *Washington Post*, 29 September 2009.

39. Letter to Albert Gallatin, 13 December 1803.

40. Tricia Welsh, "CEOs: Greenspan by a Landslide," *Fortune*, March 1996.

41. Hamilton, James D. 2009. "Concerns About the Fed's New Balance Sheet."

42. Bertrand Benoit and Ralph Atkins, "Merkel Rebukes Banks for Monetary Policies," *Financial Times*, 3 June 2009. She continued, "Our most complex task will come once we have overcome the crisis. The question will be . . . can we return to a path of virtue, as far as public debts are concerned for instance."

43. "Congress Is Losing Its Patience with the Fed: Lawmakers on Both Sides Question Power, Handling of Wall Street Bailouts," Associated Press, 22 November 2009.

44. Dodd's bill called for limiting the Fed's oversight of the financial system by curbing its authority to conduct on-site examinations of the 35 largest banks, with $50 billion or more in assets. See, for example, "Bernanke: Fed Needs Small Bank Oversight to Spot Problems," MarketWatch.com, 20 March 2010.

45. Jon Hilsenrath and Sudeep Reddy, "Bernanke Wins New Term as Fed Chief on Shaky Footing After Tough Confirmation Fight," *Wall Street Journal*, 28 January 2010.

46. Donald L. Kohn, "Federal Reserve Independence," testimony before the Sub-committee on Domestic Monetary Policy and Technology, Committee on Financial Services, US House of Representatives, 9 July 2009.

47. David Lightman, "Senate Approves GAO Audit of Fed's Bailout Record," *Business Breaking News*, 11 May 2010.

48. The lack of clarity about the reduction of potential output complicated the measurement of the amount of slack in the economy (the so-called output gap).

49. Chailloux, Alexandre, Simon Gray, Ulrich Klüh, Seiichi Shimizu, and Peter Stella. 2008. "Central Bank Response to the 2007–08 Financial Market Turbulence: Experiences and Lessons Drawn." IMF Working Paper 08/210 (September) <www .imf.org/external/pubs/ft/wp/2008/wp08210.pdf>.

50. "Monetary-Policy Maze."

51. Levin and Taylor analyze three episodes—1968–1970, 1974–1976, and 1979–1980—finding that in each, policy makers allowed inflation to pick up before starting to tighten. Levin, Andrew, and John B. Taylor. Forthcoming. "Falling Behind the Curve: A Positive Analysis of Stop–Start Monetary Policies and the Great Inflation." In Michael D. Bordo and Athanasios Orphanides, eds. *The Great Inflation*. Chicago: University of Chicago Press. Research cited in Lorenzo Bini Smaghi, Member of the Executive Board of the ECB, "Exit Strategies: The International Dimension." Speech at Euro50 Group Meeting "Is There Still a Paradigm for Monetary Policy Today?" Paris, 20 November 2009. See also "No Exit Plan for Central Banks," *Financial Times*, 27 July 2009.

52. Jean Pisani Ferry, "In Search of a Goldilocks Exit Strategy," *Eurointelligence*, 16 July 2009.

53. Loans to foreign financial institutions via other central banks dropped from more than $500 billion to $17 billion. Programs from loans to investment banks and commercial paper expired in February 2010, followed by consumer-loan market credits in March.

54. Cottarelli, Carlo, and Jose Viñals. 2009. "A Strategy for Renormalizing Fiscal and Monetary Policies in Advanced Economies." IMF Staff Position Note 09/22 (22 September).

55. See, for example, "Heavenly Regulators," *Business Standard*, 23 September 2010.

56. Ben S. Bernanke, "Central Bank Independence, Transparency, and Accountability," speech at the Institute for Monetary and Economic Studies International Conference, Bank of Japan, Tokyo, Japan, 25 May 2010.

57. Stiglitz, Joseph E. 2010. *Freefall: America, Free Markets, and the Sinking of the World Economy*. New York: Norton.

58. See Peter Wallison, "Too Big to Fail, or Succeed," *Wall Street Journal*, 18 June 2009.

59. Marvin Goodfriend, "Financial System and Monetary Policy Implementation."

60. Hamilton, James D. 2009. "Concerns About the Fed's New Balance Sheet."

61. See Calomiris, Charles W. 2009. "Reassessing the Role of the Fed: Grappling with the Dual Mandate and More?" Cato Institute paper (30 September) <www.cato.org/events/Calomiris%20Paper.doc>.

62. Goodfriend, Marvin, and Jeffrey M. Lacker. 1999. "Limited Commitment and Central Bank Lending."

63. Volcker, Paul, "Remarks at a Luncheon of the Economic Club of New York," 8 April 2008. See also Marvin Goodfriend, "Financial System and Monetary Policy Implementation."

64. Steven Gjerstad and Vernon L. Smith, "From Bubble to Depression?" *Wall Street Journal*, 6 April 2009.

65. Donald L. Luskin, "Can the Fed Identify Bubbles Before They Happen?" *Wall Street Journal*, 29 July 2009. Luskin asks whether any one of these should be different than "the price of every individual item at Wal-Mart, or the salary of every individual who works there."

66. Rajan, Raghuram G. 2010. *Fault Lines: How Hidden Fractures Still Threaten the World Economy*. Princeton: Princeton University Press.

67. John B. Taylor, "Housing and Monetary Policy," paper for panel discussion at the Federal Reserve Bank of Kansas City symposium Housing, Housing Finance, and Monetary Policy, Jackson Hole, Wyoming, 30 August–1 September 2007.

68. Ben Bernanke, "Monetary Policy and the Housing Bubble," speech at the Annual Meeting of the American Economic Association, 3 January 2010.

69. Jaroci ski, Marek, and Frank R. Smets. 2008. "House Prices and the Stance of Monetary Policy." *Federal Reserve Bank of St. Louis Review* 90.4 (July/August): 339–365 <http://research.stlouisfed.org/publications/review/08/07/Jarocinski.pdf>.

70. "The Fed's Bipolar Mandate," *Wall Street Journal*, 20 November 2010.

71. Schwartz, Anna, and Walker F. Todd. 2008. "Why a Dual Mandate Is Wrong for Monetary Policy." *International Finance* 11.2: 167–183.

72. Bernanke, Ben, Thomas Laubach, Frederic S. Mishkin, and Adam Posen, eds. 2001. *Inflation Targeting: Lessons from the International Experience*. Princeton: Princeton University Press.

73. Thorbecke, Willem. 2002. "A Dual Mandate for the Federal Reserve: The Pursuit of Price Stability and Full Employment." *Eastern Economic Journal* 28.2 (spring).

74. Fontana, Giuseppe. 2006. "The Federal Reserve and the European Central Bank: A Theoretical Comparison of Their Legislative Mandates." *Journal of Post Keynesian Economics* 28.3.

75. Thorbecke, Willem. 2002. "A Dual Mandate for the Federal Reserve."

76. Lalonde, René, and Nicolas Parent. 2006. "The Federal Reserve's Dual Mandate: A Time-Varying Monetary Policy Priority Index for the United States." Bank of Canada Working Paper 2006–11 (April) <www.bankofcanada.ca/en/res/wp/2006/wp06-11.pdf>.

77. "Greenspan: Fed's Dual Mandate," *CNBC News*, 3 December 2010.

78. Bernanke, Ben, Thomas Laubach, Frederic S. Mishkin, and Adam Posen, eds. 2001. *Inflation Targeting*.

79. de Carvalho Filho, Irineu. 2010. "Inflation Targeting and the Crisis: An Empirical Assessment." IMF working paper (February) <www.imf.org/external/pubs/ft/wp/2010/wp1045.pdf>.

80. For an excellent review, see Faust, Jon, and Dale W. Henderson. 2004. "Is Inflation Targeting Best-Practice Monetary Policy?" *Federal Reserve Bank of St. Louis Review* 86.4 (July/August): 117–143 <http://research.stlouisfed.org/publications/review/04/07/FaustHenderson.pdf>.

Chapter 6

1. R. S. Rajaratnam, "Who Will Be Number One?" *Wall Street Journal*, 22 June 1979.

2. Burman, Stephen. 1991. *America in the Modern World: The Transcendence of United States Hegemony*. New York: St. Martin's.

3. For a review of numerous accounts, see Alan Dowd, "Three Centuries of American Declinism," RealClearPolitics.com, 27 August 2007 <www.realclearpolitics.com/articles/2007/08/declinism.html>.

4. Kennedy, Paul M. 1987. *The Rise and Fall of the Great Powers: Economic Change and Military Conflict from 1500 to 2000*. New York: Vintage; and Prestowitz, Clyde. 1988. *Trading Places: How We Allowed Japan to Take the Lead*. New York: Basic.

5. Mead, Walter Russell. 1987. *Mortal Splendor: The American Empire in Transition*. New York: Houghton Mifflin.

6. The opening lines could have been written today: "[R]ecent headlines declare that the American era is over . . . economic rivals caught up. American politics gridlocked and then America went on a consumption binge, borrowing from abroad to become, by 1986, the world's largest debtor. Going into the 1990s, America seemed once again to be an ordinary power." See Nau, Henry. 1989. *The Myth of America's Decline: Leading the World Economy into the 1990s*. Oxford: Oxford University Press.

7. Fukuyama, Francis. 1992. *The End of History and the Last Man*. New York: Free Press.

8. Zoellick, Robert B. 2000. "Campaign 2000: A Republican Foreign Policy." *Foreign Affairs* 79.1 (January/February).

9. "Five Years In, Cost of Iraq War Far Exceeds Early Estimates," *PBS Newshour*, 26 March 2008.

10. Michael Hirsh, "An Unnatural Disaster: America Bears Much of the Blame for Its Waning Global Clout," *Newsweek*, 15 May 2008.

11. Bacevich, Andrew. 2008. *The Limits of Power: The End of American Exceptionalism*. New York: Metropolitan. World systems theorist Immanuel Wallerstein argued in 2003 that America had gone downhill since the Vietnam War. Wallerstein, Immanuel. 2003. *The Decline of American Power: The U.S. in a Chaotic World*. New York: Norton.

12. Walker, David. 2010. *Comeback America: Turning the Country Around and Restoring Fiscal Responsibility*. New York: Random.

13. Gabor Steingart, "A Superpower in Decline: America's Middle Class Has Become Globalization's Loser," *Der Spiegel Online*, 24 October 2006.

14. Ferguson, Niall. 2006. *The War of the World: Twentieth Century Conflict and the Descent of the West.* New York: Penguin.

15. Kupchan, Charles. 2007. *The End of the American Era: U.S. Foreign Policy and the Geopolitics of the Twenty-First Century.* New York: Random.

16. National Intelligence Council. 2009. *Global Trends 2025: A Transformed World.* Washington, D.C.: US Government Printing Office <www.dni.gov/nic/NIC_2025 _project.html>.

17. Zakaria, Fareed. 2008. *Post-American World.* New York: Norton.

18. Mead, Walter Russell. 2010. "The Carter Syndrome." *Foreign Policy* (January/ February).

19. Kagan, Robert. 2008. *The Return of History and the End of Dreams.* New York: Vintage.

20. See, for example, Day, R. H. 1992. "Complex Economic Dynamics: Obvious in History, Genericin Theory, Elusive in Data." *Journal of Applied Econometrics* 7; and, for a summary, Prokhorov, Artem B. 2008. "Nonlinear Dynamics and Chaos Theory in Economics: A Historical Perspective." *Quantile* 4 (March). An earlier version can be found at <www.msu.edu/~prohorov/paper.pdf>.

21. Goldman Sachs. 2007. *BRICS and Beyond.* New York: Goldman Sachs <www2 .goldmansachs.com/ideas/brics/BRICs-and-Beyond.html>.

22. Dadush, Uri, and Bennett Stancil. "The G20 in 2050." *International Economic Bulletin*, Carnegie Endowment for International Peace, November 2009 <www.carn egieendowment.org/publications/index.cfm?fa=view&id=24195>.

23. Gordon, Robert J. 2010. "Revisiting US Productivity Growth over the Past Century with a View of the Future." NBER Working Paper 15834 (March).

24. International differences in productivity are also affected by such variables as openness to trade, the rule of law and good institutions, private ownership, and even geographic latitude, with nations in temperate zones having greater productivity. See Hall, Robert E., and Charles I. Jones. 1996. "The Productivity of Nations," NBER Working Paper 5812 (November). Political scientists take one further step back, arguing that the public policies that propel productivity in turn hinge on political and social factors, such as electoral systems and ethnic fragmentation.

25. Data from OECD Program for International Student Assessment (PISA) <http://pisa2009.acer.edu.au>. For the insight, see McKinsey Company. 2009. *The Economic Impact of the Achievement Gap in America's Schools: Summary of Findings* (April) <www.mckinsey.com/App_Media/Images/Page_Images/Offices/Social Sector/PDF/achievement_gap_report.pdf>.

26. McKinsey Company. 2009. *The Economic Impact of the Achievement Gap in America's Schools.*

27. IHS Global Insight. 2008. "US Infrastructure: How Will The Nation Satisfy Growing Demand with Limited Funds?" (December) <www.ihsglobalinsight.com/ gcpath/PPP.pdf>.

28. American Society of Civil Engineers. 2009. Infrastructure Report Card. Washington, D.C.: ASCE <www.infrastructurereportcard.org/sites/default/files/RC2009_full_report.pdf>.

29. For forecasts, see Battelle and *R&D Magazine*. 2011. "2011 Global R&D Funding Forecast." *R&D Magazine* (December) <www.rdmag.com/uploadedFiles/RD/Featured_Articles/2009/12/GFF2010_ads_small.pdf>. For the past five decades, see Goel, Rajeev K., James E. Payne, and Rati Ram. 2007. "R&D Expenditures and U.S. Economic Growth: A Disaggregated Approach." *Journal of Policy Modeling* 30: 237–250.

30. See, for example, Goel, Rajeev K., James E. Payne, and Rati Ram. 2007. "R&D Expenditures and U.S. Economic Growth"; David, Paul A., Bronwyn H. Hall, and Andrew A. Toole. 1999. "Is Public R&D a Complement or Substitute for Private R&D?" NBER Working Paper 7373 (October); and Guellec, Dominique, and Bruno van Pottelsberghe de la Potterie. 2003. "The Impact of Public R&D Expenditure on Business R&D." *Economics of Innovation and New Technology* 12.3 (June): 225–243.

31. Wilson, Daniel J. 2007. "Beggar Thy Neighbor? The In-State, Out-of-State, and Aggregate Effects of R&D Tax Credits." Federal Reserve Bank of San Francisco Working Paper 2005–08 (August) <www.frbsf.org/publications/economics/papers/2005/wp05-08k.pdf>.

32. Hufbauer, Gary Clyde, and Martin Vieiro. 2011. "Big Business Is Good for America." *Foreign Affairs* 90.6 (November/December).

33. Ibid.

34. World Economic Forum. 2011. *The Global Competitiveness Report 2011–2012.* Geneva: World Economic Forum <www.weforum.org/issues/global-competitiveness>.

35. See Battelle and *R&D Magazine*. 2011. "2011 Global R&D Funding Forecast."

36. World Bank, Doing Business database <www.doingbusiness.org/ExploreTopics/StartingBusiness>.

37. "Unconventional Gas Hits LNG, Pipelines." *Oxford Analytica Daily Brief,* 18 September 2009; Joel Kotkin, "Play It Cool, Mr. President," Forbes.com, 22 September 2009; and Paul Kennedy, "American Power Is on the Wane," *Wall Street Journal,* 14 January 2009.

38. US Energy Information Administration. 2011. *Annual Energy Outlook.* Washington, D.C.: US Department of Energy <www.eia.doe.gov/oiaf/aeo>.

39. United Nations Department of Economic and Social Affairs (DESA). 2008. *2008 Revision of the World Population Prospects.* New York: United Nations <http://esa.un.org/unpp/p2kodata.asp>.

40. Ibid.

41. Shirk, Susan. 2007. *China: Fragile Superpower.* Oxford: Oxford University Press.

42. Olson, Mancur. 1982. *The Rise and Decline of Nations: Economic Growth, Stagflation and Social Rigidities.* New Haven: Yale University Press.

43. See, for example, Geoff Dyer, "China: No One Home," *Financial Times,* 21 February 2010.

44. See Przeworski, Adam. 2004. "Democracy and Economic Development." In *The Evolution of Political Knowledge*, ed. Edward D. Mansfield and Richard Sisson. Columbus: Ohio State University Press. See also Przeworski, Adam, Michael E. Alvarez, José Antonio Cheibub, and Fernando Limongi. 2000. *Democracy and Development: Political Institutions and Well-Being in the World, 1950–1990*. Cambridge: Cambridge University Press. They find that both the fastest-growing and the slowest-growing economies are dictatorships. But over time, dictatorships do not do better than democracies. On average, they do worse.

45. Shirk, Susan. 1993. *The Political Logic of Economic Reform in China*. Berkeley: University of California Press.

46. See Sarah Caron, "14 Big Businesses That Started in a Recession," *INSIDECRM*, 11 November 2008 <www.insidecrm.com/features/businesses-started -slump-111108>. See also Ferguson, Niall. 2009. "What 'Chimerica' Hath Wrought." *American Interest* 4.3 (January–February) <www.the-american-interest.com/article .cfm?piece=533>.

47. Among the recent examples, Fallows, James. 2010. "State of the Union." *Atlantic* (January–February) <www.theatlantic.com/doc/201001/american-decline>; and Manzi, Jim. 2010. "Keeping America's Edge." *National Affairs* (Winter).

48. Kissinger, Henry. 1994. *Diplomacy*. New York: Simon and Schuster, p. 835.

Index

Italic page numbers indicate material in tables or figures.